JOHN
WESLEY

JOHN
WESLEY

Stanley Ayling

This title now published by
Abingdon, Nashville,
order as item # 203767

William Collins Publishers, Inc.
Cleveland • New York

First American Edition 1979

COPYRIGHT © 1979 BY STANLEY AYLING

Library of Congress Cataloging in Publication Data

Ayling, Stanley Edward.
   John Wesley.

                 Bibliography: p.
   Includes index.
   1. Wesley, John, 1703-1791. 2. Methodist Church — Clergy — Biography.
   3. Clergy — England — Biography.
BX8495.W5A94   1979b   287'.092'4 [B]   79-53508
ISBN 0-529-05688-7

Printed in the United States of America

The religion of the heart; the religion which Kempis,
Pascal, Fénélon enjoyed . . .

John Wesley

I hate to meet John Wesley; the dog enchants you with
his conversation, and then breaks away to go and visit
some old woman.

Samuel Johnson

I went to the Garden of Love
And saw what I never had seen:
A Chapel was built in the midst,
Where I used to play on the green.

And the gates of the Chapel were shut,
And 'Thou shalt not' writ over the door;
So I turned to the Garden of Love
That so many sweet flowers bore;

And I saw it was filled with graves
And tomb-stones where flowers should be;
And Priests in black gowns were walking their rounds,
And binding with briars my joys and desires.

William Blake, Songs of Experience (1794)

Contents

Illustrations

Preface

It will hardly be supposed that a new life of Wesley is likely to be founded on any sensational fresh discovery of documentary evidence. There can be few Englishmen who left behind so detailed and meticulous an account of their thoughts and actions, or whose words and deeds have since been so exhaustively examined and recorded. The store of material for a biography of Wesley is vast. Primary sources alone are very extensive, and the secondary sources that have accumulated over the past two centuries are dauntingly voluminous. (The bibliography supplied at the end of this volume is in the severest sense 'select'.) I do not think, however, that an apology is required for another life of Wesley. His importance as one of the key figures of his age can hardly be questioned, and a view of him from the last quarter of the twentieth century, even using for the most part evidence which has not greatly changed, is likely to prove significantly different from a view of fifty or a hundred years ago.

There have of course been some interesting minor discoveries in relatively recent years (a number of these have appeared in the Proceedings of the Wesley Historical Society) relating either to the brothers Wesley or their parents; and some forty years ago *Son to Susanna*, by G. Elsie Harrison, made some corrections to one or two previously accepted facts concerning John Wesley's personal history. The most important of recent contributions to new knowledge upon this subject came however from V. H. H. Green's admirable *The Young Mr Wesley* (1961), and the first three chapters of my book are much indebted to Dr Green's researches.

Inevitably Wesley's own tireless pen must be the source of the great majority of matter in any book about him. It would be improper, however, to ignore the obligation any modern biographer is still under to those massively detailed, if immoderately reverential, volumes of the specialist Wesley scholars and editors of the nineteenth and early twentieth centuries – four of them in particular, Luke Tyerman, John Telford, Nehemiah Curnock and J. S. Simon.

Among the illustrations, the extract from Wesley's Oxford Diary, with its elucidation, is from Curnock's fine 1909 edition of the *Journal*, as is the little portrait of Peter Böhler. For assistance of various kinds in preparing text and illustrations, I wish to thank the Rev. Professor E. G. Rupp, who made very many helpful suggestions, but whose approval of the script I would not take for granted; the Rev. Allen Birtwhistle of Wesley's City Road Chapel; the Rev. Thomas Shaw, of the Wesley Historical Society; the London Library; the National Portrait Gallery; and, particularly, my editor at Collins, Philip Ziegler, and Dr Robert Young of Sussex University.

Introduction

RELIGION, WHEN John Wesley was born in 1703, was still almost as powerful an element in the cultural and political life of the nation as it had been over the two preceding centuries. It was religious issues which had precipitated the Revolution of 1688, and thus, not only the victory of the Church of England over its Dissenting and Romanist rivals, but also of Protestant parliament over Catholic king. The political battles of the next two reigns, of Calvinist Whig-inclined William III and High Church Tory Anne, rose mainly from religious differences. It was religion which determined the Hanoverian succession and the defeat of Jacobitism. The very political parties were to be defined in religious terms: 'By Whigs,' Dr Wooton wrote to Bishop, later Archbishop, Wake, 'we mean those that are most zealous for the Protestant succession.'

It is a mistake, though one made less often now than it used to be, to see the eighteenth century as an age of irreligion and enlightened scepticism. It *was*, however, a time of reaction against the excesses of zeal which had brought to the seventeenth century a surfeit of intolerant sectarianism. By the time of Wesley's birth there was broad acceptance of the necessity to escape from 'the smell of faggots'. The years of Queen Anne and George I had their fanatics, but the prevailing religious temper was for permitting a liberal breadth of doctrine and practice. Hence 'Latitudinarian' to describe the stance of the Whig-Anglican clergy of the day. There were, naturally, critics of this mild position, the boldest among them being the Non-Jurors, those clerics who, having once vowed loyalty to James II, had refused to unswear that loyalty when the 'usurpers' William and Mary ousted him; and some of the noisiest excitement of Anne's reign came when Dr Sacheverell, a violent opponent of toleration, roused High Churchmen and the citizenry of London against a Whig government accused of betraying the Church by over-leniency to Dissenters. Fortunately, however, after the Toleration Act which followed the 1688 Revolution, the persecuting prelate had become as much a figure of the past as the hunted Catholic priest.

The price to be paid for this advance – and some like Wesley were to see it as too heavy a price – was a loss of ardour, a luke-warmness of faith. The Latitudinarians mistrusted the poetry of religion; they were for 'prose', rational, measured, and cool. Further, among its upper ranks at least, the Church of England became rather too comfortable and worldly, running as it did in close harness with the ruling state establishment. Yet if Whig lords in government meant Low Church Latitudinarian Whig bishops in the Lords, Tory squires amid their rural acres often found themselves in accord with High Church Tory country parsons. Many of these last had sympathized with the Non-Jurors, and for years continued to hope that the Toleration Act, giving a large measure of freedom to Dissenters, might one day be repealed. There was thus, throughout the time of Wesley's youth, a good deal of tension between parish clergy and the ruling Church establishment.

Subject though it was to such strains, the Church of England was immensely strong and influential. Roman Catholics, except in Ireland, constituted now a defeated, though not persecuted, minority. Dissent was tolerated. Its contribution to the Whig cause had been too great to be ignored, and even the Tories between 1710 and 1714, though they succeeded in putting tem-porarily on to the statute book some severe anti-Dissenter measures, did not dare to repeal the Toleration Act. Dissent, however, was fragmented into many denominations, and for most of them the eighteenth century was not a time in which they flourished numerically; intellectually, especially among Quakers and Unitarians, it was a different story. Outside the churches, Deists, discrediting the miraculous and denying Christian revelation, presented an articulate challenge, but it was a small fraction of the British nation that had even heard of Deism. There was never a time when the position of the established Church seemed so secure. Anomalies, anachronisms, and abuses it had in plenty. Privilege and inequality, sometimes gross, were as much part of the Church of England as of most other departments of Georgian life. The Church did not radiate spiritual energy.

No doubt the parson's sermon, stuffed very likely with other men's learning, was as Goldsmith described it, 'dry, methodical, and unaffecting'. Communion might be infrequently celebrated. Yet in general church attendance was high. With its monopoly of Oxford and Cambridge, the Church dominated higher education. In the country districts – and, London and a handful of provincial cities apart, England was still a land of villages and country towns – the Anglican parson, by the side of the squire and justice of the peace, was the unquestioned representative of authority.

Inside the Church, well before Wesley and the Methodists, there was no lack of individuals and groups aware of its short-comings, aiming to deepen its spirituality or to extend its message by missionary work, by supplying the ignorant poor with cheap bibles and prayer books, by visiting prisons or by founding charity schools. The Society for Promoting Christian Knowledge was established at this time, with its offshoot the Society for the Propagation of the Gospel in Foreign Parts. (It was under the auspices of this last that Wesley would in the 1730s be sent out as chaplain and missionary to Georgia.) There was too a vigorously – many thought too vigorously – active Society for the Refor-mation of Manners, in which Dissenters and Churchmen co-operated. This attempted to suppress vice by prosecuting offenders, and campaigned for virtue and Sunday observance by distributing moral tracts closely akin to Wesley's own later. There were too, by the time Wesley first set up his 'godly' societies, many similar groups of earnest Christians throughout the land, particularly in the bigger towns. The eighteenth century, in fact, far from being becalmed in the doldrums of sceptical indifference, was to be rich in religious movements, in philan-thropic enterprises, in charitable and missionary endeavours of every kind. What was to make the work of John Wesley transcend them all was less any essential difference it presented than its astonishing *success*, to account for which we must surely look first to the genius of Wesley himself.

CHAPTER I

Epworth Rectory

AT THE END OF December 1700 the Rev. Samuel Wesley, Rector of the small market town of Epworth in the Isle of Axholme district of Lincolnshire, was writing, not for the first time, to his sympathetic superior and benefactor Dr John Sharp, Archbishop of York, in order to explain his shattered finances and advertise his urgent needs. Farming the glebe had been a failure. Literary work – the Rector was a prolific poet and controversialist – brought small reward. Mrs Wesley had already borne him eleven children, six of whom were still living and occasioning necessary expense. Repayments of old loans, payment of loan-interest and taxes, 'ten pounds a year I allow my mother to help keep her from starving', other charities, admittedly not all of them prudent, family and household expenses – all ate away more than his modest stipend could provide. They were making do temporarily with a single maidservant, but the parish had recently saddled him with the extra burden of an apprentice ('whom, I suppose, I must teach to beat rhyme'). In all, Samuel Wesley was £300 in debt, and his letter was a renewed cry for help from the Archbishop's charitable offices.

These again proved influential and timely. A prompt £20 from the Countess of Northampton came 'like a gift from Heaven' only one day after Mr and Mrs Wesley had 'clubbed and joined stocks, which came to but *six shillings*, to send for coals', and on the very morning when Mrs Wesley was delivered of two more children – twins, neither of whom would survive infancy. 'Last night,' wrote the Rector to the Archbishop, 'my wife brought me a *few* children, a boy and a girl, and I think they are all at present.' However, his quiver was by no means yet full. Six more Wesleys were to present themselves over the next nine years, making nineteen children in all. Of these, three sons and seven daughters would reach adulthood.

Samuel Wesley had come to Epworth in 1697, at the age of thirty-four. Like his wife, that formidable High Churchwoman, he derived nevertheless from Dissenting stock. Both his·father and grandfather had been ejected from their Dorset livings after the restoration of Charles II, and the young Samuel, after a period at the free grammar school in Dorchester, had attended two Dissenting academies in London before deciding to transfer his allegiance to the Church of England. This had enabled him to enter Exeter College, Oxford, where he became a servitor, one of those undergraduates who earned much of their keep and education by doing odd jobs and waiting on wealthier members of the college. The convert to Anglicanism proceeded to develop an antipathy to Nonconformity that later boiled over in some belligerent pamphleteering. Dissent he came to see as disloyalty. Always, once he had put school days behind him, Church and Crown represented to Samuel Wesley the pillars of the temple, as the best-known of the many colourful stories concerning him illustrates. One day towards the end of the reign of William III, he refused any longer to tolerate the neglect of his wife to say Amen after the family prayers for the reigning monarch. For Mrs Wesley, whose strength of will and of conviction was at least the equal of her husband's, William III was a usurper. She took her stand. Amen she would not say; whereupon, in her own words, Mr Wesley 'immediately kneeled down and imprecated the divine vengeance upon himself and all his posterity if ever he touched me more or came into bed with me before I had begged God's pardon and his'.

Samuel Wesley did indeed, soon afterwards, depart for London, where he intended to seek a chaplaincy in the army or navy and in fact spent a considerable time attending Convocation. He would 'take care of' their six surviving children, he assured his wife, who nevertheless was understandably concerned: 'If anything should befall him at sea we should be in no very good condition.' However, 'I'm more easy at the thoughts of parting', she wrote, 'because I think we are not likely to live happily together.' 'Since I'm willing to let him quietly enjoy his opinions, he ought not to deprive me of my little liberty of conscience.'

When Samuel Wesley did eventually return to his parochial duties and conjugal bed, his wife, it seems, had succeeded in maintaining her point. Their future marital relations, if seldom quite peaceful, were to be conducted with more mutual love and understanding than might have been then predicted. The terms of their peace treaty were never published, but the détente between the contending parties – in the late summer of 1702 – was clearly a prerequisite for the genesis of the Wesleys' fifteenth child, John, born on 17 June 1703.

To a considerable degree the elder Wesley's life as a country rector, arduously and conscientiously as he on the whole pursued it, was never more than a second best. The ecclesiastical ambitions he once entertained had been disappointed. He was obliged to labour (in his wife's words) in an 'obscure corner of the country, where his talents are buried', and to follow 'a way of life for which he is not so well qualified as I could wish'.[1] In 1694 his name had been put forward to the Archbishop of Canterbury by Lord Normanby, whose chaplain he was, for an Irish bishopric; but nothing more was heard of it, then or afterwards. He had gone from one Lincolnshire living, South Ormsby, to a somewhat more substantial one, Epworth, but advanced no further. He was rector of Epworth for the remaining forty years of his life, but regarded his parish and its cheerless reclaimed fenlands as a sort of exile, and forced himself to square up to his duties among his parishioners rather in the temper of an exasperated missionary among savage tribes. Hetty, the prettiest, most gifted, most ill-fated of the Rector's seven daughters – and none of them were to enjoy much luck in life – showed, if little else of her father's temper, at least this same view of the Axholme people when she wrote:

As asses dull on dunghill born,
Impervious as the stones their heads are found,
Their rage and hatred steadfast to the ground.

The Rector's poetry and biblical studies continued to keep his literary and polemical talents in constant exercise, but did not achieve the success he had dreamed of as a young man. To the last days of a long life he would be labouring learnedly and doggedly at his marathon Latin *Dissertations on the Book of Job*. From his Oxford days onward, the stream of his verse and prose had been ever-rolling: a *Life of Our Blessed Lord and Saviour Jesus Christ*, in some nine thousand lines ('an Heroic Poem, dedicated to her most sacred Majesty Queen Mary'), which earned him a place in Pope's Temple of Dulness in some early editions of *The Dunciad*; an elegy on the death of the same sacred Majesty – in which the crowning of Queen Mary in heaven was prepared by angels showing 'more than usual art and care',

> And first mankind's great mother rose,
> 'Give way, ye crowding souls', said she,
> 'That I the second of my race may see; –

another elegy on *John* [Tillotson], *late Archbishop of Canterbury*; a *Short Discourse on Baptism*, more or less plagiarized half a century later by his famous son and republished with trifling amendments as John Wesley's own treatise on the same subject; an *Epistle to a Friend Concerning Poetry*, some thousand lines of verse, somewhere embedded in which is the couplet which, rescued from the general annihilation and oblivion, earns the author his place in *The Oxford Book of Quotations*:

> Style is the dress of thought; a modest dress,
> Neat, but not gaudy, will true critics please.

In addition to these substantial compositions, Samuel Wesley contributed hundreds of short articles in the form of replies to readers' theological and biblical questions in a thrice-weekly penny journal, *The Athenian Gazette*, upon which as a young man he had ventured as part-proprietor, and in which he proffered answers to such diverse problems as 'Why was man not made incapable of sinning?' 'How high was Babel's tower?' 'Did Peter and Paul use notes when they preached?' 'Should women sit promiscuously with men in church?' The longest and bitterest of his articles were those attacking Baptists and Quakers.

The Rector was not the most popular man in Epworth. The inhabitants of the Isle of Axholme had only a generation or two earlier been fenmen, a race notoriously suspicious of 'foreigners', and especially perhaps of one such as Samuel Wesley, who sought to promote godly living in their midst with authoritarian rigour. More than once vandals molested his property. Ill-wishers maimed his cattle. When half of his house burned down in 1702, he was sure, though there was no firm evidence, that it had been

fired through the malice of a servant. Some of the more substantial
local families became equally his enemy, especially when in the
Lincolnshire elections of 1705 he publicly espoused the Tory
anti-Dissenter cause. He found, when he went to Lincoln to vote,
a mob of 'our isle people . . . drumming, shouting, and firing of
guns under the window where my wife lay'. They 'intended me a
mischief', he learned; 'if they got me in the Castle yard they
would squeeze my guts out'. However, 'God preserved me'.

Back home, he was soon confronted by a friend of one of the
offended Whig candidates, with a demand for immediate payment
of a £30 debt, and being unable to pay was lodged in Lincoln
jail. There, so he claimed in a letter to Archbishop Sharp, he
found 'more civility and satisfaction' than in Epworth:

> I hope [my wife] will be able to look to my family, if they do not
> turn them out of doors, as they have often threatened to do. One
> of my biggest concerns was my being forced to leave my poor
> lambs in the midst of so many wolves. But the great Shepherd is
> able to provide . . . My wife bears it with the courage which
> becomes her, and which I expected from her . . . It may be [I shall]
> do more in this new parish than in my old one; for I have leave
> to read Prayers every morning and afternoon here in the prison,
> and to preach once a Sunday . . . Most of my friends advise me to
> leave Epworth, if ever I should get from hence. I confess I am
> not of that mind, for I may yet do good there. [2]

John Wesley was two years old at the time of these misfortunes. The family never went actually hungry. To raise some
of the wherewithal to secure her husband's release, Mrs Wesley
sent her rings to Lincoln, but he returned them, preferring to
rely on the charity of well-to-do sympathizers. Within three or
four months he was home again; and a few months later Mrs
Wesley was able to report dreadful, yet unquestionably reassuring,
instances of divine support for their cause. Two Epworth
parishioners who had been most 'implacable' in doing mischief
to her husband, herself, and her family had been 'cut off in the
midst of their sins' – one of them in a fall from his horse as he was
returning drunk from Bawtry fair; 'a very sad accident', showing
nevertheless 'the severe justice of God'. [3]

Samuel Wesley's afflictions were far from over. It was fitting
that his magnum opus was to be upon the sufferings of Job. One
night in February 1709, the old parsonage, with its thatched roof,

caught fire again, and this time burned beyond repair. Nearly everything was lost – house, furniture, library, manuscripts – and thirteen years afterwards, Mrs Wesley affirmed that the family were still living in an only half refurnished home. A new building, costing £400, foursquare, substantial, tile-roofed now, was up within a year; but when Samuel Wesley's Dissenter brother Matthew, a London apothecary, visited Epworth towards the end of the Rector's life in 1731, Mrs Wesley reported him as having been 'scandalized at the poverty of our furniture and much more at the meanness of the children's habit' – adult 'children' by then. 'He wondered what his brother had done with his income, for 'twas visible he had not spent it in furnishing his house or clothing his family' – that 'numerous offspring' which he took occasion to remind the Rector had been produced 'in pursuit of his pleasure'.

When the roll was being called of the children assembled in the garden as their old rectory went up in flames, it had been discovered that one was missing. It was five-year-old John, who had slept through the first general panic. Bent on rescue, his father found the stairs impassable for smoke and flame, whereupon we are told he 'knelt down in the blazing hall and commended the soul of his child to God'. A ladder was being fetched when, espied by others in a first-floor window, the child was brought down through it, by means of one man standing on the shoulders of another. In this fortunate rescue of her Jacky there seems no very solid grounds for Mrs Wesley coming to see evidence of special divine intervention. However, so she did, resolving to be 'more particularly careful of the soul of this child, which God had so mercifully provided for'. And Wesley himself in future years frequently recalled this providential escape: was he not indeed 'a brand plucked out of the burning'?

When poor Jacky was saved [the Rector wrote] I could not believe it till I had kissed him two or three times. My wife said, 'Are your books safe?' I told her it was not much, now she and all the rest were preserved alive. A little lumber was saved below stairs, but not one rag or leaf above . . . I want nothing, having above half my barley safe in my barns unthrashed . . . I hope my wife will recover and not miscarry, but God will give me my nineteenth child. She has burnt her legs, but they mend.[4]

In the uncomfortable interim between the fire and the completion of a new parsonage, all the children except the eldest daughter Emily had to be accommodated in the households of friends and relations; and this, according to Mrs Wesley, had unfortunate results. Susanna Wesley was a woman of formidable capability. She prided herself on the efficient running of her home and godly schooling of her sizeable flock, and until the fire of 1709, she wrote,

> Never were children in better order. Never were children in better piety, or in more subjection to their parents, till that fatal dispersion of them after the fire, into several families. In those they were left at full liberty to converse with servants, which before they had always been restrained from; and to run abroad to play with any children, good or bad. They soon learned to neglect a strict observance of the Sabbath; and got knowledge of several songs and bad things, which before they had no notion of . . . A clownish accent and many rude ways were learnt, which were not reformed without great difficulty.
>
> When the house was rebuilt, and the children all brought home, we entered on a strict reform; and then was begun the custom of singing psalms at beginning and leaving school, morning and evening. Then also that of a general retirement at five o'clock was entered upon, when the oldest took the youngest that could speak, and the second the next, to whom they read the psalms for the day, and a chapter in the New Testament – as in the morning they were directed to read the psalms and a chapter in the Old; after which they went to their private prayers, before they got their breakfast . . .

This passage forms part of the well-known account Mrs Wesley sent to her son John, over twenty years later, in reply to his request to be told the principles on which she had brought up her children. When she wrote it, the youngest of them was twenty-two and the oldest over forty; she herself was sixty-three; so perhaps allowance should be made for memory's trick of tidying up the past. But with whatever pinches of salt it is taken, this detailed description of the godly severity of the Epworth parsonage regime – its eye cocked unrelentingly heavenward – provides a vivid illumination of Puritan mores in general, and in particular of the physical and spiritual climate in which the boy John Wesley grew up.

Susanna Wesley's religious convictions were based on strenuously argued theology. Her intellectual inclination was as little latitudinarian as her household organization. But High Church-woman though she was – indeed, a supporter of the Non-Jurors – she always remained the product of her Dissenter's upbringing, and life at Epworth as she directed it can sound both bracing and chilling. Her methods were certainly light years away from latter-day theory and practice. Even so, they provide their surprises. Girls, for instance, are to be treated as the scholastic equals of boys, and not to be allowed to sew before they can 'read very well'. 'The putting children to learn sewing,' she writes, 'before they can read perfectly is the very reason why so few women can read fit to be heard.'

Her system had little use for self-expression. The expression that must be striven for was that of the will of God, which must mean the extinction of self-will, 'the one grand impediment to our temporal and eternal happiness . . . Heaven or Hell depends on this alone'. The parent who indulges a child's self-will, 'the root of all sin and misery . . . does devil's work; makes religion impracticable, salvation unattainable, and does all that in him lies to damn his child, soul and body, for ever'. (Such educational views were of course far from being unique to Mrs Wesley. George Whitefield, for instance, in his *Journal* recounts how on 31 March 1738 he successfully beat an intractable child into repeating the Lord's Prayer, and adds: 'If [parents] would but have resolution to break [children's] wills thoroughly when young, the work of conversion would be much easier.')

The Wesley children, wrote their mother, were from the cradle 'put into a regular method of living'.

When turned a year old (and some before), they were taught to fear the rod, and to cry softly, by which means they escaped abundance of correction which they might otherwise have had; and that most odious noise of crying of children was rarely heard in the house.

. . . At dinner their little table and chairs were set by ours, where they could be overlooked; and they were suffered to eat and drink (small beer) as much as they would, but not to call for anything. If they wanted aught, they used to whisper to the maid that attended them, who came and spake to me; and as soon as they could handle a knife and fork, they were set to our table . . .

They were so constantly used to eat and drink what was given
them, that when any of them was ill, there was no difficulty in
making them take the most unpleasant medicine, for they durst
not refuse it, though some of them would presently throw it up.
This I mention to show that a person may be taught to take
anything, though it be never so much against his stomach . . .

Our children were taught, as soon as they could speak, the
Lord's prayer, which they were made to say at rising and bedtime
constantly; to which, as they grew bigger, were added a short
prayer for their parents, and some collects, a short catechism,
and some portion of Scripture, as their memories could bear.
They were very early made to distinguish the Sabbath from
other days . . .

There was no such thing as loud talking or playing allowed of;
but every one was kept close to business for the six hours of
school. And it is almost incredible what a child may be taught
in a quarter of a year by vigorous application . . . Rising out of
their places, or going out of a room, was not permitted, except
for a good cause; and running into the yard, garden, or street,
without leave, was always esteemed a capital offence.

There were several bye-laws observed among us . . . That
whoever was charged with a fault, of which they were guilty, if
they would ingenuously confess it, and promise to amend,
should not be beaten . . . That no sinful action . . . should ever
pass unpunished . . . That no child should be ever chid or beat
twice for the same fault . . . That every signal act of obedience . . .
should always be commended, and frequently rewarded . . . That
propriety be inviolably preserved; and none suffered to invade the
property of another in the smallest matter . . . This rule can never
be too much inculcated on the minds of children; and from the
want of parents or governors doing it as they ought, proceeds
that shameful neglect of justice which we may observe in the
world . . .

Neither was deportment to be neglected, as the seventy-year-old
Wesley remembered (apropos of the poor carriage of some of his
preachers then, who did not know how properly to walk in or
out of a room): 'My mother had a dancing master to come to her
house who taught all of us what was sufficient in *her presence*.'

Susanna, mother of nineteen children, had herself been the
youngest of twenty-four. Or was it perhaps twenty-five? Dr
Annesley, her father, admitted in conversation with a son-in-law
his inability to be quite sure whether the count was 'two dozen or

a quarter of a hundred'. A nephew of the Earl of Anglesey, he
had been prominent among the Nonconformists of his generation,
and was minister of St Giles's, Cripplegate. Like Samuel Wesley's
father and grandfather, he had been ejected from his living at the
Restoration; but, surviving without serious hardship, he was, at
the time of Susanna's marriage and until his death in 1796,
minister at a meeting-house off Bishopsgate. Plainly he had not
always been able to persuade the convictions of the young
Susanna, who very early in life must have developed – along with
considerable physical attractiveness – an unusual independence of
mind and seriousness of judgement. 'Because I was educated
among the Dissenters,' she later told her son Samuel,

> and there was something remarkable in my leaving them at so
> early an age, not being full thirteen, I had drawn up an account
> of the whole transaction, under which I had included the main of
> the controversy between them and the established church, as
> far as it had come to my knowledge, and then followed the
> reasons which had determined my judgement to the preference
> of the Church of England. I had fairly transcribed a great deal of
> it, but before I could finish my design, the flames consumed
> both this and all my other writings.[5]

After the fire she lost little time in again putting upon paper very
precise outlines of her Christian beliefs and moral principles, for
the instruction, in the first place, of her daughter Sukey, then
fourteen. No concession was to be made to a young girl's intellectual immaturity. 'Though perhaps you cannot at present
fully comprehend all I shall say,' wrote Mrs Wesley, 'yet keep this
letter by you, and as you grow in years, your reason and judgement will improve, and you will obtain a more clear understanding in all things.' There followed a careful summary of her
theological position – Mrs Wesley was not one to blur edges,
still less to entertain doubts – with an exegesis, phrase by phrase,
of the Apostles' Creed. For her own spiritual improvement,
moreover, she set time aside at morning, noon, and evening for
solitary prayer and meditation, and now began composing a
severe little manual of religious reflections, partly no doubt for
her own self-examination and edification, but partly too for her
children to employ and ponder.[6] She also assigned regular days
of the week for sessions of individual scriptural and moral

teaching for each of her children. John's day was Thursday, and he always remembered and retrospectively came to praise the thoroughness and correctness of that strict instruction. When he was a fellow of Lincoln College, Oxford, and nearly thirty, he wrote to his mother, 'If you can spare me only that little part of Thursday evening which you formerly bestowed upon me in another manner, I doubt not but it would be as useful now for correcting my heart as it was then for forming my judgement.'[7]

Samuel Wesley was content to leave the early education of his children in his wife's hands, and it is clear that young John Wesley's tenderest years were spent under a sort of matriarchy and in predominantly feminine company. Besides his mother there were five elder sisters and of course female servants; one brother was away at school or university, the other not born until late in 1707. But if Mrs Wesley dominated the nursery, she did not altogether rule the rectory roost. Samuel Wesley was no cipher, nor was he the remote library-bound figure that has sometimes been depicted, pathetically or even comically pegging away at his dry-as-dust dissertations. He scraped to find what money he could towards the education of his sons; was always paternally concerned in their well-being, and overwhelmed with pride when success came their way.

Daughters were rather a different matter; but if his judgement was often at fault and his charity sometimes wanting in his treatment of them as they grew up – and with Hetty in particular this was culpably and tragically so – it was not that he was careless of them and their happiness, but rather that he was excessively careful, authoritarian, and censorious. Patty was another of the Wesley girls whose prospects of love and marriage wilted under her father's ban, and she was moved to comment sourly on his 'unaccountable love of discord'. The sisters of John Wesley were to have an ill time of it as things turned out: with the doubtful exception of Nancy's, not a lasting passably happy marriage among the seven of them. When the spirited Hetty, exasperated by her father's vetoes on various potential husbands, eventually chose the wrong man to run away to (so briefly, for one unhappy night only), the Rector was to prove an unforgiving parent, who compounded his daughter's humiliation and wretchedness. But as a child Hetty had been intellectually precocious; she attended no school beyond her mother's kindergarten, yet at the age of eight was reading the New Testament in Greek. Mrs Wesley was no Latin scholar, and had no Greek. Who but her father could have taught Hetty? And it was from her father rather than her mother that she took her literary inclinations. The Rev. Samuel Wesley had been a tireless, if often flat-footed, poet. All three Wesley boys were to follow his example, and Hetty too became a far from contemptible poet.

When John Wesley was aged between seven and nine, his father was again more than once away in London for several months at a time, attending Convocation. At Epworth Church in his place there officiated a certain Rev. Mr Inman, who succeeded in offending many parishioners – not perhaps a difficult task – and also the absent Rector's family. He seems to have included in his sermons offensive innuendoes concerning Samuel Wesley's chronic indebtedness. Congregations fell away, and the resourceful Susanna Wesley took to holding her own services in the newly rebuilt, undeniably unconsecrated, but fortunately roomy rectory kitchen. At first only the family and servants attended, young John of course among them. Then outsiders were invited, and soon the Sunday evening flock in the kitchen outnumbered those in church on Sunday mornings. Protests from the locum priest and some of his sympathizers reaching the Rector in London, he posted off anxious enquiries to his wife. Was she not in effect conducting a conventicle, that thing of abhorrence to all devout Anglicans?

Mrs Wesley ably and eloquently rebutted the charge and defended the godly utility of her innovation. Against her were only 'the senseless objections of a few scandalous persons, laughing at us, and censuring us as precise and hypocritical'. (Her choice of adjectives already seems to presage the Oxford jibes soon to be cast at John and Charles for being so excessively methodical and holy.) After conscientious self-questioning Mrs Wesley continued on her course, reading prayers and sermons herself, and defending this heterodoxy to her husband on the very practical grounds that no man in her congregation had so carrying a voice as she, nor would any be able to read the words without having to spell them out first. Her heavenly master, she knew, approved of what she was doing; but if her earthly master should decide that the services must be discontinued,

Do not tell me that you desire me to do it, for that will not satisfy my conscience: but send me your positive command in such full and express terms as may absolve me from all guilt and punishment for neglecting this opportunity of doing good, when you and I shall appear before the great and awful tribunal of our Lord Jesus Christ.

The Rector, though still worried, issued no such veto.

CHAPTER 2

Oxford

THE WESLEYS' ELDEST SON Samuel had been to school at Westminster. He was thirteen years older than John who, although a fifteenth child, was only the second surviving son; and by 1714, when John was ten and himself ready to be sent away to school, Samuel had come down from Oxford and returned to Westminster as usher. He kept an elder-brotherly eye on John from time to time, but not quite as he would be able to do for the third brother, Charles, who was at Westminster from 1719. John was the only one of the three not to be at Westminster, his father having been glad to avail himself of the renewed benefaction of his old patron, Lord Normanby, grander than ever now as Duke of Buckingham, proprietor among much else of the brand-new Buckingham House, and donor of John's nomination for Charterhouse.

It was then, of course, a London school still, and John attended it for six and a half years, of which little is known. He must have been studious and made good academic progress. His Latin verses were competently turned. At sixteen he was already engaged on adding Hebrew, learned under the direction of his brother Samuel, to his Latin and Greek. We are told that he enjoyed talk and argument, and someone subsequently remembered seeing him harangue a group of younger boys, which does not surprise. His own strict later self judged that as a schoolboy separated from his parents' influence he slipped into some religious laxity, but even so he allowed that he always read the Scriptures and prayed twice daily. Certainly the years at Charterhouse did nothing to efface any of the teaching so painstakingly imprinted during his infant years. He went up to Christ Church, Oxford, in June 1720, a scholarly, sociable, but essentially earnest young man, just seventeen.

At Christ Church he had an exhibition worth £20 a year from
Charterhouse, but it was not long before he found difficulty in
making ends meet. Debts began to mount, in spite of a way of
life tolerably frugal, if not yet ascetic. His father was in no financial
position to help, and his mother remained concerned for her
Jacky's monetary situation until the end of his four undergraduate years, hoping nevertheless, she wrote, that 'a few crumbs
for you' would be turning up soon. (Her brother, Samuel
Annesley, of the East India Company, was expected home with
rather more than crumbs, and she went hopefully to London to
meet him, but he arrived neither then nor ever after.) 'Save
what you can,' Mrs Wesley meanwhile advised John, 'to pay
debts and make yourself easy.' John's brother Samuel, in addition
to being a schoolmaster at Westminster, also held a Studentship
at Christ Church and was able to give some practical help by
getting John's tutor to transfer to him the value of the rooms-
rent that Samuel, though non-resident, was entitled to.

Wesley never complained of the two tutors under whom he
studied as an undergraduate – the second of them, Henry Sherman,
became indeed a good friend – but of the studies themselves he
was in later life contemptuous. They had insulted common
sense; they were 'superficial', 'idle', 'useless'. At the time he was
less unhappy with them. He was, for instance, sufficiently pleased
with a pretty translation he made of some Latin verses celebrating
Chloe's favourite flea – how it strayed over 'her snowy bosom'
and found at last haven on 'her swelling lips' – to post the
composition off to his brother Samuel, that expert versifier. He
found life at Oxford enjoyable, and saw no harm in enjoying it
accordingly. As he wrote to his mother, a little after he had
taken his bachelor's degree, apropos of Thomas à Kempis, whom
'a religious friend' had advised him to read:

> I think he must have been a person of great piety and devotion,
> but it is my misfortune to differ from him in some of his main
> points. I can't think when God sent us into the world He had
> irreversibly decreed that we should be perpetually miserable in
> it. If it be so, the very endeavour after happiness in this life is a
> sin ... A fair patrimony, indeed, which Adam has left his sons, if
> they are destined to be continually wretched ..

Similarly with Jeremy Taylor's *Holy Living and Dying,* a book which nevertheless was to have deep influence on him: he could not accept Taylor's insistence that one could never know whether God had forgiven sins or no, and therefore that a true penitent must all the days of his life pray for pardon and never think the work completed till he died. Surely, wrote Wesley, God's graces are not of so little force that we cannot perceive whether we have them or no. If Jeremy Taylor's opinion was true,

> I must own I have been in great error; for I imagined that when I communicated worthily, i.e. with faith, humility, and thankfulness, my preceding sins were *ipso facto* forgiven me . . . But if we can never have certainty of our being in a state of salvation, good reason it is that every moment should be spent not in joy but in fear and trembling; and then undoubtedly in this life we are of all men the most miserable![1]

Correspondence on this subject with his mother, still first among his spiritual mentors, seems somewhat to have modified this view. Six weeks later he 'firmly' believed that 'we can never be so certain of the pardon of our sins as to be assured they will never rise up against us'. His mother's guidance was similarly sought on the subject of humility (where again he found Jeremy Taylor unsatisfying) and that oldest of theological stumbling blocks, predestination, with its trickiest of corollaries, the predetermined damnation of all but the elect of God:

> If it was inevitably decreed from eternity [wrote Wesley] that such a determinate part of mankind should be saved, and none beside them, a vast majority of the world were only born to eternal death . . . Now is this consistent with either the Divine Justice or Mercy? . . . I used to believe that the difficulty of Predestination might be solved by supposing that it was indeed decreed from eternity that a remnant should be elected, but that it was in every man's power to be of that remnant. But the words of our [i.e. the Anglican Church's] Article will not bear that sense . . . Your sentiments on this point, especially where I am in error, will much oblige and I hope improve
> Your dutiful Son.[2]

Susanna Wesley's verdict on this subject did not perhaps succeed in entirely disentangling itself from the age-old difficulty of reconciling God's benevolence with his omnipotence; but she trod with practised confidence through this well-reconnoitred logical minefield. Calvin's errors must be rejected. And that God *knew* a man would be damned must never be thought to mean that God *caused* that damnation. Divine foreknowledge must never be held to 'derogate from the glory of God's free grace, nor impair the liberty of man'. Man was 'free' to go to Heaven or to Hell, even if knowledge of his destination was lodged in God's eternal mind.

If Wesley's gaze was already concentrated towards eternity, this by no means yet involved any renunciation of the modest pleasures and decent convivialities of Oxford life. Even the pious regime of Epworth had permitted cards and dances and visits to local fairs. The Rector, though admittedly back in the friskiness of his youth, had even published a poem in praise of pipe-smoking – a lapse to be primly condemned by his Victorian biographer[3] – and now his son was not too self-denying to idle away some pleasant hours at backgammon or ombre, chess or billiards, or to find himself occasionally at a horse-race, or playing tennis two hours at a stretch, or drinking with friends in a coffee-house or tavern. He began too to develop a taste for the theatre, both in attending performances and by reading extensively among the Elizabethan, Jacobean, and Restoration dramatists – though he did not at the same time omit to study Jeremy Collier's famous diatribe against the *Immorality and Profaneness of the English Stage*. It was to be a considerable time before John Wesley's interest in theatricals was quenched. Horace Walpole indeed, forty years later, judged him 'as evidently an actor' as Garrick himself, and it is interesting to see him on three occasions jotting down in his diary in these Oxford days, 'Acted an hour' – presumably to himself in the privacy of his rooms. For the diary he was already experimenting with a system of cipher.

It was in this cipher, or in a mixture of cipher and abbreviation, or increasingly as time went by *en clair*, that he recorded his day-by-day activity, whether of profound significance or mundane unimportance; social; intellectual, spiritual; the severest self-chastisement along with a record of a breakfast engagement; friends or members of the family written to, hugger-mugger with religious exercises and rules for best employing time for the defeat of Satan; a record of books read, ranging from St Augustine or Thomas à Kempis to the light verse of Matthew Prior or Nahum Tate's translation of *Syphilis: or a Poetical History of the*

French Disease – all this side by side with such trivia as 'Collected Bennet', 'Walked round the meadow', 'Sat at the King's Head'; a note, or sometimes short criticism, of a sermon listened to, rubbing shoulders with memoranda of the steps of a new dance that needed to be learned: '. . . A gink with the other foot . . . Walk a little faster . . . First salute her, then bow, and hand her to a chair'; jottings too of verses that attracted him –

> Belinda has such wondrous charms
> 'Tis Heaven to lie within her arms . . .

– but also the sharpest self-questioning, concerning for instance the attractive companions he began seeing a good deal of, from 1725 onwards, down in the Cotswolds: 'Have I loved woman or company,' he asked, 'more than God?'

In these early diaries, begun when he was twenty-one, he was constantly reminding himself of Satan's snares and his own entanglement in them: breach of vows; boasting and pride in his own capabilities; greed for praise; peevishness; lying; 'heat in arguing'; 'sins of thought' and lustful imaginings; idleness, and in particular 'intemperance of sleep', by which he meant failure to rise, as he had resolved, by five o'clock. (Eventually four o'clock was to be his lifelong rule.)

His resolutions to counter these shortcomings were as determinedly recorded and critically reviewed, often on a Saturday evening, prior to the following morning's Communion. Against the self-accusation of inadequate devotion, for example, on Saturday 29 January 1726, he set down the necessary remedies, 'prayer and humility'; against pride, 'consider death, the Scriptures'; against idleness, 'six hours [work] every day'; against unclean thoughts, rather more mysteriously and threateningly, 'God's omnipresence'. His 'methodism' already only lacked the capital M.* He resolved to fast one day in every month. He must not fail to 'reflect' (after his mother's example) twice every day.

---

* The label of 'Methodist' was not new. It had been pinned, for instance, on a group of Catholic apologists in the 1680s. Used in the 1730s as a term of derision for Wesley and his Oxford associates, it came to be accepted by him, though at first usually with some such qualification as '*the people called* Methodists'. It is necessary to remember, however, that many people soon came to be 'called Methodists' who were followers not of Wesley but of such leaders as Whitefield, the Countess of Huntingdon, the Welshman Howel Harris, and others.

He imposed the daily task of rereading the previous week's resolutions. And, set down with as careful exactness as the state of his soul, were his everyday items of personal expenditure, whether for needles and pins, or occasionally an extravagance such as 'is. 2d. for cards at Mr Colley's'. Equally methodically, the diary entry for 9 March 1725 lists his college friends, seventeen of them.

The style of life was certainly not yet ascetic; nor even particularly severe. The self-prescribed six hours of daily study sound not inordinate, and Wesley by no means lacked modest comforts and respectable amusements. He always loved company and conversation; and among his student friends were those who, happening to come from closely neighbouring villages in the Cotswolds – at only a day's ride from Oxford – first introduced him at about this time to their families and connections.

It was probably John ('Robin') Griffiths, of New College, the Vicar of Broadway's son, who began this fortunate and, for Wesley, seductive association. Within a few miles of Broadway were the pleasant villages of Buckland and Stanton; and for the next eight or nine years after 1725, the Griffithses and Granvilles and Kirkhams and Tookers and Winningtons from the manorhouses and rectories of these few square miles along the Gloucestershire-Worcestershire border – and in particular the daughters of these substantial local families – were to play an important, if never more than subsidiary, part in Wesley's affairs. All his life, though he was to make such a lamentable hash of his various approaches towards matrimony, and eventually of marriage itself, he delighted in female companionship. Lacking inches, but with well-cut features and undeniable charm of manner, he was quickly at home in feminine company; found it easy, with his flowing talk, to get on socially and intellectually intimate terms with the several lively and attractive young women to be found among his new Cotswold connections – Robin Griffiths's sister Nancy; the two Granville sisters, Mary (Mrs Pendarves) and Anne, nieces of Lord Lansdowne and cousins of the Duchess of Queensberry; three Kirkhams, Sally, Betty, and Damaris, daughters of the Rector of Stanton; the Winnington girls of Broadway, nieces of a future Paymaster-General; Fanny Tooker; and Mrs Freeman, that 'wonderful lovely woman', as Wesley's diary saw her.

Back in Oxford, he fitted easily enough into the not over-rigorous university existence of that era, one of Oxford's more stagnant periods. The colleges had become, by and large, clerical corporations only marginally engaged in teaching. Research was generally neglected; lectures were delivered erratically or not at all; examinations were largely nominal. A high proportion of fellows were absentees. If not all, rather too many senior common rooms woke from their somnolence only to engage in college intrigue, or occasionally in less parochial and often anti-governmental university politics. For many, perhaps most, of Oxford's undergraduates and young graduates, their university terms provided a not too arduously academic interlude on the way to a country living. Of the rest, few would depend for their future way of life on what they learned or failed to learn at university. Oxford was a comfortable staging post between schoolboy youth and the life of the country gentleman.

Even however if it was intellectually in the doldrums, such a university as Oxford would never lack seriously inclined students or, as Wesley was fortunate to find, tutors prepared conscientiously to guide undergraduate studies. A great university in decay was still a centre of learning, a good place for a young man like Wesley to exercise his mind, to strengthen those walls of religious conviction whose foundations had been so solidly laid in the Epworth parsonage.

Oxford was then an essentially clerical institution, however closely its studies centred round the pagan classics. The majority of dons were in holy orders and all of them necessarily members of the established Church. Under Queen Anne their Tory and High Church inclinations were allowed to flourish. They had greeted the Hanoverian succession sourly and mistrustfully, and it had been only with difficulty that the Vice-Chancellor and heads of colleges had been able to restrain Jacobite sympathizers from rioting in 1715. Indeed there were some disturbances. In Wesley's undergraduate years, a decade or so later, the prevailing climate in Oxford remained suspicious of Whiggism in politics and Latitudinarianism in religion; mistrustful of toleration for Dissenters; and fearful of the insidious poisons of Unitarianism, Deism, or scepticism, whose potential attractions for susceptible undergraduates alarmed the conservative establishment.

Wesley was always proof against such heterodoxies. If Oxford's governing principles were politically and ecclesiastically 're-actionary', so then was he. So his father had been, underlining it when he became the ally of Dr Sacheverell in the famous impeachment affair of 1709–10, after that firebrand, from St Paul's pulpit, had violently attacked his fellow clerics of the Latitudinarian Low Church, and lambasted the Whig government for its support of Nonconformists, 'those miscreants, begot in rebellion, born in sedition'. Now it was the sermons of Sacheverell's supporter the Bishop of Rochester, Francis Atter-bury, recently exiled as a Jacobite, which were to occupy a prominent place in the reading list that Wesley kept for most of his Oxford years.

It was Jacobite leanings and association with Atterbury that were often reckoned to have hindered the advancement of Wesley's brother Samuel; and at Christ Church at least one of Wesley's closest acquaintances, who may well have influenced him during his later undergraduate and postgraduate years, was another diehard Tory of Jacobite sympathies – Jonathan Colley, Precentor of the college and presumably that same Mr Colley in whose rooms Wesley incurred his '1s. 2d. for cards'. It was Colley, twice Wesley's age, a learned, eccentric, and 'apocalyptic man, being much given to books upon the Revelation', who in May 1725 received a sharp reproof from the Dean, newly forced on Christ Church by the Whig government, for appointing a *penitential* anthem to be sung on King George's birthday.[4]

Wesley took his bachelor's degree in 1724, remaining at Christ Church with a view to proceeding to the degree of master, and then if possible securing a studentship (i.e. fellowship), which would among other things release him from worries about money. Taking holy orders would in any case mean a step forward, and he now wrote to his parents about it, not disguising the bread-and-butter considerations involved. His father's reply, while seeing no harm 'to desire getting into that office, even with Eli's sons "to get a piece of bread" ', bade him beware that that should not be his chief motive, which *must* be 'the glory of God, the service of his Church, with the edification of our neighbour'. The elder Wesley, sounding as though he had been having doubts recently about his son, professed himself sufficiently satisfied with John's recent letters to hope he would have 'no

further occasion to remember some things that are past'. (Debts?)
At first he pronounced against 'going over-hastily into orders.
When I am for taking them, you shall know'. Meanwhile he
recommended an intensive course of biblical studies – Thirleby's
Chrysostom de Sacerdotio ('master it; digest it') and other exacting
hurdles; above all, the Polyglot Bible ('compare the Hebrew, the
Vulgate, and the Samaritan'), compulsory study for mornings;
in the afternoons a free choice, 'but be sure to walk an hour, if
fair, in the fields'.

Susanna Wesley, as usual, did not quite see eye to eye with her
husband – 'an unhappiness almost peculiar to our family', as she
professed to think. She told John that she thought the sooner he
was a deacon the better. Either her persuasions or two further
letters from Oxford which the Rector found it possible to approve
must have brought him round to her point of view. He now
declared in favour of his son's intentions: 'But in the first place,
if you love yourself, or me, pray heartily. I will struggle hard, but I
will get money for your orders, and something more'.

Money troubles continued to loom throughout 1725, while
Wesley worked conscientiously at preparing himself for ordination. Only a fortnight before he was made a deacon, his father
was writing that he could not possibly 'manufacture any money',
at least for a week:

> On Monday I design to wait on Dr Morley [Rector of Lincoln
> College and also incumbent at Scotton, not far from Epworth]
> and will try to prevail with your brother [Samuel] to return you
> £8, with interest. I will assist you in the charges for ordination,
> though I am just now struggling for life . . . I like your way of
> thinking and arguing; and yet must say I am a little afraid on it.
> He that believes and yet argues against reason, is half a papist or
> enthusiast. He that would make revelation bend to his own
> shallow reason is either half a deist or a heretic. O my dear,
> steer clear between this Scylla and Charybdis . . .
>
> P.S. – If you have any scruples about any part of revelation, or
> the Articles of the Church of England, which I think exactly
> agreeable to it, I can answer them.[5]

The Rector had recently added £50 a year to his £130 from
Epworth by taking over the additional living at Wroot, a small
village five miles away across the watery flats, but this involved
paying a curate. Samuel Wesley's financial and domestic em-

barrassments, aggravated now by both his own and his wife's worsening health, were never to disappear.

Wesley's visits to the Cotswolds had begun while he was in process of determining on holy orders, during his first post-graduate year. The 'religious friend' whom he mentioned to his mother as introducing him to Thomas à Kempis was almost certainly Sally Kirkham, of Stanton Rectory. In April 1725 he noted in his diary, 'First saw Varanese. May it not be in vain.' This Cotswolds group of young friends had affected a current fashion in giving one another high-flown sobriquets, classical or literary. Thus Sally Kirkham became 'Varanese', the Granville sisters 'Aspasia' and 'Selima', John Wesley 'Cyrus', Charles Wesley 'Araspes', and so forth. It gave them a sense of being a 'set', a cosily select band of intimates.

That Wesley briefly toyed with the dream of marrying Sally Kirkham seems obvious, if the diary entry is to mean anything. Warming his hands by the fire, however, he already, as so often later, feared the flames. Besides, he had no money – indeed was still in debt. He perhaps hardly needed the advice given him by his eldest sister Emily, then suffering what she called 'the torment of a hopeless love' for one of John's Oxford acquaintances, Robert Leybourne of Brasenose College, and bitter at the breaking of a long engagement: 'Never engage your affection before your worldly affairs are in such a posture that you may marry very soon.'[6] Moreover, 'Varanese' was bespoken by the local school-master, John Chapone or Chapon, and before the end of the year was wedded to him. It proved a happy match, but the fact that 'Varanese' had married another by no means cut her off from 'Cyrus'. They remained on the closest terms of friendship – even, it might be thought, of something stronger still, which 'Varanese' herself recognized.

'I would certainly tell you,' she wrote to Wesley a few months after her marriage, 'if my husband should ever resent our freedom, which I am satisfied he never will.' Her 'esteem' for Wesley was manufactured out of 'reason and virtue' and was therefore fireproof. Thus, it appears, he might be safely allowed at least to touch her person and hold her hands while listening to the many 'obliging things' she spoke to him. It causes no surprise to find Damaris, the youngest Kirkham girl, telling Wesley afterwards that she believed John Chapone *was* jealous of him. 'Had you not

lost your dear Mrs C[hapo]n,' Wesley's sister Emily was to write
to him long afterwards '. . . you would not have been so spiritual-
ized, but something of this lower world would have had its
part of your heart, wise as you are; but being deprived of her,
there went all hope of worldly happiness; and now the mind . . .
losing its aim here, has fixed on its Maker for happiness.'[7] But
Wesley was labouring to convince himself in January 1727 that
his feelings for 'Varanese' and indeed for her sisters Betty and
Damaris, were those of a loving brother merely. It seems likely
that Damaris at least returned feelings somewhat warmer. As for
Betty, her brother Robert confided to Wesley that she often had
him in her 'thoughts', which Robert declared were accompanied
by 'inward sighs and abrupt expressions concerning *you*. Shall
this suffice?' he demanded.

During the Christmas vacation John and Charles were both at
Wroot, to whose parsonage the family had now moved temporarily from Epworth. The atmosphere there was hardly happy.
Hetty, 'ruined' by her recent desperate, disillusioning indiscretion,
found her contrition unacceptable to her father, who instead took
up with unfeeling alacrity her self-destructive offer to be married
off to the first respectable man presenting himself. This turned
out to be one William Wright, a half-literate plumber and
glazier. Patty Wesley was another who considered herself 'what
the world calls ruined', reckoning that when her father died she
would have the choice of three things – 'starving, going to a
common service, or marrying meanly' as her sisters Sukey,
Nancy, and Hetty had all done; 'what can a woman expect but
misery?' Emily, the disgruntled ex-schoolteacher, already thirty-
four ('Let me have one relation I can trust,' she begged John) was
equally fatalistic concerning her chances; resolved after her
misfortunes in love to stay single for ever and to remain at home
with her mother, whom it would be 'barbarous' to abandon. She
bemoaned 'those infinite debts my father has run into', leaden
weights round all their necks.

Between the summer of 1725 and spring of 1726 Wesley's
Oxford prospects brightened. Though nothing came of his hopes
of a Christ Church studentship, a vacancy arose for a Lincoln
College fellowship, open only to those born in the diocese of
Lincoln. Old Mr Wesley was soon busy pulling such strings as
were available to him, in particular exploiting his old political

connection with the family of the fellow of Lincoln who was resigning, John Thorold, and also his freshly tended acquaintance-ship with Dr Morley, Rector of Lincoln College. Frequently over these months John Wesley was visiting the College, canvassing his chances with its dons. He met some opposition apparently, and even some ridicule. His mother, advising him to avoid the company of irreligious mockers and 'profane wits', reminded him that many people had 'made shipwreck of faith and a good conscience merely because they could not bear raillery'.[8] Recently Wesley had resolved – once again – on a reform of his conduct and conversation, 'to set in earnest', as he put it, 'upon a new life . . . to aim at, and pray for, inward holiness'.[9] His father sent encouragement: 'Surely virtue can bear being laughed atl'

On 17 March 1726, Wesley's diary was able to record thanks to God for his unanimous election to the fellowship. 'I have done more than I could for you,' wrote his father. 'What will be my own fate before the summer is over, God knows.' There was little more than £5 to keep the family afloat till after harvest, 'and I do not expect that I shall be able to do anything for Charles when he goes to the university'. However, it was a great day for him: 'Wherever I am, my Jack is Fellow of Lincoln.'[10]

Wesley's new status, his generally friendly acceptance into the senior common room, his improved financial prospects (though he remained in debt) combined to make him for the time being well enough satisfied with life. He spent a good deal of the remainder of the year 1726 back at home – 'home' was still Wroot rather than Epworth – and he walked the many miles from Oxford, spending several months helping his father with church services and in the parsonage garden; building an 'arbour' there (in imitation perhaps of Varanese's in Stanton Rectory?); occasionally doing duty as Latin copyist for *Job*; discussing religion with his mother; reading the Restoration dramatists; shooting fowl; bathing in the river; frequently visiting friends among the more substantial local families. These apparently included even Hetty's seducer – if seduction there was – a lawyer, Will Atkins, at whose house he went dancing. This last excursion however did occasion observations in his diary con-cerning levity and scandalmongering, and indeed the diary retained its steady flow of self-reproof and self-exhortation.

Its compiler absent for a space with Cotswolds company, the

diary establishes a new character, Kitty Hargreaves, whose hands
it resolves that he must not hold any more; neither in future
must he touch the breasts of any woman.[11]

Such self-denying ordinances would frequently recur. In the
month that he wrote this one, August 1726, he also preached a
sermon at Wroot which was interpreted both by his own family
and the local population as constituting public criticism of his
father. Before preaching it, he characteristically showed it to his
mother, seeking her approval, which was probably less than
complete: 'You writ this sermon for Hetty', she said. The subject
was Universal Charity ('Be angry but for God's sake'), but an
implicit strand of its thought plainly alluded to the Rector's
treatment of his daughter – perhaps indeed to her treatment by
the family in general, with the one exception of her warm-
hearted crippled sister Molly (Maria), who had been tender and
kind. *Since* her marriage to the plumber, Wesley judged that
Hetty's conduct had been 'innocent'; yet his father remained
'inconceivably exasperated against her', had disowned her, and
never spoke of her 'in my hearing but with the utmost detestation.
Both he, my mother, and several of my sisters were persuaded her
penitence was but feigned.'

If Wesley really thought, as he seems to have done, that he
could wrap up reflections upon his father in general phrases about
universal charity and still give no offence, he was being strangely
naïve. 'You hear how he contradicts me and takes your sister's
part', the Rector complained to Charles (now eighteen, and soon
to be going up to Christ Church). Charles reported back to John,
who then decided to try making amends. The apology was 'not
without tears'. 'He kissed me, and I believe he cried too; told me
he always believed I was good at bottom . . . The next day I began
transcribing some papers for him.' Apparently Wesley felt he
was now free to stir again the same combustible embers, and it
was not long before he was preaching again, this time on Rash
Judging. Accounts of the Rector's wounded feelings reaching
Samuel junior, Wesley found he was having to defend himself at
length to his elder brother, in particular for having offended
against the spirit, at least, of that 53rd Canon of the Church
which forbids one preacher to criticize another's teaching from
the same pulpit. John was pained to find Samuel taking their
father's side.[12]

In her late fifties, Mrs Wesley was now losing that robust health which had seen her through the long years of bearing and rearing children amid chronic family difficulties. By July 1727 Samuel Wesley was warning John that he would find his mother 'much altered', with 'now and then some very sick fits' – though when, from that, John jumped to over-hasty conclusions, his father gently rallied him upon his 'supposition of her near approaching demise; to which your sister Patty . . . says . . . she cannot spare her mother yet, if it please God, without great inconvenience'. The Rector himself, proud as he was at sixty-five to walk sixteen miles in a day, and happy to encounter less hostility and better church attendance among his flock than of old, was finding his double parish a heavy burden. 'They tell me I have lost some of my tallow between Wroot and Epworth', he wrote. It was natural that he would be pleased to have his son John at home as often as possible to help in the parish work.

Wesley was now fellow of Lincoln, moderator, and college lecturer 'in Greek' (i.e. on the Greek Testament), but for the greater part of the time between April 1726 and November 1729, when he settled back in Oxford as college tutor, he was away from the university. On three occasions during 1727–8 Lincoln College granted him leave of absence. There is record of some brief lecturing when he was qualifying for his master's degree,* but in general he seems at first to have been typical of early Georgian Oxford lecturers in failing to deliver any lectures. Over this period of three years and a half he often acted for spells as part-time curate for his increasingly infirm father, not always without disputing with him.[13] At one point he toyed with the possibility of taking up the mastership of the comfortably endowed old school at Skipton-in-Craven in Yorkshire. 'A good salary is annexed to it,' he wrote, 'so that in a year's time 'tis probable that all my debts would be paid.' What chiefly attracted him was not the schoolmastering, but the fact that, the town being 'scarce accessible on any side', and he being, so he claimed, out of love with company, he would 'be entirely at liberty to converse with companions of my own choosing, whom for that reason I could bring with me'.[14] But the appointment went to another.

* He became Master of Arts in February 1727 and was ordained priest in September 1728.

Dislike of company, if it was genuine, must merely have marked a passing mood. From his two headquarters, his Oxford college and his father's parsonage, he in fact continued to busy himself with much visiting of neighbouring friends and relations. He went twice to London to see his married brother Samuel, his uncle Timothy, and other uncle Matthew, where he was able to meet Hetty. It was at Uncle Matthew's that Patty also went to live now. (A reluctant spinster at this stage, she stayed in London for six years.) Nearer home Wesley would often go over to see his other sisters; Sukey and her regrettably coarse and frequently drunken husband, Ellison, from whom she was eventually to separate; Nancy and her land surveyor, Lambert, at Gainsborough, where Wesley might join them and their friends in a quadrille or some similar diversion; Kezzy, the youngest, now a pupil teacher at Lincoln and hating it. The diary reveals also time spent 'with Miss Kitty [Hargreaves] in her closet' – presumably without the dangerous physical contact he had forsworn.

Then there was still 'Varanese', down at Stanton, with whom the talk was not always of religion. 'In the number of my friends,' she vowed, 'there is no one . . . in a stronger view than you.' And there was still Betty Kirkham and Damaris Kirkham (who rather strangely 'wished she had been a man for Wesley's sake'),[15] and Nancy Griffiths. Sometimes in this company too was the fascinating 'Aspasia', Mary Pendarves, whose seven unwilling years of marriage to a repulsive old man had left her a widow out of love with wedlock; who had just rejected the opportunity to become Lady Baltimore; and in whom Wesley claimed to find deep wells of spirituality. Mary Pendarves tried hard to find them too, if increasingly the distractions of fashionable society conspired to contaminate them. Certainly, after a game of ombre, she had fled in tears when Wesley followed her into the Stanton rectory kitchen and asked her, 'How prettily shall we reflect on our past lives thirty or forty years hence?' (In fact, not thirty or forty but fifty or sixty years later, a very old lady, the specially favoured protégée of King George and Queen Charlotte at Windsor, 'Aspasia' did reflect. She was by then a widow for the second time, having in middle life married again an older man, Swift's friend Dr Delany. Yes, she had known the Wesley brothers when they were at Oxford, young men 'of a serious turn'. Unfortunately, 'the vanity of being singular' had overtaken them and they had embraced an *enthusiasm* which 'many reasonable people thought pernicious'.) The proximity of this vivid, personable little man – so small in stature but so vibrant in personality, so searching in conversation – seems to have provoked in these susceptible young ladies a fair quantity of tears. While he was once reading aloud to them from a recently published volume which had impressed him, Betty Kirkham suddenly rushed weeping from the room.[16] The book, by one 'Lemuel Gulliver', was entitled *Travels Into Several Remote Nations of the World.* In Dublin its author, five or six years later, was briefly to make an especial favourite of the vivacious and intelligent Mary Pendarves.

A meeting of the Rector and Fellows of Lincoln in October 1729 decided that 'the interests of College and obligation to statute' required that Wesley, together with other absentees, should return to residence to carry out their duties as moderators – that is, to preside over and guide the disputations held each week-day in College Hall. Accordingly, and perhaps glad to have an excuse for relinquishing his unofficial curacy in dank, inhospitable Wroot, he returned to Oxford the following month, and was soon established there as moderator in philosophy and tutor to eleven undergraduates. For some time his personality and activities seem to have aroused little criticism from his fellow dons. He resumed his soberly convivial round. He made many social excursions. There is still mention in the diary of cards, dancing, concerts, even one or two references to some obscure gallantry. ('Hope still' is vague enough – it appears the lady in question may have been a London actress* – but 'Perhaps innocent!' baffles conjecture.) It was however a different and much more significant aspect of Wesley which after a time began to attract hostile comment in the senior common room at Lincoln and indeed eventually beyond the confines of the college.

But the Holy Club, of which he was soon the directing force, was of Charles, not John, Wesley's founding.

---

* See V. H. H. Green, *The Young Mr Wesley*, 138–9. Charles Wesley refers, not too seriously, to a once 'dear creature' of his brother's, who, so he has discovered, has had numerous lovers and is currently 'happy Mr Thompson's'. Charles himself was undoubtedly involved for a time with a young actress. Congratulating himself on escaping ensnarement, he vowed in future to be less addicted 'to gallantry and doing what Sister Hetty with less justice said you [John] did – liking woman merely for being woman'.

CHAPTER 3

The Holy Club

UNTIL HE WAS PAST twenty Charles Wesley, though he paid conventional allegiance to Christian beliefs and observances, showed no pronounced evidence of piety. Lively and good-looking (though small of stature like John), he had arrived at Christ Church from Westminster a freshman humanly susceptible to the entertainment offered by university company and by not too distant London. By then the most striking thing he had done was to reject an offer which would have given him large estates in Ireland. A rich kinsman, Garrett Wesley, having no immediate heir, was looking for a more distant relative to whom he could bequeath his property. After Charles finally decided to turn down this opportunity, it was accepted by one Richard Colley, who adopted the name of Wesley, became subsequently Lord Morning-ton, and proved to be the grandfather of the future Duke of Wellington. (The family chose late in the eighteenth century to spell their surname Wellesley instead of the earlier Wesley or Westley.)

According to John Wesley's later testimony, his younger brother's life had been 'regular' and 'harmless' enough at this time, but 'if I spoke to him about religion, he would warmly answer, "What, would you have me a saint all at once?" and would hear me no more'. In his later evangelizing days, Charles Wesley liked to paint a more lurid picture, in a style unhappily common among reformed self-styled sinners, of the unregenerate youth whose 'diversions' had kept him 'dead to God and asleep in the arms of Satan'.

After one undergraduate year of idleness, he started working but, no great scholar, he found the going hard. He wrote to

John both for advice and spiritual comfort: 'there is no one person I would so willingly have to be the instrument of good to me as you'. Should he keep a diary 'to mark all the good and ill' he did? He would be 'at a stand' till he heard. In this, his waking out of lethargy, Charles was quite aware of his brother's part.

This new-model Charles began to prove severely censorious of those round him whom he found to be indifferent Christians, wastrels, or idlers. His friend Kirkham, young brother of the sisters from Stanton Rectory, he pronounced to be 'wretchedly lazy'. As for another of his old Westminster-Oxford friends, Lushington, 'what intimacy can I ever have hereafter with a man of his morals and his gratitude?' But at the same time he was earnest in pursuit of conversion and rescue. The undergraduate in the rooms next to his own in college 'having got into vile hands', Charles had 'been, thank God, somewhat instrumental in redeeming him', helping him to celebrate Communion without his previous fears of being laughed at. To forward these and similar endeavours, and to meet frequently for prayers and discussion, Charles Wesley enlisted the collaboration of one or two like-minded college friends, though the Christ Church atmosphere was discouraging – 'the worst place in the world to begin a reformation in'. It was a wealthy, fashionable college whose prevailing conventions made small demand on student piety. To celebrate Communion as often as once a week indicated an eccentric excess of zeal; but Charles and his tiny band struggled on against the amusement of the ungodly. Against their own backsliding too: 'I won't give myself *leizure* to relapse,' wrote Charles to John, 'for I'm afraid if I have no business of my own the Devil will soon find me some.'

John had been a mentor at a distance. When he returned to Oxford in November 1729 it was natural that he should take over the leadership. As an Oxford friend, John Gambold, noticed of Charles: 'I never observed any person have a more real deference for another . . . He followed his brother entirely.' John Wesley was by four or five years the senior, outstandingly the best scholar, and also the most forceful personality among the group. For his own private 'holiness' he had to wrestle like any other, but although through most of his life he was prone to stumble into severe trouble in managing his own personal affairs, from very early he relished the directing of others. He had, wrote Gambold, 'something of authority in his countenance, though as he did not want address, he could soften his manner and point it as occasion required'. Anxious to discover proper humility before God, he had little diffidence before men. His fingers felt instinctively for the reins of authority, even while in his diary he was constantly reminding his better self of what his careless, lazy, uncharitable, snobbish, vain, proud, fleshly and generally fallible other self was up to.

He and Charles, with William Morgan (elder son of a prominent Dublin lawyer and Treasury officer), Francis Gore (of Westminster School and Christ Church, like Charles), Robert Kirkham (Varanese's brother), and John Boyce (the mayor of Oxford's son) seem to have constituted the nucleus of the so-called Holy Club by the middle of 1730.[1] It was on Morgan's initiative that in August of that year they began extending their scope by visiting prisoners in 'the Castle' (one of Oxford's two prisons) and also some of the city's destitute. According to Morgan's brother Richard, writing somewhat after this, they fasted two days in the week, almost starving themselves in order to buy necessities for the poor, including books for their religious conversion; tried to rescue prostitutes; exorcized spirits in haunted houses; and in general imagined they could not be 'saved' unless they spent every minute of their lives in God's service.

Wesley later denied to Morgan's father that Holy Club members tried to 'reform notorious whores or lay spirits in haunted houses'. As for ghosts, it is undeniable that they always did fascinate Wesley, who believed in them as unshakably as he did in the Devil himself, and claimed for them both evidential and biblical support. More than once in his letters home he tells of investigating hauntings, and once of learning of a levitation which had been vouched for by a bishop as 'the work of the Devil'. Earlier, while he was away at school, there had been much to-do about an Epworth Rectory ghost, which seems to have manifested itself in perplexingly protean guises. All his life Wesley was to remain intrigued by the phenomenon of 'Old Jeffrey', this versatile Epworth spirit. He collected all the available evidence when he was in his twenties and was writing an article about it in his eighties, finally arriving at the conclusion that the activities of this supernatural messenger had been designed to remind Samuel Wesley senior of his sin in deserting his wife in 1702.

John at first had some doubts about the propriety of the prison-visiting, and consulted among others his father. Samuel Wesley wondered whether some of these hesitations did not 'secretly proceed from flesh and blood' – which he exhorted both sons to subdue 'by fasting and prayer'. Still, he blessed God that they had grace and courage to proceed in the path their father had trod before them – for he recalled that he too had as an undergraduate gone prison-visiting. Proud of his boys, he was not inclined to deny himself some share in their merit: 'I hear my son John has the honour of being styled "the father of the Holy Club",' he wrote. 'If it be so, I am sure I must be the grandfather of it.'

Wesley consulted his father again when he began to encounter some enmity towards the Club at Christ Church, 'between mirth and anger', and heard too that at Merton, Kirkham's college, the Club 'was become a common topic of mirth'. Again Samuel Wesley breathed encouragement, this time in the Greek of 2 Corinthians vii. 4: 'Great is my glorying of you'. 'Bear no more sail than is necessary,' he advised, 'but steer steady'; surely they would not weary of well-doing because of 'the crackling of thorns under a pot'? Mrs Wesley sent her blessing too, though she did express a wish that John would not affront custom by wearing his hair long, a fashion moreover which was both bad for the complexion and injurious to health. (Wesley replied that at least it was not unscriptural, and it did save him two or three useful pounds a year in dressing and wigs.)[2] The Bishop of Oxford also gave at least his passive support, and Wesley was encouraged further to extend the Club's undertakings, visiting the local debtors' prison to pray with the inmates, to bring them small luxuries such as candles, and even, where the debt was small, to work for their release.

He had not yet turned his back on social pleasures altogether, but increasingly he would be found sitting out when the company was at cards or dancing, more especially if the day were Saturday, when Sunday's Communion was to be prepared for. But all his

days, not merely Saturdays, were soberly programmed. They
began sometimes at four, normally by five, in the morning. Each
hour was to be marked by an 'ejaculatory prayer',* every three
hours by repetition of the collect for the day; at every meal a
grace; Communion at least once a week; set time for meditation;
a relentless regularity of self-exhortation and of self-accusation
for private vows broken or pieties not properly achieved. And
amid all this of course his routine duties continued as tutor and
moderator.

No wonder that Aspasia (Mary Pendarves), removed now from
Gloucestershire to fashionable New Bond Street, should write to
him, 'The life of noise and vanity that is commonly led here
cannot possibly afford any entertainment for you.' Swept up in
the whirl of the *beau monde*, socially inclined but serious-minded,
she was still willing to be spiritually tended for a time, at a safe
distance, by her little clergyman's flattering solicitousness; and
for a year or two it was Aspasia who took pride of place from
Varanese in such dangerous dreams of feminine perfection as
Wesley's arduous disciplines permitted. 'I can't but often observe
with pleasure,' he wrote to her, 'the great resemblance between
[his feeling for her] and that with which my heart frequently
overflowed in the beginning with our dear Varanese. Yet is
there a sort of soft melancholy mixed with it, when I perceive
that I am making another avenue for grief . . .' He was aware that
the social gulf between them was wide, that he was liable to
commit 'improprieties of behaviour in which my inexperience
of the world so frequently betrays me'. 'The eternal law is
between us!', he wrote. 'I may pursue, but must not overtake! I
cannot leap the bounds.' But he might still aspire to be 'one soul'
with her, profess 'the tenderest esteem', write her long letters
which not altogether pleasantly mingle urgent proselytizing,
fulsome adulation, and sententious moralizing. He corresponded
too with Mrs Pendarves's much younger sister Ann Granville
('Selima') in self-conscious 'literary' tones which combine highly
artificial flattery with earnestly decorous exhortation. With Selima
his emotions were less involved, but his anxiety to see her
spiritually improved was no less:

* 'They had a book of *Ejaculations* relating to the chief virtues, which
lying by them as they stood at their studies, they at intervals snatched a
portion out of it' – John Gambold.

O Selima, would it but suit your health, as well as it would your inclinations, to rise at six and give the first hour of the day and part of the next to your public addresses to God, God . . . would repay it in prospering all your following employments. You would then never repent either giving what time remained of the morning to some lively writer in speculative divinity, or your calling in from the afternoon or evening . . . an elegant poet or judicious historian.

Ann Granville's professions of pleasure in being thus 'taught the happiness of being above trifles' at least started out, we may believe, in sincerity; but the road turned stony, and little Cyrus's recommended reading proved of a density impenetrable to her. Both sisters, while expressing effusive gratitude and *promising* to read a digest Wesley specially prepared for them of the Bishop of Cork's *Procedure, Extent, and Limits of Human Understanding*, very soon discovered, modestly and realistically, the limits of their own – and at the same time, perhaps, of Cyrus's understanding of their generally conventional, decently pleasure-loving, upper-class selves.

While she read his letters, however, Mary Pendarves found herself 'carried above the world'. 'O Cyrus . . . how are you adorned with the beauty of holiness!' As for the imputation he told her was being ascribed to him in Oxford, of 'carrying things too far in religion', she was ready enough to pronounce it 'extraordinary'. On the contrary, he was rather 'in a state to be envied', unlike those among whom her life was now led, where many made 'an open profession of having no religion at all'. She sought his opinion on the prospects in a future life of a London acquaintance, a man of every social and personal virtue, yet one who denied the Trinity and the divinity of Christ; but Wesley's reply could offer only an unhopeful prognosis for this friend's eternity. The Gospel was exceeding plain: 'He that believeth not shall be damned'.

Wesley begged his Aspasia to protect herself not merely against the vanities that surrounded her in London, but more particularly against 'those choicest instruments of mischief, "they that do no harm" . . . May you ever remember that we are to resist, not stand still . . . that to be innocent we are to be active.' For another friend of Aspasia's who was suffering from 'a coldness' when she said her prayers, Wesley had ready a prescription that 'seldom failed to be of service' if the draught were only taken regularly (it is not likely that he was in any degree shaken by Aspasia's helpless reply, that her friend had already tried this physic, and it had reduced her 'to death's door'):

> Are you inattentive in prayer? pray oftener. Do you address to God twice a day already? then do so three times. Do you find yourself very uneasy before the sacrament, though you receive it every month? Your next resolution, with God's leave, should be to receive it every week.'[3]

On several occasions during 1730 and 1731 Wesley found time for short stays with his Cotswolds circle of friends, walking and talking, preaching at Stanton, sitting in Varanese's arbour, taking tea with the ladies, attending a dance or two, being 'much tempted' to play cards. Aspasia and Selima were not there; and to Aspasia in June 1731 he wrote, after a week of 'almost uninterrupted conversation' with 'dear Varanese', of how tenderly they remembered their distant friends. 'On this spot she sat', 'Along this path she walked'; and then, forelock-touching again, 'Here she showed that lovely instance of condescension'.[4]

Already in the preceding January Mary Pendarves had requested that he should burn all her letters to him, and in August 1731, again insisting that he must,* she added, 'Pray don't make use of any epithet before my name when you write to me. I have not time to tell my reasons.' Excusing herself for not having written earlier, she rather weakly pleaded eye-strain. Once when Wesley was up in London with Charles, she and her sister found themselves, first, 'obliged to go abroad for supper' and so with little time to spare, and then again 'obliged to put off the favour you designed', this time owing to a dubious-sounding indisposition. Wesley had been anxious to see her again, so that he might speak what he could not write. Had perhaps some 'indecent or foolish expression' displeased her? He had 'a thousand things to say, would time permit; but, O believe, I can never say half of what I feel!'

In September 1731 Mary Pendarves left London for Dublin, where she received from Wesley a further instalment of his diagnosis of her unnamed friend's spiritual sickness. 'O Aspasia,' he burst forth, 'how amiable do you appear while you are em-

* Apparently he did, but methodically made copies.

ployed in such offices as these, especially in the eyes of him who seeth more clearly than man seeth! . . . Watch over me too for good, Aspasia.'[5] But the hum of Dublin's life and the attractions of its 'vanities' were no less than London's. 'Company is come'; Cyrus's letters remained unanswered. There were parties, dinners, balls, ridottos; there were Dr Swift and his friend and champion, Dr Delany. 'Cyrus has by this time,' she wrote in March 1732, 'blotted me out of his memory; or if he does remember me, it can only be to reproach me . . . I declare 'tis want of time!'[6]

Of course he was hurt. When at last she did write again it was only to say, 'I never began a letter with so much confusion . . . I find it impossible to say anything in my justification . . . To tell you my engagements with the world have engrossed me . . . will be enlarging my condemnation.' 'Alas, Aspasia,' Wesley wrote sadly in reply (his last letter to her), 'experience has shown how far my power is short of my will. For some time I flattered myself with the pleasing hope, but I grow more and more ashamed of having indulged it . . . Doubtless you acted upon cool reflection . . . I sincerely thank you for what is past; and may the God of my salvation return it sevenfold into your bosom.'[7]

He was writing this in July 1734, when he was thirty-one. For a year or two before that, his work in Oxford had been attracting considerable notice, some of it approving, some critical. Among those who saw in the Holy Club promise for a revival of a sterner and purer Christianity, and gave money towards its charities, was the veteran parliamentarian and philanthropist Sir John Philips, whose great wealth had already contributed to assist recently formed movements to promote free schools in Wales, the propagation of the gospel, and the reformation of manners. (His benevolent intentions had some decades previously embraced a parliamentary act to make blasphemy, profanity, or denial of the Trinity punishable by imprisonment, and adultery by death. The Commons had jibbed at this last.) Of the hostile criticism greeting the Holy Club, some was conventional ridicule. More seriously, some fastened on the dangerous fanaticism of its members; in the vocabulary of the day, their *enthusiasm*. In 1732 this condemnation was fortified when one of the Club's founder members died – in effect killed himself, it was alleged, by an excess of fasting and self-mortification.

William Morgan's earnestness for God proved too much for

him. His weakened body fell an easy victim to tuberculosis; his mind collapsed in religious hysteria and, at the end, maniac raving. Ill in the preceding year, he had then (according at least to Wesley's own later account)[8] professed himself 'exceedingly well pleased' with the prospect of early death. His father, however, not able to share this sanguine fatalism, wrote insisting that the allowance he paid his son should be used for health and education and reasonable recreation, and not for the indulgence of extravagant and eccentric evangelizing. 'You can't conceive,' he wrote, 'what a noise that ridiculous Society which you are engaged in has made here.'

In February 1732 Wesley wrote a long letter to his mother, consulting her opinion on the doctrine of the Real Presence,* and sermonizing in very rhetorical vein on the renunciation of the world and the fear of death – being too much 'afraid of dying before one has learned to live'. Apropos of 'thoughts of dying', he added a few words about William Morgan which sound impatient and even callous. By this time Morgan could not 'bear to have [his approaching death] named, though he can neither sleep, read, stand, nor sit. Yet without hands, or feet, or head, or heart, he is very sure his illness is not increased. Surely now he is a burthen to himself and almost useless in the world . . .'

With difficulty they got Morgan home to Dublin and he died there, insane, in August. It was of the Wesley brothers, his father wrote, that he raved most of all towards the end. Aware that people in Oxford were accusing the brothers of causing his death, Wesley hastened to defend himself to Mr Morgan: 'I am obliged to clear myself . . . Your son left off fasting about a year and a half since.' The letter swelled to become a long apologia for 'the Godly Club' and its practices, which did admittedly include 'observing the fasts of the Church, the general neglect of which we can by no means apprehend to be a lawful excuse for neglecting them'. What Wesley showed no hint of understanding was the danger to sanity inherent in the impact of fanatical zealotry on a naïve sensibility and immature mind. He had convinced himself, and seems to have persuaded Mr Morgan, that

---

* 'We cannot,' Wesley thought, 'allow Christ's human nature to be present in [the sacrament of the Communion] without allowing either con- or trans-substantiation. But that his divinity is so united to us then . . . I firmly believe, though the manner of that union is utterly a mystery to me.'

fasting had played no part in William Morgan's original illness or eventual death. Instead, all was glory. The young man had 'acted like a faithful and wise servant, who, from a just sense that his time was short, made haste to finish his work before the Lord's coming'.[9]

Mr Morgan was sufficiently persuaded of Wesley's sincerity and reliability to allow his younger son, Richard, to enter Lincoln College in October 1733 as a gentleman commoner with Wesley as his tutor, though he hoped he might 'be excused of being solicitous' to prevent him falling into his elder brother's extremes. It soon appeared that between Wesley's interpretation of 'extremes' and the younger Morgan's there was a gulf. On his arrival Richard Morgan fell in with current undergraduate trends and fashions, which included keeping a greyhound in college rooms – a matter on which Wesley 'spoke to' him. Besides this, Morgan soon found himself being given what he considered excessive moral and spiritual attention by his tutor, and therefore complained to his father who, with the earlier tragedy in mind, suggested to Wesley that 'for young people to pretend to be more pure and holy than the rest of mankind is a dangerous experiment'. Wesley, watchful and conscientious, but quite failing to understand his pupil's resentment at being told what hours he must keep, what dogs he must not keep, what books he must read and not read, what taverns, coffee houses, and other sensual snares he must avoid, what pangs of eternal damnation must await sinners, stumbled one day in Morgan's rooms on an unposted letter to Mr Morgan senior, bemoaning the barrage of holy fire he was being subjected to, and the life that was being forced on him:

> The whole College makes a jest of me, and the Fellows themselves do not show me common civility, so great is their aversion to my tutor . . . He has lectured me scarce in anything but books of devotion. By becoming his pupil I am stigmatized with the name of Methodist, the misfortune of which I cannot describe . . .

Mr Morgan, while threatening to disinherit his son if he should persist in idleness, extravagance, or vice, advocated a sensible moderation on both parties. But Wesley, aggrieved and persevering, considered – it seems rightly – that in the campaign for Richard Morgan's soul he had lost a battle but not the war. In no time he had succeeded in persuading the young man that 'few can be saved'. Within six months (according to Charles Wesley) Morgan was 'in a fairer way to becoming a Christian than we ever yet knew him'. Wesley's unrelenting pressure told. Morgan joined the Holy Club and remained a member when in 1735 Wesley embarked for Georgia.

Not all Wesley's successes in Oxford proved as lasting. To make converts to godliness was relatively easy; to retain them, more difficult. In particular, when the two brothers were on vacation, the Club's membership was inclined to languish. This had happened when they visited home in the summer of 1731 (walking the nearly three hundred miles there and back, and reading as they went). 'Since our return,' Wesley wrote to his mother, 'our little company that used to meet us on a Sunday evening is shrunk into almost none at all.' Again in the spring of 1733, after Wesley had been away from Oxford for seven weeks, visiting his parents, he found on his return that many of the weaker members had been seduced from their strict allegiance – by the fear of appearing singular, by a taste for secular books, by Dr Frewin's common-sense counsels against fasting, by the attractions of warm beds and regular meals. Where twenty-seven had previously attended the weekly Communion, the number had fallen to five.

Wesley's hold on members who were not his own pupils could not hope to be complete; but with those who were, his persistence was unremitting. His diary for 1733, for instance, discloses the battering into eventual submission of two of his Lincoln undergraduates, Matthew Robinson and John Robson. Many times they resolved, after their tutor's adjurations and reminders of God's powerful justice, to rise early, to communicate regularly, to observe appointed fasts, to eschew pagan authors, to deserve grace. Repeatedly the flesh rebelled, and (we may suppose) intellect too, once their tutor's heavy guns were temporarily resting. There would follow scenes, tears, remorseful rededications to godliness, renewed relapses. When in September 1735 he was due shortly to leave for America Wesley was still bombarding John Robson with his authoritative rulings and fervid exhortations: dining in college hall on Friday was 'utterly unjustifiable', although the Wednesday fast, while probably apostolical, was *not* strictly obligatory. Fasting must be regarded as a means not simply to chastity, but to the twin desiderata of 'deadness to pleasure and heavenly-mindedness'. In such measure as it agreed with health, it was therefore necessary 'to all persons in all times of life'. As to giving 'offence . . . by adhering to the gospel of Christ', Robson was told, 'till a man gives offence he will do no good'. He should try to avoid 'luke warm company', or if he strayed among it, should 'pray before, after, and during' his stay in it 'fervently and without ceasing'. We cannot be wholly surprised if young Robson should have found this way rather too strait for him, but as he wavered and pondered the more comfortable paths of unrighteousness, he was left with his tutor's accusing challenge staring up from the paper: 'I charge Mr Robson in the name of the Lord Jesus that he no longer halt between two opinions.'[10]

Others of those under Wesley's tutelage at this time were two of his future brothers-in-law: John Whitelamb, of Wroot (the crippled Molly's future husband), who had earlier been employed as copyist by Wesley's father and entered university at the late age of twenty-two – a young man of whom, at this time, Wesley still had high expectations; and Westley Hall, of a good Salisbury family, a gentleman commoner, whom Wesley at first found 'holy and unblameable in all manner of conversation', and in whom Mrs Wesley (when John brought him home on a visit to Epworth in 1734) thought she discovered 'extraordinary piety and love to souls'. He did indeed seem sincerely, even immoderately, pious. Only Samuel Wesley junior, a shrewder judge of character than his brothers, saw through him from the first, thinking him at once smooth and shifty, with something 'foul at bottom'. He was indeed to prove an unscrupulous and unstable hypocrite, whose plausible charm wrought havoc with two of Wesley's sisters. First, allegedly under God's direction, he proposed marriage to Kezzy, the youngest Wesley girl, even fixing the day for the wedding. Then, after listening to some anti-Kezzy propaganda from John Whitelamb,[11] and being vouchsafed a change of instructions from the Almighty, he suddenly transferred his marital intentions to Patty, who unluckily accepted him. For this treachery and 'perfidy', Charles, Kezzy's champion, castigated the older sister in some lines of bitterly violent censure,[12] and both he and John always held Hall responsible later for poor Kezzy's slow decline and eventual death. Hall was to become as wide-ranging in his doctrinal as in his sexual attachments. From

Methodism he turned to Moravianism, then to Antinomianism, and finally to a sort of Deism, eventually preaching a polygamy which would have lent legality to his own long-standing practice. Before he ultimately deserted her and went off with a mistress to the West Indies, Patty was to bear him ten children, every one of them dying in infancy or childhood. Of all Wesley's 'failures', Westley Hall would be perhaps the most spectacular.

In the Oxford of the early and middle 1730s the brothers drew into their company many more soberly devout supporters, several of whom were to become of importance to their movement. There was John Gambold of Christ Church, who would one day become the first English bishop of the Moravian Church; John Clayton, fellow and tutor of Brasenose College, a strong High Churchman and Jacobite; William Clements of Lincoln, and afterwards Magdalen, College; James Hervey, of Lincoln; the Yorkshireman Benjamin Ingham of Queen's; and among others, some time during 1733, the nineteen-year-old George White-field, of the Bell Inn, Gloucester, and Pembroke College.

Whitefield, like Wesley earlier, the young Samuel Johnson, and so many others, had been deeply impressed by William Law's *Serious Call to a Devout and Holy Life*. He had attended the Holy Club's Communion service at the Castle prison, and then, by his own account, 'strenuously defended them when I heard them reviled by the students'. Soon, through an introduction to Charles Wesley, he began like the Methodists 'to live by rule . . . to the glory of God'. His interpretation of that rule was harsh indeed, and he was one of those who starved themselves into a state of extreme debility. God, he claimed, 'was pleased to permit Satan to sift me like wheat'. From that enemy's wiles, however, and the 'long night of desertion and temptation', during which he had been 'groaning under an unspeakable pressure both of body and mind for above a twelvemonth', he was eventually delivered by the grace of God and John Wesley's 'excellent advice and management'.[13] The philanthropic Sir John Philips helped to sustain him at Oxford with a grant of £30 a year; at twenty-one, 'abashed with God's goodness to such a wretch', he was ordained at Gloucester; and the following year, at Bristol, he began astonishing himself and rapturous congregations with the fervid flow of his eloquence.

*

As he aged and grew more infirm, the Rev. Samuel Wesley became more and more accident-prone. He fell from a stumbling horse and was dragged after it. His boat, alternative means of transport between his two parishes, was wrecked in foul weather and he had to be rescued by John Whitelamb (still at that time his assistant and amanuensis). Then in June 1731, when he was sixty-eight, a fall from one of his farm wagons left him seriously disabled. Sixteen months later Mrs Wesley feared he had 'but a short time to live', and in January 1733 his life was despaired of. He recovered, but at seventy-one he relinquished his watery parish of Wroot – and the hand of his daughter Molly – to John Whitelamb, who was by that time down from Oxford and doing service as curate. 'They love the place, though I can get nobody else to reside on it', the Rector explained. But he still looked towards resigning his main Epworth living to a successor who would provide security of tenure for himself in his last days, for his wife (or, as he expected, his widow), and for any remaining unmarried daughters. This must argue an arrangement within the family, without which their future prospect would look comfortless indeed – the subscriptions taken up for *Job*, whose elephantine gestation proceeded, remaining less than satisfactory.

The Rector's first approach was to his eldest and favourite son. But the Rev. Samuel, junior, churchman, poet and schoolmaster, had recently left his assistant-mastership at Westminster for the headmastership of Blundell's School, Tiverton, in Devon, and was not minded to change his course. In any case, he thought the cure of Epworth was the obvious destination of his brother John, to whom the Rector next addressed himself. (Charles was not yet ordained.)

Wesley's refusal disappointed and grieved the old man, who charged his son with being more concerned with his 'dear self' than with 'the glory of God', and begged him to think again,

> if you are not yet indifferent whether the labours of an aged father, for above forty years in God's vineyard, be lost . . .; if you have any care for our family, which must be dismally shattered as soon as I am dropt; if you reflect on the dear love and longing which this poor people have for you . . .

The five thousand or so words of Wesley's letter of refusal,[14] methodically numbered in sections 1–26, are among the most unpersuasive and unattractive things he ever wrote. He would have come better out of this exchange with his father if only he could have brought himself simply to say, 'I cannot give Oxford up, I like it here too much; and only here at Oxford can I be free of parochial and domestic trivia, and wield the influence for good I feel capable of.' But in his over-anxiety to justify himself, he exposes a number of his less lovable characteristics – an in-sensitivity in human relations, a certain priggish-sounding complacency, a holier-than-thou-ness.

His attempted apologia for the life-style of his choice is transparently, even disastrously, honest. Which of the alternatives before him, he asked, the life of the college or of the country parish, would conduce more to his *own* improvement? Em-phatically Oxford must better promote his 'holiness'; and 'where I am most holy myself, there I could most promote holiness in others'. There was 'no other place under heaven where I can always have at hand half a dozen persons nearly of my own judgement and engaged in the same studies . . . constantly watching over my soul'. At Oxford he was blessedly free from the frivolity of commonplace persons and the company of 'luke-warm Christians'. The petty cares of the world were largely removed from his shoulders: income, meals, 'my laundress, barber, etc.,' were always to hand. And to complement these comforts and amenities there was the joy of being able to earn a degree of his fellows' contempt, 'a part of that cross which every man must bear' if he would follow his 'Saviour's judgement . . . A man cannot be saved without being despised'. Contempt indeed was to be earned at Epworth too (he grants that his father earned a great deal of it), but the strong implication is that to earn it in Oxford would be both more tolerable and more salvation-worthy.

And with what sort of profit, he argued, could he undertake the care of 2000 souls in a parish like Epworth? 'I see not how any man living can take care of an hundred.' As for the par-ishioners, what would happen when he came 'to tell them plainly that their deeds are evil'?

> Alas, sir, do I not know what love they had for you at first? And how have they used you since? . . . What have you done there in so many years? Nay, have not the very attempts to do good . . . brought such contempt upon you as has in great measure

disqualified you for any future success? And are there not men in Oxford who are not only better and holier than you, but ... being universally esteemed, are every way fitter to promote the glory of God in that place?

Following on these cruelly frank words, the letter's closing paragraph rings singularly false:

> ... As for the flock committed to your care, whom for many years you have diligently fed with the sincere milk of the Word, I trust in God your labour shall not be in vain ... You shall come to your grave, not with sorrow, but as a ripe shock of corn, full of years and victories. And He that took care of the poor sheep before you was born will not forget them when you are dead.

What Wesley is really saying, behind all the letter's long sermonizing and bandying of texts, is that he cannot accept a life of day-by-day contact with ordinary people. He hungers for righteousness, and to be persecuted for righteousness' sake, but not amid Epworth's humdrum acres, with their 2000 souls, their 'trifling acquaintance' and 'impertinent company'. He aspires to take up his cross daily, give 'the word of exhortation' to paupers, jail-birds, tender minds, 'babes in Christ to be instructed and perfected in all useful learning' – but it is to be where he can keep his 'eye single' in a haven of retirement. For a man who only five years later was to claim the world as his parish, his horizon was still surprisingly close-bounded within his academic groves.

When his brother Samuel, again taking their father's part, accused him of having broken an engagement made at his ordination to undertake the cure of a parish, Wesley rebutted the charge, even applying to the bishop who ordained him to obtain written testimony that it was unfounded. But positively as he continued to assert that he could not give up any part of his Oxford life 'without manifest hazard' to his salvation, he was plainly shaken, and driven to re-examine the rectitude of his position afresh. Perhaps, he conceded, he *would* take a parish. Lincoln College disposed of four locally, and – still intending to retain the college fellowship – 'I do not know but I may take one of them at Michaelmas'.

CHAPTER 4

Georgia

WHAT HAPPENED OVER the next few months to shake his determination to remain at Oxford is not clear, but family events must have played a considerable part. By April old Mr Wesley was on his deathbed, and John and Charles were there with him in bedside prayer and Communion before he died. There must then have been many family discussions of their various futures, and it seems likely that Wesley for a time was influenced by concern for his mother's in particular. Certainly at one stage he decided, despite all that he had so recently vowed, to take over his father's rectorship if the succession could be arranged. But by then it was apparently too late. Others had applied for Epworth, and the Lord Chancellor, patron of the living, bestowed it on a Mr Hurst. So, after thirty-eight years, Mrs Wesley was obliged to leave the Rectory. She went to live, over the next few years, at different times with her children Emily, Patty and Samuel. Both Emily and Patty were married shortly after their father's death (leaving only Kezia a spinster) – Patty to the still seeming-godly Westley Hall, and the unhappy, unlucky, and often bitter Emily (now forty-four) to Robert Harper, an unprospering Epworth apothecary, with Wesley officiating at the ceremony. Emily's was very far from a love match and certainly did not change her luck. Her husband could never afford to keep them both, and she continued to teach in Gainsborough. Her brother John she called 'the dear partner' of her 'joys and griefs'; to him alone, she wrote, her 'heart lay open at all times'.

During the summer of 1735 Wesley employed himself tidying up the final stages of his dead father's ten years' labour on *Dissertationes in Librum Jobi* and preparing them for publication. A

copy was formally presented by him on 12 October to its dedicatee,
Queen Caroline, who gave 'many good words and smiles', and
declared it 'prettily bound' before laying it 'down in a window
without opening a leaf'. The world's reaction to it proved not
greatly dissimilar.

Two days later Wesley was at Gravesend, from where the ship
Simmonds was to take him, first to Cowes Roads, and thence to the
not at all Oxonian destination of Savannah in Georgia, the newest
and rawest of Britain's American colonies. (It was less than three
years after the arrival of the first shipload of settlers.) On board,
in the Thames and Solent, he was already 'instructing and
exhorting the poor passengers . . . catechizing the children,
explaining the Scriptures, and applying them in private conversation' – and not forgetting, when writing to his brother Samuel,
to beg him to remove from his pupils' studies such 'poisonous'
works as Ovid's, Terence's *Eunuch*, and Virgil's *Aeneid*, which
tended 'to inflame the lusts of the flesh' and feed 'the pride of
life'. In Georgia he expected to be isolated from the lusts of the
eye, the palate, or the flesh (he would see 'no woman but those
which are almost of a different species from me'). Moreover, by
preaching to the heathen Indians, whom he took to be 'as little
children, humble, willing to learn', he would himself learn 'the
purity of that faith which was once delivered to the saints'.[1]

In January he had argued that only in Oxford could he reach
such godliness as his salvation demanded. Now, in October, he
could not see that there was anywhere in England where he
might 'attain the same degree of holiness' as in Georgia. The
initiative in persuading him to undertake this mission had come
from Dr John Burton of the Society for the Propagation of
Christian Knowledge, one of the colony's Board of Trustees and
an old Oxford acquaintance. Wesley had then briefly but strenuously consulted his friends, his brother Samuel, his mother (who
expressed approval), and not least his Maker. 'I shall plainly
declare the thing as it is,' he wrote to Dr Burton. 'My chief
motive, to which all the rest are subordinate, is the hope of
saving my own soul.' It is an important admission. John Wesley
would never be one with the Ancient Mariner, from whom the
albatross fell away only when, upon an impulse of wonder and
benevolence, *unaware* he blessed the water-snakes:

Sure my kind saint took pity on me
And I blessed them unaware.

Wesley was far from unaware. He had viewed in the distance the
heavenly city through whose gate so few might pass, methodically
mapped out the road towards it, and planned the fitness exercises
necessary for the journey. The 'chief motive' for his chosen way
of life was acknowledged as openly to others as to himself.

The *Simmonds* was one of two ships, protected by a naval sloop,
carrying emigrants that autumn to Georgia. On board was James
Oglethorpe, soldier, member of parliament, and philanthropist,
the prime mover in the establishment of that still infant colony,
which was intended by its charitable founders as a land of refuge
and fresh opportunity for British debtors and physically able
unemployed, for Highland Scots, and for oppressed European
Protestants. The government saw in it a valuable forward
position to protect the Carolinas against the Spaniards to the
south, as well as an adjunct to 'the trade, navigation, and wealth
of his Majesty's realms'. [2]

The company aboard the *Simmonds* was a variegated assortment:
a jail-delivery of discharged debtors and their families; twenty-six
men, women and children of the pietist sect of 'primitive
Christians' known as the Moravian Brethren;* besides Oglethorpe,
one or two other 'gentlemen' connected with the new colony,
and emigrants not 'on the charity', with their wives and servants;
Wesley himself; his young associate the Rev. Benjamin Ingham
and still younger devotee Charles Delamotte; Wesley's brother
Charles, recently ordained and appointed to be Oglethorpe's
secretary; and of course a ship's crew of not noticeably religious
complexion, including a second mate 'insolent and turbulent'
enough to be removed to the escorting sloop. Westley Hall and
his wife Patty had planned to be of the party too, and got as
far as Gravesend; but they turned back, for Hall to take up an
English benefice. Still in Spithead, Wesley quickly made his

---

* Their origins went back to the fifteenth century in Bohemia and Moravia,
but the Thirty Years War had almost annihilated them. The persecuted
remnants fled to Germany, and during the 1720s the movement was re-
founded by Christian David and redirected under the protection of Count
von Zinzendorf, on broadly Lutheran principles but with the ambitiously
ecumenical aim of restoring unity to Christianity. Harassment however did
not cease; and this, together with their missionary zeal, had taken some of
them to Georgia.

influence felt by causing one of the gentlemen's maids, 'who was a known drunkard and suspected of theft and unchastity' to be put ashore.³ Another gentleman quit the ship because he found it an 'inconvenience' to have 'the great cabin' used by Wesley and his group for public prayer.

From the outset they were proselytizing. Of the eighty or so passengers, between thirty and forty were soon attending prayers, and as many as twenty-one the Communion services – figures methodically noted in the diary,* as indeed in neat tabular form and elliptical shorthand were each day's incidents and occupations: how hourly ejaculatory prayers were adopted among their 'company', dropped, readopted, and then dropped again by majority decision; how on occasions Wesley found Charles 'perverse' or Oglethorpe 'open and friendly'; how God significantly caused a child to stop crying at the very moment when Wesley began reading in Law's *Christian Perfection*; how Charles and he agreed to turn teetotal and vegetarian at least for the voyage's duration; how he spent from nine to twelve most mornings with the Moravians, learning German; how Mrs Moore, one of Oglethorpe's woman servants, appeared very 'serious' when she was ill and seemed ready to take stiff doses of Norris's *Christian Prudence*, but how 'in a few days she recovered from her sickness and her seriousness together' – and later she, and her husband and others, were 'so angry at me that they resolved (and prevailed on some others to do the same) never to be at prayers more'; and a great deal more, in the most painstaking and revealing detail.

The women aboard brought Wesley, the indefatigable soul-saver, high if over-credulous hopes to begin with, but in the end little but acrimony and disillusionment. There was Mrs Lawley, recovering in her cabin from illness, whose initial receptiveness to the Word failed to survive Wesley's prolonged readings from William Law and his well-intentioned efforts to heal her feud with other passengers. One of these, Mrs Hawkins, wife to an apothecary-surgeon and reckoned by Wesley to be a 'gay young

* Now for the first time to be somewhat incorporated into what became the *Journal*. A fair sample of the diary's shorthand reads: 8 re c ap p s h s c 1 2 3 4 p t b x – which seems to mean, 'At eight a.m. read chapter appointed; prayed; sang hymn; said the Creed, and Collects 1, 2, 3, and 4; Tate and Brady's metrical version of the Psalms; expounded.' The day's entries would begin with a 4, his usual hour of rising.

woman', seemed to him however to be so affected by his repeated ministrations – 'always attentive', he noted, 'and often much amazed' – that he admitted her to Communion, against the wishes of Ingham, Charles, and others of the ship's congregation, who judged that she was merely acting piety. Both Wesley brothers were to discover later in this Mrs Hawkins one of the most explosive of their Georgia problems.

Then there was Mrs Welch, advanced in pregnancy, who was thought to be dangerously ill and for much of the voyage therefore was bedded in the obliging Oglethorpe's own cabin, while he slept in a hammock. (This too was to have repercussions later.) Wesley was convinced that her health began its recovery from the moment she received Communion from him; but, as with others of the ladies, he eventually perceived that he was 'getting no good' – an expression much in evidence in the diary. When finally Mrs Welch, four days after arriving in Georgia, was safely delivered of her child, Wesley was present (with, he explains, 'only a door between us') and found his sense of the fitness of things outraged that this woman experiencing 'one of the deepest distresses which life affords', groaning away with only 'very short intermissions', should have been surrounded, *not* by 'strong cries to God', *not* by 'exhortations . . . to fear Him who is able to inflict sharper pains than these', but 'with laughing and jesting, at no time convenient, but at this least of all. Verily,' he then concludes in the *Journal*, adopting his least likeable vein of censorious piety, 'if they hear not Moses and the Prophets, even the thunder of His power they will not understand.' Eleven days later, baptizing the baby and alert as ever to discern divine intervention, he saw evidence of that power afresh: the child, who had been ill, *recovered from that hour*.[4]

Wesley's failure to comprehend the ways or detect the wiles of the women aboard the *Simmonds* – members of his future flock – worried him. Before long he would be seeking advice on the subject from one of the leading Moravians in America, August Spangenberg, who passed on to him a quotation from Thomas à Kempis, freely interpreted by Wesley to mean, 'Speak to Mrs Hawkins seldom and in few words, and earnestly pray God to do the rest'. The dangers he saw in his situation were heightened by his apparent attractiveness to many women; and some of these fellow voyagers and future parishioners of his were young and

Friday March 26. I find great many unclean thoughts arise in prayer [or devotions], and discovered these temptations to it.

a. Too much addicting myself to a light behaviour at all times.
b. Listening too much to idle talk, or reading vain plays or books.
c. Idleness, and lastly—
Want of devotion—consideration in whose presence I am.
From which I perceive it is necessary
b. To labour for a grave and modest carriage.
a. To avoid vain and light company; and
c. To entertain awful apprehensions of the presence of God,
d. To avoid idleness, freedom with women, and high-seasoned meats.
e. To resist the very beginnings of lust, not by arguing with, but by thinking no more of it or by immediately going into company; lastly
To use frequent and fervent prayer —

- - - - - - - - - - -

FRIDAY, *March* 26. I found a great many unclean thoughts arise
in prayer [or devotions], and discovered these temptations to it :
 a. Too much addicting myself to a light behaviour at all times.
 b. Listening too much to idle talk, or reading vain plays or books.
 c. Idleness, and lastly—
 Want of devotion—consideration in whose presence I am.
From which I perceive it is necessary
 a. To labour for a grave and modest carriage ;
 b. To avoid vain and light company ; and
 c. To entertain awful apprehensions of the presence of God.
 d. To avoid idleness, freedom with women, and high-seasoned
 meats ;
 e. To resist the very beginnings of lust, not by arguing with, but
 by thinking no more of it or by immediately going into
 company ; lastly
 To use frequent and fervent Prayer.

One of Wesley's Sets of Rules and Resolutions in cipher, prefacing his Oxford Diary.

James Oglethorpe

Peter Böhler

Susanna Wesley

Mary Granville,
Mrs Pendarves

attractive too. He was, he felt, 'in jeopardy every hour', and would soon be asking (in the prudent intimacy of Greek, since letters in Georgia tended to be intercepted) for the assistance of his brother Charles's prayers that he should 'know none of them after the flesh'.[5]

Jeopardy more immediate arose from the Atlantic storms. A foretaste of these, experienced while they lay in the relative shelter of Cowes Roads, had already demonstrated to him his unfitness, because unreadiness, to die. Time and again, during his crossings of the Atlantic and the dangers he was to experience in Georgia, he was smitten by this terrifying realization that, were he to die at that moment, he could not be certain of salvation. As the Bible seemed undoubtedly to threaten, and as his mother had so constantly and menacingly taught to all her children, there were few indeed who might expect to be saved.

Ten days after the storm in the Solent, in mid-ocean, he wrote:

> The sea broke over us from stem to stern; burst through the windows of Mr Oglethorpe's cabin, where three or four of us were sitting with a sick woman, and covered her all over . . . About eleven I lay down . . . and in a short time fell asleep, though very uncertain whether I should awake alive . . . O how pure in heart must he be who would rejoice to appear before God at a moment's warning![6]

On subsequent days the gales grew fiercer still, the sea once coming 'with a full, smooth, tide over the side of the ship' and bowling him clean over. On another occasion, when the mainsail was split and some of the English aboard took to 'terrible screaming', he found it significant when the Moravians, in mid-psalm, 'calmly sang on'. Seemingly these German brethren, and also their womenfolk and children, owned an assurance which the English – including alas himself! – lacked.

When, a day or two after arrival in America, Spangenberg enquired of him whether he 'knew Jesus Christ', whether he *knew* that he was a 'child of God' and 'saved', he found himself equivocating in his replies. 'Do you know yourself?' asked Spangenberg. 'I do,' Wesley answered; 'but,' his *Journal* adds, 'I fear they were vain words.'[7] In Georgia the Moravian Brethren continued to impress him with their sober meekness and wisdom, the mutual harmony of their existence, their fidelity to the teachings of the primitive Church. He was to spend much time among them, lodging with them at first, and incidentally fast improving his German. Soon after arriving in Georgia, he was present among them when they elected a bishop. It was an occasion whose simple solemnity prompted in Wesley a fancy that seventeen centuries had been momentarily rolled back: it was as if he was one of a company 'when Paul the tent-maker or Peter the fisherman presided'.[8]

The *Simmonds* anchored off Savannah on 5 February 1736, and within a week or so Wesley had made contact through a woman interpreter with the local chief of the Creek Indians, one who had previously been brought over to England under the auspices of the Georgia trustees, and had expressed willingness to hear the Great Word of the white man. For a time Wesley's view of the Indians remained hopeful, indeed starry-eyed. They had such 'gentleness', such 'softness of tone and manner'. But Oglethorpe was realistically wary of letting unprotected missionaries loose on what Wesley regarded as the prime task he had come to America to undertake. Nothing was to come of various pious and courteous exchanges with the Creek chiefs, and when in June 1736 Wesley asked to be allowed to make an expedition to the more distant and (as he heard) less 'corrupted' Choctaws, Oglethorpe objected. It was too dangerous; and, moreover, the Choctaws were associated with the French. There was more than enough for Wesley to do, ministering to Savannah and the smaller Georgia settlements. In time, the idea of an Indian mission was completely set aside amid the demands of his pastoral work among the settlers; and his eventual, second-hand judgement upon the 'poor heathens', whom he had come to give God's word to but had succeeded in making such insignificant contact with, plummeted sharply: 'all, except the Choctaws', were apparently 'implacable, unmerciful' – drunkards, thieves, dissemblers, liars, abortionists, adulterers, murderers. Sons killed fathers; mothers cut children's throats; 'whoredom they account no crime'.

Life at Savannah, or at Frederica (to which brand-new settlement, a hundred miles to the south, Charles departed in company with Ingham and Oglethorpe immediately after landing) was in itself tough enough. Savannah, ten miles from the Atlantic coast up the Savannah river, was a struggling new gridiron-style townlet of a hundred or so houses, only just beginning to emerge from the wilderness clearing and the first temporary encampment of wooden huts. It had a court-house, but as yet no church. Its pioneers, coming from so wide a variety of classes, backgrounds, religions, and even nationalities, labouring to adapt to a new environment, in a hot climate, were living under great physical and moral pressures.

Oglethorpe, not an 'enthusiast' but a convinced and philanthropic Christian, was as anxious as the rest of the Georgia trustees to maintain moral standards among his heterogeneous community. He approved and did his best to enforce the trustees' bans on rum, Negro slavery, and unlicensed trading with the Indians. He would not presumably have disapproved of Wesley's first exercise of authority on arrival at Savannah: staving in the rum casks which had been aboard the *Simmonds* and with whose contents the crew and some passengers were celebrating the safe completion of their passage, a step which cannot have made him the most immediately popular of men. Oglethorpe respected Wesley's rigid principles, while demurring at some of the more fanatical of their manifestations. He allowed himself without protest to be reproved by Wesley for irregular attendance at divine service, and to be persuaded into issuing an order that fishing and fowling should cease on Sundays. On the other hand, to live on dry bread, or sometimes bread and butter, and water, as Wesley did for a considerable time – and not merely in Lent – struck him as eccentrically abstemious. He begged the minister to make it known to his flock that eating animal food or drinking wine was not positively wicked. (Wesley, however, tackling meat and wine again, was quite persuaded they gave him a five days' fever.)⁹ What Oglethorpe obviously did recognize in Wesley – and found lacking in his brother Charles – was business efficiency. More and more during Wesley's stay in Georgia he found himself employed, sometimes for up to six hours a day, as the Governor's secretary and personal assistant.

It is surprising that in Savannah, with its adult population of some one hundred and eighty professing Anglicans, Wesley should have gained even as many adherents as he did. He made what most might reasonably have thought impossibly exacting demands. To be accepted as 'serious', that is as a communicant, his flock were expected regularly to attend his morning service, usually at five, though sometimes at six or as late as eight o'clock.

'I mean,' he explained, 'every morning, winter and summer, unless in the case of sickness.'[10] All prescribed fasts were to be strictly observed. While he required absence from Communion to be satisfactorily explained, credentials for being allowed to partake in it were rigorously scrutinized. Thus Dr Bolzius, one of the pious Salzburgers for whom he had the deepest personal respect, he still felt obliged to bar from the Sacrament.* On the other hand he employed exclusion from Communion as a means of priestly discipline, for repeated absence from services for instance, or for doing some 'wrong to neighbours, by word or deed'.[11] One of the presentments eventually lodged against him before the Savannah Grand Jury in August 1737 was that he had refused celebration of the Lord's Supper to those who would not conform 'to a grievous set of penances, confessions, mortifications, and constant attendance of early and late hours of prayer, very inconsistent with the labour and employments of this Colony'.[12]

Another cause of dissatisfaction was his refusal, even with such influential citizens as one of the town bailiffs and his wife, to baptize a baby other than by 'dipping', which the bailiff, among others, would not allow. It was a maturer Wesley who, some fourteen years later, wrote to a Baptist minister: 'I wish your zeal was better employed than in persuading men to be either dipped or sprinkled. I will employ mine by the grace of God in persuading them to love God with all their hearts and their neighbours as themselves.' At this most stiff-necked stage of his development, Wesley was an out-and-out stickler for the rubric and his own interpretation of it; and if this gave offence, then he would glory righteously in giving it. 'If therefore,' he wrote, 'striving to do good, you have done hurt, what then? So did St Paul.' He was outraged when, on his return from one of five visits he made to Frederica, where he had been officiating in place of Charles, he discovered that the military chaplain substituting for him in Savannah had baptized 'several strong healthy children in private houses' and married 'several couples

* He later came to see the folly of such rigidity. Remembering this exclusion of Dr Bolzius, he wrote in 1749: 'Can any one carry such High Church zeal higher than this!' In a similar vein of self-criticism the aged Wesley recalled in 1789: 'In my youth I was not only a member of the Church of England but a bigot to it, believing none but the members of it to be in a state of salvation'. (*Letters*, viii. 140)

without first publishing the banns'. 'O Discipline,' he lamented rhetorically, 'where art thou to be found?'[13]

His behaviour, personal and priestly, gave occasion for both puzzlement and indignation. 'I like nothing you do,' he was told straight by one Horton, magistrate at Frederica during the temporary absence of Oglethorpe; 'all the people are of my mind, for we won't hear ourselves abused.' People sometimes wondered, Mr Horton implied, whether Wesley was not some sort of Catholic. 'They cannot tell what religion you are of . . . They do not know what to make of it. And then your private behaviour – all the quarrels that have been here since you came have been 'long of you . . . You may preach long enough; but nobody will come to hear you.' 'I had nothing to do,' Wesley comments, 'but to thank him for his openness, and walk away.'[14] He undoubtedly thought it his duty to brave, even actually to court, unpopularity. When for instance a gentleman issued invitations to a ball, Wesley, that once energetic dancer, set about organizing the forces of righteousness against this occasion of worldly vanity, claiming the victory when that day the attendance at worship outnumbered the ballroom's.

For eighteen months in Georgia he worked with the intensest concentration – up usually at four, conducting service frequently by five; meditating, praying, *singing* (giving fervent religious voice was a regular feature of the Wesley day); performing the many pastoral chores of a parish priest, 'going from house to house exhorting the inhabitants to virtue and religion';[15] spending much time with the Germans, translating into English verse several of their hymns, which he included in a collection he now began preparing for publication;* beginning to learn Spanish, hoping thereby in the future to be able to communicate with the handful of Georgia Jews; giving French lessons to good, genteel Miss Bovey; even conducting services in their native languages for the benefit of small Protestant communities from France and

---

* This, the first of *sixty-two* collections of religious verse to be composed or compiled by one or both of the Wesley brothers John and Charles between 1737 and 1785, was published in Charleston. Some of the hymns and metrical psalms were of his own composition; there were renderings from the German; and about a third were by Isaac Watts whom, Dissenter though he was, Wesley admired. Verses by the Catholic John Austin were slightly adapted to fit them for Protestant worship, and George Herbert, too, received some editing. Both Samuel Wesleys, father and son, were represented.

Italy; reading the proofs of his brother Samuel's latest collection
of poems; studying constantly in the library of devotional and
theological works he had brought with him; writing home, once
to Varanese, and among many others to his mother, who was
now in severe trouble, having to be rescued by her son Samuel
from arrest for debt (in the circumstances Wesley's exhortation
to his mother and sister Emmy to 'renounce the world, deny
yourselves, bear your cross with Christ, and reign with him'[16]
sounds singularly gratuitous); writing to two of the Georgia
trustees, to request their support in the attempt to stop Carolina
trampling unscrupulously upon Georgia's charter rights to
control, by licence, her trade with the Indians; conscientiously
visiting, in addition to Frederica, such outlying small settlements
as Cowpen, Skidoway, Thunderbolt, and the Salzburgers' village
of Ebenezer; always ready to rough it on often arduous and
sometimes dangerous journeys on foot, by river, or along the
coastal waters of Georgia.

He was proud of his stamina and ability to make light of
physical hardship, though still disturbed by his unreadiness to
die, 'to be dissolved and to be with Christ'. His diary entry for
20 May 1736, its writing betraying in places the motion of the
little open boat in which he was then journeying towards
Frederica with Delamotte, will give an example of his terse,
sometimes cryptic, but minutely thorough jottings, as well as a
record of one not untypical day. The figures tell the time:

3½ [a.m.] Rowed; conversed. 4 Rowed; conversed. 5 Rowed:
prayer, conversed . . . 6 Great trouble, Mr Delamotte drest me
[Wesley was suffering from what he variously describes as 'St
Anthony's Fire' (erysipelas) and boils.] 7 Set out; translated
German. 8 Translated German. 9 Began de Renty [i.e. reading a
life of a seventeenth-century French mystic]. 10 de Renty. 11
Washed feet. Verses. Lay by. 12 Dined; very hot; conversed.
1 Set out; read Renty; wind rose. 2 Renty; very rough! 3½ On
Millikin's Island; on business. 4½ Greek Testament. Supper;
conversed with two; no water. 5 Conversed. Set out; verses;
water; rough! afraid! 6 Water, S. Katherine's Sound. Rough!
7 On the sand; conversed; exceedingly afraid! 8 Conversed. 9½
on S. Katherine; could not find water! . . . 10.30 Found water.
Lay on shore.

Once, journeying from Savannah to Frederica by flat-bottomed barge, Delamotte and he anchored one evening

> near Skidoway Island, where the water, at flood, was twelve or fourteen feet deep. I wrapped myself up from head to foot in a large cloak, to keep off the sand-flies, and lay down on the quarter-deck. Between one and two I waked under water, being so fast asleep that I did not find where I was till my mouth was full of it.

He swam and climbed his way out of that particular misfortune, not failing to add in his account of it, 'Thou art the God of whom cometh salvation: Thou art the Lord by whom we escape death.' But getting soaked to the skin was nothing unusual, and lying at night in the open, under rain or dew or even frost, would harm none, he was sure, whom the Lord had in his arms and whose constitution had not been 'impaired by the softness of genteel education'.[17]

At Frederica Charles Wesley began his brief disastrous career as Oglethorpe's secretary for Indian affairs. It did not take him long to discover how ill-suited he was to both the secretarial and pastoral duties expected of him. Obviously, many of Frederica's brand-new settlers – sweating to establish themselves in what was still mainly a palmetto hut encampment won from the wild, with the Spaniards dangerously close to the south of them – were soon to find the behaviour of their resident priest provoking, even infuriating. In this rough-and-tumble frontier environment, with its far from godly assortment of pioneers, ex-debtors, adventurers, and misfits, he looked likely to prove the greatest misfit of them all.

Several times a day (Mrs Hawkins said four) he summoned them all to public prayers by roll of drum. He buttonholed them tirelessly to discuss and ameliorate their spiritual condition. Like his brother, he held very closely to the rubric, refused to baptize infants other than by trine immersion, and demanded absolute observance of the Sabbath. He was seen as the cause of Hawkins the apothecary-surgeon being confined in the lock-up because he had gone shooting during divine service. Charles Wesley regarded it as his duty to enquire conscientiously into reported breaches of the Commandments, and his perhaps especial concern for the seventh led him to be duped by the malicious inventiveness of two women who had obviously become exasperated with him.

Mrs Hawkins, the apothecary's wife, and Mrs Welch (the godlessly cheerful circumstances of whose recent confinement had so shocked Charles's brother) together seem to have agreed penitently to confess to the busily interested priest that they had shared the bed of Governor Oglethorpe – and then complained virtuously to Oglethorpe that the minister was spreading abroad this scandalous slander concerning them. It appears that they then succeeded in persuading Oglethorpe, who was for various reasons now quite ready to consider his secretary a knave as well as a fool, that it was Charles Wesley himself who was the amorous villain of the piece. (His unwise late night visits to Mrs Welch had been motivated, as he explained to an angry and frustrated Oglethorpe – who was anxious only to get on with protecting Frederica against the Spaniards – by his honest desire to put her on the road to salvation.) Oglethorpe had more substantial complaints against Charles. He idolized the *forms* of religion, with the result that 'the people came slowly'. More heinously, where the success of the new colony was touch and go, he was guilty of 'stirring up the people' to desert it. This was 'mutiny and sedition'.[18]

It is not surprising that Charles should have become lonely, despondent, and ill. He was aware that every man's hand was against him. His congregation dwindled – in the end almost to zero. He was largely ostracized, and denied some of the barest necessities of existence. His life was threatened, and it seems that once he was indeed shot at. There was hardly sufficient recompense in being enabled, as he wrote in his *Journal*, 'to pray earnestly for my enemies, particularly Mr Oglethorpe, whom I now looked on as the chief of them'.[19] In alarm for his friend, Ingham set out to find John in Savannah and added his own disquieting details to those supplied in Charles's letters. Immediately John made the difficult journey to his brother's help. He found him 'exceeding weak, having been for some time ill of a flux; but', John's *Journal* adds, 'he mended from the hour he saw me. This also hath God wrought!'[20]

Wesley stayed at Frederica for a week, preaching at Sunday service 'in the new store house' on sin and salvation; reading, or hearing read, Charles's private diary ('!!!!' is the comment in John's own); doing his best to unknot the Oglethorpe-Charles-

Mrs Hawkins-Mrs Welch tangle. 'God will reveal all', he assured himself, but meanwhile he tirelessly assisted, interviewing Oglethorpe and Hawkins – both apparently 'very angry' – and trying to get truth and sincerity out of Mrs Hawkins and Mrs Welch, a slippery and even at times hazardous undertaking, yet one whose fascination was not to be resisted. He was indefatigable in pursuing these heart-to-heart exchanges, but found both women baffling subjects, either for analysis or for improvement. One moment Mrs Welch appeared to be 'soft, open and affected', the next 'dark' and 'dissembling'. Was she making a fool of him, as she had of Charles? Or was she perhaps as passionately and neurotically inclined as her collaborator in mischief Mrs Hawkins? Or had the whole thing been a plot hatched by Mrs Hawkins (as Mrs Welch once alleged) that they might be rid of the parsons and then have Oglethorpe all to themselves?[21]

This apothecary-surgeon's wife, the 'gay young woman' of the voyage over, has always figured as the villainess in the recounting of these notoriously unfortunate episodes in the Wesleys' careers. Plainly she was a dangerous and violent woman, though one does sometimes feel that it might be illuminating to have had *her* version of events. According to Charles, she spoke in 'a loose, scandalous dialect', 'joking about prayers, declaring she would be no longer priest-ridden'. She certainly seems to have had a low threshold of exasperation, which both the brothers – and perhaps life in general in this raw, hot, frontier outpost – managed soon to cross. But she may not have been simply the licentious calculating termagant and liar usually depicted. (Charles's *Journal* actually describes her as not only a 'complete hypocrite' but implausibly as 'a common prostitute'.)

Wesley, in his frequent intimate soul-examinations with her, found her sometimes 'sad', 'melancholic', 'in tears'. 'There is none of those who did run well whom I pity more,' he wrote. 'When I reflect on her condition my heart bleeds for her.'[22] She may well have had 'seriousness' enough in some moods to be 'much affected' by the persuasive earnestness of this eloquent, vigorous saver of souls. Sometimes his diary notes her to be 'open and mild', 'very civil and serious and open'. Then suddenly she turns 'cold', 'reserved', 'out of humour', or on occasions violently resentful and hysterical, 'in a passion and utterly unreasonable'. After first hearing from Charles, Wesley was

originally convinced that she and Oglethorpe had been lovers.
Then he became, after his researches, *almost* sure for a time that
they had not. 'Mrs Hawkins and Oglethorpe,' his diary records
on 16 April 1736, 'seem innocent; Amen! She quite angry.'
But then, mysteriously to complicate the scenario: 'Mrs Welch
in a swoon. Open my eyes!'

Oglethorpe, who saw no reason to disclaim having pursued
some earlier amorous adventures, both denied and pooh-poohed
this one. After his easily understandable anger was expended,
his comment to Wesley was dismissive: 'The thing itself is a
trifle. Tis not such things as these that hurt my character – they
would pass for gallantries and rather recommend me to the
world.' After John had set out to return to Savannah, Oglethorpe
said to Charles: 'I took pains to satisfy your brother, but in vain.
He here renews his suspicions in writing. I could clear up all, but
it matters not.' He was just off on an expedition against the
Spaniards from which he thought he might not return. His
relations with Mrs Hawkins (which Charles, at least, now voted
not guilty) were of very minor importance.

In mid-May 1736 Charles found himself both ashamed and
delighted at being allowed temporarily to leave Frederica, in
order to dispense at Savannah the Governor's licences for
Indian trade, and during May-June he and John exchanged
places for a month. By July, however – back in his dreaded
'furnace' of Frederica – Charles decided to resign his post and
return to England, Oglethorpe finding it convenient to employ
him as one-way transatlantic courier and use instead his much
more efficient brother as secretary. The Governor parted with
Charles on kindly terms, sending him off with the significant
advice that he should abandon celibacy, to which he appeared by
nature unsuited: 'You would find in a married state the difficulties
of working out your salvation exceedingly lessened.'[23]

Celibacy: its spiritual and pastoral advantages had been long
debated among the little Methodist company at Oxford. John
Wesley's convictions now directed him sternly away not only
from sensual allurements but equally from even the chastest
matrimony, which could not, he thought, fail to dilute the
concentration of his quest for salvation. So argued the mind and
the spirit, but the flesh over the coming months was to prove
agitatingly vulnerable. 'Miss Sophy', the eighteen-year-old niece

of the wife of Savannah's chief magistrate and keeper of public stores, Thomas Causton – a girl whose 'soul appeared to be wholly made up of mildness, gentleness, longsuffering', who was 'all sympathy, tenderness, compassion', yet who preserved 'in all that yielding easiness a modesty pure as the light' – came to exercise so disturbing an influence on the natural man struggling within this austere seeker after salvation, that eventually, by February 1737, he found himself groaning under the weight of 'an unholy desire'.[24]

Sophy Hopkey possessed many attributes to recommend her as a wife to Wesley. Not the most important, but not altogether least, was her ownership of property which Wesley saw might offer him 'all the truly desirable conveniences of life'.[25] (This worked both ways, for might desirable conveniences be just what ought *not* to be desired?) Miss Hopkey was devout, declaring herself once, in answer to Wesley, as 'ready to die' – always encouraging evidence to both Wesley brothers of spiritual mettle. Indeed, a challenging enquiry on this subject was a not unusual gambit posed to their acquaintance, somewhat as others might ask how the weather suited. Miss Sophy, Wesley informs us, was intelligent and quick to learn – she was in effect for many months his pupil. When – which was almost daily – he was reading to her from Law's *Serious Call* or Dean Young's *Sermons* or George Hickes's *Reformed Devotions* or *The Abridged French Grammar*, she was 'all stillness and attention'. Neat but plain in dress, she disregarded 'those inconveniences of life in Georgia which most English gentlewomen's delicacy would abhor'. She was, so he wrote, 'born without anger' – though Wesley's subsequent behaviour was to engender some in her. Her unhappiness at home with her aunt and uncle made her especially susceptible to marriage offers, despite inclinations which she at times expressed towards lifelong spinsterhood. Alternatively she sometimes threatened to return to England, she was so wretched in Georgia.

While he was seeing much of Sophy Hopkey at Frederica in the summer of 1736, Wesley's persistence in pursuit of the elusive soul of Mrs Hawkins, and more particularly his carelessness in letting other people see some very private observations written to him earlier by Charles, brought him into deep and oddly ludicrous trouble. (Charles, at least, reckoned it carelessness, but perhaps it was simply that in Frederica the private post was public property.) The letter had contained two very damaging words – *in Greek*, to defeat potential prying eyes – to describe the wicked women of Frederica. Mrs Hawkins and Mrs Welch could not translate Greek, but guessed the drift easily enough. To whom, they demanded of John, might Charles have been referring, *all* the women, or just *two?* Innocent of prevarication, John rashly explained matters to Mrs Hawkins. The thing was written earlier, 'when all things were dark', but Charles had undoubtedly meant 'only two persons, you and Mrs Welch'.

Wesley's reward next day for this frank elucidation was 'such a mixture of scurrility and profaneness' from Mrs Welch as he had never before heard; and the day following, Mrs Hawkins sent one of her servants to demand his presence. Greeting him in her bedroom, where she was professedly indisposed, with a pistol in one hand and a pair of scissors in the other, she forced him down on the bed, and swore she would have either his hair or his 'heart's blood', threatening her servants meanwhile if they dared to impede her. The apothecary, appearing on this field of lively activity to demand 'what the scoundrel did in his house', warned off neighbours and a town constable who had now arrived, and held the ring while his wife simultaneously vindicated her virtue and assuaged her frenzy by getting her teeth (since Wesley was prudently gripping her wrists) into his cassock sleeves and ripping them to pieces. Finally Mr Hawkins 'took her round the waist and lifted her up' to prevent further and less reparable mayhem.[26]

The sorely-tried Oglethorpe was immediately appealed to and, doing his best to lower the temperature, dissuaded Wesley from taking the assault to court. As the *Journal* explains, 'something like an agreement was patched up, one article of which was that we should speak to each other no more. Blessed be God who hath at length given me a full discharge . . . from all intercourse with one "whose heart is as snares and knots and her hands as bands" '. However, on 24 January 1737, the day before he finally left Frederica in 'utter despair of doing good there', his private diary records that Mrs Hawkins visited him and that after evening prayers he 'conversed and prayed' with her and her husband.[27]

Safely back in England, Charles, reading towards the close of the year 1736 his brother's account of this imbroglio in the latest passages of the *Journal* (which crossed the Atlantic in instalments to circulate among the Georgia trustees and other interested parties), allowed himself the surely unmerited luxury of savouring his own superiority of judgement: 'All this,' he wrote, 'will teach him a little of the wisdom of the serpent, of which he seems as utterly void as his dear friend Mrs H. is of the innocency of the dove.'[28]

Wesley's misadventures with the snareful and knotted Mrs Hawkins proved as nothing to the torments awaiting his association with the docile, devout, and – however she might sometimes deny it – patently nubile Sophy Hopkey. Sophy had recently escaped from the matrimonial intentions of a desperate-sounding character named Thomas Mellichamp, currently in custody for fraud, to whom she had rashly once promised that if she did not marry him she would marry no one, while he had threatened that murder would be done if she broke her word. Her uncle and aunt Causton, who were as anxious to get her off their hands as she was to escape from theirs, gave her into Wesley's charge when in October 1736 she left Savannah for Frederica. Mr Causton offered the minister a blindingly plain hint. 'Sir, what direction do you give me with regard to her?' Wesley had asked, and Causton replied, 'I give her up to you. Do what you will with her. Take her into your own hands. Promise her what you will. I will make it good.' He told Wesley he would offer a maintenance to her future husband if he was poor: 'let him be but an honest man, an honest, good man'. 'The girl will never be easy till she is married.'[29]

Returning to Frederica, 'that ignoble spot', for a fourth visit, Wesley found Sophy so depressed that she was half resolved to return to England. Disappointedly he noted her down as 'open but not affected' – not, apparently, even by Hickes's *Devotions* or Ephrem Syrus ('the most awakened writer, I think, of all the ancients'), or by frequent sessions of prayer and singing of psalms and hymns. Only when Wesley 'pressed her upon the head of friendship' not to leave Georgia did her determination weaken. She must surely have expected that this friendship was headed towards the altar – the more so when Wesley 'told her Mr Causton's engagement to make good whatever I should promise her'.

Oglethorpe told him that he ought to take the unhappy girl back to her uncle in Savannah. 'In what boat?' asked Wesley. 'She can go in none but yours, and indeed there is none so proper', replied Oglethorpe, who we know approved of marriage for socially inclined priests, and may well have reckoned that a week in an open coastal boat by day and on uninhabited islands by night, with only a servant and the boat's small crew for company, might well assist the ripening of Wesley's intentions. Wesley himself saw his peril looming, and methodically analysed it, 'with a good hope I should be delivered out of it'.

The journey down that lonely coast carried its own, different, perils and considerable hardships, in the overcoming of which Wesley had opportunity to observe his charge's behaviour more nearly, and to be increasingly impressed by her courageous equanimity, her open honesty, her 'sweetness', her receptivity to 'serious' conversation (on Christian holiness, on 'lying in order to do good', on readiness for death). At St Katherine's Island, however, in the middle of a cold night, serious considerations of a different sort thrust themselves obstinately forward. 'Observing in the night, the fire we lay by burning bright, that Miss Sophy was broad awake,' Wesley was moved 'as the expression of a sudden wish, not of any formed design', to something very near indeed to a proposal of marriage. Sophy burst into tears, remembering the jealous threats of her former suitor Mellichamp. She would not marry that 'bad man'; but her promises and his menaces meant that she might marry no one else. 'Sir,' she said, 'you don't know the danger you are in.'

It seems likely that if Wesley had chosen to risk that particular danger and pressed on with a lover's ardour, he might not have been long in overcoming the girl's objections on this score (which vanished rapidly enough when she accepted Wesley's rival later). As it was, the moment passed, and the conversation retreated towards safer waters, and 'ended with a psalm'. Wesley's inhibiting fears of losing his road to salvation – which must involve 'deadness to pleasure'* and freedom from the lures and

---

* It was impossible to be fully consistent on this theme, of course; and, accused of austerity, he denied and pronounced against it. He approved, so he wrote in March 1737, of having 'as much cheerfulness as you can' in religion, and as for pleasure, he admitted that *eating* afforded him much (though at one time he and Delamotte subsisted for weeks on plain bread). He was not, he said, 'for a stern, austere manner of conversing', yet un-

comforts of matrimony – reasserted themselves powerfully, and held firm on the next island the following night, when Miss Sophy 'hung her apron on two small sticks, which kept off a little of the north wind from her head, and lay down on the ground under the canopy of heaven, with all the signs of perfect content'.[30]

Back in Savannah, he consulted his friends. Should he break off all contact with Sophy, in view of her continued daily proximity and the snares of marital temptation. Their replies being at this stage ambiguous or uncertain, the situation drifted. Sophy still came regularly to early morning prayers at Wesley's, stayed to breakfast (à trois with Delamotte present), took her French lessons, listened through many a devotional reading, shared 'serious' conversation and the singing of hymns and psalms. People 'wondered', she told Wesley later, what she could have been doing so long with him – wondered, she must surely have meant, if he had not been an avowed suitor.

After a final visit to Frederica, by the end of January 1737 Wesley was back, 'in a great strait', with his demurely enticing Sophy and his old problem. Again he weakly offered her a half-proposal, a hint, of marriage, and she as weakly failed to close with it. If she had, 'my judgement', wrote Wesley, 'would have made but a faint resistance'. Instead she reminded him meekly of his view that clergy should be 'unencumbered'. Therefore, for her part, she would marry no one.

Wesley then took his troubles to the Moravian pastor, and was 'amazed to the last degree' at actually receiving encouragement to marry. Ingham and Delamotte, however, thought he should not; and Wesley finally took Ingham's advice that he should leave Savannah to clear his bemused head. 'I find, Miss Sophy,' he wrote, 'I cannot take fire into my bosom, and not be burnt. I am therefore retiring for a while to desire the direction of God.' Being obliged to spend an hour of one day back in Savannah during his week of attempted mind-clearing four miles away, he found himself distracted, in a torment of frustrated sexual longing. His 'heart was with Miss Sophy all the time'. But God, though 'hiding his face' at first, spoke pretty firmly by the end of these days of retirement. So at least Wesley maintained, though

deniably – vide Matt. xii. 36, Cor. iv. 6, Eph. iv. 29 and v. 4 – trifling conversation was unequivocally forbidden.

what he actually wrote down after all his prayer and self-examination looks confused and contradictory: 1. He would not marry till he had fulfilled his purpose in coming to America, and gone among the Indians. 2. He was in any case 'not strong enough to bear the complicated temptations of a married state'.

On 14 February, when Sophy came as usual for early prayers and readings, this time from Dr John Owen's collection of Puritan devotions, Wesley imparted to her, walking in the garden, the first of his above conclusions. The girl's bruised response showed plainly enough what, for all her protestations about staying single, she had been expecting and hoping. She would, she declared, not come to see him any more alone. There was no point in her taking further French lessons. And when, by agreement, Wesley called to see her at her uncle's, he found her 'in such a temper' as he had never before seen in her, 'sharp, fretful, and disputatious'. He next told her he might be returning to England, whereupon 'she changed colour several times, and then broke out' that in that case she had no tie in America left.

Wesley was still far from being out of the toils. Calling upon the Caustons one day, he found Sophy there alone. 'Her words, her eyes, her air, her every motion and gesture, were full of such a softness and sweetness! I know not what might have been the consequence had I then but touched her hand. And how I avoided it I know not. Surely God is over all.' The following day, however, he subjected God's guidance to the severest test. Alone with her again, he did touch her hand, and found her 'not displeased' by this perilous advance. Almost, almost, he then and there engaged himself to her for life. But, again, an ever watchful providence reminded him, prompt on the cue, that *she* had vowed to stay single for ever.[31]

Delamotte, nevertheless, still thought that Wesley was 'losing ground daily'. Together therefore they considered, fasted, prayed, and agreed at last to put the great Searcher of hearts to the appeal direct. Accordingly they prepared three lots. On one was written 'Marry'; on one, 'Think not of it this year'; on the third, 'Think of it no more'. Delamotte – we must hope there was no legerdemain – drew the third. They then organized a second of these sortileges, and the finger of God, which did indeed seem to have clear objection to John Wesley committing

George Whitefield, by J. Woolaston

Wesley, by J. Williams

Above right John Fletcher
Above One of Wesley's electrical
machines
Right Plaque of Charles and John Wesley
in Westminster Abbey

himself to Miss Hopkey, pointed again: 'Only in the presence of Mr Delamotte'.[32]

Within three days Wesley was allowing himself briefly to elude this directive when in the Caustons' garden Sophy caught hold of his hands and spoke to him 'with the most engaging gesture, look, and tone of voice'. Causton however calling from the house, he was delivered anew from temptation, before his resolution had broken 'in sunder as a thread of tow that has touched fire'.

It was finally rescued from this threatened annihilation two days later, when Mrs Causton asked him to publish the banns of marriage between Miss Sophy Hopkey and Mr William Williamson. This Williamson had appeared as a contender for Sophy only recently. He was not among the more devoted churchgoers of Savannah. Wesley indeed was somewhat comically convinced that Sophy might never have succumbed to this dangerously undevout (and moreover unhandsome) person had not he, Wesley, persuaded her 'to sup earlier and not immediately before she went to bed . . . By this began her intercourse with Mr Williamson'. So small a circumstance, so pregnant perhaps with the destruction of his own happiness, 'in time and eternity!'[33]

Afterwards Wesley came to think that he had been the intended victim of a ploy to have his own hand forced, and that he was lucky not to fall for it; but his diary tells well enough how at the time he was desolated:

> . . . 10 [a.m.] Mrs Causton's, in talk with her. Miss Sophy to be married; meditation . . . 12 . . . quite distressed . . . 2 Took leave of her, ½ [hour] at home. Could not pray! 3 Tried to pray, lost, sunk . . . 6 Kempis; Germans. Easier! . . . 8 Miss Sophy et cetera, ½ [hour] within with her, ¾ with Delamotte, prayer. No such day since I first saw the sun. O deal tenderly with Thy servant. Let me not see such another![34]

Still he did not know whether he more hoped than feared what might happen, should Delamotte leave the two of them alone when Sophy came for evening prayers. The risk was one which Williamson for his part was not prepared to run for long; Sophy cried too ominously after returning. He therefore demanded that her conversations with Wesley should cease till after the wedding. Causton tried one last time to push Wesley into an eleventh-hour proposal. If he loved her, why on earth had Wesley not pressed her, 'when she was so much moved'? Wesley 'consulted the oracles of God' – opened, that is, the Bible at a chance page and derived such guidance or consolation as was offered (obscure or irrelevant to a neutral eye, but charged for him with meaning and comfort) by the verses there divinely indicated.

Williamson and Sophy did not wait for Wesley to publish banns. They had become engaged on 8 March. On the 11th they left for a little town twenty miles up the Savannah valley, just over the border into South Carolina, and on the following day were married there – if not illegally at least irregularly, Wesley maintained, in the absence of banns. He went on referring to Mrs Williamson as Miss Sophy.

For a time he continued to admit her to Communion, exhorting her 'not to be weary of well-doing'. Significantly, though, he counselled her to obey her husband only in 'things of an indifferent nature', when this did not conflict with the will of God. Then, as the spring and summer of 1737 went by, Wesley noticed that Sophy's attendance at services grew more erratic. He checked the register: she had failed to communicate on nine (presumably weekly) occasions during April-June. He began too a private enquiry into her conversations with friends concerning her earlier relations with both Mellichamp and Williamson. She had, it transpired, 'dissembled', not told Wesley the whole truth of her feelings towards these men. Taxing her then with these failings, he noted that the more he spoke of them 'the more angry she appeared, till after a few minutes she turned about and went abruptly away'.[35] It was the last time he spoke to her.

His mind was now made up, his duty clear; she could no longer qualify for admittance to Communion. He determined to proceed 'with all the mildness and prudence' God should give him, but a letter he wrote to her on 5 July was hardly notable for either of these virtues; unsparingly frank, harshly censorious, demanding a full confession both of her shortcomings in observing her Christian duties (public prayers, fasting, communicating) and of her 'deliberate dissimulation' and guile in personal matters. A few days later she miscarried – which Mrs Causton and others, though not Sophy herself, attributed to

Wesley's chiding. A month passed, and then – foreseeing the consequences, he claimed – he took the extreme step, exercising his priestly rights, of turning her away when she attended for Communion, 'for the reasons specified in my letter of 5 July, as well as for not giving me notice of her design to communicate after having intermitted for some time'.[36]

Was this merely the authoritarian rubric-conscious parson riding his High Church high horse, or did there lie behind it, however repressed and submerged, the resentment and sense of grievance of the failed and disappointed lover? If he really foresaw the consequences of his action he must have been expressing a death-wish upon his stay in Georgia, for inevitably he was seen to be publicly insulting Sophy Williamson, and showing a vindictiveness which would be forgiven only by the circle of his strict followers. Sophy had herself told him, a week after her marriage, of 'many instances of his anger and resentment' that had been reported to her.[37] Now her uncle Causton (whom Wesley had tried to forewarn in vague terms of what he was going to do, pleading 'duty') became leader of the outcry against him – perhaps all the more willingly because Wesley had recently taken upon himself to be the mouthpiece of public complaints against Causton,* which had multiplied during Oglethorpe's temporary absence in England during 1737.

The next day a warrant was issued for 'the body of John Wesley, clerk' to be brought to court to answer charges made by Sophy Williamson and her husband that he had defamed her character and denied her the sacrament of the Lord's Supper in a public congregation. Williamson formally demanded £1000 damages. By Wesley's very credible account, Causton now began suborning those members of the grand jury who were not already hostile to their parson, and bribing them from the public stores. Prepared at first to sit at home 'easy' and commit his case solely to God, Wesley decided later to defend his actions before his congregation, from which the Causton-Williamson party were naturally now absentees. For their part they prepared an affidavit, which among much else of an unfriendly nature to which Sophy

---

* These may well have had good foundation. He was held to have abused his powers as keeper of the public stores and acted against the policies of land allocation laid down by the Georgia trustees. Oglethorpe, on his return to the colony in 1738, removed him from office. William Williamson was at about the same time appointed Recorder in Savannah.

put her signature, asserted that Wesley had many times unsuccessfully proposed marriage to her. Their version of the
affair – partial and distorted, no doubt, but most plausible – was
that 'Mr Wesley had done this merely out of revenge because
Sophy would not have him'.[38]

The grand jury numbered forty-four, being a sizeable proportion of the population of Savannah and according to Wesley's
contemptuous account of it containing a score of Dissenters, one
Papist, one infidel, and one Frenchman unable to understand
English. Nine out of the ten presentments against him concerned
his ecclesiastical practice and were therefore dismissed by him
out of hand as being *ultra vires* for a civil court; the one remaining, defamation of Mrs Williamson's character, he contested.
'Uncouth' though he called the ecclesiastical complaints, several
of them do strongly indicate the resentment widely occasioned
by his stern regime: refusing Communion to all whose religious
observance did not meet his grievously strict requirements;
teaching wives and servants 'absolutely' to follow his rules
'without any regard to the interest of their private families';
'searching into and meddling into the affairs of private families';
'refusing to baptize the children of such as will not submit to his
innovations' – for instance, 'dipping'; 'refusing the Office of the
Dead to such as did not communicate with him'; *et cetera*.[39]

A sufficient majority of the grand jury found a true bill on all
counts, but twelve of the forty-four agreed on a 'minority
report' in favour of Wesley which they dispatched to the trustees
in London. The whole set of charges, they alleged, had been
'an artifice of Mr Causton's designed rather to blacken the
character of Mr Wesley than to free the colony of religious
tyranny'.[40]

For three more months Wesley, debating with himself and
friends whether or not he should return to England, continued
ministering and preaching in Savannah, although his Sunday
congregation, which earlier had sometimes reached several
score, was by this time very small, with few of the more substantial citizens present.[41] Towards the end of November he
posted a notice announcing his coming departure, and went to
Causton to request an allocation of funds for his return journey.
As late as June he had written to his youngest sister Kezzy
suggesting that she should come to Georgia to live with him, so

there can be no doubt that his decision to leave the colony arose out of the Sophy Williamson crisis.

Mr Williamson, however, had not forgotten that he had sued Wesley for £1000, and publicly advertised a reminder of the fact, while the magistrate proceeded to issue an order requiring no one to assist, and officials to prevent, Wesley leaving. Refusing to enter into a bail which they demanded (with a £50 penalty attached for breakage), he now saw clearly, so he wrote,

> the hour has come for me to fly for my life, leaving this place; and as soon as evening prayers were over, about eight o'clock, the tide then serving, I shook off the dust of my feet, and left Georgia, after having preached the Gospel there . . . not as I ought, but as I was able, one year and nearly nine months.[42]

It is very likely that no real attempt was made to detain him, the Savannah authorities being only too glad to see him go. After an arduous and perilous ten days' journey, tramping for the most part through the forests, plantations, and swamp-lands of South Carolina, in the company of three similarly desperate travelling companions, he arrived finally at Charleston where, as he characteristically recorded, 'I expected trials of a quite different nature, and far more dangerous; contempt and hunger being easy to be borne: but who can bear respect and fullness of bread?'[43]

CHAPTER 5

By Faith Alone

IT WAS NOT MERELY his material affairs which were at a crisis. Although he was as yet unready to attribute his failure in Georgia to any unwisdom in his conduct there, personal or ecclesiastical, he did nevertheless discover severe sickness when he once again now examined his spiritual condition. He had indeed constantly employed, as was his prescribed duty, all the *means* of grace; but did he have grace? The answer was a depressing, a terrifying, no; he did not. His heart was 'corrupt and abominable'; he was still a child of wrath, an heir of hell. He laid upon himself the appalling accusation (though in later years in a note added to his *Journal* he questioned the justice of it) that he 'who went to America to convert others' was himself 'never converted to God'. He lacked 'that faith which none can have without knowing that he hath it'; his was of the kind which even 'the devils' have, those 'strangers to the covenant of promise'. During the Atlantic storms which his homeward voyage met, he experienced that same sudden vacuum of faith that had troubled him on the voyage out, the 'sinne of fear', which Donne had so regretfully discovered within himself,

> . . . that when I have spunne
> My last thread, I shall perish on the shore.

'I asked myself long ago,' he wrote, ' "What must I do to be saved?" ' And he gave himself credit for a fair record of virtue and endeavour. *If the gospel were true*, then, he thought, 'verily . . . I am safe'. But when the waves ran mountain-high and the storm raged, Wesley's great edifice of belief which might have been thought so tempest-proof, was disturbingly shaken:

I think, what if the gospel be not true? Then thou art of all men the most foolish. For what hast thou given thy goods, thy ease, thy friends, thy reputation, thy country, thy life? For what art thou wandering over the face of the earth? – A dream, a cunningly devised fable! O who shall deliver me from this fear of death? . . . A wise man advised me some time since, 'Be still, and go on.' Perhaps this is best, to look upon it as my cross . . .[1]

'Being still', schooling one's soul to correspond in tranquillity with the divine afflatus, was the way of the mystics and quietists, and of the Moravians too, but it could never be Wesley's. He could never wait in patience to be enfolded by God's pinions, to be embraced in the everlasting arms. His way was to pound strenuously along that straight path that led to salvation, forever wary of false tracks and alluring byways.

Down some of these he was aware of having perilously strayed. There was the error of laying too much stress on good works merely, 'as the Papists do'. *Per contra*, an 'overgrown fear of Popery', which had infected so many Calvinists and Lutherans – and himself too, once – had magnified faith 'to such an amazing size that it quite hid all the rest of the Commandments'. In the course of his penetrating self-inspection during the voyage back to England, he reproved himself for falling into these doctrinal errors, and into an even worse one: he confessed to a passing love affair with those mystical writers who preached 'internal religion' – affirming that love, and union with God, were all that mattered; offering plenary dispensation from fulfilling the rest of the divine commands. (Fifty years later, an old man of eighty-five, he was still recalling 'that poisonous mysticism' with which both he and his brother Charles were somewhat 'tainted' before they went to America.) Of all the Christian enemies of true Christianity these mystics were most dangerous:

All the other enemies of Christianity are triflers. The Mystics . . . stab it in the vitals; and its most serious professors are most likely to fall by them. May I praise Him who hath snatched me out of this fire likewise, by warning all others that it is set on the fire of hell.[2]

Such incandescent language might persuade one that Wesley thought mysticism more poisonous a brew than Deism, which he always equates simply with infidelity, or 'having no religion at all';

but he cannot really have considered so. Elsewhere, again on his theme of over-reaction by the English against Catholicism, he is at pains to allow it, for all its many errors, to be preferable to Deism. A Catholic was merely in serious danger of hell-fire; a 'baptized infidel' was assured of it.[3]

For Wesley, 'stillness' and inaction brought no spiritual balm. He must be always up and doing; and he realized now, aboard the *Samuel* homeward bound from Charleston, that his 'fearfulness and heaviness' remained with him only until he took a resolve to 'apply the word of God to every single soul in the ship', even though only one, even though *not* one, of them should hear it.

Back in London, he lodged for a time with the family of a printer and bookseller, John Hutton, procuring lodgings also nearby for four Moravian Brethren just arrived from Germany. Once again Moravianism, catching Wesley now in a phase when he was to an unusual degree both spiritually and doctrinally vulnerable, was to play a vital part in shaping his convictions. One of the four Brethren was Peter Böhler, who was quick to observe that Wesley 'knew he did not properly believe in his Saviour, and was willing to be taught'.[4] Böhler, still only twenty-six (to Wesley's thirty-five), had been tutor to the son of Count Zinzendorf, the leader of the Moravians in Germany, and was now in England *en route* for missionary work in Carolina and Georgia.

First Wesley had to account to the Georgia trustees for his sudden and unauthorized abandonment of his duties. There followed several awkward interviews; Wesley's ministering authority in America was revoked; and Oglethorpe told Charles there was 'strong spirit' against his brother for his hostile attitude towards the colony.[5] According to the Earl of Egmont, 'In truth the Board [terminated Wesley's authority] with great pleasure, he appearing to us in a very odd mixture of a man, an enthusiast, and at the same time a hypocrite, wholly distasteful to the greater part of the inhabitants, and an incendiary of the people against the magistracy.' Wesley's own version of events implies that the trustees were treated to some straight talk they did not much care for. Certainly within a few weeks of his return, his uncompromising language from the pulpits of nine different London churches could not have been to the taste of their incumbents or the more influential among their congregations. He was left in no doubt that he would not be asked to preach in these places again. In the pulpit, at least, he was in fighting mood, and he recorded that of these recent sermons of his, his favourite was one in condemnation of prudence: 'it pleased God to bless this most, because it gave most offence'.[6]

He was soon energetically scurrying round half England, preaching, visiting friends of past Oxford and Holy Club days, as far away as Manchester; seeing his mother at Salisbury, she being confined to bed at her married daughter Patty's; being prevented from proceeding to Tiverton to visit his brother Samuel only by receiving news of Charles lying seriously ill with pleurisy at Oxford, where he hastened instead; neglecting no opportunity to 'awaken, instruct, or exhort' fellow travellers on the road, and incidentally feeling the need to censure himself for being weak enough once to ease the path towards 'seriousness' by a little prefatory light conversation: 'Lord, lay not this sin to my charge!'[7]

During March-April 1738 Wesley several times met Böhler again, conversing with him – and later corresponding – in Latin, neither Böhler's English nor Wesley's German being quite adequate. 'He is a poor sinner,' wrote Böhler, 'who has a broken heart and who hungers after a better righteousness than that which he has had up till now.' It was over these weeks that Böhler finally convinced Wesley that the doctrine which only a short time before aboard the *Samuel* he had been condemning – that salvation can come from faith *alone* – was indeed true; that he, John Wesley, was deficient in this necessary faith; but that the surest way by which he might reach it would be to preach it. There would be no doubting; he would eventually, and suddenly, *know* when he had arrived at it. This would mark the decisive 'change' which the faithful called 'conversion', or 'new birth'. It was an error to think it might come gradually. Conversion was always instantaneous, though this at first Wesley found hard to believe. He would receive, said Böhler, God's grace by virtue of unquestioning belief, when the encumbrances of his *'philosophia'* had been stripped away. He would know then that he was assured of salvation, 'translated out of darkness into light, out of sin and fear into holiness and happiness'. On Sunday 23 April Wesley entered in his *Journal*: 'Here ended my disputing. I could now only cry out, "Lord, help thou my unbelief." '[8]

He asserted now that for the past twenty years or so he had mistakenly grounded his hope of salvation upon his own righteousness and good works. In Georgia, he decided, he had been 'beating the air', 'carnal, sold under sin', 'ignorant of the righteousness of Christ', anxious only for his own. Böhler had convinced him that there was only one road to salvation, the road of 'saving faith', 'justifying faith', but that this road was open to *every* soul who earnestly and perseveringly sought it, and not merely to the few, as he had always been taught and always believed. Faith, hope, charity; the greatest of these, St Paul to the Corinthians notwithstanding, was faith. It was a doctrine, of course, for which there was also Pauline *support* (not least Luther's decisive *Romans* i. 17), but as at least the Moravians taught it, it had developed nice distinctions. It seems that, although Böhler had begged Wesley to cast aside his philosophy, his fellow Moravians were not strangers to the mysteries of balancing angels on the point of a pin. As Wesley explained to Charles:

> We ought to distinguish carefully . . . between faith (absolutely speaking), which is one thing; justifying or saving faith, which is a second thing . . .; the assurance of faith, where we know and feel that we are justified; and the being born again which they say is a fourth thing, and often distant in time . . . from all the rest.[9]

While Böhler over these crucial weeks became Wesley's spiritual shepherd, one of the most trusted of earlier guides, William Law, whose *Practical Treatise upon Christian Perfection* and *Serious Call to a Devout and Holy Life* had made such a deep impression on him, was now brusquely rejected. Several times in days past he had sought out Law personally for guidance, but now he found him guilty of muddying the waters of truth with Germanic mysticism, and of having failed in the duty of directing Wesley towards 'a living faith in the blood of Christ'. As incapable of indirectness as of tact, he took Böhler along with him to tell Law so, and then wrote to tell him so again. Law understandably retorted with tartness, and some sarcasm concerning Böhler, this 'man of God [who] had shown you the poverty and misery of my state', inventing things 'as false as if he had charged me with picking his pocket'. As for Wesley himself, his accusations plainly exasperated Law. 'Who made me your teacher?' he demanded, 'or can make me answerable for any defects in your knowledge? You sought my acquaintance. You came to me as you pleased, and on what occasion you pleased, and to say to me what you pleased . . . Pray, sir, be at peace with me.'[10]

Wesley had begun preaching salvation by faith alone in March 1738, the first person to receive from him this message of eternal promise being a prisoner under the sentence of death. (Until this time Wesley declares he had disbelieved the possibility of death-bed or scaffold's-edge repentance, so it becomes harder to value his earlier preaching to capitally convicted prisoners at Oxford in the days of the Holy Club.) It was presumably his passionate concentration now on this uncompromising doctrine of justifying faith, the master-key to eternity, 'God's free gift' to all men – though he still sometimes felt his grasp upon it fumbling – which caused him to be *persona non grata*, the parson not to be re-invited, in a number of London's churches. Certain now of his dogmatic position, he seemed to be preaching what could hardly fail to sound extremist and alarming to many thoughtful Christians who thanked God that in their day there had been a slackening of the fierce religious tensions which had plagued the previous century. Goodness, lacking the talisman of faith, so Wesley now preached, would avail men nothing:

A man before he is justified may feed the hungry, or clothe the naked . . . These are in one sense 'good works' . . . but it does not follow that they are, strictly speaking, good in themselves, or good in the sight of God. All truly good works . . . follow after justification [by faith] . . . All works done before justification . . . have the nature of sin.[11]

This was a doctrine tough indeed for everyday untheological Christian intellects to digest, and Wesley was to be repeatedly reproached for belittling good works. As repeatedly he defended his position, as for example in his reply to the influential journal *The Craftsman* in June 1745. By faith, he then explained, he did not understand what *The Craftsman* seemed to understand. He meant 'faith working by love', a faith 'zealous of good works. Nor do we acknowledge him to have one grain of faith who is not continually doing good . . . to all men.' And in reply to Bishop Lavington's allegation against him in 1749 that he disparaged good works, Wesley's rebuttal attempted to explain: 'There must be something good in the heart before any of our works are good.

Insomuch that "though I give all my goods to feed the poor" and have not *this*, it profiteth me nothing.' Paul's *'this'* was of course what the King James Bible translated as 'charity'; certainly not as 'faith'. If Wesley was being consistent, and these two last extracts are compared, 'charity' for him must be logically if complicatedly rendered as 'faith working through love'; the best of both worlds indeed.

Having been convinced by Böhler and his own renewed scriptural researches that 'conversion' was always instantaneous, he looked with anxious expectation towards his own instantaneous conversion. Charles, who had been ill again and was now lodging in London with a certain Mr Bray, 'a poor ignorant mechanic, who knows nothing but Christ, yet by knowing him, knows and discerns all things',[12] had as recently as 25 April found 'very shocking' his brother's belief that even gross sinners might believe in an instant and be saved, but only a week later was won over by Böhler on the day before this most persuasive Moravian set sail for America. Charles soon found himself astonished that he should ever have thought justification by faith alone a *new* doctrine: 'Who would believe,' he cried in simple joy, 'that our Church had been founded on this important article?'[13] His surprise is itself surprising, Articles Eleven and Twelve of the Thirty-nine being explicit enough,* widely though they may differ in letter and spirit from many New Testament passages – notably from chapter two of the Epistle of James.

There followed for Charles, still a sick man, three weeks of intense religious emotion, troughs of despondency in violent alternation with spells of something near to frenzy, as he first despaired of his 'new birth', and then prayed his way towards it. After 'sighs and groans unutterable', and 'tears that flowed freely', by the night of Whit Sunday, 21 May, he claimed finally to *see that by faith he stood.*

> I walked under the protection of Christ, and gave myself up soul and body to him. At nine I began a hymn upon my con-

---

* 'We are accounted righteous before God, only . . . by Faith, and not for our own works and deservings; wherefore that we are justified by Faith only is a most wholesome Doctrine . . .' (Article 11). 'Albeit that Good Works, which are the fruits of Faith, and follow after Justification, cannot put away our sins, and endure the severity of God's Judgement . . .' (Article 12).

version, but was persuaded to break off, for fear of pride. Mr
Bray coming, encouraged me to proceed in spite of Satan. I
prayed Christ to stand by me, and finished the hymn . . .

The following day, towards ten in the evening,

My brother was brought in triumph, by a troop of our friends,
and declared, 'I believe.' We sang the hymn with great joy, and
parted with prayer. At midnight I gave myself up to Christ;
assured I was safe, sleeping or waking.[14]

It was the day of John Wesley's attending, in an initially depressed
state of mind, the meeting of a religious society at Nettleton
Court, off Aldersgate Street. There, after listening to the reading
of a translation of Luther's preface to Paul's *Epistle to the Romans*,
he rose to testify to what he felt to be the great moment of his
conversion. As the *Journal*'s famous phrase put it, he felt his heart
'strangely warmed'. But that there is any clear boundary between
Wesley's life before a quarter to nine on the evening of 24 May
1738, and his life after that point, is a proposition which accords
neither with the apparent facts nor even with a good deal of
Wesley's own subsequent testimony, however lovingly he might
sometimes luxuriate in this legend himself, and paint the rescued
sinner's conventionally cautionary picture of his unregenerate
past.

It has been suggested that if this Aldersgate experience 'had
not been entered in the first extract of the *Journal*, it is quite
possible that Wesley would have entirely forgotten all about it'.[15]
Certainly for many months after it, he was to be subject to moods
of spiritual despondency, when his hold on the certainty of faith
and assurance of salvation weakened. Even as early as a few
minutes after his 'conversion' he felt, if only momentarily – and,
as usual, was honest enough to record it – that 'the enemy', not
finally defeated, was still tugging at his soul. 'This cannot be
faith,' he wrote, 'for where is thy joy?' And there continues to be
a good deal of contradiction in his *Journal*'s record. 'I have
constant peace,' he attests: 'not one uneasy thought. And I
have freedom from sin; not one unholy desire.' Then, in no time
at all, he still finds 'soreness' in his heart, 'so that I found my
wound was not fully healed . . . O God, save Thou me, and all
that are "weak in the faith . . ."' Neither the words nor the
sentiments are greatly distinguishable from when he was 'not a

Christian till May the 24th last past'.[16]

A year later he is writing to tell the Huttons' son James that he is 'still dead and cold' except when he is preaching. 'Pray,' he begs him, 'that when I have preached to others, I may not myself be a castaway!'[17] It is not that his conversion was of no significance. The something which was held to have occurred that May evening was to be important both for Wesley's own personal myth – his theory of himself – and for the Methodist following in general. Conversion in any case was a prerequisite for the saving of sinners. Of itself, Wesley's changed nothing in his theological position. By the time it occurred, he had already moved away from his earlier belief in salvation through righteousness and good deeds. He knew Article XI of the Church of England well enough, and Böhler had merely confirmed him in what he was now passionately sure was the old true belief. Indeed, 'true' added to 'old' was for Wesley tautological: 'Whatever doctrine is new' – so he preached – 'must be wrong . . . No doctrine can be right, unless it is the same which was from the beginning.'[18] As he wrote in June 1740: 'After we had wandered for many years in the *new path* of Salvation by faith and works, about two years ago it pleased God to show us the *old way* of Salvation by faith only.'

However, that John Wesley Part One was now a closed volume, and John Wesley Part Two was in circulation, was a thesis he was now energetically asserting. A few of his friends showed some alarm, or even revulsion. Mr Hutton senior, when Wesley informed the devout company gathered at his house that they too were not yet Christians, told him to have a care how he despised the benefits bestowed by the sacraments. Hutton and his wife were worried by the influence Wesley obviously wielded over their two children; and Mrs Hutton, after more 'wild speech' from Wesley, answered him with some point, 'If you was not a Christian ever since I knew you, you was a great hypocrite, for you made us all believe you was one.'[19] A friend and one-time neighbour of the Samuel Wesleys junior, she posted off news of Wesley's strange aberrations to Tiverton: 'Such visions as will surprise you to hear of. If there cannot be some stop put to this, and he can be taught true humility, the mischief he will do among the ignorant but well-meaning Christians will be very great.'[20]

Samuel Wesley, the Blundell's School headmaster, a good orthodox conventional churchman who shared the mistrust of his fellow clerics for religious fanatics, 'canting fellows . . . who talk of indwellings, experiences, getting into Christ, etc., etc.', suspected that John had gone dangerously mad. Perhaps 'perpetual intenseness of thought, and want of sleep' had disordered him. 'God deliver us from visions that shall make the law of God vain!' he wrote to Mrs Hutton, 'I heartily pray God to stop the progress of this lunacy.'[21] Samuel's wife, who had always had a tart tongue in her head for her brother-in-law, needed no persuading to agree too. From his side, it occurred to John Wesley that Mrs Samuel Wesley resembled a character called Susurrus in Law's *Serious Call*, who 'had a mighty inclination to hear and discover all the defects and infirmities of all about him'. Hence, in 'affectionate' correction, he told her so – twice – listing with the kindest intentions several of her other failings which he would be 'false to God' if he did not acquaint her with, and on the second occasion including brother Samuel as a Susurrus too. The pair of them had this fault of which they were 'more guilty than any other persons I have known in my life'. 'O brother,' John wrote at the end of a blunt, earnestly censorious and didactic letter on 30 October, 'would to God you would . . . beg of God to fill up what is yet wanting in you!'[22]

A few days before Böhler left them for America, James Hutton, with Charles and John Wesley and others, had founded another of those small 'companies', like the Holy Club earlier or the little group set up by Wesley in Savannah, to which Methodism traces its origins. Such godly societies were nothing unusual, and this one's claim to be specially remembered lies in its share in the ancestry both of the Methodist movement and of the English Moravians, for the allegiance of its members was soon to be split. Its nine founder members met first at the house of the young bookseller James Hutton, himself eventually to become a Moravian; but the group is commonly known as the Fetter Lane Society, from the situation (off Fleet Street) of the room where it met from September 1738. Its initial loyalty to the Church of England was absolute. Its rules, however, drawn up 'in obedience to the command of God by St James, and by the advice of Peter Böhler',[23] foreshadow a good deal of subsequent Methodist organization and practice. Meetings were to be weekly, 'for prayer, singing, mutual confession of faults, and for each member to speak freely, plainly, and concisely as he can, the real state of his heart'. As its numbers increased – they reached fifty-six within four months, forty-eight men and eight women – the society was to be divided into 'bands' of between five and ten. New members were to be admitted under two months' probation. Those breaking the rules might after three warnings be expelled. Every fourth Saturday was to be a day of intercession, and on the Sunday evening eight days following there was to be a three-hour love-feast (in imitation of the primitive Christian *agape*), a simple communal meal taken after celebration of the Lord's Supper and in token of the brotherhood of believers.

On 13 June 1738, two days after 'preaching faith in Christ' from the pulpit of St Mary's, Oxford, Wesley, in company with his one-time companion in Georgia, Ingham, and the Moravian Töltschig, set out from Gravesend on a tour of the Moravian settlements in Germany. This took him through Holland – to his traveller's eye so clean with its brick-paved streets and neat avenues – then to Cologne, 'the ugliest, dirtiest city I ever yet saw', with its 'huge, misshapen' cathedral, and thence by the swift-running Rhine to Mainz, to make a first stay among the Moravians at Marienborn near Frankfurt. Here he met Count Zinzendorf, heard him preach, and wrote home to Samuel with at this stage unqualified enthusiasm for the Moravians: 'Oh how high and holy a thing Christianity is! and how widely distant from what is so-called . . .' Germany in general, however, found little favour with him. There was altogether too much *non*-Reformation in the Church services, and a 'senseless inhuman usage of strangers' by the petty bureaucracy of 'almost every German city' they passed through. (They experienced some vexation too from Frederick William of Prussia's famous giant Guards, who at Halle sent them to and fro 'from one gate to another, for nearly two hours').

He found a better welcome at Jena University, where the Moravians were in some strength, and finally at Herrnhut, where he remained a fortnight and would, he said, gladly have spent his life. It must be doubted. Wesley's energies were not made to be dissipated in acceptance of the meek disciplines of Herrnhut. A letter to the brethren there, which he began after his return but left unfinished and unposted, reveals his reservations concerning their community. Were the brethren not mere shadows, and Count Zinzendorf 'all in all'? Were they in general serious enough? Did they not sometimes fall into trifling conversation? Had they not too much worldly prudence? Was their speech open and plain enough? (Wesley was fanatical at this time for absolute directness and plainness of speech, in the pattern, so he believed, of the Apostles and early Christians.) Did the brethren not neglect fasting? Were they not secretive, guileful, dissimulating? And did they not see their Church as bigger and more important than it really was? These criticisms, however interrogatively set down, were pretty comprehensive, coming from the pen of one who had a few short months before been so willing a disciple of Böhler and, more recently still, found among the Moravians of Marienborn 'a Church whose conversation is in heaven'.[24]

The flirtation with Moravianism had been brief. Even at Herrnhut, where there had been so much to admire, he had been quick to seize on any of their practices which he found 'unscriptural'. (One of these, so he judged,[25] was making evening prayers silent rather than spoken; this was too close to the 'stillness' of the mystics which he now passionately disapproved of.) Wesley's devotion to the forms and doctrines of the English Church did not seriously falter; nor would it do in the future. He would always regard his Methodists as essentially truer members of the Church of England than the 'almost Christians' who constituted its respectable majority. The question for him was and remained, not whether he should stay loyal to the Church, but whether a Church lacking 'priests that believe' could stay loyal to itself.[26]

The alleged decadence, worldliness, and torpor of the eighteenth-century Church of England is the occasion of much pained reproof in the nineteenth- and early-twentieth-century accounts of Wesley and the 'moral and spiritual reformation of England' which he inspired, thus turning back the 'flood of profligacy and unbelief'[27]; and less indignant or committed historians never found themselves short of evidence to point to the Church's many anachronisms and abuses. Its bishops, Walpole's in particular, have taken a good deal of righteous hammering, and certainly many of them were appointed more for their political reliability than for any intellectual or spiritual quality. (Even so, an episcopal bench supporting such representatives as Warburton, Butler or Berkeley can hardly be treated as entirely rotten wood.) No less than the state, the Church was of course imprisoned in the class structure of the age. Appointment and preferment were dependent upon connection. Non-residence, both among the higher clergy and parish parsons, was undoubtedly very common; pluralism equally, its corollary – though neither of these abuses was particularly special to the eighteenth century. What made them inevitable, and often perhaps in the circumstances justifiable, was the extreme discrepancy between ecclesiastical emoluments, many livings providing nothing like a living. Some were worth £5 a year, some £500; one in eight carried an annual stipend of £20 or under; over half were worth £50 or less. Curates were notoriously, sometimes grossly, underpaid. Certainly the organization of the Church cried out to be reformed, and it was above all on organization that the Wesleyans would eventually outpoint it. Unadaptably rural in its parish structure, the traditional Church was to find itself overtaken and largely stranded by the Industrial Revolution while the tide of Methodism ran strongly into the new manufacturing territory. There would be no Parson Woodfordes to write their charming civilized diaries among the parishes of Manchester or Bradford or Birmingham.

But all this was some distance away. There were many of the likes of Parson Woodforde, or Cole of Blecheley, or Fielding's Parson Adams, or Goldsmith's Vicar of Wakefield, or Dr Johnson's Zachariah Mudge among the clergy of Wesley's day. The proportion of them who were charitable and tolerably conscientious was probably no lower than in earlier or subsequent times. The once conventional picture of an eighteenth-century Church whose congregations (or absentees from the congregations) were as hungry sheep who looked up and were not fed, whose candidates for ordination were scandalously ignorant of the Bible, whose parsons, when they were not drinking port or fox-hunting with the squire, preached as if 'their sole aim was to fit men for *this* world', was very considerably overdrawn. (The complaint of Samuel Johnson, himself no mean ornament of the Church, was rather that most parsons did not know how to shed their 'polished periods and glittering sentences', and so preached over the heads of common folk.)

It may well have been broadly true, as Lecky wrote, that the old religion was loosening round the minds of men. With the coming in the previous century, for the first time in western history, of scientific modes of thought, a movement was begun which never subsequently lost impetus, even during the palmy days of Victorian church-going. This process of secularization has made irregular but relentless headway through every religious revival of the past three centuries, Wesley's – the biggest and most important of them – not excluded. However, most thoughtful Christians of Wesley's day felt that they had very satisfactorily come to terms with the new science. The discoveries culminating in the work of Newton all seemed to proclaim the activities of a beneficent, consistent, and rational deity. In Addison's famous hymn, the spacious firmament on high, the spangled heavens, the unwearied sun, the moon, the planets, the stars – all, in their orderly, intelligible, and majestic way,

> Confirm the tidings as they roll,
> And spread the truth from pole to pole . . .
> For ever singing as they shine,
> 'The hand that made us is divine.'

As a label for early- or mid-Hanoverian Britain, 'the age of reason' can apply only if Christianity is included as seeming generally reasonable. Though the pagan classics underlay most literary and artistic taste and dominated formal education, that is not of course to say they had unseated Christianity from its central situation in the minds of men. Sectarian ferocity had happily decreased; 'enthusiasm' was generally deplored; there was greater religious tolerance than in any earlier epoch. But if among the educated well-to-do and in the fashionable society of London and the spas there was much easy-going detachment concerning religion – to be seen nowhere better than in the insouciant pages of Horace Walpole's letters – it must be considered that the *beau monde* was a very small world indeed; and even Walpole would go to church to set the servants an example. The bulk of the nation, however vaguely, variously, or confusedly, would not have dreamed of calling itself, or thinking itself, anything other than Christian. It is true that the century's greatest British philospher, Hume (whom Wesley naturally detested) was a sceptic; and so was its greatest historian, Gibbon. But Gibbon's bland ironies at the expense of Wesley's admired primitive Christians were found rather shocking; and the age's *favourite* philosopher was not Hume but Locke, author not only of the famous works on *Government, Toleration,* and *The Human Understanding,* but also *The Reasonableness of Christianity as Delivered in the Scriptures.*

Scripture sat little disturbed upon its throne, its authority, for most, still absolute. Difficulties, lacunae, apparent contradictions, might be satisfactorily explained, reconciled, disposed of. Wesley's own prescription for this was beguilingly straightforward. 'The general rule for interpreting scripture,' he said, was as follows: 'the literal sense of every text is to be taken, if it be not contrary to some other texts; but in that case the obscure text is to be interpreted by those which speak more plainly.'[28] 'Obscure'; not 'corrupt', never 'unreliable'; he was always to insist on the absolute reliability of the Bible's every word. Once you conceded that any biblical text contained a falsehood, you were lost, and might as well be a Deist or an atheist: 'Nay, if there be any mistakes in the Bible, there may as well be a thousand.'[29] For Wesley, 'unscriptural' always remained the most conclusively dismissive epithet.

It would be a long time yet before any Lyell or Darwin or Huxley would polarize the conflict between reason and scripture, or set science and religion in opposing camps. From his entrenched scriptural position, Wesley always regarded himself as essentially the *champion* of reason, whether against infidels, or Christian mystics, or for instance Luther's commentary on *Galatians,* which he rejected specifically because it 'decried reason'.[30]

Certainly the Deists presented the churches with a challenge, repudiating as they did divine revelation, miracles, and the reliability of Christian records, but they were not widely thought to have had the best of the argument with Christian theologians; and even the Deists, though they appeared heathenishly horrible in the eyes of Wesley and sound Christians, were (as their name insists) very far from being atheists. Theirs was primarily a system of ethics and morality, but it unequivocally postulated the existence of a God or Supreme Being. The very vehemence of the outcry against them serves to correct the proposition that

the age was irreligious.* Charges of irreligion were of course
brought against it, as they are in all ages professedly religious.
But it would be a mistake to accept without severe qualification
Southey's pronouncement that 'there never was less religious
feeling either within the Establishment or without, than when
Wesley blew his trumpet and awakened those who slept'; and
Montesquieu's assertion, that not more than four or five members
of the British Parliament regularly attended church, must surely
be greeted with scepticism.

Wesley himself, with his readiness to write off his fellow clergy
(as well, of course, as his own 'unconverted' self before May
1738) as non-Christians, or at best 'almost Christians', is a witness
to be approached with caution. When, for instance, he denounces
the run-of-the-mill church service of his day, conducted by 'a
poor humdrum wretch who can scarce read what he drones out
with such an air of importance', with the singing of metrical
psalms in 'the miserable scandalous doggerel of Hopkins and
Sternhold', 'the solemn addresses to God interrupted by the
drawl of a parish clerk, the screaming of boys who bawl out
what they neither feel nor understand, or the unseasonable and
unmeaning impertinence of a voluntary on the organ', this lively
representation (which he contrasts with a godly Methodist
service conducted by 'one whose life is no reproach to his
profession') can hardly be less of a caricature than any of Hogarth
or Rowlandson on the same subject.

Shortly after his return from Herrnhut, Wesley counted *ten*
Church of England ministers he knew who taught 'the way of
God in truth', to which meagre tally he was prepared to add one
Baptist and 'one, if not two' Presbyterians.[31] 'My brother and I
are not permitted to preach in most of the churches in London', he
wrote. Perhaps there was a little exaggeration here; Wesley was
apt to make as much as possible of being thought 'vile' and
suffering discrimination, if not actual persecution, for righteousness' and Methodism's sake. 'Till a man gives offence he will do
no good.' In fact over these weeks his *Journal* records a considerable number of London churches (for Charles these included
Westminster Abbey) where he was still able to speak 'strong
words', 'the truth as it is in Jesus', 'strange doctrine to a polite

* *Christianity as Old as the Creation*, by Matthew Tindal, best known of the
Deist writers, elicited 150 or more clerical counterblasts.

audience', without any immediately resulting ban. (Within a few years, however, there *was* to be hardly a church left in London where either Wesley was invited to preach. By 1747 there was one only.) Outside church, in hall, or meeting-room, the brothers continued to 'publish the word of reconciliation every evening . . . sometimes to twenty or thirty, sometimes to three or four hundred persons'. And there were more visits to Oxford, to preach at the Castle prison and 'expound' to various religious societies. 'Saturday the 11th [November], spent the evening,' John wrote, 'with a little company at Oxford. I was grieved to find prudence had made them leave off singing psalms. I fear it will not stop here. God deliver me . . . from what the world calls Christian prudence.'32

The brothers' preaching did cause stir and hostility enough for its acceptability to be investigated by Dr Gibson, the Bishop of London. At this stage, however, he showed a tolerant and even friendly neutrality; so too did Archbishop Potter of Canterbury, who merely cautioned them 'to give no more umbrage than was necessary' for their own defence. Certainly to Charles during one interview Dr Gibson burst out, 'Oh, why will you push things to an extreme?' But in matters of doctrine, particularly on 'assurance' and 'justification by faith', he found nothing to fault the Wesleys on yet, even if there were hints of impending difficulties. There was for instance the troublesome question of whether the religious society meetings constituted conventicles, which were illegal under the Acts of 1664 and 1670. There was also the Wesleys' practice of rebaptizing ex-Nonconformists which, although Gibson strongly opposed it and ruled it irregular, he did not expressly forbid. Another sensitive matter concerning the societies involved preaching by laymen, which was certainly impermissible but seems to have been a subject not yet raised by the bishop. James Hutton, who preached at Fetter Lane, thought it advisable not to advertise the fact, in particular to his disapproving father. Wesley himself recorded later that it was during this year 1738 that he was for the first time in England assisted by a lay preacher, one Joseph Humphreys – though previously in Georgia the unordained Charles Delamotte had substituted for him.33

Lay preaching was to be one of the chief future sources of complaint against Methodists. Another was to be open-air or

'field' preaching. With Wesley, the practice seems to have begun
at a Tyburn hanging. On 8 November 1738 John and Charles
Wesley were at Newgate 'to do the last good office to the condemned malefactors . . . the most glorious instance', John was
convinced, 'of faith triumphing over sin and death'. His diary
indicates the programme of the day with its usual terse precision:

> 7 [a.m.] communion, prayers, preached; 9 in the coach, meditated,
> singing; 10 at St Giles' [-in-the-Fields, where the procession
> customarily halted for the condemned prisoners to receive a bowl
> of ale]; 10.30 Tyburn . . . 11 in the cart, prayer, singing, prayer,
> all cheerful; 12 . . . prayer, preached to the mob . . .

'All cheerful'; no painting the scene's horrors; no disgust at the
punishment or the spectacle; no social criticism, but instead joy
at introducing sinners to faith and the hope of blessedness – and
then off to Islington for dinner and prayer; then to Basinghall
after tea to preach at 5.30; looking in at Mr Richter's love-feast;
'8.15 at J. Harris's, singing, etc.', home by 10.30; conversation,
prayer; in bed by eleven; one more businesslike no-moment-
wasted day in the service of salvation. Ministering to condemned
felons was not a new experience for him, even if Tyburn itself
was. The significant novelty in the day's record was surely
'preached to the mob'.

Charles had earlier spoken a 'few suitable words' to the Tyburn
crowd after a hanging some months previously. By his almost
ecstatic account, the six felons who died that day after receiving
his ministrations showed 'no natural terror of death . . . I never
saw such calm triumph . . . We sang several hymns . . . I could do
nothing but rejoice: kissed Newington and Hudson; took leave
of each in particular . . . They expressed some concern how we
should get back to our coach. We left them going to meet their
Lord, ready for the Bridegroom. When the cart drew off, not one
stirred, or struggled for life, but meekly gave up their spirit.'
For both Wesleys there was never to be occasion for reproach
or horror in the hanging of repentant criminals who confessed a
true faith.

CHAPTER 6

The Campaign Begins

WHITEFIELD HAD ARRIVED in Savannah six months after Wesley left, and on this first of his American missions had fared much more successfully than either of the Wesleys; swelled the congregations; discovered even sin-laden Frederica to be full of good people hungry for the Word; and in general reckoned America 'an excellent school to learn Christ in'. He arrived back in London in December 1738, finding the new-old doctrine of justification by faith 'much revived' by the Wesley brothers; and flowing from it he discerned 'a great pouring out of the spirit'. Straightway he entered on a hectic round of preaching, taking packed congregations by storm with the uninhibited flow of his eloquence. Between sermons, he was busy 'expounding', 'praying extempore', and love-feasting with the London religious societies, feeding his devout and devoted admirers 'like new-born babes . . . with the sincere milk of the Word', and never omitting to pray with charitable vigour for 'opposers of the New Birth' whose palate rejected this nutriment. ('Lord, open Thou their hearts and eyes'.)*

Wesley, attending together with Charles, Whitefield, Ingham, and sixty or so others the all-night New Year love-feast-cum-intercession at Fetter Lane, records 'awe and amazement' (in that King James Bible vocabulary which had come to impregnate his writing, so that that part of it which was not direct textual quotation was often unconscious biblical imitation) at the power

* Whitefield's *Journal*, 15–16 January 1739: 'Read a pamphlet written against me by a clergyman, I bless God, without any emotion; prayed most heartily for the author . . . Preached to a thronged and affected audience at St Helen's. After this, I expounded twice to two companies, and prayed by name for the author of the pamphlet; left my auditors in tears.'

of God coming mightily upon them at 3 a.m., 'insomuch as many cried out for exceeding joy, and many fell to the ground'. Were such phenomena symptomatic of 'enthusiasm'? Wesley was prepared to pose himself the question but rejected the imputation. Enthusiasm was something different, something to be eschewed: it was 'false, imaginary inspiration', 'thinking to attain the end without the means'.[1] He was anxious to profess wariness of those claiming God-given psychic powers. Attending a séance of one of the currently-much-talked-of Camisard refugees, a 'French prophetess', he was not altogether convinced by her 'strong convulsive movements' and prophecies concerning the imminent Second Coming, but expressed no hostility or distaste, and noted that several of his companions present were 'much affected'.[2] In fact his journals and correspondence over the coming months and years contain scores of accounts of men and women at his services 'falling into extreme agony both of body and soul', being pierced 'as it were by a sword' so that they cried aloud 'even in the street', calling upon God 'as out of the belly of hell', suffering 'violent sweats and heavings of the breast', or gnashing of teeth, or convulsive trembling, dropping to the ground 'as if thunderstruck', enduring such 'pangs [of the New Birth] as I never saw before', 'strainings as it were to vomit', 'groaning for deliverance'. Whether or not later in life he was inclined to deprecate such public displays of emotional struggle, he certainly did not yet. Repeatedly, while still disclaiming 'enthusiasm', he records these scenes as welcome evidence of work well done, prayer truly prayed, crises agonizingly but triumphantly surmounted in the quest for grace.

Many among the educated public saw these 'extacies' either as the effect of religious mountebanks working on weak minds or simply as an exhibition of bogus sensationalism. Among Wesley's more temperate critics was his brother Samuel. Were the main body of these ecstatics, he enquired suspiciously, 'good sort of people beforehand, or loose and immoral?' He refused to accept Wesley's conviction that divine intervention was at work: 'Your followers fall into agonies. I confess it. – They are freed from them after you have prayed over them. Granted. They say it is God's doing. I own they say so. Dear Br[other] *where is your ocular demonstration*? Where indeed is the *rational proof*? Their living well afterwards may be a probable and sufficient argument that they believe themselves; but it goes no further'.[3]

Wesley was inclined to view these painful pre-conversion scenes – as men and women, and sometimes children, struggled to cast out their devils and win through to 'faith in the blood of Christ' – in a consciously New Testament spirit. As earnestly as any of the early apostles he was looking for signs and wonders. At a religious society meeting in April 1739, for instance, a young woman, after typically enduring 'a short agony', was with three others 'fully set at liberty'. When she began to be in pain, Wesley wrote to Hutton,

> We asked God to give us a living witness that signs and wonders were now wrought by the name of his holy child Jesus. We asked for one, and he hath given us four.[4]

On another occasion, when preaching on the falsity of pre-destination, he interrupted the flow of his argument to beg God to give a sign of divine concurrence in the truth of it – a daring and dramatic, not to say risky, procedure surely. If this was God's truth, however, he would not delay to confirm it.

> Immediately the power of God fell upon us: one, and another, and another, sank to the earth: you might see them dropping on all sides as thunderstruck ... In the evening I made the same appeal to God, and almost before we called he answered. A young woman was seized with such pangs as I never saw before, and in a quarter of an hour she had a new song in her mouth, a thanksgiving unto our God.[5]

His belief in God was matched by a no less absolute belief in a living Satan. When, following a Wesley sermon, Thomas Maxfield roared hysterically and beat himself against the ground 'so that six men could scarcely hold him', the *Journal* explains simply that he was being 'torn by the Evil One' – a phrase echoed on many other occasions. Wesley seems often to have envisaged his war against the Evil One as a kind of personal combat. The Enemy took possession of the souls of men and women, who became his troops in action. Wesley in the armour of God's Word fought them off; and then 'the Devil, knowing his kingdom shook', would 'stir up his servants ... to make a noise' to drown the preacher. When a hostile crowd shouted down his reading from the book of *Acts*, it was 'the prince of the air' making 'another attempt in defence of his tottering kingdom'.[6] Even rebelliousness in his horse he was prepared to ascribe to diabolical possession. At one particularly 'stupid, senseless' place in Ireland, where during April 1748 he felt his preaching was obviously being wasted, he could write:

> I do not wonder that Satan was sorely unwilling I should go out of this place. The moment I mounted my horse, without any visible cause he began to boggle and snort and drew backward, and from one side to the other, as if there were a stone wall just before him. Brother William whipped him behind and I before, but it was lost labour. He leaped from side to side, till he came to a gateway, into which he then ran backwards and tumbled head over heels. My foot was under him but I arose unhurt. He then went on as quiet as any horse in the world. Thus far only could Satan go.[7]

The evil spirits which infected mankind with 'sin and death' were, if not materially tangible, much more real than any metaphor; if not figures of flesh and blood, much more than figures of speech. *Not* to believe in spirits (or similarly in witchcraft or ghosts) was clearly 'unscriptural'; such phenomena possessed not only the backing of common experience but also the unanswerable authentication of biblical record. When, a dozen years on, in 1751, he was answering publicly charges brought against him by Bishop Lavington of Exeter, who had quoted critically the many devil-references in Wesley's own *Journal* – fits of insane laughter inspired by diabolical possession, opposition to Methodist services inspired by the Prince of Darkness – Wesley simply replied, 'I own the whole charge. I did say all this. Nay, and if need were I should say it again.'[8] As for the physical reality of angels, he offered the opinion that 'the several instances of music heard before or at the death of those that die in the Lord' might literally be the singing of the heavenly choir. The voice of an angel might affect 'the auditory nerves, as an apparition does the optic nerve or retina'.[9]

It was surely reasonable to believe that a God who had intervened in terrestrial affairs as directly and repeatedly as the Bible indicated would not be unready to offer guidance to those Christians who now sought it in faith; and Wesley and his associates, like the Moravians, made habitual use of lottery and bibliomancy. Should Wesley break with Sophy Hopkey? It was to a choice between slips of paper that Delamotte and he had resorted, to ascertain God's intentions. When Charles's friend Miss Claggett hovered tearful and trembling on the brink of conversion, he naturally consulted 'the oracles of God' for her, and reassuringly opened the book at Isaiah, xxx. 18; whereupon Miss Claggett consulted too, and hit upon the comfort of Corinthians, v. 27. When Charles was so 'full of heaviness' for his tragically unfortunate and still unconverted sister Hetty that he could not sleep, he got up to open the Bible at random and met with the meaningful words of Jehu, 'Let none escape out of your hands.' And when this was crowned by a clap of thunder and violent rain, what must it be but 'a sign that the skies would soon pour down righteousness'?[10]

For both brothers indeed there was always 'a special providence in the fall of a sparrow'. No circumstance was so trivial that the hand of God might not be seen in it. When John put into print that twice, being 'in violent pain' he had 'prayed to God, and found immediate ease', he was attacked for 'claiming miraculous gifts'. He jibbed somewhat at the phrase (though he had himself originally written of enjoying 'miraculous cures'); but he would not deny that he had experienced 'signal instances of God's particular providence', 'not strictly accountable for by the ordinary course of natural causes'.[11] This sort of thing was always to be held against the Methodists as evidence of 'enthusiasm'. A lifetime later Sydney Smith, in an 1808 *Edinburgh Review* article berating both Methodists and Evangelicals, made it one of his many complaints: their 'belief that Providence enters into all the little actions of our lives' encouraged 'the grossest superstitions'.

In the early months of 1739 Whitefield's potent eloquence had had sensational success in Bristol and Bath, though both the manner and matter of his preaching had given offence to the Church establishment there. Being excluded from many pulpits and seeking also to reach those people, like the rough colliers of Kingswood, for whom there *were* no pulpits, he took to preaching in the open. A natural crowd-compeller, all vehemence and passion and fervour, sentimental to a fault, a master of gesture and histrionics, he was sometimes so moved by his own oratory that it was in danger of being drowned in his own tears. Squint-eyed he might be ('Dr Squintum' soon to the caricaturists), but to be able just to pronounce *Oh* as Mr Whitefield pronounced it,

Garrick once said he would give a hundred guineas. One of his outdoor platforms was on a Bristol bowling green, where he addressed crowds of as many as five thousand. 'Blessed be God,' he said, 'that the bowling green is turned into a preaching place' – a token, he trusted, that assembly rooms and playhouses, those 'strongholds of the Devil' would soon be put to similar use. At Coal-Pit Heath, where the audience, largely colliers and their families, reached two thousand, he preached beside the village maypole, and 'took occasion to warn them of misspending their time in revelling and dancing'. 'Oh,' he wrote, 'that all such entertainments were put a stop to. I see no other way to effect it, but by going boldly, and calling people from such lying vanities in the same of Jesus Christ.'[12] It is not difficult to see why Whitefield was accused of being a rabble-storming 'enthusiast', a crypto-Dissenter, but he strongly protested his Anglican orthodoxy. 'What evil have I done?' he demanded of the Bishop of Bristol. 'I answer, None, save that I visit the religious societies, preach to the prisoners in Newgate, and to the poor colliers of Kingswood . . . Many are brought to the Church by my preaching, not one taken from it.'

He took his preaching tour also to South Wales – he was raising funds to build an Orphan House in Georgia, to which colony he was proposing soon to return – and when he wanted to take his mission back to London, he needed someone to succeed him in Bristol and sustain the impetus of the work he had so sensationally begun there. Best of all would be someone who combined evangelical zeal with organizing ability, since many were 'ripe for bands' – ready, that is, to be grouped into units for regular meeting. Who better than his admired master and honoured friend John Wesley? whom he therefore begged to come, if the brethren 'after prayerful direction' should approve. Some of them did not, including Charles Wesley, until, appealing to the oracles of God, he allowed himself to be divinely overruled. Others in the already schism-threatening Fetter Lane society hung out longer, until they agreed to determine the issue, first by an obscurely indecisive lottery and then by further resort to bibliomancy, which produced some esoteric responses from the second Book of Samuel and seemed to require a very Procrustean interpretation of 2 Chronicles, xxviii. 27; 'And Ahaz slept with his fathers, and they buried him in the city, even in

Jerusalem' – a text of bafflingly arcane significance, unless perhaps Wesley read it as having some connection with his own death, which for no obvious reason he appears at this time to have regarded as imminent. 'I believe I have nearly finished my course', he wrote to his brother Samuel; he expected to finish his days 'in the body' at Bristol. Many years later he explained that as a young man he sometimes 'spat blood'. In fact he generally enjoyed, and except for brief periods continued to enjoy into old age, wonderfully robust health. It was Samuel who had nearly finished his course.

Wesley arrived in Bristol on 31 March 1739. Whitefield left two days later, and was before long giving great crowds in London their first taste of his soul-storming field preaching. Wesley, that stickler for decency and order, while reminding himself that the Sermon of the Mount did set 'a pretty remarkable precedent', took to the practice only with reluctance. Yet, very soon, phenomena like those Whitefield had engendered were being repeated by Wesley, who set about Bristol and its environs like a whirlwind sent by God. By the evidence of his printed sermons merely, this might give some cause for surprise. In them, he is a preacher as far removed from the style of Whitefield as one might expect a fellow of Lincoln to be from the son of a Gloucester innkeeper. They are severely structured, logically argued, learnedly scriptural; forceful and devout, but generally unemotional and never fanatical. His more impromptu discourses, by the evidence of their impact, must often have been of a character more immediately stirring. Especially in this early stage of his half-century of missioning, there were numerous instances of crowd hysteria, of psychological breakdown both public and private, of alarming physical symptoms arising from inner tension and overpowering consciousness of sin, all meticulously related by Wesley in his letters and journals with a mixture of astonishment and awe – and of thanksgiving when, after his prayers and ministrations, the struggler escaped from the curse laid upon Adam's children and won through, by God's grace and sincere affirmation of faith, to 'justification' and the hope of a blessed immortality. He thought it in no way strange that frustrated evil spirits, or Satan, seeking to 'discredit the work of God', would 'tear those that are coming to Christ'.[13]

The psychology and physiology of religious conversion and

of the more sinister-sounding 'brain-washing', are subjects particularly apt for consideration in this propaganda-drenched age. (Whitefield and the Wesleys perhaps would have preferred the expression 'soul-washing': washing souls clean in the blood of the Lamb.) The physical and mental behaviour of the brain-washed victims of Stalin's purges, of prisoners-of-war undergoing re-education, of mass-evangelized religious converts, of initiates to Voodooism, even of Pavlov's dogs,* enormously different in most significant respects, presents one common sequence of phenomena. A tremendous assault on the emotions or physique, or on both together, induces a condition of intense stress and frequently collapse. But out of this pit of prostration a road of escape must be offered. The Communist re-educator to his prisoner, the evangelist to the sinner appalled by his conviction of sin, Pavlov to his dogs, offers the prospect of reward. The new behaviour pattern, political conviction, conversion, 'new birth', is achieved.

It would be offensive to push too far a parallel between the techniques of Wesley and those of Stalin's police or the Communist Chinese in Korea. But his earnest eloquence, his powerful hammering on the theme of the innate sinfulness of unregenerate man and the punishment awaiting those who rejected the offer of God's grace and forgiveness, his 'thunderclap upon the conscience', provided all necessary material in susceptible minds (and sometimes too in mockers who found their resistance weaker than they thought) for the all but intolerable psychological crisis that preceded conversion. And the reward which the Wesleys held out to their potential converts was 'certain' and beyond price; open not merely to the elect, as Calvinism taught, or to the few, as they themselves had been brought up to believe, but to every man and woman who took the road of faith: 'the *free gift* of God'. Eternal punishment was presented only as the result of *rejecting* the offer of salvation through faith.

---

* See W. Sargant, who writes in *The Battle for the Mind* (p. 78): 'Fear of everlasting hell . . . affected the nervous system of Wesley's hearers very much as fear of drowning did Pavlov's dogs in the Leningrad flood.' Wesley's own attempted interpretation (*Works*, viii. 127) of these '*extraordinary* circumstances' is not altogether out of step with Dr Sargant's: 'How easy is it to suppose, that a strong, lively, and sudden apprehension of the heinousness of sin, the wrath of God, and the bitter pains of eternal death, should affect the body as well as the soul . . . and put nature out of its course.'

'I met Miss Jeffreys, the Quaker,' records Charles in October 1739, 'whom I had so laboured to convince of sin.' His words, he notes hopefully, had 'sunk deep'. 'An horrible dread has over-whelmed her. Her flesh trembles for fear of God . . . She sees herself . . . every moment sinking into hell.' Some lives of Wesley, reflecting the milder thinking of their own day, have perhaps wished to minimize his insistence on the threat of eternal damnation awaiting the unbelieving unrepentant sinner. It is true that he advised his preachers, in conference, to stress the love rather than the wrath of God: too much talk of the latter, he suggested to them, 'generally hardens them that believe not, and discourages them that do'.[14] But for him the sombre reality of hell, and the dread warning it offered mankind, were never things to be comfortably brushed aside. 'I preached, at five,' he writes on an Irish mission in 1748, 'the terrors of the Lord in the strongest manner I was able.'[15] Isaiah's 'everlasting burnings', Revelation's 'lake of fire burning with brimstone', Mark's fire which 'is not quenched', and more than enough similar texts showed damnation to be as 'scriptural' as salvation. It was what must await unrepentant sinners, an unhappily numerous band composed no less of so-called Christians than of non-Christians, whom he saw alike 'posting to hell and fancying it was heaven', 'on the brink of the pit, ready to be plunged into everlasting perdition'. 'The great decree of God, eternal, unchangeable', was ' "He that believeth shall be saved; he that believeth not shall be damned".'[16]

This was no mere metaphor, and this he never ceased to preach. When he was approaching seventy, of a congregation in Port Glasgow he suspected of 'gaiety' he wrote: 'I spoke strongly of death and judgement, heaven and hell. This they seemed to comprehend, and there was no more laughing among them.' When some of an 'elegant' congregation in Pembroke in 1777 came to his service 'dancing and laughing, as in a theatre', he soon subdued their levity and had them 'as serious as my subject – Death'. At Wincanton, 'one of the dullest places in the county [of Somerset]' he applied the same shock treatment to attack the inhabitants' spiritual lethargy: 'I preached on Death in the evening, and Hell in the morning.' And he expressed outrage at the sug-gestion of the 'madman' Swedenborg that the damned were not actually *burned* in hell. Swedenborg's unforgivably unscriptural account of hell left 'nothing terrible in it; for, first, he quenches the unquenchable fire'.[17]

From April to June 1739 Wesley spent ten uninterrupted weeks preaching, evangelizing, and 'driving out evil spirits' in the Bristol-Bath district, returning there later in the year after a preaching campaign in London and attempts to restore harmony to the troubled affairs of Fetter Lane. As with Whitefield, the crowds who assembled to hear him were very large – indeed vast, if we are to accept Wesley's own estimates, which range, perhaps not always quite reliably, up to twenty thousand. He now fully accepted the necessity of field-preaching and street-preaching, whether the Church approved or no; he had, in his own strange phrase, 'submitted to be more vile'. (This was of course another biblical reference, echoing David, where in 2 Samuel, vi. he 'shamelessly uncovered himself' to his servants' handmaids.) Not all the churches in the Bristol neighbourhood were closed to him, but he accepted that most would be. He continued busily 'expounding' and 'exhorting' to the quickly expanding religious societies; and it was here, in the often highly charged atmosphere of their meetings, that a large proportion of the scenes of 'enthusiasm' occurred. He supervised the organizing of new Methodist converts into 'bands' on the model of Fetter Lane, the men and women meeting separately under leaders chosen by lot. He pressed ahead with the building of a school for colliers' children at Kingswood which Whitefield had begun, and at the same time started work on a new meeting-house in the Horsefair, Bristol, for two of the religious societies. To this a small charity school was soon to be added.

Naturally he gave offence by invading other priests' parishes, and it was aggravated by the nature of the dangerous fanaticism which accompanied Methodist meetings. Even some of his earlier sympathizers proved critical. It was in reply to one of these, James Hervey, his former pupil at Oxford and a Holy Club member, that Wesley wrote:

You ... ask, 'How is it that I assemble Christians, who are none of my charge, to sing psalms and pray and hear the Scriptures expounded? and think it hard to justify doing this in other men's parishes, upon catholic principles.

Permit me to speak plainly. If by catholic principles you mean any other than scriptural, they weigh nothing with me ... God in

Scripture commands me, according to my power, to instruct the ignorant, reform the wicked, confirm the virtuous. Man forbids me to do this in another's parish: that is, in effect, to do it at all; seeing I have now no parish of my own, nor probably ever shall. Whom then shall I hear, God or man? . . .

Suffer me now to tell you my principles in this matter. I look upon all the world as my parish . . .[18]

A few years later, he wrote from Dublin: 'Wherever I see one or a thousand men running into hell, be it in England, Ireland or France; yea, in Europe, Asia, Africa, or America, I will stop them if I can . . . Were I to let any soul to drop into the pit whom I might have saved from everlasting burnings, I am not satisfied God would accept my plea, "Lord he was not in my parish".'

Criticism from inside the Church was severe. According to Dr Joseph Trapp, for instance, the Methodists were 'teaching absurd doctrines, and seconding them with such absurd practices, as to give countenance to the lewd and debauched, the irreligious and profane'. 'Can it,' he asked, 'promote the Christian religion to turn it into riot, tumult, and confusion? to make it ridiculous and contemptible, and expose it to the scoffs of infidels and atheists? . . . Go not after these impostors and seducers; but shun them as you would the plague.' A few years later the bishop of Exeter, George Lavington, was at once attacking and ridiculing their 'sanctified singularities, low fooleries, and high pretensions'. Carried away by 'the intoxicating vapours of the brain or the uncouth effects of a distempered mind and body', Wesley and his followers were accused by Lavington of 'the ostentation of sanctified looks . . . swelling words of vanity and loud boastings . . . a strain of sophistry, artifice and craft, evasion, reserve, equivocation, and prevarication'. Against such criticisms, and there were many of them, it is pertinent to set the very different picture presented by one of Wesley's own preachers, John Hampson: 'His attitude in the pulpit was graceful and easy; his action calm and natural, yet pleasing and expressive; his voice not loud, but clear and manly; his style neat, simple, perspicuous, and admirably adapted to the capacity of his hearers.' And Dr Johnson, while complaining against those enthusiasts who claimed to have an 'inner light' (you 'could not tell where you were' with such people) spoke up unfashionably, in his own way, for the preaching of the Methodists, whose success he declared (30 July 1763) was 'owing to their expressing themselves in a plain and familiar manner, which is the only way to do good to the common people'.

In Bath Wesley had a public brush with Beau Nash, the acknowledged arbiter of the city's style and demeanour, who levelled the pertinent accusation that Wesley's open-air meetings were in breach of the Conventicle Act. 'Beside,' Nash added, not without some justice, 'your preaching frightens people out of their wits.' Wesley was satisfied that he managed to rout this revel-master of Bath's Vanity Fair by turning the laugh against him, but the argument he employed elsewhere in these same exchanges, that the Conventicle Act could not apply to his meetings, being concerned only with those that were 'seditious', was in fact misinformed.[19] On the way back to where he was lodging, after conducting prayers for the spiritual improvement of Beau Nash, he also reports dealing summarily, and again to his own satisfaction, with 'several ladies' who had followed him home.

> The servant told me there were some wanted to speak to me. I went to them and said, 'I believe, ladies, the maid mistook; you only wanted to look at me.' I added, 'I do not expect that the rich and great should want either to speak to me or to hear me; for I speak the plain truth – a thing you little hear of, and do not desire to hear.'[20]

His attitude towards 'the rich and great' was hardening. It was not many years since the contemplation of 'Aspasia's' obliging condescension had brought him humble joy. Now, and increasingly as the decades of his ministry followed, it was 'Christ's poor' who provided his main concern. Not that an anti-aristocratic implied any sort of democratic inclination. His temper, if rebellious, remained authoritarian. Christ's poor must be offered the benison of faith and opportunity of salvation, but never any hint of majority rule. The Methodist bands, for example, were not to choose their own leaders. The principle of election by lot cast responsibility where it must properly belong, with God; and Wesley was never in doubt who among Methodists would remain God's principal interpreter and vice-gerent.

Personally, he could reasonably claim at least associate membership of the society of the poor. As fellow, albeit absentee

fellow, of Lincoln, he received, while celibate, an annual payment
– fluctuating complicatedly by dint of room rentals, share of
college fines, and other variables[21] – which on average amounted
to rather more than country curates might then expect but less
than most country parsons. Charles, a Student of Christ Church,
received payments not dissimilar. Then, as prolific authors and
hymn-writers, both brothers would soon be taking in modestly
substantial earnings, adequate for them comfortably to survive
the loss of college income upon marriage. Their style of life was
simple, even spartan. Wesley ate and drank frugally, though no
longer on the extreme teetotal-vegetarian lines he had adopted on
going to Georgia. He required no amusement, and little entertainment beyond serious conversation with friends. He troubled
few tailors and no wigmakers, wearing his own hair, partly on
principle and partly from economy; but he was always, however
soberly, neatly dressed, with hair well brushed; a trim, tidy man.
He did not need a house of his own, though sometimes (in the
new Bristol meeting-house, for instance) he was glad to have a
room set aside for his use. When he was travelling the country –
which was constantly – his bed and board would be usually
provided by the hospitality of fellow Methodists. He did require
the expense of horse hire and coach or chaise travel; and his
outlay on boot leather cannot have been negligible. But, proud
of poverty, he would not flaunt it, like a 'poor preacher'. He
remained his gentlemanly, businesslike self. When funds lagged,
he was inclined to plunge ahead on his own, trusting to the
promise of what he might raise from sympathizers. In the
building of the new meeting-house, for instance, when his
appointed 'feoffees' proved men of straw, he personally engaged
to supervise and underwrite the project, quickly running up a
debt of £150; 'nothing doubting', he writes, that the Lord would
provide – as indeed He did, it seems largely through the philanthropic agency of William Seward, one of Whitefield's wealthier
followers.* Seward would soon be accompanying and helping to
support Whitefield in the early stages of his second American
tour. Returning, on a preaching mission in company with the

---

* By 1748 there was money enough to build an entirely new meeting-
house and chapel on the site of the older one and able to hold double the
congregation. The New Room still stands, at the heart of Bristol's modern
shopping centre.

Welsh evangelist Howel Harris, having by then broken with the Wesleys, he was twice assaulted by hostile mobs. A stone blinded him in the first attack. In the second he was killed.

William Seward had several brothers, and two of them were involved in the sort of family recriminations which not uncommonly resulted from Methodist evangelizing. At Bengeworth, near Evesham, Henry Seward, 'mad with passion' at Charles Wesley's influence over his brother Benjamin Seward, organized an anti-Methodist counter-meeting, which had the support of the local ale-house, manor-house, and vicarage. Charles had a message from the vicar that if he did not immediately quit the town, Mr Henry Seward could easily raise a mob, and then – let him look to himself.

John and Charles both learned to take these 'children of Belial' in their stride. At Reading, John found the 'zealous mob' so enraged 'they were ready to tear the [meeting-] house down'. Once at Bristol 'the street was filled with people, shouting and cursing and swearing', who were not dispersed till the Mayor's officers took the ringleaders into custody. In Cardiff's Shire Hall he found an attentive audience with 'many gentry', but at his next stop in Newport met 'the most insensible, ill-behaved people', including one 'ancient man' who spent Wesley's sermon-time in non-stop swearing and cursing, and in repeated attempts to throw a 'great stone', which fortunately proved too heavy for him. At Upton, near Bristol, 'the devil knew his kingdom shook, and therefore stirred up his servants to ring bells and make all the noise they could. But my voice prevailed.' The occasional sermon from a church pulpit proved hardly less liable to inflame. After he had preached at matins in St Mary Arches, Exeter, he was told by the rector, 'Sir, you must not preach in the afternoon. Not that you preach false doctrine . . . But it is not guarded. It is dangerous. It may lead people into enthusiasm or despair.' As Charles observed, 'The word has turned them upside down'; some were 'wounded' (i.e. impressed by their state of sin); some were hardened; 'I hear of no neuters.'[22]

Mrs Kirkham, that old intimate acquaintance of Cotswolds days, was another who voiced strong hostility to the Methodists. Charles, about to preach in the street at Gloucester (the minister said he dared not lend him his pulpit for fifty guineas) found her barring his path with 'What, Mr Wesley, is it you I see? Is it possible that you, who can preach at Christ Church, St Mary's, etc., should come hither after a mob?' 'I cut her short', writes Charles; 'I continued my discourse till night.' He was now classing such 'well-dressed ladies' (*vide* Isaiah iii. 16–24) among those daughters of Zion and the rest of the sinful company of profligates alike condemned by the Prophet:[23] 'In that day the Lord will take away the bravery of their tinkling ornaments about their feet and their cauls, and their round tires like the moon . . . Instead of sweet smell there shall be stink and burning instead of beauty.'

With Charles even more than with John, it seems that a large proportion of the 'newly born' were women, particularly young women, who also provided a majority of the dramatic conversion episodes and the incidents of hysteria and 'demoniacal possession'. Both brothers' journals abound with instances: 'a woman cried out, and dropped down under the weight of sin'; another 'raged more and more for about two hours, and then our Lord gave her rest'; another 'screamed for mercy'; another sank down 'with groaning that could not be uttered'. 'Many were ready to cry after Jesus for mercy . . . Miss P. declared her soul's cure before two hundred witnesses, many of them gay young gentlewomen.' The prostitute 'J.T.' in a 'flood of tears . . . is washed, but she is justified!' 'The thousand distortions' of an illiterate nineteen-year-old showed 'how the dogs of hell were gnawing at her heart. The shrieks intermixed were scarce to be endured.'

Of this last painful case of 'anguish, horror, and despair' John wrote with a touch of incipient caution, 'The fact I nakedly relate, and leave every man to his own judgement of it'.[24] Charles, like his brother, learned in time to be wary in his reaction to such occurrences. He found it necessary, for instance, to 'talk sharply' to one Jenny Deschamps, aged twelve, who eventually confessed that she had feigned all her fits and cryings out ('above thirty of them'),[25] 'that Mr Wesley might take notice of her'. Then there was a drunkard 'who fell into a fit for my entertainment'. Charles also had occasion once to remove to a far corner of the meeting-house room some 'unstill sisters' who always took care to stand near him and 'tried which should cry loudest'.[26] There were indeed, Charles wrote, 'many counterfeits', and he noted at Newcastle in 1743, having discouraged 'the fits', that he found the local gentry less hostile.

'Margaret Austin tells me', wrote Charles innocently, 'she has longed for my coming as a child for the breast.' Without his presence she felt she could not remain fast in the faith.[27] Was there something specially personal, some element of sexuality, in all this? It seems most likely. Both brothers had always been attractive to women; and James Hutton, for one, noted in alarm the threat this posed to the spiritual equilibrium of some female bands. Both John and Charles appeared to present 'dangerous snares to many young women. Several are in love with them', he wrote; 'I wish they were married to some good sisters.' He added, with apparent uncharitableness but perhaps also a degree of discernment, ' – though I would not give them one of mine, even if I had many'.[28]

In September 1739, during one of Wesley's short open-air preaching tours in London, he found time to call on his mother, who had removed there from Salisbury – still with her daughter Patty and son-in-law Westley Hall. For John a conversation with his mother was always likely to involve more than trivial family chatter. It seems that she had earlier been perturbed by reports she had heard of him. Doctrinally, however, all was now well. Best of all, it had suddenly been borne in upon her, at Communion, she said, ('while my son Hall was delivering the cup to me') that what John now gloried in teaching was true: salvation was not, after all, 'the peculiar blessing of a few', but 'the privilege of all true believers'. Surely she was to be included among them.

Other family news was less satisfactory. Samuel died at Tiverton on 5 November, and later that month John and Charles travelled down there from Oxford, preaching and expounding as they went. Samuel had always been an opponent of his younger brothers' Methodism. Now his no less critical widow was able to report to them that before his death Samuel had been given by God 'a calm and full assurance of his interest in Christ'. With that archaic-sounding phrase John closes the book on brother Samuel; no word of sentiment, shock, regret; not another sentence.

Of his six surviving sisters, there was little joyful to celebrate. (Molly, the cripple, married to John Whitelamb of Wroot in 1733, had died a year later in childbirth with her baby.) True, 'sister Wright', the unfortunate Hetty, with whom once or twice John took tea, was reconciled to her mother and came sometimes to see her. All but one of her many children had died; her husband, only occasionally violent, nevertheless was frequently drunk and provided no kind of moral support or intellectual companionship. Charles and John both tried to bring her to 'justification', not yet with any success, though the day would eventually arrive when sick, sad, ill-used Hetty *was* to discover grace. Indeed John once commented, long after her death, that though in general his relations, apart from Charles, had been of little assistance to him in his great work, the one exception was Hetty towards the end of her life – of whom he would 'least have expected it'. She died in 1751. One who knew her towards the end of her life wrote: 'She was an elegant woman, with great refinement of manners; and had the traces of beauty in her countenance, with the appearance of being broken-hearted'.[29]

Emily, the eldest sister, whom John had married off at the age of forty-three to Robert Harper of Epworth, the failed apothecary, was unhappy and poverty-stricken. She had never seen eye to eye with John in religious matters, and it seemed to her that he now thought God intended us to deny all our bodily 'desires and tendencies'. She could not agree. Unhappily for luckless Emily, all *her* desires and tendencies were frustrated. Her one baby died. Her husband's various attempts to earn a living all failed, and of course she was unable to keep *him* from her little school in Gainsborough. They drifted apart. By the end of 1738 she was nearly on the rocks, 'ready to give up the ghost with grief', as she wrote to John; 'almost always sick'; selling clothes for bread; owing two years' rent, 'and 'tis a cold time of year to be turned out of doors'. Her other two brothers had helped her through the previous summer. Here was John now expecting her to show interest in the condition of Christianity in Germany – his letter apparently having been full of Herrnhut and the Moravians. 'For God's sake,' wrote Emily, 'tell me how a distressed woman, who expects daily to have the very bed taken from under her for rent, can consider the state of the churches in Germany . . . You seemed to love me from your infancy; I am sure of my side . . . I loved you tenderly. You married me to this man, and as soon as sorrow took hold of me you left me to it . . . You, who could go to Germany, could you not reach Gainsborough?'[30]

This was not the only time hard words were exchanged between these two. But when Emily left Lincolnshire for London in 1740 it was her brother John who would give her lodging, first at his Moorfields headquarters next to his mother, and later in rooms in the preachers' house attached to his chapel at Seven Dials. For the last thirty of her fourscore years, Emily was to be wholly maintained and supported by Wesley.

Of his other sisters, Sukey (Susanna) also separated from her husband, the unsatisfactory Ellison, and went to live in London with her four children. Ellison was another of Wesley's brothers-in-law to suffer constant business misfortune (from fire, flood, and misjudgement). 'A coarse, vulgar, immoral man', old Mrs Wesley called him; and John's brother Samuel considered that he lacked religion, good nature, and good manners. However, Ellison too, indirectly, through Wesley's influence in disposing of a legacy, received some desperately needed financial help later.[31]

Of Nancy, Mrs Lambert, ('lusty Ann' of one of her brother Samuel's verses) the rest of the family saw and heard little. She was certainly no Methodist, and her husband too was reported as having 'little religion'. Patty (Martha), who was to survive into her mid-eighties, enjoying for a time the respectful friendship of Dr Johnson, was still in the early years of her ill-starred marriage to the Rev. Westley Hall, beginning the bearing and burying of her many children. Her husband, as promiscuous in his sexual as in his religious attachments, was to prove a pattern of infidelity. Kezzy (Kezia), the unmarried youngest daughter, was troubled in body and soul; as she herself said, 'a weak, entangled, wretched thing'. She was nearest, in years and sympathies, to her brother Charles, and helped to nurse him through his illness in 1738. She prayed that *he* would pray for her and with her. He wrestled for her soul. She wept; he was sure her wretchedness came from not 'loving God'. He 'used Pascal's prayer for conversion'; but the dove would not descend. Kezzy fell slowly into a decline and died, aged thirty-two, in 1741.

The physical toughness and inexhaustible energy of the man who had professed to think that he was going to Bristol to die,*

---

* Wesley, though he often enthusiastically hailed 'triumphant' deaths in others and prematurely heralded his own many times, did not habitually indulge the propensity for necrophily often affected by his brother and Whitefield. 'What would I give to be on that death-bed,' wrote Charles of a woman he had just left, 'ready for the Bridegroom'; and again, 'I visited our

may be gauged from a single twelvemonth's itinerary (August 1739–July 1740) listing those towns at which Wesley either preached or expounded – usually both, and often at each town on the route: Bristol-Wells-Bradford on Avon-Bath-Bristol-London - Oxford - Burford - Gloucester - Chepstow - Pontypool - Newport - Cardiff - Bristol - Bradford on Avon - Bristol - Reading - London - Oxford - Burford - Bristol - Exeter - Bristol - Malmesbury - Burford-Oxford-London-Oxford-Burford-Malmesbury-Bristol-Newbury-Reading-Windsor-Reading-Bristol-Cardiff-Pontypool-Bristol-London-Bristol-Malmesbury-Oxford-London. He was of course to keep this sort of travel up year in, year out, for half a century to come.

That final 'London' was of rather special significance. He returned there in the summer of 1740 determined upon a show-down with the opposition at Fetter Lane. Disputes had been growing in violence and numerically the Wesley party had been having the worst of the battle against the Moravians, with their teaching of an inward religion which needed no churchgoing or ordinances or sacraments or other 'means of grace'. The seeker after 'assurance', according to the Moravians, must simply wait in quietness for grace to descend. Attempts to earn assurance by good deeds would be self-defeating, by tending to destroy the 'freedom' of God's gift. Nine out of ten of the brethren, Charles lamented, were 'swallowed up in the dead sea of stillness',[32] and amid his comings and goings John had 'observed every day more and more the advantage Satan had gained'.

The most influential of Satan's agents at Fetter Lane had been the German, Philipp Molther, who when he first attended reported to Zinzendorf how shocked and alarmed he had been at all the 'sighing and groaning and whining and howling' which attended the expression of the members' religious feelings. But it was Wesley's turn to be shocked when Molther convinced one woman member that she never had any faith at all, and 'advised her, till she received faith, to be "still", ceasing from outward works'.[33] When later Molther was taken ill, Wesley optimistically discerned the hand of God. It was Satan, however, who made the faster progress. Even some of the Wesleys' most intimate stalwarts, such as James Hutton, were seduced; 'the

sister Webb, dying in child-bed. We sang that hymn over her corpse, "Ah lovely appearance of death", and shed a few tears of joy and envy.'

honest, plain, undesigning Jacob', Charles complained, 'is now turned a subtle, close, ambiguous Loyola.'[34] From his side of the fence Hutton complained of John Wesley's dictatorial temper: 'he will have the glory of doing all things. I fear, by-and-by, he will be an open enemy of Christ and His church.'

The two factions became locked in controversies as personally bitter as they were theologically complicated. Intense animosities were now aroused over whether there could, or could not, be *degrees* of justifying faith, and over its essential immediacy or possible gradualness. 'I assert', wrote Wesley, 'that a man may have a degree of justifying faith before he is wholly freed from all doubt and fear, and before he has, in the full, proper sense, a new, a clean heart.' With a sort of grieving ferocity, he accused the still brethren of being unscriptural, of having been corrupted by the German mystics – Böhme in particular, though he reckoned Law hardly better; of conforming too closely to the world in wearing 'gay and costly apparel', and of depreciating self-denial and good works (except 'to their own people'). This last he ascribed to the influence of Luther, whose decrying of reason and 'blasphemous' teaching on good works and God's law, 'constantly coupling the law with sin, death, hell, or the devil' were 'the real spring of the grand error of the Moravians'.[35]

Wesley, after consulting with Charles and his other supporters, decided on physical secession, insisting that doctrinally it was the others who had seceded. On 20 July, at a love-feast (an irony quite unperceived in Wesley's account), he read the company a paper which concluded with the words,

> I have borne with you long, hoping you would turn. But . . . nothing now remains, but that I should give you up to God. You that are of the same judgement, follow me.

Only eighteen or nineteen men did then follow him, but of the fifty women in the society 'seven or eight and forty', an interesting disparity.[36] The English Moravians soon set about organizing their own Church; and Hutton, the Delamotte brothers, Gambold, Ingham later, Westley Hall for a time, and several more of those closely tied earlier to the Wesleys, joined it. At one point early in 1741 Wesley was even afraid his brother Charles might go with them. John should not 'think so hardly' of the Moravians, Charles told him. Was there not in John's breast 'envy, self-love, emulation, jealousy?' Was he not afraid lest they should eclipse his own 'glory'? 'O my brother', John replied, 'my soul is grieved for you; the poison is in you; fair words have stolen away your heart.'[37] But not, as it proved, for long.

Wesley could hardly erase, and indeed had no wish to forget, what he had written in tribute to the Moravians in Georgia, or at first in Herrnhut; but *corruptio optimi pessima*: though good men, they had joined Satan's legions. Subsequent attempts to reunite his movement with theirs never stood much chance. Doctrine apart, neither Zinzendorf nor Wesley was likely to have brooked a rival commander. Even so, when Wesley met Peter Böhler again in April 1741, he wrote, 'I marvel how I refrain from joining these men. I scarce ever see any of them but my heart burns within me.'

A second schism already threatened. To Whitefield Wesley was still 'Honoured Sir', his deeply respected master and brother; but the pupil's teachings, on two or three essential points, were seriously at variance with those of his teacher. One of these was of an importance as fundamental as its ancestry was ancient, the eternally vexed question of predestined 'election'.

Already, a year before the break-up at Fetter Lane, Whitefield had written to tell of his shock to hear that Wesley's sermon on Free Grace was to be published for general consumption. His heart was as 'melted wax' at the thought of it. And could it be true that Wesley had expelled brother Stock because he believed in predestination? Several times Whitefield entreated Wesley, preserving that 'cordial union and sweetness of soul' which he prayed might continue between them, to hold his peace on this subject. 'Hearken to a child who is willing to wash your feet', he wrote from Savannah, on his second American tour. How glad the Lord's enemies would be to see the two of them divided! The squire-preacher Howel Harris, chief ally of the Methodists in Wales, protested in similar terms. He was sure Wesley himself *was* one of God's elect, and 'the more I write, the more I love you' – but, if Wesley in 'a stiff, uncharitable spirit' persisted in expelling society members for professing the doctrines of election and reprobation (that some were fore-ordained for heaven, some for hell), he would soon have to exclude 'brother Whitefield, brother Seward, and myself'.[38]

It was not in Wesley's nature to delay long in grasping a nettle

such as this. The thing must be settled, the argument thrashed
out. His sermon on Free Grace, delivered earlier in Bristol,
where the predestinarians were gaining ground, *would* be published. Although it carried a prefatory request that its opponents
should observe Christian meekness and charity in any of their
criticisms, it also quoted Jesus's appeal, 'Father, forgive them, for
they know not what they do.'

The dogma of predestination, his sermon argued, made all
preaching vain. It removed all motive for holiness. It destroyed
'the chief comfort of religion, the happiness of Christianity'. It
effaced zeal for good works. It blasphemed God by making him a
hypocrite who pretended a love he did not have, 'a gross deceiver
of the people'. It made him invite the weary and heavy-laden to
come unto him, while knowing they *could not* come:

> Here I fix my foot . . . You represent God as worse than the Devil.
> But, you say, you will prove it by Scripture. Hold! What will you
> prove by Scripture? That God is worse than the Devil? It cannot
> be . . .

If predestination were to be accepted, what then? Wesley's
answer, in the passage that follows, may give some inkling of the
power of his preaching at its passionate best:

> O how would the enemy of God and man rejoice to hear those
> things were so! How would he cry aloud and spare not! How
> would he lift up his voice and say, To your tents, O Israel! Flee
> from the face of this God, or ye shall utterly perish! But whither
> will ye flee? Into heaven? He is there. Down to hell? He is there
> also. Ye cannot flee from an omnipresent, almighty tyrant. And
> whether ye flee or stay, I call heaven, his throne, and earth, his
> footstool, to witness against you, ye shall perish, ye shall die
> eternally. Sing, O hell; and rejoice, ye that are under the earth!
> For God, even the mighty God, hath spoken, and devoted to
> death thousands of souls, from the rising of the sun unto the
> going down thereof! Here, O death, is thy sting! They shall not,
> cannot escape; for the mouth of the Lord hath spoken it. Here, O
> grave, is thy victory! Nations yet unborn, or ever they have done
> good or evil, are doomed never to see the light of life, but thou
> shalt gnaw upon them for ever and ever! Let all those morning
> stars sing together, who fell with Lucifer, son of the morning!
> Let all the sons of hell shout for joy! For the decree is passed, and
> who shall disannul it?[39]

Such a breach on such a subject stood little chance of being fully healed. Whitefield, not ceasing to pray that one day Mr Wesley might see the light, continued his appeals to his Dear and Honoured Sir: 'Do not oblige me to preach against you; I had rather die', a brave and brotherly avowal he soon revoked. 'Dear, dear Sir, give yourself to reading. Study the covenant of grace. Down with your carnal reasoning. Be a little child.' Wesley after all was only 'a babe in Christ, if so much. Be humble; talk little; think and pray much.'[40] 'You do not believe original sin aright . . . Dear Sir, consider how you dishonour God by denying . . . the amiable doctrine of election.'

There was also a cognate subject of vital dispute. According to Whitefield, grace once received, conversion once accomplished, was for ever. Wesley saw in this belief an acute danger of Anti-nomianism – that the elect, deeming themselves irrevocably and immutably immune from God's wrath, might presume to set themselves with impunity outside the moral law, as had most notoriously happened with some groups of Anabaptists. These were grounds for disputation and of scandal as ancient as the primitive Church itself. Wesley's was essentially the central argument of the Dutchman Arminius (Hermanns) against Calvinism a century and a half before, of the 'Arminian' party in the Church of England against the seventeenth-century Presbyterians, and of the Jesuits against the Jansenists in France; predestinarianism opened a logical door to Antinomianism and moral anarchy. Wesley, unlike Whitefield, taught that conversion and justification gave only *present* pardon for sins: 'If a justified person does not do good, as he has opportunity, he will lose the grace he has received, and . . . will perish eternally.'[41] There was no everlasting guarantee, but there *was* the opportunity to labour towards 'sanctification' and the possibility of attaining 'Christian perfection', a condition of earthly sinlessness.

For the remainder of Whitefield's life (he died in 1770) he and Wesley would on many occasions make sincere gestures of mutual respect and affection, even sometimes by the one officiating or preaching at the other's services, or by both taking part in the same love-feast. Wesley avowed a wish that they might 'trample on bigotry'; and when Whitefield called on him in 1755, he rejoiced that 'disputings were no more; we love one another'.[42] Seven years later the Calvinist Countess of Huntingdon, Whitefield's patron, actually presided over a Methodist Conference, and seven years later again Wesley preached in her theological college at Trevecca in South Wales. All this, however, amounted to little more than papering over a deep crack. Moreover the personal regard of the two principals in the quarrel was often far from extending to their followers, or from either one of them to the lieutenants of the other.

CHAPTER 7

'Surely God is Over All'

SOME MONTHS BEFORE walking out of Fetter Lane, Wesley had already established an alternative London headquarters. This was at an old cannon foundry near Moorfields which had lain derelict since an explosion had wrecked it twenty-four years earlier. He first preached there eight months before the Fetter Lane show-down and, like the good businessman he was, set about buying the lease of the property, borrowing the £115 from sympathizers, and at the same time organizing a subscription list towards repayments and repairs. The Moorfields 'Foundery' eventually cost some £800. It comprised a chapel seating 1500 (the sexes always segregated in it); adjoining accommodation for Wesley, his guests or dependants; a book-room for the sale of Wesley's works; and a large room to house meetings of the bands and classes, the regular five o'clock service, the twice-weekly prayer meetings, and desks for a little school.

It was at the Foundry that Wesley, arriving to preach on 1 February 1741, found being given away to his society members, as they arrived, printed copies of a letter Whitefield had sent him earlier from America, controverting free grace and universal redemption. Wesley tells how he reacted:

> Having procured one of them, I related (after preaching) the naked fact to the congregation, and told them, 'I will do just what I believe Mr Whitefield would were he here himself.' [This was to say the least somewhat doubtful.] Upon which I tore it in pieces before them all. Everyone who had received it did the same.[1]

He was just then in the middle of bitter dissensions in Bristol and Kingswood. Only recently he had been giving glory to God

for the moral reformation Methodism had brought to Kingswood's rough mining community – though one is brought
sharply to question the nature of some of that reformation when,
for instance, reading the story of one James Rogers, a fiddle-
playing miner who thought it proper to celebrate his rescue from
sin by going home and smashing up his fiddle.[2] Some edifying
emotions are no doubt stirred by the famous passage in Whitefield
telling of the tears tracing their clean watercourses down miners'
grimy cheeks as these poor heathen received the preacher's
message; but the story of the battered violin and the many others
akin to it in the evangelists' accounts of their work constantly
reveal the puritanical severity of their piety.

'Dost thou think, because thou art virtuous, there shall be no
more cakes and ale?' They did, even literally so: 'I do not frequent
taverns,' Charles explained primly to Henry Seward, who had
asked him to step inside the Crown to continue their conversation. No more cakes and ale, no more 'dancing and revelling'
– Charles lumped such abominations in with other lusts of the
flesh and boldly set up his pitch at village fairs to persuade the
merrymakers that they were 'dead souls';[3] no more playhouses or
assembly rooms or card parties, alike schools of vice; no more
'gay apparel'; no more trifling conversation or reading – John
(for the time being at least) had now turned his back on secular
literature. No more 'carnal' music either – only the psalms and
hymns he was so uplifted to hear the miners singing in the
Kingswood fields; and (needless perhaps to add) none of those
forbidden pleasures decorously referred to as 'company-keeping'.

The quarrels at Bristol and Kingswood chiefly concerned
matters more theological than these. John Cennick, Wesley's
appointed lay preacher at Kingswood and self-appointed schoolmaster there, had sided with Whitefield and the Calvinists, and
during the winter of 1740–1 Wesley was made to feel the strength
of these opponents. His congregations at society meetings in
December several times numbered no more than 'two or three
men and as many women'; the rest had gone to hear Cennick.
'The poison of Calvin,' Charles reported, 'had drunk up their
spirit of love . . . Alas, we have set the wolf to keep the sheep.'
There followed in March 1741 another painful schism, fifty-two
of the Kingswood flock following Cennick (who was later to
desert in turn the Calvinists for the Moravians) and 'upwards of

ninety' Wesley.⁴ The 'universal redemption' party in the Bristol
society gave powerful if intolerant voice to their feelings when in
June Howel Harris, having been fraternally invited by Charles
Wesley to speak 'in God's name', found himself unable to resist
entering upon Calvinist doctrines. Stung by this 'ungenerousness',
Charles sprang up to protect the 'soul's blood' of those present,
appealing to them to know if Harris should be permitted to
continue.

> A woman first cried out . . . 'The wounds of Jesus answer "No".'
> Then many others repeated 'No, no, no'; and a whole cloud of
> witnesses arose, declaring 'Christ died for all.'

Charles Wesley clinched his victory by giving out a hymn. 'O
what a burst of joy was there in the midst of us!' 'You thrust me
out?' Harris enquired. No, he might stay 'as a child of God', but
not to corrupt the flock with his Calvinism. Then they sang
another hymn to silence Harris's heresy of damnation:

> Praise God, from whom pure blessings flow,
> Whose bowels yearn on *all* below . . .⁵

A similar clash was at least temporarily avoided when John
Wesley was campaigning in South Wales in the following
October. When a dispute threatened, Howel Harris 'hasted to
stand in the gap once more; and with tears brought them all to
follow after the things that lead to peace . . . so that we parted
with much love'. In August 1742 Wesley sent Harris an emotionally fraternal letter, pleading for a doctrinal truce so that they
might 'rise up together against the evil-doers'; but unity proved
impossible to achieve, and the Welsh Methodists were to go their
separate Calvinist way.*

Round the Celtic fringes, Cornwall was to provide more
fruitful preaching ground for Wesley than Wales. His own first
descent upon Cornwall did not come until 1743, but his followers
were busy there some time earlier preparing the soil. Throughout
1741 and the early months of 1742 Wesley was kept busy culti-
vating and recultivating his original fields of endeavour between
London and Bristol, moving for the first time also beyond
Oxford to the Midlands. Neither did he neglect to weed. There

---

* They were eventually to become, in this century, the Presbyterian
Church of Wales.

were always backsliders, 'disorderly walkers', the records of whose offences he would systematically investigate. If the evidence, of which he was always ultimately sole judge, looked convincing such members would be denied society membership. His purging of the London society brought its strength in 1741 down to about a thousand; a later purge in 1744 reduced the total to 'under nineteen hundred'. Such cleansing operations were always to remain an essential feature of the Methodist polity. At Bristol on 9 December 1741, Wesley expelled ('for their edification and not destruction') thirty members, and again on 27 December, 'after diligent inquiry made', another batch 'whose behaviour or spirit was not agreeable to the gospel of Christ: openly declaring the objections I had to each, that others might fear and cry to God for them'.

Just what sort of objections these were may reasonably be deduced from an analysis Wesley himself made during a later purge on one of his northern tours – though the most numerous category of condemnation, 'lightness and carelessness' does leave a great deal to the individual imagination. Of sixty-four expelled on that occasion, twenty-nine were accused under this elastic charge; seventeen more were struck off for drunkenness; four for 'railing and evil-speaking'; three for brawling; three for constant lying; two for swearing; two for habitual Sabbath-breaking; two for retailing spirituous liquors; and one each for idleness and wife-beating. The Methodist societies should embrace Christ's poor, but never Christ's riff-raff, and only those who were seen to walk orderly were privileged to carry the Methodist 'ticket'. This was the membership card, renewable quarterly, superscribed with one of a variety of godly emblems or scriptural texts, and bearing authorization either of Wesley himself or of one of his chief lieutenants.

Wesley was always the unquestioned commander-in-chief, but so fast-growing a company needed subordinate officers, and the system which had originated in Bristol was soon found to be wonderfully suitable. It was in the early days of the Bristol societies that he had first delegated two or three capable 'stewards' to supervise the collection and accounting of members' con-tributions. The expanding numbers of these officers eventually provided a nation-wide arrangement efficiently to manage, under God and John Wesley, the movement's business affairs. To collect the penny-a-week contributions towards repaying Wesley and his creditors for the new Bristol buildings, the members there had been divided into 'classes' each a dozen strong, with its class-leader responsible ultimately to Wesley, who was quick to perceive the 'unspeakable usefulness' of this arrangement. Henceforward as a unit of Methodist organization the 'band' would be less important than the 'class'. The appointed class-leader met the remaining members of his little group weekly, at first by house-to-house individual visits, but soon all together at an agreed convenient place. There he would begin and end meetings with singing and prayer, and spend some part of every session talking with each member alone.

For Wesley, no system would ever be wholly perfect unless he could contrive to discover for it some precedent in the practices of the ancient Church. Thus 'upon reflection', he wrote,

> I could not but observe, this is the very thing which was from the beginning of Christianity . . . The first preachers met these *catechumens*, as they were called, apart from the great congregation, that they might instruct, rebuke, exhort, and pray with them, according to their several necessities.[6]

To those who objected that not all class-leaders would be fitted for their work he replied that if one were found 'remarkably wanting in gifts or grace' he would be noticed and removed. The whole system remained under the ultimate control of its bene-volent dictator and creator. To assure himself, as well as his growing flock, that it was running smoothly, and to ensure 'the separation of the precious from the vile', he *himself* undertook 'at least once in every three months to talk to every member'[7] – though of course a time would come when that would be im-possible even for him. Possession of the Methodist ticket, said Wesley, was to be understood as *his* recommendation that the bearer 'feared God and worked righteousness'.

He expected the Methodist societies to perform some part of that righteousness in the relief of poverty and sickness among their own members. As early as the winter of 1740–1 the Moor-fields society room was being used to occupy twelve of its poorest women members, together with an instructor, in carding and spinning cotton. 'And the design answered', Wesley wrote; 'they were employed and maintained with very little more than the produce of their own labour.' Not only was physical want thereby avoided, but also idleness, for which Satan would be ever quick to find mischief. In the following spring Wesley aimed to enlarge these welfare activities. He therefore asked his London members to donate any surplus clothing, plus a penny a week 'or what they could afford', to relieve their fellows' poverty and illness. Twelve members were given the combined duty of visiting the sick every other day, and of supervising the labour of those unemployed women who asked for it, in knitting. 'To these', wrote Wesley, 'we will first give the common price for what work they do; and then add, according as they need.'[8] Trying to adapt organization to meet a swelling demand, in 1743 he mapped out London into twenty-three districts, two visitors being allocated to each. The next year he made repeated appeals to the classes for extra contributions towards relieving the deserving poor. Both in London and the main provincial centres of Methodism this charitable endeavour was energetically pursued, but it proved uphill going. By 1750, when Wesley reviewed 'all in the [London] society who were in want', he found himself soon discouraged, 'their numbers so increasing upon me, particularly about Moorfields, that I saw no possibility of relieving them all, unless the Lord should, as it were, make windows in heaven'.[9]

Of the various innovations assisting the spread of Methodism during the 1740s, lay preaching must be reckoned the most significant. Outside the Roman and Anglican churches, it was of course nothing new, as Wesley was quick to point out after he had finally managed to convince himself of its necessity. Was Jesus a priest? Were any of the early apostles? Was Calvin ordained? Indeed was ordination held to be a prerequisite for preaching among any of the continental Protestants? Even in some Anglican churches, and in cathedrals too, did not a lay clerk conduct the entire service? 'Nay, is it not done in the universities themselves? Who ordained that singing man at Christ Church, who is likewise entirely unqualified for the work, murdering every lesson he reads, not endeavouring to read it as the word of God, but rather as an old song?'[10] This was Wesley writing in 1745, but he had not come easily to such sentiments.

What had made the problem urgent was the hostility towards Methodism of a big majority of bishops and parish priests. Even some among the few clergy who originally had joined Wesley had now defected, either to the Moravians or to the Calvinists. Two brothers, even two so formidably tireless, could hardly methodize alone the whole of the kingdom. Yet, as at first with field-preaching, lay-preaching took some time to be accommodated into Wesley's tenacious traditionalism. When the fluent exhortations of his convert Thomas Maxfield 'riveted' Lady Huntingdon and, more importantly, a great number of humbler folk, an untypical double negative had at first to be found to avoid expressing disapproval: 'I am not clear that brother Maxfield should not expound at Greyhound Lane' (Whitechapel). Yet he could 'not do without him'.[11] Old Mrs Wesley – who now that the Westley Halls had returned to Salisbury, was lodged in her son's quarters adjoining the Moorfields Foundry – warned him to think hard before he issued any ban: 'that young man', she was sure, 'is as surely called of God to preach as you are'. In any case, the thing was happening of its own momentum. Although Wesley himself remained at heart a High Churchman (and indeed was often ridiculously enough accused of having papist sympathies), there was much in his message and methods to appeal to the spirit of old Dissent, which retained a long tradition of laymen publicly expounding and testifying.

There was a numerous company of such men waiting to be used, gospel-preachers no rubric was likely to silence; some unlettered, some largely self-taught; latterday Bunyans, whose *Pilgrim's Progress* was indeed for many a sort of educational primer. One of the most remarkable of them was a stonemason from Birstall in Yorkshire, John Nelson, who was recruited to Methodism on hearing Wesley at Moorfields and would one day publish his own *Journal*.* Within two years of accepting Maxfield, Wesley had approved the instatement of thirty-five such preachers.

After recommending Maxfield, Mrs Wesley is heard of no more until in the summer of 1742 the *Journal* reports her as being

* Something of its flavour may be sampled from his accounts of dreams. He saw Satan in the shape of a red bull making 'directly at me, as if he would run his horns into my heart. Then I cried out, "Lord, help me!" and immediately caught him by the horns, and twisted him on his back, setting my right foot upon his neck, in the presence of a thousand people.' Or again, 'I thought I saw Satan coming to meet me in the shape of a tall, black man, and the hair of his head like snakes ... But I ... ripped open my clothes, and showed him my naked breast, saying, "Here is the blood of Christ." Then I thought he fled from me as fast as a hare could run.'

'on the borders of eternity'. 'Three or four' of her daughters were present with John round her deathbed, and sang with him 'a requiem for her passing soul'. Her death on 30 July was improbably laid at the door of 'gout', that eighteenth-century jack-of-all-diseases. All five surviving daughters attended the funeral ceremony conducted by their brother in Tindal's Burying Ground (Bunhill Fields), a few steps only from the Foundry. Charles was not present, but composed for her headstone some lines which afford better testimony to the consistency of early Methodist theology than to the author's judgement of the fitness of things. Even devotees of his prolific verse (he averaged at this time a hymn a day) have boggled at the poem's opening:

> True daughter of affliction, she
> Inured to pain and misery
> Mourned a long night of griefs and fears,
> A legal night of seventy years.
> The Father then revealed his Son . . .

Then'? After seventy years of miserable error, a 'night' unlit by God's law? It makes a chill verdict on Susanna Wesley's three-score years and ten, even if conversion 'in the broken bread made known' did come in the nick of time, like the rescuing hero in the last act of a melodrama, to give a happy ending and allow Susanna to be 'meet for the fellowship above'. But what a narrow shave, and how vivid an insight into the Methodist mind's uncompromising insistence on the necessity of 'justification'!

Probably it is some similar dogmatic considerations which explain a letter John sent his brother (part in longhand, part shorthand, part Latin) at the time of their mother's death: 'My heart does not, and I am absolutely assured God does not, condemn me for any want of duty towards her in any kind, except only that I have not reproved her so plainly and fully as I should have done.'[12] Reproved, one must suppose, for incorrectness of belief. It must be remembered also that intermittently after the death of her husband, Mrs Wesley had lived under the roof, and perhaps in some degree the persuasions, of her eldest son, who had latterly been driven to the exasperated opinion that Methodists deserved to be housed in Bedlam.

In May 1742 Wesley for the first time took his mission north, staying on the way at Donnington Park, the estate of the Earl of Huntingdon, whose pious Countess had more than once asked him to come – for one thing to give spiritual consolation to a woman friend, now dying, who had read the *Journal* and admired Wesley from a distance; more generally to spread the gospel among the heathen, especially the heathen colliers. Riding northwards, Wesley did not let slip an opportunity of demonstrating to a fellow horseman, casually met on the road, the mistakenness of his beliefs – though on his travels a year earlier (he explains) he had briefly experimented, Quaker-wise, with 'speaking to none concerning the things of God' unless the spirit imperiously moved him. But then, he asked himself in one of his rare sallies in the direction of humour, what was the consequence? – 'Why (1) that I spoke to none at all for four-score miles together . . . (2) that I had no cross to bear . . . and commonly in an hour or two fell fast asleep (3) that I had much respect shown me . . . as a civil good-natured gentleman.'

This was not at all the usual Wesley practice. 'Observing three or four sailors standing together', he says as though the thing were a simple matter of course, 'I began explaining to them the nature of religion.' And Charles too repeatedly records how he chips in on his journeys to reprove such a one for swearing – and is, he assures us, thanked 'most heartily' for his kindness, or else the profane offenders depart 'with their eyes full of tears'; or how in the London-bound coach he preaches 'faith in Christ' to a lady who takes umbrage at his attempt to convince her that she deserves 'nothing but hell', and refuses to be mollified by his admission that *so does he*.[13] Now, on 20 May 1742, John Wesley, bound for Newcastle, fell in with 'a serious man' who positively invited argument:

> I told him over and over, 'We had better keep to practical things, lest we should be angry at one another.' And so we did for two miles, till he caught me unawares and dragged me into the dispute before I knew where I was . . . He told me I was rotten at heart, and supposed I was one of John Wesley's followers . . . I told him, 'No, I am John Wesley himself.' Upon which . . . he would gladly have run away outright. But being the better mounted of the two, I kept close to his side, and endeavoured to show him his heart, till we came into the street of Northampton.[14]

From Donnington Park Wesley moved on to Birstall in the

West Riding of Yorkshire, in which neighbourhood John Nelson the stonemason and Benjamin Ingham, Wesley's erstwhile associate in Georgia, had for some time been spreading their respective versions of the Methodist and the Moravian message. (Ingham, who established forty of his own societies in Yorkshire, would soon be marrying into the nobility – the Countess of Huntingdon's sister-in-law.) In Birstall Wesley lodged in Nelson's cottage, preached on Birstall Hill and nearby Dewsbury Moor, and continued towards Newcastle, where on arriving he saw that there would be work indeed to do; 'so much drunkenness, cursing, and swearing (even from the mouths of little children) do I never remember to have seen and heard before in so small a compass of time'.[15] However, the large crowds that came to hear him – or perhaps just to watch him, for he was sure that there were more present than even his strong tones might reach – were not hostile. He set up his stand on Sunday 'in the most contemptible part of the town, began singing the Hundredth Psalm, and preached, at first to three or four people, eventually to twelve or fifteen hundred'. Then,

> observing the people to stand gaping and staring at me with the most profound astonishment, I told them, 'If you desire to know who I am, my name is John Wesley. At five in the evening, with God's help, I design to preach here again.'[16]

When he had done so, he tells, 'the poor people were ready to tread me under foot, out of pure love and kindness'. In other towns at other times he was to be trodden underfoot from less friendly motives.

By the summer of the following year he had made three more visits to Newcastle, with its surrounding towns and villages; between times Charles was busy there too; and in December 1742 the first stone was laid of the building intended by Wesley partly as a home for orphans, partly to house the newly founded local Methodist society. He said later that his Newcastle Orphan House was founded on faith in God's readiness to provide, plus the twenty-six shillings which constituted his own existing capital assets. But as in Bristol earlier, he was not slow to find benefactors of substance, including a Quaker well-wisher who donated £100, one-seventh of the total cost. The Orphan House was to become for the North-east what the Foundry was for

London or the Bristol New Room for the West country, a Methodist regional headquarters.

It was the 'heathen' colliery districts round Newcastle which offered Wesley his sternest and therefore most welcome challenge. Mining villages like Pelton, Chowden (near Gateshead), and Plessey (inland from Blyth) were his Kingswoods of the North-east. Of Chowden he wrote:

> Twenty or thirty wild children ran round us, as soon as we came, staring as in amaze. They could not properly be said to be either clothed or naked . . . My heart was exceedingly enlarged towards them; and they looked as though they would have swallowed me up.[17]

Plessey he found

> inhabited by colliers only, and such as had been always in the first rank for savage ignorance and wickedness of every kind. Their grand assembly used to be on the Lord's Day; on which men, women and children met together, to dance, fight, curse, swear, and play at chuck-ball, span-farthing, or whatever came next to hand. I felt great compassion for these poor creatures . . . And as most of these had never in their lives pretended to any religion of any kind, they were the more ready to cry to God . . .[18]

His hostility by this time to all forms of games (playing on Sundays merely made bad worse) sounds today – and indeed surely was – severely unimaginative and puritanical; but how altogether more wholesome and admirable a John Wesley it is whom we follow on these tirelessly benevolent endeavours (and they were of course only just beginning), compared with the self-absorbed, rather priggish young dogmatist of five, ten, fifteen years earlier. He is still a zealot for salvation, but now it is the salvation of others; he has ceased to be obsessed by his own; his heart is spontaneously 'enlarged' towards these wretchedest of his wretched fellow sinners.

And yet, and yet – what is one to make of the want of empathy, the insensitivity, of the man who, while intending every brotherly friendliness, could write at this time to his sister Patty, Mrs Westley Hall (still having to bear her unstable husband's*

---

* Hall was in a Moravian phase, openly hostile to Wesley, who however was giving quite as good as he got. 'Dear Brother,' he wrote, 'You are angry . . . compose yourself . . . You are a weak, injudicious, fickle, irresolute

unkindnesses and the steady succession of his babies so soon to
lie under the ground) in words like these:

> Dear Sister – I believe the death of your children is a great instance
> of the goodness of God towards you. You have often mentioned
> to me how much of your time they took up! Now that time is
> restored to you, and you have nothing to do but to serve our
> Lord . . .[19]

We may only conjecture Patty's reaction to reassurance of such
monumental crassness. We do know, however, what she thought
of her brother Charles's sentimentally morbid hymn on the
same subject,

> Ah lovely appearance of death!
> What sight upon earth is so fair?

Understandably she detested it.

In 1743 Emily Wesley, deeply as ever submerged in poverty
and bitter against life's injustices, wrote to her brother John
flatly accusing him of unkindness to her, which she said 'I impute
. . . to one principle you hold – that natural affection is a great
weakness, if not a sin'. He replied, ridiculing the charges, reminding her that he was not as well off as people said, was
indeed almost continually in 'straits', and had in any case already
housed her rent-free for three months. He then concluded with a
severity more magisterial than fraternal:

> I have now done with myself, and have only a few words con-
> cerning you. You are of all creatures the most unthankful to
> God and man. I stand amazed at you . . . Surely, whenever your
> eyes are opened, whenever you see your own tempers, with the
> advantages you have enjoyed, you will make no scruple to
> proclaim yourself (whores and murderers not excepted) the very
> chief of sinners.[20]

However, if this may be thought to carry Wesley's desideratum
of plain speech a little far, we should remember that Emily, whom
life had disappointed, could be no less sharp; that her brother

man . . . a fit tool for those who apply to your weak side, vanity . . . After
God had put you under my care, without preconsulting me you courted
my poor sister Kezzy, to which I cannot but ascribe her death . . . You may
remember you fathered all upon God! You then jilted one of my sisters and
married the other . . . Your life has been one blunder ever since . . . indeed,
my brother, you need a tutor now more than when you first came to Oxford.'

continued to house and maintain her, in quarters adjoining the West Street chapel he acquired in 1743; and that she was to live there and worship at the adjacent chapel for another thirty years.

Wesley was not under the illusion of thinking that, because he had managed to convert a number of poor sinners, they would necessarily stay converted. In March he methodically totted up the number (76) who had deserted or drifted away from the Newcastle society since December, carefully setting down the reason proffered in each case. He expelled sixty-four more for backsliding. At Tanfield, another village near Newcastle, he found 'terrible instances' to remind him

> that the devil himself desires nothing more than this, that the people of any place should be half-awakened and then left to themselves to fall asleep again. Therefore I determine, by the grace of God, not to strike one stroke in any place where I cannot follow the blow.[21]

One such place was his own home town, in whose neighbourhood he found an already established religious society, which he judged to be in sad confusion from the doctrines of Ingham and the 'still brethren'. Wesley was of course by now something of a celebrity, and Epworth mustered a big crowd during a week in June 1742 when he preached every evening from the vantage-point of his father's tombstone, the church's pulpit having been denied to him. He spoke similarly the next year on visits to 'follow the blow' in January and July, and three or four times between 1742 and 1745 he sat among the congregation while the Epworth priest-in-charge, John Romley, delivered what Wesley called 'false', 'bitter', 'railing' sermons. The first, in 1742, was pointedly against 'enthusiasm'. Romley in 1743 refused Communion to Wesley much as Wesley had once refused it to Sophy Williamson, because he was 'unfit'. He was that same John Romley who in his youth, when he taught in the local school, had set his cap at Wesley's sister Hetty, until her father removed her from his attentions by dispatching her to Grantham. He had nevertheless for a time been old Mr Wesley's curate and, like John Whitelamb, copyist for *Job*. John Whitelamb himself, still Rector at Wroot, was among those who listened to his old Oxford tutor preaching in the churchyard; Wesley's presence, he wrote, always inspired him with awe. It seems however that Wesley had

his doubts about brother-in-law Whitelamb, all the graver as
Whitelamb – who remained at Wroot for the rest of his life –
developed his own doubts about the sort of Christianity Wesley
stood for, and even professed an inclination towards 'Mother
Church', meaning presumably Rome. When he died in 1769,
Wesley's verdict on him was harsh; Whitelamb, like Hall, was
one of his failures; 'O why did he not die forty years ago?' wrote
Wesley, 'while he knew in whom he believed?'[22]

Having set in train the evangelization of the North, the Wesley
brothers in 1743 turned towards Cornwall, where an 'imbruted'
heathenism was held to be no less rife. Here it was Charles who
blazed the Methodist trail, and a rough time he had of it on the
whole. At first he ventured to think that the Devil's children were
in retreat; more and more were 'convinced that we speak as the
oracles of God'. Outside St Ives 'near a thousand' tin miners
assembled to hear him, many he claimed in tears, and at St Just
'about two thousand, mostly tinners'. But the enemy, stirred up
in particular by the local clergy, were soon out in strength. At
St Ives, although his 'soul was calm and fearless', they first
drowned his words with shouting and drumming, and then
proceeded to a fair-sized riot. At Wednock it was no better: 'the
minister's mob fell upon us . . .* I bade them strike me and spare
the people', wrote Charles; 'many lifted up their hands and
weapons, but were not permitted to touch me . . . My time was
not yet come'. Both the biblical echo of this sentence and the
implication of his 'not permitted' are pure Wesley: each brother
records time and again how sticks and stones fly furiously
but – and how if not by some higher influence? – are diverted
from their course, deprived of their target.

The first of John Wesley's many Cornish expeditions followed
soon after his brother's. He took John Nelson with him and
another lay preacher, and if they did not exactly find the fields
white unto harvest, as Charles had declared them, at least John
seems to have encountered less violent hostility than Charles.
It was more often a case of 'much goodwill . . . but no life', or
even 'huge approbation but absolute unconcern'. When the
rabble threatened at St Ives, the mayor helpfully posted a town

* The church accounts at Illogan in Cornwall seem to show that such
activity might be reckoned a chargeable expense: 'On driving the Methodists,
nine shillings.'

alderman 'so that no man opened his mouth' while Wesley expounded. The local society already numbered over a hundred, but Wesley was a better realist than his brother; 'Which of these', he wondered, 'will endure to the end?'

Still, at Gwennap Pit near Redruth, in the grassy hollow among the hills which was to become in time his most famous outdoor auditorium, it was estimated, he wrote, there were 10,000 present to listen. Even if we must, as always, be cautious in accepting his figures, it must certainly have been a fine turn-out. In later years he rarely gives an estimate below 20,000 for the audience at his many preachings in Gwennap Pit. At St Just, Morvah, Zennor and Land's End he had quiet receptions, and was delighted to find a *providentially* ready-made congregation on St Mary's in the Scillies, among the soldiers, sailors and labourers assembled there to fortify the island against the threat of French invasion. 'After the sermon I gave them some little books and hymns, which they were so eager to receive that they were ready to tear both them and me to pieces.'

It was much more literally and alarmingly that he was nearly torn in pieces when in the following month he proceeded to Staffordshire. Here in the Wednesbury-Darlaston-Walsall district the Methodist society had grown to number some three hundred, and this was Wesley's third visit. There had been trouble earlier, arising partly from the anti-clerical ranting of some visiting preachers, who had provoked the vicar of Wednesbury, not unfriendly at first, to condemn Methodism from the pulpit in the bitterest terms. Charles Wesley had faced stone-throwing and manhandling when he was there in May, being knocked over twice, once before and once after delivering the blessing – proceedings which lend some oddity to his comment: 'they reviled us, but had no commission to touch an hair of our heads'. After he left, attacks on Methodists' houses, property and persons continued, and for a time a protection racket seems to have flourished. The disturbances offer some parallels with the 'throne and altar' riots in the neighbouring Birmingham district half a century later. In the forties it was the Methodists who suffered; in the nineties it was the Dissenters, accused as they then were of anti-patriotism and republicanism. On both occasions the rabble had some encouragement, usually passive but sometimes quite open, from magistrates and clergy.

In the eighteenth century rioting was common enough. Hooliganism and gang rivalry are not twentieth-century novelties; and, as Wesley found, it was no joke to be fought over by the rival scrums of Darlaston and Walsall. He had been preaching one afternoon at Wednesbury when a mob some hundreds strong laid siege to the house where he was. When they dispersed Wesley missed his opportunity to escape. They returned, and kept yelling, 'The minister! Bring out the minister!' After parleying with their ringleaders, he agreed to accompany them to the nearest magistrate's. At the end of the dark, wet, two-mile trudge, however, the magistrate refused to be seen or become involved. The company therefore proceeded with their as yet unmolested captive to the house of a second magistrate, of Walsall, but he like the other sent word out that he was in bed and not to be disturbed. The Darlaston mob at this began to break up, about fifty of them still convoying Wesley. Unluckily this reduced band, with among it some Methodist supporters and a woman who had appointed herself as the minister's guardian-in-chief, then met some bigger battalions from Walsall and had the worst of a mêlée, though Wesley's protectress 'knocked down three of four men, one after another' before being battered and overpowered.

The men of Walsall, having captured Wesley, marched him from one end of the main street to the other, knocked him about, threatened to beat his brains out, and eventually fell to quarrelling among themselves, while Wesley argued, remonstrated, prayed aloud, and finally gained some sympathy and support from 'an honest butcher' and others. These rescuers, while some of the hostile mob held the bridge, helped him to escape by going 'on one side over the mill-dam, and thence through the meadows, till, a little before ten, God brought me safe to Wednesbury, having lost only one flap of my waistcoat and a little skin from one of my hands'.[23]

Charles's second-hand and less phlegmatic account of these hostilities (he hurried to join forces in Wednesbury) adds a bloody nose and gashed mouth. Angels had borne his brother up, and the spirit of glory had rested on him as he reasoned composedly with the rabble. 'He did not wonder', Charles writes, '(as he himself told me) that the martyrs should feel no pain in the flames, for none of their blows hurt him.' The mayor of

Walsall had refused him the protection of his house for fear the rioters would pull it down, and he had finally been carried across the river on the shoulders of one who had earlier been leader of the mob and the greatest profligate imaginable but had now turned Methodist himself, 'upon trial'. Wesley, so Charles has this spectacular convert proclaiming, was 'a mon of God; God was on his side, when so mony of us could not kill one mon'.[24]

It had, of course, been divine interposition: 'I never saw such a chain of providences before', wrote Wesley; 'so many convincing proofs that the hand of God is on every person and thing, over-ruling all as it seemeth him good.' Characteristically he appended a careful list of these proofs, eight in number – among them, that 'the very first men whose hearts were turned were the captains of the rabble . . . one of them having been a prize-fighter at the bear-garden'; and that 'a lusty man just behind struck at me several times with a large oaken stick . . . but every time the blow turned aside, I know not how, for I could not move to the right hand or the left'.[25]

Both Wesleys claimed continually that they received this peculiar protection and preservation from God. It might be some quite trivial matter, a head aching, or a horse going lame: precisely those two minor misfortunes, so Wesley found one day in March 1746, God would even cure simultaneously: 'Cannot God heal either man or beast, *by* any means, or *without* any?' he asked himself, and found, after relevant prayer, 'immediately my weariness and headache ceased, and my horse's lameness in the same instant'. In the previous July, during an anti-Methodist riot at Falmouth, 'although the hands of perhaps some hundreds of people were lifted up to strike or throw, yet they were one and all stopped in the mid-way'. Time and again, aware that the sun was shining uncomfortably into the eyes of Wesley as he was about to preach, God would interpose a kindly cloud; or when it was raining as the field-sermon began, ordain a considerate cessation – for was 'anything too small', he reflected, 'for the providence of him by whom our very hairs are numbered?' When a torrential storm brought ruinous loss to some Gloucestershire villages, his bland comment upon the ordering of things outdoes Dr Pangloss: 'How frequent', he writes, 'would accidents of this kind be if chance, not God, ruled the world.' Attacked by an 'old disorder' which seemed to be resisting medication, 'I was

John Wesley in 1766 by N. Hone

The 'Foundery', Moorfields

The City Road Chapel

considering', the *Journal* declares, 'I had not yet asked help of the
Great Physician; and I resolved to delay no longer. In that hour
I felt a change. I slept sound that night and was well the next day.'

Well aware of the sceptical smiles greeting these stories and the
disparagement of his judgement that they occasioned, he was
often quick to add a defiant coda: 'What I aver here is the naked
fact: let every man account for it as he sees good'; or, 'I relate the
naked fact . . . Now he that will account for this by natural
causes' – the revival this time of a man whose speech, senses,
and pulses had all vanished – 'has my free leave. But I choose to
say, this is the power of God.' In expounding once a chapter in
Ezekiel, Wesley was suddenly seized with such a pain in his side
that he could not speak: 'I knew my remedy', he wrote, 'and
immediately kneeled down. In a moment the pain was gone.'
When his horse fell, pinning him underneath it, and some women
ran out from a house near by to take him in, the *Journal*'s next
sentence reads simply, 'I adore the wisdom of God'. On an
autumn night in South Wales when it was too dark to see the
horses' heads, 'the promise of God did not fail; he gave his
angels charge over us, and soon after ten we came safe to Mr
Williams' house'.[26] When the doctor pronounced that one Mr
Meyrick could not last the night, and Wesley found him 'as it
seemed dead already', he and others present

> all kneeled down and called upon God with strong cries and tears.
> [Meyrick] opened his eyes and called for me; and from that hour
> continued to recover his strength till he was restored to perfect
> health. I wait to hear who will disprove this fact or philosophically
> [i.e. scientifically] account for it.[27]

Charles Wesley's *Journal* is not less studded with such instances.
Had providence not ordained that Thomas Maxfield and he
should meet unexpected delays in their travels on a June morning
in 1740, it was they instead of another who would have been
murdered by a highwayman on the Oxford road. During 1743
he once lost his way near Selby in Yorkshire, and 'some hours' of
prayer (plus, admittedly, help from a sailor he met) were needed
to get him back on the right road. When in February 1747 the
Devizes mob, incited by certain of the gentry and the local
curate, and having already battered and played the town fire-
engine upon the house where he and his followers were sheltering,

proposed to break in and throw him into the horsepond, it was only tireless prayer and the protection of 'the invisible hand' that stopped them from being 'torn to pieces'. More sensationally, he gives willing credence later that year to a tale he had been told, that someone who had been among the Methodists' 'fiercest persecutors' had died, and actually *stayed dead* for some hours until he was miraculously revived 'as a monument of divine mercy'.[28]

If the going, in the teeth of ill-wishers and hooligans, often proved rough, so too it was in the face of travel in all weathers, at all seasons, to every nook and cranny of the kingdom where Satan ruled or threatened to regroup his forces. Amid the riotous mêlées which accompanied Wesley's evangelizing, particularly during its first two decades, on many occasions he showed notably calm courage and steadiness – if also, when he deemed it necessary, a belligerence in counter-attack against the authorities who permitted or even encouraged such outrages. He never gave up easily; was remarkably unflappable; and his year-in-year-out progress round the country, with that relentless schedule which he did not like upsetting, often demanded its own courage and fortitude. Wesley was a little man, but wonderfully tough-fibred. He expected trouble and hardship, and took them in his matter-of-fact stride. His record of a few days' journeying during February 1747 may exemplify many others not much different:

Tues. 10 – My brother returned from the north, and I prepared to supply his place there.

Sun. 15. – I was very weak and faint; but on *Monday the 16th* I rose soon after three, lively and strong, and found all my complaints were fled away like a dream.

I was wondering the day before, at the mildness of the weather; such as seldom attends me in my journeys. But my wonder now ceased: the wind was turned full north, and blew so exceedingly hard and keen that when we came to Hatfield neither my companions or I had much use of our hands or feet. After resting an hour, we bore up again, through the wind and snow which drove full in our faces. But this was only a squall. In Baldock Field the storm began in earnest. The large hail drove so vehemently in our faces that we could not see, nor hardly breathe. However, before two o'clock we reached Baldock, where one met and conducted us safe to Potton. About six I preached to a serious congregation.

Tues. 17. – We set out as soon as it was light; but it was really hard work to get forward, for the frost would not well bear or break; and the untracked snow covering all the roads, we had much ado to keep our horses on their feet. Meantime the wind rose higher and higher, till it was ready to overturn both man and beast. However, after a short bait at Buckden, we pushed on, and were met in the middle of an open field with so violent a storm of rain and hail as we had not yet had before. It drove through our coats, great and small, boots and everything, and yet froze as it fell, even upon our eyebrows, so that we had scarce either strength or motion left when we came to our inn at Stilton.

We now gave up our hopes of reaching Grantham, the snow falling faster and faster. However, we took advantage of a fair blast to set out, and made the best of our way to Stamford Heath. But here a new difficulty arose, from the snow lying in large drifts. Sometimes horse and man were wellnigh swallowed up. Yet in less than an hour we were brought safe to Stamford. Being willing to get as far as we could, we made but a short stop here, and about sunset came, cold and weary, to a little town called Brig Casterton.

Wed. 18. – Our servant came up and said: 'Sir, there is no travelling today. Such a quantity of snow has fallen in the night that the roads are quite filled up.' I told him: 'At least we can walk twenty miles a day, with our horses in our hands.' So in the name of God we set out. The north-east wind was piercing as a sword, and had driven the snow into such uneven heaps that the main road was unpassable. However, we kept on, afoot or on horseback, till we came to the White Lion at Grantham.

Some from Grimsby had appointed to meet us here, but not hearing anything of them (for they were at another house, by mistake), after an hour's rest we set out straight for Epworth. On the road we overtook a clergyman and his servant; but the toothache quite shut my mouth. We reached Newark about five. *Thurs. 19.* – The frost was not so sharp, so that we had little difficulty till we came to Haxey Carr; but here the ice . . . would not bear, nor readily break . . . We committed ourselves to God, and went on. We hit all our fords exactly; and, without any fall or considerable hindrance, came to Epworth in two hours, full as well as when we left London.

And here he is again, bound once more for Epworth eleven years later and determined to honour his engagement on time:

Mon. 6 March 1758 – I took horse [from London] about seven

o'clock. The wind being east, I was pleasing myself we should have it on our back; but in a quarter of an hour it shifted to the north-west, and blew the rain full in our face; and both increased, so that when we came to Finchley Common it was hard work to sit our horses. The rain continued all the way to Dunstable, where we exchanged the main road for the fields, which, having been just ploughed, were deep enough . . . On
Thursday the 9th I rode to Bedford, and found the sermon was not to be preached till Friday. Had I known this in time, I should never have thought of preaching it, having engaged to be at Epworth on Saturday.

It was the assize sermon, which he preached to a 'very large and very attentive' congregation; after which the judge invited him to dinner.

Having no time, I was obliged to send my excuse, and set out between one and two. The north-east wind was piercing cold, and, blowing exactly in our face, soon brought a heavy shower of snow, then of sleet, and afterwards of hail. However, we reached Stilton at seven, about thirty miles from Bedford.

Rest was now more sweet because both our horses were lame. However, resolving to reach Epworth at the time appointed, I set out in a post-chaise between four and five in the morning; but the frost made it so bad driving that my companion came with the lame horses into Stamford as soon as me. The next stage I went on horseback; but I was then obliged to leave my mare and take another post-chaise. I came to Bawtry about six. Some from Epworth had come to meet me, but were gone half an hour before I came. I knew no chaise could go the rest of the road, so it remained only to hire horses and a guide. We set out about seven, but I soon found my guide knew no more of the way than myself. However, we got pretty well to Idlestop, about four miles from Bawtry, where we had just light to discern the river at our side and the country covered with water. I heard that one Richard Wright lived thereabouts, who knew the road over the moor perfectly well. Hearing one speak (for we could not see him), I called, 'Who is there?' He answered, 'Richard Wright.' I soon agreed with him, and he quickly mounted his horse and rode boldly forward. The north-east wind blew full in our face, and I heard them say, 'It is very cold!' But neither my face, nor hands, nor feet were cold, till between nine and ten we came to Epworth. After travelling more than ninety miles, I was little more tired than when I rose in the morning.

CHAPTER 8

Polemics and Alarums

WESLEY NEVER CEASED FROM reinforcing his spoken word by the written. The edition of his collected works first published in 1771, when he still had another twenty busy years to live, ran to thirty-two volumes. The new Oxford University Press edition of all his prose works is being planned to consist of thirty-four, each of them (if we may judge from the first to be issued) of about six hundred pages. In all, during his life he published some four hundred books and booklets. The two years 1743 and 1744 may be taken as offering a fair sample: they contain a score of diverse publications: the latest batch of his and his brother's hymns; a three-volume thousand-page anthology of *Moral and Sacred Poems* (which cost him a £50 indemnity for the piracy of Young's *Night Thoughts* and other poems 'the property of Mr Robert Dodsley' the publisher); a little book of family prayers and another of Methodist society rules; his Oxford sermon of August 1744; an instalment of his *Journal* for 1739–41; a book of *Instructions for Children*, with the advice that the young should be made to memorize them; a number of pamphlets, including one directed at soldiers, and another, whose arguments were destined to rebound against him, recommending the spiritual advantages of celibacy; several abridgements of authors he admired, among them Henry Scougal, John Bunyan, Jonathan Edwards the New England evangelist, and – despite earlier criticism and continuing reservations – William Law and Count Zinzendorf; most considerable of all, Wesley's own *Earnest Appeal to Men of Reason and Religion*, fifty-three pages of trenchant polemics, which went quickly into a second edition (and eventually during his lifetime to eight more), encouraging the prompt composition of a

Farther Appeal . . . (1744–5) four or five times as long.

The earlier *Appeal* a 'short, rude sketch of the doctrine we teach' and an apologia for Methodism and Methodists (those *truest* upholders of authorized Church of England teaching), was directed both towards unbelievers who claimed nevertheless to be men of reason, and more particularly towards pretending Christians and his fellow clergy. The tract is Wesley at his persuasive, plain-speaking, *buttonholing* best. ('Bear with me yet a little longer: my soul is distressed for you . . . You see, then, it is not *we* that say this, but the Lord . . .') Near his conclusion, he defends himself sturdily against those amongst the clergy who were whispering that he was doing well financially out of his activities:

> For what price will *you* preach (and that with all your might, and not in an easy, indolent, fashionable way) eighteen or nineteen times every week? And this throughout the year? What shall I give *you* to travel seven or eight hundred miles, in all weathers, every two or three months? For what salary will *you* abstain from all other diversions than the doing good and the praising God? I am mistaken if you would not prefer strangling for such a life . . .
>
> I will now simply tell you my sense of these matters . . . I have what is needful for life and godliness. And I apprehend this is all the world can afford. The kings of the earth can give me no more. For as to gold and silver, I count it dung and dross: I trample it under my feet . . . I only fear lest any of it should cleave to me, and I should not be able to shake it off before my spirit returns to God . . . And hear ye this, all you who have discovered the treasures which I am to leave behind me: if I leave behind me ten pounds (above my debts and the little arrears of my fellowship) you and all mankind bear witness against me that 'I lived and died a thief and a robber'.[1]

The university sermon he preached in August 1744 was Wesley's farewell to Oxford; no fond farewell but, instead, a denunciation. He had come near to delivering similarly harsh sentiments on the previous occasion he had preached at St Mary's, in 1741 – the obligatory sermon was a triennial affair – but then Lady Huntingdon, to whom he had shown his draft, had pronounced against its wisdom, whereupon he toned down his strictures. This time he pulled no punches, being resigned to dissociating himself entirely from the world of Oxford – though for a few years yet he held on to his Lincoln fellowship. He had come to take as poor a view of the university's academic as of its moral standing: 'I see not', he wrote, 'why a man of tolerable understanding may not learn in six months' time more of solid philosophy than is commonly learned at Oxford in four (perhaps seven) years.'[2] (With the passing years, however, some nostalgia crept in. In his old age he confessed 'I love the very sight of Oxford.' The place had improved in everything, *except religion*.)[3]

'I preached, I suppose for the last time, at St Mary's', his *Journal* records on 24 August. 'Be it so. I am now clear of the blood of these men. I have fully delivered my own soul.' He praised, as ever, 'the wise providence of God' when after the service the vice-chancellor, as resentful as the many heads of colleges present, sent his beadle to demand the script of the sermon, thus ensuring that it 'came to be read, probably more than once, by every man of eminence in the university'. Two editions were indeed published within a month or two of its delivery; Wesley hoped thereby that 'men of reason might judge for themselves'.

He had castigated Oxford professedly 'in tender love, and in the spirit of meekness'; but the carefully considered words bit very sharply:

> Ye venerable men who are more especially called to form the tender minds of youth, are you filled with the Holy Ghost? . . . Do you inculcate upon them, day by day, that without love all learning is but splendid ignorance, pompous folly, vexation of spirit?

He proceeded to accuse senior members of the university of 'pride, haughtiness of spirit; impatience and peevishness, sloth and indolence, gluttony and sensuality, even proverbial uselessness'. And then:

> What shall we say concerning the youth of this place? . . . Do you not waste day after day, either in reading what has no tendency to Christianity, or in gaming, or in – you know not what? . . . Are not drunkenness and uncleanness found among you? Yea, and are there not of you, who glory in their shame?

By swearing to observe customs and statutes of which they were wholly ignorant, were they not forsworn and perjured?

What is perjury, if this is not? May it not be one of the consequences of this, that so many of you are a generation of triflers? triflers with God, with one another, and with your own souls? How few of you spend, from one week to another, a single hour in private prayer? How few have any thought of God in the general tenour of your conversation? . . . Would you not take it for granted, if one began such a conversation, that it was either hypocrisy or enthusiasm? In the name of the Lord God almighty I ask, What religion are you of? Even the talk of Christianity ye cannot, will not bear. O my brethren, what a Christian city is this? It is time for thee, Lord, to lay to thine hand.[4]

What manifestation of divine anger was being invited by this final threatening declaration may hardly be ascertained. It should perhaps be regarded as only another instance of the scripture-echoing rhetoric into which he lapsed with such facility. It is unlikely that he actually foresaw Oxford being engulfed by God's vengeance in any form so unmistakable as, say, an earthquake. Yet both he and his brother took such natural disasters very seriously as instances of God's displeasure; Oxford undoubtedly merited one.

In a few years' time (following some alarming earth tremors) Charles Wesley preached four sermons specifically upon earthquakes, 'of all the judgements which the righteous God inflicts on sinners here, the most dreadful and destructive'. One of these was subsequently and mistakenly included among *John* Wesley's published sermons, and indeed its message might equally be his. After the congregation had set before them recent examples of these works of the Lord – Sicily and Jamaica in 1692, Peru in 1746 – they were invited to consider : 'Was the earth just now to open its mouth and swallow thee up, what would become of thee? Wouldest thou not have died in thy sins, or rather gone down quick into hell?' Even if they were by good fortune to escape the earthquake, they were to remember, 'God will never want ways and means to punish impenitent sinners. He hath a thousand other judgements in reserve.' But the escape route was, as ever, clearly indicated: 'Repent and believe the gospel. Believe on the Lord Jesus, and ye shall yet be saved'. ('Repentance *alone* will profit you nothing.') When this sermon came to be published, it was given the boldly remarkable title, *The Cause and Cure of Earthquakes.*[5]

The widespread tremors of 1750 brought a notorious sermon from Whitefield too. There had been a well-publicized prophecy, made by a soldier 'enthusiast', that London would be engulfed in a great earthquake on 4 April. Sceptics smiled, but thousands of the credulous did not. Tyerman writes:

> Places of worship were packed, especially the chapels of the Methodists, where crowds came during the whole of that dreary night, knocking and begging for admittance. At midnight, amid dense darkness, and surrounded by affrighted multitudes, Whitefield stood up in Hyde Park, and, with his characteristic pathos, and in tones majestically grand, took occasion to call the attention of listening multitudes to the coming judgement, the wreck of nature, and the sealing of all men's destinies.[6]

It is not surprising that the great Lisbon disaster of 1755 elicited a timely tract from John Wesley, *Serious Thoughts on the Earthquake at Lisbon*.* It ran quickly into six editions. And after prolonged earth tremors, with heavy falls of rock at Whiston Cliff, near Thirsk in Yorkshire, in that same year 1755, Wesley was moved to ask:

> What, then, could be the cause? What, indeed, but God, who arose to shake terribly the earth; who purposely chose such a place, where there is so great a concourse of nobility and gentry every year; and wrought in such a manner that many might see it and fear; that all who travel one of the most frequented roads in England might see it . . . a visible monument of his power, all that ground being now so encumbered with rocks and stones that it cannot be either ploughed or grazed . . .[7]

In the mid-1740s sporadic anti-Methodist rioting often coincided with anti-Jacobite scaremongering. That the two should be associated seems curious until we remember that even in his Georgia days Wesley had by some been suspected of Catholic hankerings; that in a panicky year like 1745 anyone known to be at odds with the Church establishment, yet hostile also to Dissent, might well be the object of such ignorant suspicion; and that, even four years afterwards, one of the most widely read of the many clerical assaults on Wesley and his followers, by the Bishop of Exeter, George Lavington, was entitled *The Enthusiasm*

* 'Directed, not as I designed at first, to the small vulgar, but the great – to the learned, rich, and honourable heathens, commonly called Christians.'

of Methodists and Papists Compar'd. (He judged Methodist 'ecstasies and raptures, apparitions and visions' to be all too closely akin to the alleged experiences of St Francis of Assisi, St Dominic, St Ignatius, and St Teresa – supporting his thesis with unkind selective quotations from Wesley's own *Journal.*) During 1745 the two Wesleys found it necessary to attest, even formally before magistrates, their hostility towards Rome and loyalty to King George. 'Every Sunday damnation is denounced against us', complained Charles, 'for we are Papists, Jesuits, seducers, and bringers-in of the Pretender.' Such wild charges were so persistent that Wesley was moved to compose a loyal address to the King on behalf of 'the Societies in England and Wales in derision called Methodists', a document whose chief interest lies less in its affirmation of Protestant patriotism and detestation of Romish doctrines than in its implicit acceptance of the separate existence of a Methodist sect. It was indeed on these grounds that Charles objected to it; an early indication of fraternal rift ahead. The address, he wrote, 'would *seem to allow* that we are a body distinct from the national Church, whereas we are only a sound part of that Church. Guard against this . . .'[8]

Separate sect or no, its efficient organization busily occupied Wesley. Towards perfecting it, he convened on 25 June 1744, following a love-feast the preceding evening, a meeting which became in effect the first Methodist Conference and thus the parent of Methodism's subsequently annual convention. At these initial sessions he was assisted by his brother, four other clergy of the Church of England, and four invited lay preachers. The agenda had been prepared with his usual thoroughness: what they were to teach, how they were to teach it, internal discipline, society rules and organization, rules for itinerant and local lay assistants, guidance for stewards, band leaders, class leaders, sick visitors, school teachers, housekeepers.

The crucial question of schism could hardly be avoided. It was asked, 'How far is it our duty to obey the Bishops?' – to which difficult question they replied: only insofar as conscience permitted. Methodists must not seek to separate from the Church. However, if the Church by its errors and shortcomings were to separate from *them*, this would be regarded as a regrettable accident. 'The Church in the proper sense, the congregation of English believers, we do not weaken at all.' Minutes of this

conference and its successors were recorded largely in the form
of question and answer – essentially of course the answers were
Wesley's own. For example,

> Q ... Is it not probable that your hearers after your death will
> be scattered into all sects and parties? or that they will form
> themselves into a distinct sect?
> A ... We are persuaded the body of our hearers will, even after
> our death, remain in the Church, unless they are thrust out.
> We do, and will do, all we can to prevent these con-
> sequences ... but we cannot with good conscience neglect
> the present opportunity of saving souls ...[9]

As it chanced, Wesley found himself in Newcastle at the height
of the Jacobite alarums, when its citizens, Prince Charles Edward
having taken Edinburgh, were now awaiting his expected advance in their direction. Wesley's visit coincided with an emer-
gency meeting of householders convened by the mayor. Though
not a householder, Wesley nevertheless thought it wise to send his
respects and assurances of loyalty by letter. This gave him at the
same time the opportunity, Jacobites or no Jacobites, to plead
the ever-pressing cause of moral reformation. Could the mayor not
use his influence to check the 'overflowings of ungodliness' and
of 'open, flagrant wickedness' in his city? When, after the Pretender's victory at Prestonpans, Newcastle was suddenly the
headquarters of an Anglo-Hanoverian army of 15,000 men,
which did nothing to purify the prevailing moral atmosphere,
Wesley wrote to the mayor again: 'The continued cursing and
swearing, the wanton blasphemy of the soldiers in general, must
needs be a torture to the sober ear ... Can it be expected that
God should be on their side, who are daily affronting him to his
face?' If only through the mayor's friendly offices, he might be
allowed to preach to the troops, they would soon find he was
not out to 'fill their heads with peculiar whims and notions',
but rather with 'plain principles of manly, rational religion'.[10]
Permission was obtained. Wesley was even able to exercise his
rusty German on some of the foreign troops hanging disconsol-
ately about the Town Moor (they 'drank in every word'); but he
was not able to claim any electrifying results among the English
redcoats. They listened on the whole politely; but 'the words of a
scholar did not affect them like those of a dragoon or a grenadier'.[11]

Over the years, the decades, Wesley would go on trying: whenever his travels took him near military camps, in England or in Ireland, he was shocked anew at their profanity and godlessness, and he never neglected an opportunity of seeking permission to plant the seed among them, stony as the ground proved. 'The whole tenor of their behaviour', he regretfully concluded, 'speaks "Let us eat and drink, for tomorrow we die".' And as for ships of war, those 'mere floating hells', where was there to be found 'more consummate wickedness, a more full, daring contempt of God and all his laws, except in the bottomless pit?'[12]

But were military and naval sinners in much worse case than the generality of his countrymen? Contemporary moral corruption provided of course a theme he endlessly reverted to, but in particular the second part of his *Farther Appeal to Men of Reason and Religion*, published in 1746, became one long excoriation of English sinfulness. 'What a weight of sin lies on this nation!' he lamented, and proceeded to spare hardly any aspect of its life. 'To prove at large that the luxury and sensuality, the sloth and indolence, the effeminacy and false delicacy of our nation are without parallel, would be but lost labour.' It was labour, nevertheless, he was prepared apparently to lose. Even, he wrote, Solomon in his glory, archetypal of such hedonism, knew nothing of such modern abominations as horse-races, theatres, balls, assemblies, ridottos, masquerades. And where in England was male chastity to be found? Among the nobility? Among the gentry? Among the tradesmen? Among the common people of England? How few laid claim to it at all! (What preconception, or perhaps sense of delicacy, made him omit female unchastity?)

However 'now restrained', were there not also signs observable of 'the wild, turbulent, ungovernable spirit' of Englishmen, whose 'histories witness such a series of mutinies, seditions, factions, and rebellions as are scarce to be paralleled in any other kingdom since the world began?' – a boldly comprehensive charge indeed. And was not violence still to be found everywhere, 'even in our streets'? 'Even in the open streets' too, 'how many buy and sell on the day of the Lord . . . Money is their God, and gain their godliness.' Then, because of swearing, did not the land, like Canaan, mourn? Not merely 'light swearing' either, but clear wilful perjury, in which offence were to be found particularly and peculiarly guilty (for reasons set out at length) constables, grand jurors, churchwardens, ship's captains, customs officers, and voters in parliamentary elections. Again, did not all kinds of theft abound throughout the land, even though death was the punishment for it? And what of British justice? 'Suppose a great man to oppress the needy; suppose the rich grinds the faces of the poor. What remedy against such oppression can be found in this Christian country? . . . If you have money enough, you may succeed; but if that fails, your cause is gone.'

Denunciations followed of the legal profession (how much honester was a pickpocket than an attorney!); and of the general easy acceptance of mendacity, whether from convention and fashion, or from a desire to please or make a profit. 'A well-bred person is not *expected* to speak as he thinks . . . And if the rich and great have so small regard to truth . . . what wonder can it be that men of lower rank will do the same thing for gain?' As for religion, did not the 'men of quality' in England lack belief 'in any God at all – or at best but an epicurean God, who sat at ease upon the circle of the heavens, and did not concern himself about us worms of the earth'. 'In tender love' he enquired ('I speak to you, my brethren, who are priests and prophets of the Lord'): did *their* ranks not include adulterers and drunkards? Were not too many of them socially obsequious? Who among the clergy 'dares repel one of the greatest men in his parish from the Lord's table? Yea, though he openly deny the Lord?' How great the damnation would be of those who destroyed souls instead of saving them! ' "Ye have caused many to stumble . . . Therefore have I also made you contemptible and base before all the people." '

He summarily dismisses the standing and practice of Presbyterians, Baptists, Quakers, sceptics and Roman Catholics, the Quakers' inconsistencies occupying him longest. Quakers, like Methodists, *professed* plainness; but did they never 'compliment' and 'flatter and dissemble?' Moreover,

> Do not many of your women wear gold upon their very feet? And many of your men wear 'ornaments of gold'? . . . Have you not seen . . . their canes and snuff-boxes glitter, even in your solemn assembly, while ye were waiting together upon God . . . This woman is too strict a Quaker to lay out a shilling on a necklace. Very well; but she is not too strict to lay out fourscore guineas

in a repeating watch . . . What multitudes of you . . . will not put
on a scarlet or crimson stuff, but the richest velvet, so it be black
or grave . . . Surely you cannot be ignorant that the sinfulness of
fine apparel lies chiefly in the expensiveness. In that it is robbing
God and the poor.

'Such at present' was the religion of Christian England. And yet
was there ever a nation more careless and secure? More un-
apprehensive of the wrath of God! . . . Surely never was any
people more fitted for destruction.'[13]

Nevertheless there *were* some who, seeing the 'abominable
hypocrisy' of conventional religion, and drawn towards God
with the cords of love, had earned the right to expect his mercy.
If another Flood was justly deserved – it was not his metaphor,
but the sense was strongly implied – the Methodist membership
card ought to qualify as a passport towards a place on the Ark.
'Two or three clergymen of the Church of England' had in-
augurated a movement. Thousands had listened, repented,
believed, and were now inspired 'with every holy and heavenly
temper'.

The drunkard commenced sober and temperate. The whoremonger
abstained from adultery and fornication, the unjust from oppression and wrong. He that had been accustomed to curse and
swear now swore no more. The sluggard began to work . . . The
miser learned to deal his bread to the hungry, and to cover the
naked with a garment. Indeed the whole form of their life was
changed . . . They began to experience *inward* religion . . . The
love of God constrains them to love all mankind . . . And in
whatsoever state they are, they have learned therewith to be
content . . . There is scarce a city or considerable town to be
found where some have not been roused out of the sleep of
death . . . No less remarkable is the purity of the religion which
has extended itself so deeply and swiftly . . . It is likewise rational,
as well as scriptural; it is as pure from enthusiasm as from superstition . . .[14]

This lavish testimonial, almost in the very same words, was
repeated[15] in Wesley's forthright *Letter to the Right Reverend the
Lord Bishop of London, occasioned by his Lordship's Late Charge
to his Clergy (1747).* 'Pure from enthusiasm and superstitition' was
just what most of the bishops, and indeed most of the clergy and
educated laity, did *not* think Methodism to be. The enthusiasm of

Whitefield in particular had from the beginning offended Bishop Gibson of London. Upon the Wesleys at first he had merely urged caution; but by now Methodists, both Whitefieldite and Wesleyan, as well as the Moravian Brethren, had all fallen under his official episcopal condemnation. They were guilty of 'annoying the established ministry and drawing over to themselves the lowest and most ignorant of the people, by pretences to greater sanctity and more orthodox preaching'. Their effusions were 'wild and indigested' and spread doctrines, of which he listed six, 'big with pernicious influences'. (One was Wesley's troublesome tenet of the possibility of 'sanctification' and 'Christian perfection' in *this* life.) Their 'restless and vagrant teachers' prided themselves upon 'extraordinary strictness and severities . . . beyond what the rules of Christianity require'. Moreover they encouraged working people towards exaggerated religious observance 'to the neglect of the business of their stations'.

'My Lord, this is not so', was Wesley's terse comment on this last. It was a point on which his advice to his own people was always particular, and he objected to being misrepresented. On the bishop's six doctrinal points much of his counter-offensive was similarly valid. He had every right to complain when Gibson casually lumped together the alleged errors of John Wesley with those of men he had broken with on doctrinal grounds, with for instance the dangerous Antinomianism of men whom Wesley considered 'the firstborn children of Satan'.* The lord bishop was magisterially reproved:

> Before I proceed, suffer me to observe, here are three grievous errors charged on the Moravians, Mr Whitefield, and me conjointly, in none of which I am any more concerned than in the doctrine of the metempsychosis! But it was 'not needful to charge particular tenets on particular persons'. Just as needful, my lord, as it is not to put a stumbling-block in the way of our brethren;

---

* The *Journal* for 23 March 1744 relates with horror a conversation he had with one of these elect brethren who claimed immunity from the moral laws governing the non-elect: 'Do you believe you have nothing to do with the law of God?' 'I have not; I am not under the law; I live by faith.' 'Have you, as living by faith, a right to everything in the world?' 'I have; all is mine, since Christ is mine.' 'May you, then, take anything you will anywhere? Suppose out of a shop . . .?' 'I may if I want it, for it is mine. Only I will not give offence.' 'Have you also a right to all the women in the world?' 'Yes, if they consent.' 'And is not that a sin?' . . . '. . . Not to those whose *hearts are free*.'

not to lay them under an almost insuperable temptation of condemning the innocent with the guilty. I beseech your lordship to answer in your own conscience before God, whether you did not foresee how many of your hearers would charge these tenets upon *me*? Nay, whether you did not design they should? If so, my lord, is this Christianity? Is it humanity? Let me speak plain. Is it honest heathenism?[16]

'Let me speak plain': his writing is always best when he does; when he rations his inexhaustible supply of scriptural texts; when he pitches in to his critics for their wrong-headedness, their misrepresentations, their want of the truth. He was a formidable polemicist, writing often with a challenging scorn, a controlled passion, which still keeps wide awake the modern reader whom some of the theological arguments and ecclesiastical disputes might easily incline towards a yawn. *Cet animal est méchant; quand on l'attaque, if se défend.* 'Sir', he demands of Bishop Lavington (who had compared at length the 'enthusiasm' of Methodists and Papists) – 'Sir, has your passion quite extinguished your reason?' 'Have fierceness and rancour left you no understanding?' 'Sir, away with your flourishes and write plain English.' 'O Sir, when will you deviate into truth?' 'Tedious as it is to wade through so many dirty pages, I will follow you, step by step.' 'Sir, you run very fast. And yet I hope to overtake you by and by.' Then, when he is sure he has the bishop cornered, 'Now, Sir, where is your loophole to creep out?'[17]

The three *Letters* Wesley published in reply to Gibson's and Lavington's strictures occupy between them some hundred reproachful fighting pages. But though he hit very hard, he refused to bear rancour, and for Gibson at least he continued to retain, and even publicly to express, respect. To Lavington he had ended his *Second Letter* (*1751*): 'You regard neither mercy, justice, nor truth. To vilify, to blacken, is your one point. I pray God it may not be laid to your charge. May he show mercy, though you show none!' But eleven years later, only a fortnight before Lavington's death, he was writing:

> I was well pleased to partake of the Lord's Supper [in Exeter Cathedral] with my old opponent, Bishop Lavington. O may we sit down together in the Kingdom of our Father![18]

Wesley also published replies in letter form, some seventy

Selina, Countess of Huntingdon

Augustus Toplady, after J.R. Smith

William Romaine

Rowland Hill

Wesley at 86, after
Romney

Ordination of Francis
Asbury by Thomas
Coke, at Baltimore,
Maryland

thousand words in all, to two of the weightier attacks among the many made against him at this time, one by Thomas Church, a prebendary of St Paul's (*Remarks on Mr Wesley's Last Journal, 1744*) and the other by Conyers Middleton, a fellow of Trinity, Cambridge (*A Free Inquiry into the Miraculous Powers supposed to have subsisted in the Christian Church, 1748*). Wesley was at pains to acknowledge Thomas Church's 'calm manner of writing (some paragraphs excepted)' and hence his own rejoinder was correspondingly civil. Church had accused him both of inconsistency in his views of the Moravians and of a too ready indulgence of their errors. Wesley painstakingly, even pedantically, rebutted the charges; but the truth was that there was a real ambivalence in his attitude to the Moravians. He loved them, he loved them not. He could never forget his early admiration for them, or his own personal debt to Böhler. Yes, he now wrote, the Moravians did 'excel in sweetness of behaviour'. He acknowledged everything his *Journal* had published in their praise. But – the 'buts' were meticulously set down; and if he had been writing, say, five years later, in 1750 or '51, they would have been considerably harsher.

By that time he had just read and reacted very strongly against Count Zinzendorf's autobiography: 'O when will he learn (with all his learning) "simplicity and godly sincerity"? When will he be an upright follower of the Lamb, so that no guile may be found in his mouth?' And when he readily took down, the following year, a long deposition from a lapsed Moravian, detailing one man's experience of the 'haughty and tyrannical' behaviour of the 'management', the excesses and hypocrisies among the brethren (whoredom, masturbation and 'other abominations') and the prevalence of abortions among the sisters, Wesley held forth in righteous lamentation:

> Was there ever so melancholy an account? Oh what is human nature? How low are they fallen who were once burning and shining lights, spreading blessings wherever they came![19]

It happens to be true that during the later 1740s and the 1750s Moravianism in Germany did become decadently self-indulgent, not least in the luscious vocabulary of its devotion, which tended to bathe luxuriantly in the Blood of the Lamb and wallow in the wounds of Jesus – 'the dearest little opening of his sacred, precious, and thousand-times-beautiful little side', and so forth.[20] No doubt translation makes bad worse, but all those untranslatable diminutives must sound nauseous enough in their original German. And a first-hand, if admittedly strait-laced, report published in England in 1753 of the goings-on at a celebration in Marienborn of Zinzendorf's forty-sixth birthday makes very curious reading – the young folks at this 'love-feast' beginning 'to grow wanton, laughing, sporting, jesting, leaping, throwing one another on the floor, and struggling till they were quite out of breath, besides many filthy, gross indecencies'.[21] Methodism, while Wesley commanded it, would never be allowed to tolerate such enthusiastic extravagances, though a watchful eye for eccentricity and fanaticism was always needed, and at much this same time he did have to enquire sharply into allegations of some scandalous practices among certain of his own preachers.

Wesley's public controversy with Conyers Middleton concerned not the Gospel miracles, which he accepted, but those credited to the early leaders of the Church. 'The primitive Christians were perpetually reproached for their gross credulity', Dr Middleton had written, not precisely adding but certainly believing and implying, that contemporary Methodists were in like case. Primitive Christians indeed *were* so reproached, Wesley countered, but by whom? – 'why, by Jews and heathens'.[22] This was a contest on his home pitch; it involved Justin Martyr, Irenaeus, Tertullian, Origen, Cyprian, and the rest of them, whose texts he knew like the back of his hand. He would not have his early Fathers supposed to be 'fools or knaves, or both'. Once one began to doubt their credibility, the floodgates would be open:

> Then it is plain all the history of the Bible is utterly precarious and uncertain; then I indeed may presume, but cannot certainly know, that Jesus of Nazareth was ever born, much less that he healed the sick and raised either Lazarus or himself from the dead. Now, sir, go and declare again how careful you are for 'the credit of the Gospel miracles'.[23]

The consequences of Conyers Middleton and his like (we might venture the anachronism of calling them liberal churchmen) could only be 'to free the good people of England from all that prejudice, bigotry, and superstition vulgarly called Christianity'. But for Wesley it was really too tragic for such irony.

No one reading these considerable polemics of Wesley's middle years will easily agree that 'his Christianity was almost totally devoid of intellectual content . . . wholly ethical and emotional', as Paul Johnson asserts in his *History of Christianity*.[24] Of many of his followers such a view would indeed be tenable. Methodists tended to lapse rather easily into sentimental emotionalism (just the offence Wesley found most nauseous among the Moravians), or into preachifying cant. Intellectually they come poorly out of a comparison with late eighteenth or nineteenth-century Unitarians or Quakers. Among British Methodists there were to be no great writers or artists or composers. The architectural meanness of the houses of worship with which they were to fill the country arose not only from the relative poverty of their congregations, but also from an inherent mistrust of sensuous beauty. They inherited the Puritan suspicion, even hatred, of decorative art. Certainly signs of some of these attitudes may be noticed in Wesley himself – a horror of display, a fear of the senses, a refusal to acknowledge any art or literature or even science that was not 'improving'.* But none of this robs him of 'intellectual content'. Not many educated Christians could today go along with his biblical fundamentalism, and few even among modern Methodists could fully accept all the premises from which his teaching and polemic flowed. But given those premises, he never lacks logic or adroitness in controversy or intellectual vigour. It was Lecky, the historian of rationalism and the decline of the miraculous, who rated him as 'one of the most powerful and active intellects in England'.

* It was characteristic of Wesley that when, one day in 1748, he 'spent an hour in observing the various works of God in the Physic Garden at Chelsea' [Sir Hans Sloane's botanic garden] he commented that somebody ought to make 'a full and accurate inquiry into the uses and virtues of all these plants. Without this, what end does the heaping them thus together answer, but the gratifying an idle curiosity?'

CHAPTER 9

Bodies and Souls

SIDE BY SIDE WITH the relatively weighty *Appeals* and *Letters*, Wesley, having as he claimed 'a desire to furnish poor people with cheaper, shorter, and plainer books', poured out a stream of pamphlets, usually of a dozen or so pages, on a great variety of matters, political, social, moral. It was a practice he would tirelessly continue. In later days no one needed to be in ignorance of Mr Wesley's *Thoughts* or *Words*, on smuggling, on the American question, on the issue of slavery, et cetera. Among this earlier output of the 1740s came *A Word to a Drunkard, A Word to an Unhappy Woman, A Word to an Englishman* (loyalty, 1745), *A Word of Advice to Saints and Sinners, A Word to a Methodist* (printed also in a Welsh translation), *A Word to a Protestant*, and *A Word to a Freeholder* (against accepting bribes in parliamentary elections). These sold handsomely, generally at a penny each, and so, as he put it, he 'unawares became rich'.[1] Inevitably, malicious rumours came to be spoken and printed concerning his new-found wealth, most of them exaggerating grossly and some of them insinuating misappropriation of his societies' funds. To this he replied with proper ridicule, and indeed no such charges would ever be made to stick against one who so obviously despised creature comforts and worldly possessions. Wesley always ploughed his profits back into the business.

The business was of course the saving of souls; but there was the important sideline of saving bodies too. Among the Methodist poor there were many chronically sick and unable to afford a doctor. Could something be done for them? Ever enterprising and practical, Wesley decided in 1746 to open a dispensary, employing 'an apothecary and an experienced surgeon'; re-

solving not to get out of his depth with 'difficult and complicated' or acute cases, but to offer the rest 'the best advice I
could and the best medicines I had'. He would be accused, he
knew, of quackery, but he possessed 'numberless proofs that
regular physicians do exceeding little good'.

Some disorders of course might be banished simply by prayer.
He cured his own toothache thus on 12 November 1746. Mr
Spear's rupture, declared by the most eminent physicians to be
untreatable, was by the same means 'perfectly cured'.[2] At the
London dispensary (a second was soon started in Bristol),
among the first to attend was

> one William Kirkham, a weaver . . . I asked him, 'What complaint
> have you?' 'O Sir,' said he, 'a cough, a very sore cough. I can
> get no rest day nor night.' I asked, 'How long have you had it?'
> He replied, 'About threescore years; it began when I was eleven . . .'
> I looked up to God, and said, 'Take this three or four times a day.
> If it does you no good, it will do you no harm.' He took it two
> or three days. His cough was cured, and has not returned to this
> day. Now, let candid men judge, does humility require me to
> deny a notorious fact? If not, which is vanity? To say I by my
> skill restored this man to health, or to say God did it by his
> almighty power?[3]

Within five months over five hundred had attended the London
dispensary, and he 'did not regard whether they were of the
Society or not'. He claimed seventy-one complete cures in that
time, and 'nine out of ten . . . remarkably altered for the better'.
So far as he knew, no one had died of Dr Wesley's physic. The
work of the dispensaries continued.

He had long nurtured his own notions upon correct diet and
healthy living, many of them echoing the theories in Dr Cheyne's
Book of Health and Long Life; and these he never hesitated to
advance, both privately and publicly. Privately in particular to
his preachers, from whom God's work would require fit bodies.
Thus he wrote to one: 'Never sit up later than ten o'clock, no,
not for any reason (except a watchnight) . . . In general, I desire
you would go to bed about a quarter after nine' – which would
permit seven or eight hours' sleep for rising sharp by five or
earlier. To another, John Downes, who was delicate: 'Your
water should be neither quite warm (for fear of relaxing the tone
of your stomach) nor quite cold. Of all flesh, mutton is the best

for you; of all vegetables, turnips, potatoes, and apples (roasted, boiled, or baked) if you can bear them . . . How apt is the corruptible body to press down the soull'[4] To a preacher beginning work in Northern Ireland he counselled:

> If you regard your health, touch no supper but a little milk or water gruel. This will by the blessing of God secure you from nervous disorders . . . Avoid all familiarity with women. This is deadly poison both to them and you. You cannot be too wary in this respect . . . Avoid all nastiness, dirt, slovenliness . . . Do not stink above ground . . . Whatever clothes you have, let them be whole . . . Let none ever see a ragged Methodist. Clean yourself of lice . . . Do not cut off your hair, but clean it, and keep it clean. Cure yourself and your family of the itch: a spoonful of brimstone will cure you . . . Use no tobacco unless prescribed by a physician. It is an uncleanly and unwholesome self-indulgence . . . Use no snuff . . . Touch no dram. It is liquid fire . . . a sure though slow poison.[5]

Ideally Wesley approved of, and indeed for some years practised, vegetarianism, but after being attacked by 'a violent flux' in Ireland he thought it advisable to return to animal food.

Then there was the question of tea. The rich drank it to excess; the poor wasted money on it they could not afford, and it manifestly impaired their health. Wesley himself had been consuming it liberally for over a quarter of a century; but in July 1746 he resolved to abjure it, persuading his London class-leaders to join him in setting an example. Let Methodists put into the poor-box the money they saved each week by not buying it. His own deprivation cost him, he said, a three days' headache and a sudden loss of memory; but timely prayer again righted him, and for twelve years – until his doctor prescribed it for him again – he abstained from the poisonous herb, thus ridding himself, he concluded, of a shaking of the hand ('paralytic complaint') and saving, together with his fellow-Methodists in London, Bristol, Kingswood and Newcastle, fifty pounds a year to help feed the hungry and clothe the ragged.

Another of Wesley's initiatives in social welfare was a charitable fund for offering small interest-free loans to the needy among his London members, usually of a few shillings only, to meet emergencies. The maximum was later fixed at £5; the principal was to be repaid within three months. Two hundred and fifty were thus assisted during 1747 alone. Looking back, however, years later on these philanthropic activities – what he called 'temporals' – he recognized what a tiny surface they were scratching, compared with the 'spirituals' of Methodism:

> It is certain we have barely the first outlines of a plan with regard to temporals. The reason is, I had no design for several years to concern myself with temporals at all. And when I began to do this, it was wholly and solely with a view to *relieve* not *employ* the poor, unless now and then with respect to a small number; and even this I found was too great a burthen for me, as requiring both more money, more time, and more thought than I could possibly spare. I say, than I could spare; for the whole weight laid on me. If I left it to others, it surely came to nothing.[6]

He was angrily contemptuous of the 'wickedly, devilishly false' upper-class view that the poor stayed poor only because they were idle. The genuineness of his pity and indignation shines through the occasional sarcasm of the *Journal*'s account of his visiting of the sick and poor in the districts on the Thames south bank during the winter of 1753 – even though his American comparisons may seem somewhat rose-spectacled:

> Such scenes, who could see unmoved? There are none such to be found in a pagan country. If any of the Indians in Georgia were sick (which indeed exceeding rarely happened, till they learned gluttony and drunkenness from the Christians), those who were near him gave him whatever he wanted. O who will convert the English into honest heathens?
> On Friday and Saturday I visited as many more as I could. I found some in their cells under ground; others in their garrets, half-starved both with cold and hunger, added to weakness and pain. But I found not one of them unemployed, who was able to crawl about the room . . . If you saw these things with your own eyes, could you lay out money in ornaments or superfluities?[7]

In the same part of London lay Marshalsea Prison, where the conditions appalled him no less than they did Howard a generation or Dickens a lifetime later: 'a nursery', proclaimed Wesley, 'of all manner of wickedness. O shame to man, that there should be such a place, such a picture of hell upon earth! And shame to those that bear the name of Christ, that there should need any prison at all in Christendom!'[8]

To rid Christendom, 'so-called', of vice and crime was asking

too much; but at least something practical and immediate might
be done towards improving the health of the common people.
To this end in 1747 Wesley had first published *Primitive Physick,
or an Easy and Natural Method of Curing Most Diseases*, a little
manual of medical self-help which was to be reprinted twenty-one
times by 1785;* it was always on sale at Methodist chapels.
Much of it was sensible and practical enough by the standards
of the day, but it is rather by its frequent oddities that it is now
chiefly remembered. To remedy hoarseness, rub the soles of the
feet with garlic and lard well beaten together. To heal sores,
apply a poultice of powdered coal. To cure baldness, rub the
scalp with honey and onions. For a twisted gut, swallow three
pounds of mercury ounce by ounce. For jaundice, wear leaves of
celandine under and upon the feet. To treat bruises, apply treacle
spread on brown paper. To correct an over-voracious appetite,
place in the nostrils small pieces of bread dipped in wine. To
combat old age, take a little tar-water night and morning, or a
decoction of nettles – but remember, the only *cure* is death.

Brown paper, spread this time with powdered sulphur mixed
with egg white, figures again in the *Journal*'s account of Wesley's
illness towards the end of 1753 when, having just authorized an
inscription for his own tombstone in expectation of imminent
death, he laid the home-made application to his side, whereupon
'the pain ceased in five minutes, the fever in half an hour'. Since,
however, this occurred at just the hour that 'some of our brethren
in London had set apart for joining in prayer', we are left to
wonder whether the brown paper or the prayers had the greater
share in his restoration. By 1760 he was ready to claim that he
had been 'preternaturally restored more than ten times'; and he
once told a correspondent that in 1753 he was delivered from
'the third stage of a consumption. And physicians have long
since agreed that this is not curable by any natural means.'9

It was like him to call his little book '*Primitive* Physick'.
With him that adjective invariably implied commendation.
Methodism itself set out to emulate a supposedly primitive
Christianity. When Wesley and his London stewards set up a

---

* When in 1776 William Hawes, physician to the London Dispensary,
accused Wesley in *Lloyd's Evening Post* of being a dangerous quack, Wesley
jauntily replied in the same journal that since Dr Hawes's attack on his book
there had been 'a greater demand for it than ever'. He hoped therefore for
the favour of 'a few farther remarks'.

Methodist poor-house to provide a home for aged and infirm widows (which however failed to last), he rejoiced that they had copied 'another of the institutions of the apostolic age'.[10] But this conscious traditionalism sometimes surprisingly went hand-in-hand with an enthusiasm for the new-fangled which did nothing to lessen the charges of charlatanism made against him. When for instance medical and 'philosophical' circles began to buzz with controversy over the new electrical machines, Wesley championed them energetically – and of course then proceeded to publish a little monograph in their praise. In April 1753 he recounts in the *Journal* various cases of disorders – paralysis, 'inveterate pain' in the stomach or the side – which the machine ameliorated or cured. 'Who can wonder', he asked, 'that many gentlemen of the faculty, as well as their good friends the apothe-caries, decry a medicine so cheap and easy, as much as they do quicksilver and tar-water?' Three years later he procured an apparatus of his own whose 'surprising medicine' he found so popular and, he claimed, efficacious that he soon had it at work in four different London centres treating 'hundreds, perhaps thousands' of patients. Neither his enthusiasm for electrifying nor his confidence in his own diagnoses diminished with the years. Electrification mended his lameness in 1764. At the age of seventy he was certain a friend's 'gout in the stomach' was in fact angina pectoris: 'I therefore advised him to take no more medicines, but to be electrified through the breast'; and, as we might have predicted, 'the violent symptoms immediately ceased'.[11]

His educational activities could hardly affect a public as large as the one that read his little medical *vade mecum*. They had begun in 1740, with the school, originally Whitefield's idea for colliers' children, three miles outside Bristol at Kingswood. The small school Wesley set up subsequently at Moorfields in London was similarly for the poor. Those few of the parents who could afford it did pay a small fee, but most did not, and some indeed might have their children clothed from Wesley's funds. The pupils, aged six and upwards, were taught ten hours a day; neither holidays nor play-times were permitted; and since the prime reason for the school's existence was to rescue children from the vice and heathenism they would pick up in the streets, to the 'three R's' was of course added that much more vital fourth, religion; in Wesley's language, 'to read, write, cast accounts, and know God'.

At Kingswood in 1748 a rather different sort of establishment was begun, side by side with the existing charity school, primarily for the convenience of Wesley's growing band of lay helpers, many of them itinerant preachers, the education of whose families presented obvious difficulties; but other Methodists also might enter their children. Eight hundred pounds of the money for this foundation was donated by a wealthy Mrs Gumley, one of the few among the upper classes who looked kindly on Methodism.* It was intended to be, as well as a school, a sort of college or seminary where Wesley could from time to time gather together his preachers for instruction; and this was what he was doing for instance during Lent in 1749, with seventeen of his helpers present. He planned a girls' boarding school at Kingswood too, and proceeded at least as far as establishing rules for it; the fees, like those for boys, were to be £10 for a 365-day year, board and tuition. As for putting one's daughter to an existing boarding school, he thought all 'pious, sensible women' agreed 'one might as well send a young maid to be bred in Drury Lane';[12] – or as he once exclaimed, 'Methodist parents, who would send your girls headlong to hell, send them to a fashionable boarding school!'

At the new boys' school, no child under six or new entrant over twelve was to be admitted; over-twelves would be liable to introduce too much of the outside world's contamination. Since 'children may unlearn in one week as much as they have learned in several; nay, and contract a prejudice to exact discipline which never can be removed', there were to be no holidays. The regime was to be the same, winter and summer: rise at four, service at five, breakfast at six; lessons from seven to eleven; a break till noon for working indoors and walking or working in the gardens; dinner at twelve; lessons again from one till five; private devotion from five to six; after six, working, walking, praying, supper; and bed at eight, with a master sleeping in the dormitory. Edu-

* None put their distaste more baldly than the Duchess of Buckingham, writing to the Countess of Huntingdon: 'These Methodist doctrines are most repulsive and strongly tinctured with impertinence and disrespect towards their superiors in perpetually endeavouring to level all ranks and do away with all distinction . . . I cannot but wonder that your Ladyship should relish any sentiments so much at variance with high rank and good breeding.'

cationally speaking, John Wesley was his mother's son, and Rousseau's polar opposite. The libertarianism of *Emile* would shock him deeply (it was published while Kingswood was still struggling to survive) and confirm his low opinion of 'enlightened' *philosophes*.

Wesley had no doubt that Satan lurked unceasingly for idlers. If his daily time-table looks punishing, the curriculum he proposed appears worse than Draconian: reading, writing, arithmetic; English, French, Latin, Greek, Hebrew; history and geography; rhetoric, logic and ethics; geometry and algebra; 'natural philosophy' (science) and metaphysics. He forthwith set about writing and publishing a set of grammars, one for each of the five languages, and also sundry text-books. Those classical texts he was prepared to allow were to be carefully expurgated, and the post-Augustan authors were, with a few minor well-edited exceptions, to be altogether excluded.[13] (From his own reading he had for a time banished pagan books altogether. Now he was ready again to explore them when more serious tasks permitted. Reading the *Iliad* as he rode towards Newcastle in August 1748 he reflected on Homer's 'amazing genius' and even found 'a vein of piety' in him, though with such improprieties intermixed 'as are shocking to the last degree'.)[14] Envisaging Kingswood School as a training ground for future ministers of the church, he proposed, for those who lasted the four-year primary course, a secondary course with a programme of work which would not have disgraced a university faculty. One may catch the rigour of his requirements, which he set out in characteristically careful detail, by noting one small item in mid-syllabus: 'Universal History'. This was lightly thrown in, together with a *Compendium of Ethics* and Euclid's *Elements*, between Origen, Tertullian, Cyprian, Chrysostom, Augustine, Pascal, *The History of the Council of Trent*, Burnet's *History of the Reformation* and a good deal else that appeared to demand unusual stamina and stoicism in his adolescent students. Even Spenser's *Faerie Queene*, which looks at first as if it were included as light relief, was then regarded, it must be remembered, as a vindication of the Protestant virtues.

However, all this represented only the intention; the prospectus, as it were, inside Wesley's mind. Reality fell disappointingly, often even disastrously, short. Rules which, Wesley announced, 'would not be broken in favour of any pupil whatsoever', were ignored continually. The masters fell out among themselves and with the boys; the housekeeper was found wanting; even the maids were divided into hostile camps. Pupils failed to avail themselves of their opportunities and had to be excluded. Numbers fell within two years from twenty-eight to eighteen. The staff had to be pared down to two masters, one housekeeper, and one maid. Still there was trouble. More of the senior pupils were expelled as 'incorrigible' after one of Wesley's visitations, and others were found to be 'very uncommonly wicked'.

Four years later he was still labouring to regulate the school as he wished it. 'I spent more money, and time, and care on this', he wrote, 'than almost any design I ever had; and still it exercises all the patience I have.' In 1766 it was the same story, after eighteen years, of disappointment and perseverance: 'I will have one or the other – a Christian school or none at all'; and then at last, during the few years immediately following, it seemed that his single-minded determination was beginning to reap a reward. He sensed 'a revival'. Numbers rose to forty, all boarders; and there was evidence of truly revivalist fervour among both the staff and boys. 'O what a work is it to train up children for heaven!' Wesley wrote in 1767.[15] What one of the masters joyfully reported to him in 1768, however, though it may have brought comfort to Wesley, is perhaps likelier now to provoke feelings of pained embarrassment:

> God broke in upon our boys in a surprising manner ... While they were in their private apartments, the power of God came upon them, even like a mighty, rushing wind, which made them cry aloud for mercy. Last night, I hope, will never be forgotten, when about twenty were in the utmost distress. But God quickly spoke peace to two of them ... A greater display of his love I never saw ... We have no need to exhort them to pray, for that spirit runs through the whole school ... While I am writing, the cries of the boys, from their several apartments, are sounding in my ears. There are many still lying at the pool, who wait every moment to be put in ... Since I began to write, eight more are set at liberty, and now rejoice in God their Saviour ... Their age is from eight to fourteen. There are but few who withstand the work ...[16]

After a good deal more of this sort of thing, it is a relief to learn that boys still continued to be boys. Human nature proved no less resilient than John Wesley; Satan no less persistent. Indeed, Wesley thought Satan must have 'a peculiar spite at this school'.

Kingswood's troubles soon loomed again; 'the devil is more deeply concerned against this school', Wesley believed, 'than against any other in England'; and in 1783, his eightieth year, the Methodist Conference was obliged to decide that either the school should cease,* or the rules of it be particularly observed; particularly, that the children should never play, and that a master should be always present with them.[17]

'This sect increases as fast as almost ever any religious non-sense did'; so in May 1749 judged Horace Walpole, a writer understandably not much to the taste of Wesleyans.[18] There were some eighty local Methodist societies by that time. Whether it was nonsense or the pure milk of the Word, Methodism was being carried with vigour and enterprise to all corners of the land – including, since 1746, Ireland – despite strong ecclesiastical disapproval, a degree of petty persecution from certain magistrates, mayors, and others in local authority, and unpleasantly frequent outbursts of violence from riotous mobs.

With his fifteen to eighteen sermons week after week, his endless hours in the saddle traversing and criss-crossing the country (covering four or five thousand miles in an average year, always with a book ready in his pocket for reading as he rode), writing his own books, his pamphlets, hymns, handbooks and school primers, preparing his abridgements and anthologies,† keeping his regular journal, conducting a busy, varied, and often protracted correspondence – John Wesley was undoubtedly a prodigy of zeal and energy. Plainly too, both in public and in private, his personality commanded a rare magic. Walpole might consider that as a preacher he was a good *actor* – 'towards the end he exalted his voice, and acted very ugly enthusiasm' – but

---

* It did not 'cease'. The modern Kingswood School, removed to Bath since 1851, is its direct descendant.

† In 1748 in a letter to Ebenezer Blackwell, a banker friend, he projected a *Christian Library*, extracting 'all that is most valuable in the English tongue ... to provide a complete library for those that fear God'. It duly appeared between 1749 and 1755, a massive and edifying compilation of potted biography and 'practical divinity': writings from the early Fathers; from Catholic, Dissenting, and Latitudinarian divines; from a wide diversity of English, Scottish, and continental theologians. Wesley was a didactically selective editor, excising passages he could not approve.

even Walpole granted him 'parts and eloquence';[19] and clearly
he must have possessed in outstanding measure the popular
preacher's gift of moving consciences and scouring souls. 'I
was like a wandering bird!' wrote John Nelson,

> cast out of the nest, till Mr John Wesley came to preach his first
> sermon in Moorfields. O, that was a blessed morning to my soul!
> As soon as he got upon the stand, he stroked back his hair, and
> turned his face towards where I stood, and I thought fixed his
> eyes upon me . . . I thought his whole discourse was aimed at me.
> When he had done, I said, 'This man can tell the secrets of my
> heart . . .' That evening, under Mr Wesley's sermon [a subsequent
> one, on Kennington Common], I could do nothing but weep, and
> love and praise God for sending his servant into the fields to
> show me the way of salvation.[20]

But what gave Wesleyan Methodism its especial momentum,
the ingredient which made it unique among the rival or rebel
religious movements of the day (of Howel Harris for instance,
in Wales, of Ingham and the Moravians, or of Whitefield and
Lady Huntingdon – and there were not a few others) was the
thoroughness of its discipline and organization. What counted
was not so much the emotional conversion as the well-managed
follow-up. It was relatively easy, given the suitably charged
atmosphere, the practised evangelist, the suggestible audience,
to find converts desperately ready to off-load their weight of sin.
The country was full of people most unlike Horace Walpole;
aware vaguely that they ought to be good Christians but instead
feeling themselves full of guilt; some of them churchgoing but
untouched by the prescribed services and by sermons that went
over their heads; many altogether neglecting or neglected by the
Church, yet remaining mistily and distantly 'Christian'; very
many struggling amid the evils and insufficiencies of their earthly
situation, starved (on a Christian diagnosis) of the nutriment
without which man is a spiritual cripple, or deprived (on a
Marxist) of the opium which might serve to mitigate the severity
of their lot. There could never be a shortage of potential converts. The fields were always 'white unto harvest' – the metaphor
was one so constantly employed by the early Methodist evangelists
that it declined into a cliché – but the real test came with the
harvest itself and the storing of the grain.

During his lifetime Wesley's Methodism remained effectively an autocracy. Ultimate control of its doctrines, practices, administration, and finances rested with him only. The annual Conference was a meeting less for decision-taking after debate than for receiving rulings and exhortation from Wesley, to be passed on as necessary to society members. Methodist membership itself rested finally at his discretion, even after numbers became too large for every individual's worthiness to be regularly inspected by him personally. But the system of enrolment in classes, weekly class meetings for prayer and worship and communal confession, the organization of the bands, the collection and management of local funds by stewards accountable to Wesley, the ever-increasing employment of lay preachers, some like the Wesleys themselves itinerant over the whole country, some confined to their own locality or 'circuit' – all this worked with remarkable success. This is not to say that the Methodist classes and bands were everywhere compact of mutual love and Christian understanding. On the contrary, there is plenty of evidence of backbiting, tale-telling, and petty quarrels. But the tendency towards fission inherent in a popular movement such as Wesley's was held in check, at least during his lifetime, partly by his own paramount prestige, but no less by the fact that ultimately all the preachers and local office-holders were not so much representatives of their various Methodist flocks as delegates (if need be immediately dismissible) of Wesley himself.

He recruited his lay helpers with conscientious care – they were 'to be strictly examined on three points, Have they grace, gifts, and fruit?' – and he always regarded them, even after they in several instances had become his personal friends, as essentially his pupils, or even servants. 'To me', he wrote, 'the preachers have engaged themselves to submit, to serve me as sons in the gospel.' Even if often operating of necessity at a distance, he was again a tutor, and one wielding wider influence than ever he could at Oxford; doctrinal instructor, spiritual guide, moral adviser, director of studies, father figure to a fervent and fast growing band of enthusiasts – all of them in the modern and not a few in the current pejorative sense. By 1747 they numbered between fifty and sixty in all, twenty-two fully itinerant. From its inception a number of them were invited to attend the annual Conference. The one held in 1747 issued specific advice on how

they were to preach, and thought it necessary among other
things to pronounce, wisely no doubt, against their singing
hymns of their own composition. More general counsel to his
preachers was set out by Wesley in the form of a set of rules to
guide their conduct:

> Be diligent. Never be unemployed. Never be triflingly employed.
> Never *while* away time. Be serious . . . Avoid all lightness, jesting,
> and foolish talking. Converse sparingly and cautiously with
> women, particularly with young women. Take no step towards
> marriage without solemn prayer to God and consulting your
> brethren. Believe evil of no one unless fully proved . . . Speak
> evil of no one . . . Tell every one what you think wrong in him,
> lovingly and plainly, and as soon as may be, else it will fester in
> your own heart. Do not affect the gentleman . . . Be ashamed of
> nothing but sin; no, not of cleaning your own shoes when
> necessary. Be punctual . . . Do not mend our rules, but keep
> them . . . You have nothing to do but to save souls. Therefore
> spend and be spent in this work . . .[21]

Many of the men he was addressing, then mostly young or in
their early middle years, were later encouraged by him to write
an account of their life. From these (some, like Nelson's or
Walsh's, full-scale autobiographies) it appears that most of them
came from the families of yeomen, small manufacturers, tradesmen or craftsmen. To look at a few of them: John Nelson, stonemason, was the son of another stonemason; Thomas Mitchell,
also from Yorkshire, had been a stonemason's apprentice; John
Haime of Shaftesbury had been apprenticed to his uncle, a
button-maker, before he joined the army. Peter Jaco of Newlyn
in Cornwall was a fisherman's son, Christopher Hopper of
Ryton in Durham a farmer's. So was William Hunter from
neighbouring Northumberland, and the orphan Thomas Olivers
was brought up by his Welsh farmer uncle. John Pawson was the
son of a 'respectable' farmer-cum-builder near Leeds. Alexander
Mather, son of a 'reputable' baker in Brechin, having first 'on a
childish frolic' joined the rebels at the age of thirteen and escaped
from Culloden, became a baker too, and one who successfully
maintained opposition to baking on Sundays. George Story
from Harthill in the West Riding (who was brought up, he
says, among books and before he was six 'had read the Bible
through several times') became a printer, and Joseph Cownley

of Leominster a magistrate's travelling secretary.

For all the diversity of their upbringing, their character, and early experience, there emerges a pattern of similarities. Most of them had received the sort of schooling then thought adequate for boys of their station. In general, their capabilities were probably above the common run. Nearly all of them seem to have been brought up in the ways, or at least the formalities, of religion, and most of them later tormented themselves with self-accusations of adolescent guilt and the sins of early manhood. Some (writes Southey) 'passed through struggles of mind that bordered on madness'. John Pawson relates how 'he roared for the very disquietness of his soul', Thomas Olivers how he was 'one of the most profligate and abandoned young men living', John Nelson how at nineteen he found himself 'in great danger of falling into scandalous sins' until God rescued him by giving him a wife. Christopher Hopper 'greedily pursued all the pleasures of the world . . . whatever the devil brought to town or country'; and John Haime, more specific, was 'much given to cursing, swearing, lying, and Sabbath-breaking . . . card-playing, lewdness, and like works of darkness, but not easy in these ungodly practices', being afraid that the Devil would 'carry him away'.

There were indeed times when Haime was convinced the Devil was in the room with him, and was sure that once, having on an impulse of rebellious blasphemy hurled a stick heavenwards at God, he was visited by the apparition of a brown-and-black swan-like giant bird which made hostile passes over him and then alighted forty paces away and glared at him in a very sinister manner; Southey, but not Wesley, was convinced it must have been nothing more devilish than a bustard. George Story, the printer, was unusual among Wesley's preachers in being converted to Methodism from settled sceptical convictions. The majority, reared in orthodox Christian beliefs, found themselves sooner or later at a crisis in their lives, longing for the strength to cast off their overmastering sins and discover a fresh path to godliness. They were prime candidates for being 'born again' into a new life under God's grace. Among such men the fields were indeed white unto the Wesleys' harvest. Their stories are akin to that of the young John Bunyan a century earlier – the Bunyan of *Grace Abounding to the Chief of Sinners*, a book which as it happens this same John Haime singled out for

its powerful influence upon him. The case of the Bedford tinker
had been much like his own; much like that of dozens more of
Wesley's lay recruits. Bunyan tells how he was beset by remorse
for his wild transgressions in general, and in particular for
having just played tipcat on a Sunday:

> A voice did suddenly dart from heaven into my soul, which said,
> Wilt thou leave thy sins, and go to heaven? or have thy sins, and
> go to hell? At this I was put to an exceeding maze; wherefore,
> leaving my cat upon the ground, I looked up to heaven, and was
> as if I had with the eyes of my understanding seen the Lord Jesus
> looking down upon me, as being very hotly displeased with
> me . . .[22]

Sampson Staniforth, Methodist convert and subsequently lay
preacher, claimed *his* vision of Jesus on the cross remained
constantly with him 'for about ten weeks'; and that Wesley
should have published Staniforth's own account of it without
one qualifying remark, Southey comments severely, was 'obviously to encourage wild and dangerous enthusiasm'.[23]

Wesley had not chosen his preachers for their docility, and not
all of them remained his obedient followers. Of the four privileged
to be invited to the first Conference, in 1744, three later broke
ranks: Thomas Richards, Thomas Maxfield and John Bennet.
All three of the men appointed to be Wesley's first lay preachers,
Joseph Humphreys, Thomas Maxfield and John Cennick, left
him either for the Calvinists or the Moravians (or in Cennick's
case each in turn). The Moravian Brotherhood also claimed
Charles Delamotte, who to speak strictly had become the very
first Methodist lay preacher of all, when he deputized for Wesley
in Georgia. There were other defectors, and not a few whom
Wesley felt bound to be rid of. While his personal influence
over the majority remained immense, there were always to be
many who found his dominance irksome.

Charles Wesley not only looked anxiously at the doubtful
Anglican loyalty of some of his brother's preachers but also seems
to have viewed the social origins of some of them with misgiving.
He wrote to John Bennet to tell him, 'A friend of ours' – John
Wesley – 'has made a preacher of a tailor; I, with God's help,
will make a tailor of him again.' There were times ahead when he
was inclined to sympathize with Laurence Sterne's contemptuous

verdict: 'illiterate mechanics, much fitter to make a pulpit than to get into one'.

At the level of personal friendship, there can surely never have been anyone more disinterestedly candid, more fearlessly direct in his advice and criticism, than Wesley. With his subordinates, his preachers in particular, it was no doubt to be expected, since he was at once their censor of morals, postal tutor, professional counsellor, and father in God. He wrote to them and of them as 'brothers'; the tone, however, whether commendatory, hortatory, advisory, or (as not infrequently) reproving was never other than paternal. But it is the line he adopted towards those who would have rated themselves his social equals, or often superiors, that sometimes astonishes by its refusal to consider any tempering of the wind, its uncompromising contempt for convention or even elementary tact. Tact did not rate high in Wesley's order of virtues. If faults and failings were there to be discerned, it was his business in the name of God and the cause of salvation to point them out, not least to those personally close to him; indeed to them most earnestly of all.

This missionary concern is well seen in various letters to his business adviser and friend Ebenezer Blackwell, banker and Methodist benefactor, the man within the comforts of whose fine house in Lewisham Wesley lay in the autumn of 1753, when he thought he was dying. Why, asked Wesley, did Blackwell remain an 'almost' rather than an 'altogether' Christian, despite a real desire to please God? Was it because he was too sanguine, possessor of 'a natural cheerfulness of temper, which, though in itself it be highly desirable, yet may easily slide into an extreme?' Did he not suffer from an excessive desire to please all men? Was he not ashamed of holiness rather than sin? 'I have feared that you are not so bold for God now as you was four or five years ago ... O sir, let us beware of this! ... You have a thousand enemies – the flattering, frowning world, the rulers of darkness of this world, and the grand enemy within ... O may God warn you continually by his inward voice ...'[24] And again in the following year: 'Since I left London I have had many thoughts concerning you, and sometimes uneasy ones.' Was Mr Blackwell falling back? What had occasioned 'this feebleness of mind?'

Was it because he conversed more than was necessary with men that were 'without God'? Did even his apparently innocent enjoyment of his garden occupy too large a place in his thoughts and affections? 'I know Mrs Blackwell and you desire to please God in all things. You will, therefore, receive these hints as they are intended . . .'[25]

If we pay Wesley the compliment of respecting the nakedness of his candour we must likewise concede merit for his unruffled readiness to receive counter-criticism – though this was not the same thing as accepting its justice. 'With regard to myself', he told Blackwell,

> You do well to warn me against 'popularity, a thirst of power and applause, against envy producing a seeming contempt for the conveniences and grandeur of this life, against an affected humility, against sparing from myself to give to others from no other motive than ostentation'. I am not conscious to myself that this is my case. However, the warning is always friendly . . . considering how deceitful my heart is and how many the enemies that surround me.[26]

Most revealing too is a long adjuration of Wesley's addressed to Sir James Lowther, of Whitehaven, who as magistrate had once acted very fairly towards the Methodists on the occasion of a riot against them in 1749. Now the year was 1754, and Sir James lay dying. He was, though with a penny-pinching reputation, easily the wealthiest man in the locality, reckoned to be worth '£40,000 a year, and some millions in ready money'. One day Wesley paid him a visit, and within a few hours had hammered home by letter the uncomfortable message he had just in person delivered:

> . . . I rejoice that I have seen you this once, and that God enabled you to bear with patience what I spoke in the simplicity of my heart . . . You are on the borders of the grave, as well as I; shortly we must both appear before God. When it seemed to me, some months since, that my life was near an end, I was troubled that I had not dealt plainly with you. This you will permit me to do now . . . I reverence you for your office of magistrate; I believe you to be an honest, upright man . . . But so much the more am I obliged to say (though I judge not; God is the judge), I fear you are covetous, that you love the world. And if you do, as sure as the word of God is true, you are not in a state of salvation . . . [Sir

James is then accused of not having given enough of his money
away.] You cannot go about to look for poor people; but you
may be sufficiently informed of them by those who can . . . I
rejoice that you have given some hundreds of pounds to the
hospitals, and wish it had been ten thousand. To the support of
the family I did not object; but begged leave to ask whether this
could not be done without giving ten thousand a year to one who
had so much already . . . I likewise granted that the family had
continued above four hundred years; but observed meantime that
God regarded it not one jot the more for this . . . Is not death at
hand? . . . Will you then rejoice in the money you have left behind
you . . . to support the pride and vanity and luxury which you
have yourself despised all your life long? O sir, I beseech you,
for the sake of God, for the sake of your own immortal soul,
examine yourself whether you do not love money. If so, you
cannot love God. And if we die without the fear of God, what
remains? Only to be banished from him for ever and ever.

   I am, with true respect, sir,
   Your servant for Christ's sake
    John Wesley[27]

Then there was Samuel Furly, setting out in life at much the
same time as Lowther was leaving it. An undergraduate at
Cambridge destined for the priesthood, Furly seems to have been
a serious young man, looking towards Wesley as auxiliary tutor,
in matters both academic and spiritual; and Wesley's many
letters to him and his sister (she married one of the cleverest of
Wesley's preachers, John Downes*) tell a good deal more of the
sender than the recipients.[28]

That Cambridge was a perilous place to be at, Wesley was in no
doubt. For one thing, there was the danger of frequent conversation with 'good natur'd honest triflers'. 'The less you speak', he
counselled, '(unless to God) the better . . . Fight your way
through.' But Satan sowed mischief: young Furly frankly confessed to a hankering after some female charmer. 'Dear Sammy',
Wesley replied sternly, 'conquer desire, and you will conquer
fear . . . Never write to that person at all, nor of her, and continue
instant in prayer. Cut off the right hand and cast it from you;

---

 * Downes had a bent for mathematics and mechanics – 'by nature,'
Wesley roundly asserted, 'full as great a genius as Sir Isaac Newton'. When
Downes's health began to fail, he set him up in London to supervise his
printing.

otherwise you will be a dastardly wretch all your days.' The girl, on whom of course Wesley had never set eyes, was 'a poor silly worm like yourself . . . Fight, Sammy, fight!' And from Dublin, on Good Friday 1756, Sammy received the sternest of reprimands:

> How? Going up to town? Are you stark, staring mad? Will you leap into the fire with your eyes open? Fly for your life, for your salvation. If you thus tempt the spirit of God any more, who knows what may be the consequence? I should not wonder at all to hear you was confined at St Luke's hospital. [If Sammy should find he could not stick to his studies at Cambridge] quit the college at once . . . Come away to me . . . You are on the brink of the pit . . .

Far from falling in, Sammy survived pretty respectably as a country parson and devout evangelical; but Wesley's concern for him had been only imperfectly rewarded, for Furly became 'a regular clergyman unconnected with the Methodists'. Certainly, as Wesley admitted to Miss Furly, this was the best way to preferment; but it was *not* 'the best way to heaven or to good upon earth'.

CHAPTER 10

Grace Murray

AMONG THE BETTER EDUCATED of Wesley's preachers was John Bennet. Born of Dissenter parents in Derbyshire, intended at one time for the Christian ministry, but setting up in business as a carrier at the age of twenty-two, converted soon thereafter to Methodism, introduced to Wesley by Lady Huntingdon, he was soon one of the most successful evangelists in the counties of Derbyshire, Cheshire and Lancashire. In 1746 he fell ill, and for six months remained at the Orphan House at Newcastle, being looked after there by the housekeeper-in-charge, Mrs Grace Murray, a widow in her late twenties. A mutual attachment arose, and John Bennet came to be more or less accepted as Grace Murray's intended second husband.

Born and brought up in Newcastle, at the age of twenty she had been married to a Scottish master mariner, Alexander Murray. Then, when she was staying with her sister in London during an absence of her husband at sea, and was perhaps emotionally vulnerable just after the death of a baby, she had gone to hear Whitefield and the two Wesleys preach and had become a Methodist, thereby incurring her husband's anger on his return. On his next voyage he was drowned. One of her letters preserved in Charles Wesley's journal of May 1740 shows well enough the converted Mrs Murray's evangelical cast of thought, her recent psychological crises and religious self-examinings, her full-blooded adoption of the vocabulary of the saved:

> I had seen myself a lost sinner, bound with a thousand chains ...
> My soul was like the troubled sea. Then did I see my own evil
> heart ... I cried out in bitter anguish of spirit, 'Save, Lord, or I

perish.' In my last extremity, I saw my Saviour full of grace and
truth for me . . . My peace returned . . . Now my joy is calm and
solid; my heart drawn out to the Lord continually . . . Dear Sir,
I have spoke the state of my heart, as before the Lord. I beg your
prayers . . .[1]

Remaining for a time in London, she was made a band leader at
Moorfields by Wesley, but returned to Newcastle soon after the
opening of the Orphan House there, and by the time she came to
be tending John Bennet in his illness was already Wesley's
leading woman Methodist in Newcastle, assisting the preachers
and both addressing and inspecting the women's bands.

John Bennet was not the first who had made overtures in the
direction of this comely and capable young widow. An earlier
projected union seems to have fallen through because of her
suitor's religious inadequacies, and thereafter for a time she had
undergone spells of depression. Obviously Grace Murray was no
light flirt, as some in retrospect came to allege; on the contrary,
she was highly charged with that 'seriousness' which Wesley so
uncompromisingly insisted on; she was 'filled with God'. Both
Bennet and Grace Murray indeed stood very high in Wesley's
estimation. Bennet he was disposed to treat much more nearly on
terms of equality than most of his helpers. As for Mrs Murray,
he decided that she was endowed with 'every qualification'.

> She understands all I want to have done. She is remarkably neat
> in person, in clothes, in all things. She is nicely frugal, yet not
> sordid. She has much common sense; contrives everything for
> the best; makes everything go as far as it can go; foresees what is
> wanting and provides it in time; does all things quick, and yet
> without hurry. She is a good work-woman; able to do the finest,
> ready to do the coarsest work, observes my rules . . . and takes
> care that those about her observe them . . .

The desirability of celibacy in priests and preachers, so often
commended by Wesley both verbally and in print, was plainly
about to face a critical challenge from the even greater desirability
of such a proximate paragon; and the proximity was emphasized
when in August 1748 it was Wesley's turn to be ill, with sickness
and headache; was it, he wondered, animal food that did it? At
Newcastle he took, if only briefly, to his bed and his grains of
ipecacuanha, becoming thus, like Bennet two years before, the
subject of Mrs Murray's efficient care.

John and Charles had mutually agreed that neither would
marry without first consulting the other; and Charles's celibate
intentions too were weakening very noticeably at this time. At
Newcastle there was Mrs Murray. At Garth on the Wye in
Breconshire there was the no less charming and socially rather
more exalted Miss Sarah, or Sally, Gwynne (daughter of Marma-
duke Gwynne, landowner and magistrate), in whom Charles
was displaying a persistent interest. The future for the Wesleys'
celibacy did not look promising. As for John, it was not that
during his indisposition at Newcastle the kind attentions of the
amiable, pious and efficient Mrs Murray entirely swept him off
his feet. He did not exactly propose to her then and there. As
with Miss Hopkey in Georgia, now with Mrs Murray, he found
himself in a disturbing quandary. *Exactly* and unequivocally to
propose marriage to anyone was not something of which Wesley,
now forty-five, seemed capable. But what he did say to Grace
Murray was quite enough to put her in a state of indecision even
more disturbing than his own. 'If ever I marry', he was moved to
inform her, 'I think you will be the person.' She was not so
irrevocably attached to John Bennet that words like those from
so admired and dynamic a man as Wesley, a figure famous
throughout the land by then, could fail to set up in her heart a
turmoil of emotions. She certainly did not discourage him; 'It
was so great a blessing that she knew not how to believe it. It
seemed all as a dream.'[2]

That she was held in special esteem was further clear when,
immediately after this, she was invited to accompany him,
together with Bennet, William Mackford of Newcastle, and that
'mad' Rev. Grimshaw of Haworth on a preaching tour of the
Yorkshire West Riding and Lancashire. Thus, as it happened,
she came to be involved with them in one of the more vicious of
anti-Methodist riots, in the neighbourhood of Colne in
Lancashire, where the curate played some part in whipping up
popular feeling against them. Wesley's party were punched,
stoned, clubbed, dragged by their hair, thrown into the river;
and at one stage in these proceedings taken forcibly by a roaring
(and Wesley said drunken) mob to see the curate, who then
demanded an undertaking that the Methodists would stay
permanently away from his parish. Wesley's verbal reply was
substantially incorporated within hours in a long letter of

protest to the curate, and this in turn was itself incorporated in
the next-to-be-published instalment of the *Journal.* He 'would
sooner cut off his hand than make any such promise'. As for Mr
Grimshaw, 'he was ready to go to prison or death for Christ's
sake'.[3]

When the time came for Wesley to move again southward,
Grace Murray travelled with him, riding pillion, part of the way
from Newcastle. Then, with an ill judgement unnatural in a
serious wooer, he left her in the company of Bennet, his obvious
rival, and made off on further rounds of preaching, in the home
counties, the Midlands, the West Country, Cornwall, Wiltshire,
Essex; examining the bands betweenwhiles in London, in
Bristol, in Kingswood; writing tracts, pamphlets, hymns; interviewing, editing, extracting for his *Christian Library* – a routine
autumn and winter's labour. Bennet, again close to Grace,
renewed his attentions. Was there 'anything between' her and
John Wesley? he wanted to know. There was not, she said,
though she would not consent to marry Bennet without Wesley's
approval. Both of them then wrote to him; and, part of him
feeling depressed, even betrayed, another part perhaps half-
relieved at being spared the necessity of making so mind-racking
a decision, he did give his consent to a marriage which Grace's
letter had supposed 'the will of God'. There were delays, however.
Grace even declared that she would 'live and die with John
Wesley'; and still, by the spring of 1749, she remained Mrs
Grace Murray, widow.

Wesley then sent her a letter making a straight proposal; not
indeed of marriage, but that she should accompany him (and a
lay preacher named Tucker) on his forthcoming, third, tour of
Ireland. According to Wesley he had arranged this with her the
previous August. Her special duty would be to address, interview,
and 'regulate' the female classes. She was to meet him at Bristol.
Fluttered anew by the prospects reopening before her, she wrote
to Bennet that if he loved her, he should arrange to see her *en
route* at Sheffield, for she was 'sent for to Ireland', and if he did
not come she 'could not answer for what might follow'. He did
not come.

She met Wesley as arranged, and was with him in Bristol when
Charles arrived, with his friend Charles Perronet, from London.
Charles Wesley had finally tied up the negotiations for the hand

of his Sally and was about to be married. The pre-nuptial trans-
actions had not been concluded without difficulty. Though
emphatically a gentleman and in general well received in the
Gwynne household, Charles had no money; and Mrs Gwynne,
to whom her husband surrendered the business of treaty-making,
insisted that their daughter must have an adequate settlement.
Charles had already consulted his brother about marrying, in
accordance with their agreement; and then it had been *John* who
'proposed three persons' as acceptable choices for his brother,
Sally Gwynne fortunately being one of the three. Had either
John or Mrs Gwynne, or of course Sally herself, maintained an
objection, Charles declared he would have treated it as 'an
absolute prohibition from God'. (The objection of Sally's brother,
though 'vehement', luckily did not carry the same power of
veto.)

John had again to be consulted over Mrs Gwynne's required
£100 a year settlement for her daughter, and eventually promised
it from the proceeds of his own books, an undertaking of whose
practicality and reliability Mrs Gwynne first requested independent
assurances.

When all appeared to have been amicably settled, and Charles,
united with his brother and Grace Murray and Billy Tucker, was
setting out with them for Wales, John suddenly 'appeared full of
scruples, and refused to go to Garth at all'.[4] What these were
exactly Charles does not tell us; with the Wesleys, weddings and
scruples were always inextricably interlocked; but in the end,
agreeing to nominate God as final arbiter, they crossed the
Bristol Channel to Wales. There Charles 'did not take kindly' to
the delays involved in John's insistence on keeping strictly to
his full preaching programme; but John was pleased at his
reception and the calm good humour of the crowds assembled
to hear him. At last, on 7 April 1749, four days late, they arrived
at Garth. John who, on the 3rd Charles had thought 'quite
averse to signing his own agreement', did sign after a conversation with Mrs Gwynne had dispelled his reservations.

So John Wesley married his brother to Sarah Gwynne in
Garth Church, a celebration according to Charles 'cheerful
without mirth, serious without sadness'. He thought his brother
'the happiest person among us' – an odd comment, surely, from a
cheerful bridegroom, whose journal moreover adds: 'A stranger,

that intermeddleth not with our joy, said, "It looked more like a funeral than a wedding".'

Wesley spent three months on this Irish tour (April-July 1749). Methodists in Ireland were necessarily a minority of a minority, but he did not at all despair of his mission there. He had some 'triumphant' hours among his societies, proud of 'the many who did run well', endeavouring to see 'all who were weary and faint in their minds', preaching away as tirelessly as ever. At Athlone at 5 a.m. on 7 May he claimed to have among his con- gregation 'great numbers of poor papists (as well as protestants) maugre all the labour of their priests'. In Cork, however, the Catholic mob was so dangerously rampant that it was as much as Wesley could do to get quickly through the town towards territory safer for Protestants.

Throughout this Irish evangelizing Grace Murray was his fellow labourer. 'She examined all the women in the smaller societies, and the believers in every place. She settled all the women bands, visited the sick, prayed with the mourners.' As for the closeness of their relationship, Wesley always maintained that even in Newcastle the previous summer, though their engagement was 'not so explicit as would stand good in law', it was still such a one 'as ought in conscience to have prevented any other till it should be dissolved'. In Dublin he took it a stage further: still no formal engagement, but an exchange of vows described learnedly by Wesley as a contract *de praesenti.**

But Grace Murray,[5] whose emotional inconstancy was a match for Wesley's procrastinating indecisiveness, began back in Bristol again to blow hot and cold. She took offence at what she considered to be his over-affectionate conduct towards sister Molly Francis. (However innocently, he could never resist being indiscreetly charming to young ladies.) Grace thereupon resumed correspondence with Bennet, who promised to meet her when she travelled north again. During the intervening month she remained with Wesley, part of the time at Kingswood, where among the pupils was little Jacky Murray, Grace's one surviving child, and where Wesley on 1 August, spending 'a solemn hour' with the children, once more 'settled all things there'. If he married Grace, and God gave them offspring, these also were to

* There were many legal precedents for such verbal contracts being subsequently held to be binding.

be sent at the earliest permissible age to Kingswood, so that he
and she might continue their labour in the field together, disturbed
as little as possible by domestic hindrances. (Did she, one wonders,
find this undoubtedly great and good, as well as attractive, John
Wesley of hers a shade inhuman?) With some of the sisters in
London she took to discussing her emotional predicament, and
it was not reassuring to be told by one of them that she did not
have enough 'humility, or meekness, or patience' to be kindly
accepted as Mrs Wesley: 'if you love him', one said, 'never think
of it more'.

The two of them journeying north at the beginning of September had reached Epworth when they ran into Bennet, to whom
meanwhile Grace had forwarded all Wesley's letters to her.
There followed an unhappy confrontation. Bennet claimed Grace
as of right. Wesley asserted the superiority of his own claim, but
then (for the second time) agreed to abandon it in Bennet's
favour. Grace pronounced she would have John Bennet; then,
overwrought, took to her bed. When Wesley visited her, again
she reversed course. 'My dear sir', she cried, 'how can you
possibly think I love any other better than you? I love you a
thousand times better than ever I loved John Bennet in my life.
But I know not what to do. I am afraid if I don't marry him he
will run mad.' Very shortly after this she again told Bennet it
was he she would have.

However, it was with Wesley that she and the drama moved
north to Newcastle, from where Wesley dispatched to Bennet,
by a messenger who never delivered it, a long, bitter letter of
passionate accusation. Bennet had been treacherous and unfaithful. He well knew that Grace was 'such a person as I had
sought in vain for many years, and then determined not to part
with'. Wesley even claimed that he had been forming her 'to his
hand for ten years'. He had been *robbed*.

> Was this consistent with gratitude or friendship? nay, with
> common justice? . . . Oh that you would take scripture and reason
> for your rule instead of blind and impetuous passion! . . . You
> may tear her away by violence. But my consent I cannot, dare not
> give: nor, I fear, can God give you his blessing.[6]

Yet when, still in Wesley's company as they rode on to Berwick,
Grace besought him to marry her forthwith, his answer puts one

in mind of a ploy by some latterday politician, scared of the possibility of some proposal being actually implemented, and recommending that the whole matter should be examined by a royal commission: 'I told her before this could be done it would be needful (1) to satisfy John Bennet (2) to procure my brother's consent, and (3) to send an account of the reasons on which I proceeded to every helper and every society in England, at the same time desiring their prayers.'

Grace, it seems moderately enough, said that she could not wait longer than one year for these preliminaries to mature; whereupon Wesley offered the encouragement of hoping it might not take all that time. Grace went on (one must surely guess meltingly) to relate the whole story of her love for her bold sea captain, yet how in the end she had defied and even threatened to leave him, sooner than abandon the Christ whom Wesley and his Methodists had shown her. To these confidences, and perhaps one should say appeals, Wesley's own account of his response – though Bennet accused him of pursuing Grace 'inflamed with love and lust' – reads with a depressingly limp inadequacy. 'This', he wrote, 'endeared her to me more than before; and yet at the same time strongly inclined me to believe that the severe discipline was designed to prepare her for a comforter of many, a mother in Israel.' ('A mother in Israel': in the current Methodist vocabulary a stock commendatory phrase for such women as 'did run well'.)

Never less than thorough, Wesley took care at about this time to enquire what other brothers and sisters in and around Newcastle thought of his intended wife. Some of the replies hardly witness to that exemplary charity and mutual respect which he loved to claim for his society members: Grace Murray was proud; she was insolent; she should not have ridden pillion behind Wesley; she had bought a new 'joseph' before the old one was worn out; she had been known to wear a fine holland shift, had spent far too much on a new apron, etc. Having started the enquiries, Wesley resolved to ignore them: 'jealousy and envy', he decided, 'were the real ground of most of the accusations'.

At Grace's request the verbal contract first made in Dublin was now renewed, before the lay preacher Christopher Hopper; and John wrote, as arranged, to his brother to tell him of his marriage intentions. Then, leaving Grace with friends at Hindley, near Allendale in Northumberland, he set off westwards through the Lake District to Whitehaven, where he was engaged to preach.

At this juncture a hitherto subsidiary character in the unfolding drama suddenly assumed the centre of the stage. Charles Wesley was by no means sure that his brother should contemplate marriage. In any case, it most certainly ought not to be to Grace Murray, the daughter of labouring folk and a woman who was, after all, only his brother's servant. The more he contemplated the preposterous proposition the clearer appeared his Christian duty to put a stop to it.

Storming post-haste to Newcastle, he had just enough time to reinforce his prejudices by collecting such unfavourable verdicts upon Mrs Murray as were available among the Methodists there, before setting off again towards Whitehaven and his allegedly besotted brother. There he excitedly spilled forth his objections: Grace's lack of social standing, the fact that she had travelled in company with Wesley for six months, and people would say he was marrying his mistress; and finally, that she was in any case promised to another with a prior claim, John Bennet.

Wesley's reaction to his brother's outburst was apparently mild, reasonable, yet determined. He brushed aside the issue of class: 'Whoever I marry I believe it will not be a gentlewoman. I despair of finding any such so qualified.' That Grace had lived under one roof with him so long merely argued that he was not likely to be deceived in her. That she had travelled the country with him was another positive recommendation: he would never marry any woman till he had proof that she both could and would share the hardships of itinerancy. When the unconvinced and unappeased Charles had ridden off to return to Hindley and Mrs Murray, John sat soberly down and methodically put on paper the pros and cons of his marrying her. He concluded at last that the pros 'totally set aside' the cons.

Charles meanwhile, armed with a letter he had composed for his 'dear sister and friend' Grace, was riding hard to deliver it to her personally. Arriving at Hindley, he first kissed her, then breathlessly accused her of breaking his heart, and next collapsed in a faint, recovering to deliver her his very unpleasant-sounding letter. This began by again accusing her of having 'wellnigh broke' his heart:

. . . Neither my soul nor my body will ever recover the wound: this life I mean. But *there* the weary are at rest, *there* all tears are wiped away from our eyes. Fain would I hope you can say something in your defence . . . which now I know not . . . [John Wesley's] doing such an action would destroy himself and me and the whole work of God . . . Had not the Lord restrained you, what a scandal had you brought upon the Gospel. Nay, and you would have left your name as a curse upon God's people. But I spare you and hope in ignorance you did it. Be not therefore troubled overmuch. I never intend to speak a hard word to you about it, but pray for you and love you, till we meet at the marriage supper of the Lamb.

The conditional tenses make it clear that Charles was already confident that he had rescued Methodism from disgrace and spiked his brother's guns.

All action again, within two hours he had Grace on his pillion and was heading her towards Newcastle before John might be able to get upon the scene himself. Apparently he imagined his brother was after them, and he even 'used several stratagems to elude his pursuer', losing his way as a result and having to put up at the house of an acquaintance during a night which at least for weak, wavering, storm-tossed Mrs Murray was wretched and sleepless. Leaving her temporarily behind now, Charles went on to meet John Bennet and his sympathizers at the Orphan House, where sister Murray and even Wesley himself seemed to retain few staunch friends. She was his whore – worse, one he had tired of and was now ready to thrust into a corner. John Wesley was 'a child of the devil'. 'If John Wesley is not damned there is no God.'

His strength renewed 'after a flux for some days', Wesley had in fact followed his brother to Hindley, but arrived two hours too late. His host, James Broadwood, broke down in tears. If Wesley also did, he does not record it: 'I said, "The Lord gave, and the Lord hath taken away: blessed be the name of the Lord!" '

Broadwood soon after rode off to Newcastle to try to bring Grace back; but Wesley, having 'calmly committed the cause to God', turned his thought towards the text he was to expound that evening. Perhaps it was not quite a coincidence that he chose the twentieth chapter of Revelation, at the identical verse upon which he had preached at his mother's funeral. 'It was', he said, 'as though we were already standing before "that great white throne".' The next day – 'a day never to be forgotten' – he spent in fasting, prayer and self-examination, not least on the question whether his love for Grace Murray was or was not 'inordinate'.

> I need add no more, than that if I had had more regard for her I loved than for the work of God I should now have gone straight on to Newcastle, and not back to Whitehaven. I knew this was giving up all; but I knew God called, and therefore on Friday the 29th I set out again for Whitehaven. The storm was exceedingly high, and drove full in my face, so that it was not without difficulty I could sit my horse; particularly as I rode over the broad backs of those enormous mountains which lay in my way. However I kept on as I could, till I came to the brow of Hartside. So thick a fog then fell that I was quickly out of all road, and knew not which way to turn. But I knew where help was to be found, in either great difficulties or small. The fog vanished in a moment ... I set out early on Saturday the 30th, and in the afternoon reached Whitehaven. Today I resumed my spare diet, which I shall probably quit no more.[7]

He recorded (though not in the *Journal* for publication) how ghoulishly the vision of Grace pursued him in sleep. He dreamed that he was watching her being taken out at some place like Tyburn to execution:

> She spoke not one word, nor showed any reluctance ... The sentence was executed, without her stirring either hand or foot. I looked at her, till I saw her face turn black. Then I could not bear it, but went away. But I returned quickly, and desired she might be cut down. She was then laid upon a bed. I sat by mourning over her. She came to herself and began to speak, and I awaked.[8]

George Whitefield, also on a preaching tour in the North country, had run into his old friend and first mentor Charles Wesley; heard where John was; and written to Whitehaven suggesting that they meet in Leeds, which happened to fall in with Wesley's originally proposed plans, before the past few days' darkness had closed round him. ('Only so long as I was preaching, I felt ease. When I had done, the weight returned.') It was thus Whitefield to whom the uneasy task fell of confirming to Wesley, directly after an exhausting day's ride of sixteen hours, that Grace and

Bennet were to be married. Lying beside him on the bed, Whitefield, tearful as he was ever liable to be,

> said all that was in his power to comfort me, but it was in vain.
> It was his judgement that she was my wife, and that he had said
> so to J.B.; that he would fain have persuaded them . . . not to
> marry till they had seen me; but that my brother's impetuosity
> prevailed and bore down all before it.[9]

In fact the wedding had by this time already taken place at
Newcastle. Two days later Charles, Bennet and Grace were also
in Leeds. John did not wish to see Charles, and Charles at first
announced he would have no further dealings with John – which
Wesley wrote was 'only adding a drop of water to a drowning
man!'

> Poor Mr Whitefield and John Nelson burst into tears. They
> prayed, cried, and entreated till the storm passed away. We
> could not speak, but only fell on each other's neck. J.B. then
> came in. Neither of us could speak, but we kissed each other and
> wept. Soon after I talked with my brother alone. He seemed
> utterly amazed. He clearly saw I was not what he thought, and
> now blamed her only . . .

This convenient conclusion seems to have provided a formula
which allowed Charles to calm down. A public breach between
the brothers was thus avoided. Wesley then being invited to
visit the Bennets, there ensued another emotional scene, with
Bennet kneeling on one side of Wesley to beg forgiveness for the
harsh things he had said, and Mrs Bennet in like posture on the
other side, repeatedly protesting, when her sobs allowed, that
she 'never had spoken or could speak' ill of him. Bennet even
left the two of them for a while after dinner to talk alone. Then,
within a few days – days of 'business as usual', preaching to 'a
crowded audience . . . crying aloud to them all, scarcely knowing
when to leave off' – Wesley was back on the road to Newcastle
again, composing in the saddle on his journey a largely auto-
biographical poem of thirty-one six-line stanzas treating, inevitably, of profane and sacred love: of the former, when

> Oft as thro' giddy youth I roved
> And danc'd along the flow'ry ways;

when

> . . . love's envenomed dart
> Thrilled thro' my veins and tore my heart,

to the day when

> My soul a kindred spirit found,
> By heaven entrusted to my care;

through protest:

> Oh why dost Thou the blessing send?
> Or why thus snatch away my friend?

to resignation:

> What Thou hast done I know not now!
> Suffice I shall hereafter know;

and finally,

> Teach me from every pleasing snare
> To keep the issues of my heart.
> Be Thou my love, my joy, my fear!
> Thou my eternal portion art . . .

For a little while he tried to forgive Bennet; but only a month after the wedding he had come round to writing a letter full of that 'plain speaking' he was so constantly advocating. The marriage had been against the will of God, 'inconsistent either with justice, mercy, or truth'. 'You tore her from me . . . I think you have done me the deepest wrong.' Furthermore, it seemed that Bennet's theology was running too closely towards Whitefield's. It was so; within two years, after denouncing Wesley and his 'popery' from the pulpit, he persuaded all but twelve members of the Bolton society and almost all those of Stockport to secede from Wesley's connection to one of his own leading; and later became minister of a Calvinist chapel at Warburton, near Warrington. Grace Bennet had five sons by him, and after his death, at the age of forty-five in 1759, she came back into the Wesleyan fold and remained in it until her death in 1803, well over a half-century after those hectic fourteen months of vacillation and trauma when she had so nearly become the wife of John Wesley. Once in 1788, three years before his death, she met Wesley again and spoke briefly with him. If, all those years before, he had proved a less hesitant, less scrupulous, more convincing lover, or she had been more determined to hold out against Charles Wesley's ill-judged interference, might the future of Methodism have been significantly different? It does not seem likely. A *sine qua non* of marriage for Wesley was that it should not be allowed to interfere with his overriding passion, his life's one task, the saving of souls. What might however have turned out very differently, and altogether less dismally, was Wesley's own marital fortunes.

CHAPTER 11

Breaches and Purges

WHITEFIELD'S BROTHERLY TEARS during the dénouement of the Bennet-Wesley-Grace Murray tangle are a reminder of the continuing ambivalence in the relationship between him and Wesley. They had begun together, first as master and pupil then as fellow labourers. In doctrinal separation, they never lost mutual respect, and many times protested mutual love. They regarded one another as branches of the same tree, the ancient oak of the Church of England. Seeing their methods and their style, the heady excitement of their followers, their similar outdoor preaching and popular appeal, the public regarded them as twin manifestations of the same phenomenon. So it was also with Howel Harris and Daniel Rowlands, rival leaders in Wales, or with the various societies founded by Ingham and other revivalists in the North. The 'enthusiasts' tended all to be lumped together as Methodists, and not only by the ignorant; Wesley was repeatedly having to remind his clerical detractors that they must not blame him for the errors of Moravians and predestinarians.

Even for the Moravians some of his old love lingered; for Whitefield considerably more. Yet Calvinist predestinarian Whitefield unarguably was, and the error of it was heinous beyond compromise. In Whitefield's view John Wesley preached two undoubted heresies: universal redemption and Christian perfection. Among men who rated doctrinal correctness as imperative and unnegotiable, the likelihood of further fission and schism was ever-present.

Lady Huntingdon sincerely lamented that there should be any gulf between two such beneficent christianizing influences as

Wesley's and Whitefield's. During 1749, therefore, she tried hard
to reconcile them, and to bring in Howel Harris too. On 3
August Charles Wesley's *Journal* records: 'Our conference this
week with Mr Whitefield and Mr Harris came to nought; I
think, through their flying off.' Yet only two months later he
writes to the banker, Blackwell, 'George Whitefield, and my
brother, and I, are one – a threefold cord which shall no more be
broken'; and by January 1750 Whitefield was offering to assist
occasionally at Wesley's West Street chapel in London. He was
'ready to help all that preach and love the Lord Jesus in sincerity';
and accordingly he and Wesley for a week or two at West Street
jointly officiated at services, alternately sharing prayers and
sermons, sermons and prayers. It was a moment for general
rejoicing and congratulation. Howel Harris joined in by accepting
Wesley's invitation to preach at the Moorfields Foundry. People
might indeed say with justice, remarked Lady Huntingdon, 'See
how these Christians love one another!'[1] Yet even while praising
God for removing a stumbling-block, Wesley could not resist
mixing a dash of judicious censure with his praise of Whitefield:
'How wise is God', he observed, 'in giving different talents to
different preachers. Even Mr Whitefield's little improprieties,
both of language and manner, were a means of profiting many
who would not have been touched by a more correct discourse,
or a more calm and regular manner of speaking.'

Selina, Countess of Huntingdon, that energetically pious great
lady, saw herself as the champion of *all* the Methodists, though
Whitefield had long been the object of her especial admiration.
She had followed the revivalist banner of the Wesley brothers
when she was only twenty-one, in the days of the Fetter Lane
society. Indeed it seems very probable that she had been one of
that company of Wesleyan seceders who in July 1740 marched
out of Fetter Lane, leaving the Moravians and their sympathizers
in control. Her three Hastings sisters-in-law, the Ladies Frances,
Catherine and Margaret, were no less evangelically inclined.
These 'exalted females' (as their kinsman-chronicler describes
them*) '. . . drank in, like thirsty travellers, the refreshing streams
of consolation; they made open profession of faith, and ex-

---

* *The Life and Times of Selina Countess of Huntingdon*, by 'A Member of the
Houses of Shirley and Hastings': a thousand hagiographical pages genteelly
redolent of the earnest piety of early Victorian evangelicalism.

hibited a bright example of female excellence to the world . . .
They were amiably condescending to their inferiors, even to the
poorest, and more especially to the pious poor.' Indeed one of
them, Lady Margaret, went so far in amiable condescension as
to be tied in matrimony to that same Benjamis Ingham who had
gone to Georgia with Wesley and whose north of England
religious societies around the mid-century competed against the
Wesleyan connection there, prospering in some districts to
Wesley's concern and chagrin.

The Countess of Huntingdon's principal mission was less to
condescend to her inferiors than to convert her peers. She
thought highly of both the Wesleys, and eventually collected
round her a kind of ginger group of evangelical Anglican
preachers; but it was Whitefield (when he was available from his
American missioning) whom she deployed in the vanguard of her
assault on the souls of her fellow aristocrats. 'The Methodists
love your big sinners as proper subjects to work upon', wrote an
amused Walpole, 'and indeed they have a plentiful harvest.
Flagrancy was never more in fashion . . . Methodism in this town
is more fashionable than anything but brag; the women play very
deep at both.' There were of course some who refused to play.
The Duchess of Buckingham found it monstrously insulting to
be 'told that you have a heart as sinful as the common wretches
that crawl on the earth'. The King's discarded mistress, Lady
Suffolk, though deaf, was not too deaf to hear that she was being
got at. And the dowager Duchess of Marlborough, while finding Lady Huntingdon's invitation 'obliging' – 'God knows we
all need mending' – had commented that 'women of wit, beauty
and quality cannot bear too many humiliating truths'. The
Duchess of Queensberry was briefly bowled over, but never in
serious danger of permanent capture. It was however alleged that
Frederick Prince of Wales was near to conversion, when death
interposed. Even that ageing unbeliever and former roué Lord
Bolingbroke expressed high approval of Whitefield's oratory; so
too did the Earl of Chesterfield. He wrote to Lady Huntingdon
of the preacher's 'unrivalled' eloquence and 'unequalled' zeal;
not to admire them 'would argue a total absence of taste'. But
while he was willing to contribute £20 towards the building of
Whitefield's new tabernacle in Bristol, he must beg his name 'not
to appear *in any way*'.[2] Perhaps it would not be unfair to see these

distinguished men of the world, and a high proportion of the
fashionable ladies present in Lady Huntingdon's drawing-room,
as coming there to enjoy the shock of a spiritual sauna bath.

It was not John Wesley's milieu at all, though he did preach
several times at Lady Huntingdon's. The more genteel and
socially conventional Charles was comfortably at home in this
setting. He was soon on terms of 'intimate friendship' with Lady
Huntingdon, and 'frequently preached and administered the
sacrament in her ladyship's house, to personages of great distinction'.[3] This was in Park Lane where, following his latest
return from America in 1748, Whitefield preached – or as scoffers
like Walpole might prefer to say, performed – twice weekly. By
that time he had been appointed chaplain to the Countess. By
virtue of her title she was legally permitted to retain such private
clergy, whose numbers during the fifties and sixties would
increase, and include such noted Anglican evangelicals as William
Romaine, Henry Venn and Martin Madan. John Fletcher of
Madeley, Augustus ('Rock of Ages') Toplady, Rowland Hill,
William Grimshaw of Haworth and John Berridge of Everton
in Bedfordshire were others who came to be among Lady
Huntingdon's favoured divines.*

John Wesley was aware that some prominent Methodists
seemed excessively obsequious to the aristocracy, and as early as
August 1744 he was carefully justifying to a critic his own very
different attitude to Lady Huntingdon. A place was reserved for
her at the West Street chapel, he said, only till the Creed. 'If she
does not come before then, anyone takes it that is next, as also
when she is out of town. I doubt', he added, 'whether this respect
to her be not too great; but I yield on this point to my brother's
judgement . . . We have no 5s. or 2s. 6d. places at the Foundery,
nor ever had, nor ever will.'[4] It is an illuminating commentary on
the crowd-pulling power of the leading Methodist preachers that
seating had to be a matter of first come, first served.

As he grew older, his distaste for the grand and the mighty of
this world was to increase. We find him writing as an old man of
seventy-eight, having just attended one of the fashionable

* It was not until 1761 that she began building the first of her own chapels,
at Brighton. Sixty-three others eventually followed, a large proportion of
them in places of affluence and fashion. She was in her seventies before in
1779 a consistorial court ruled them impermissible within the Church of
England, and obliged her to register them all as Dissenting houses.

concerts presented by his musician nephews, Charles's two sons:
'I was a little out of my element among my Lords and Ladies. I
love plain music and plain company best'.[5] Whitefield, on the
other hand, bowed and scraped rather more than was becoming.
That he was 'sensibly touched' by Lady Huntingdon's piety
there is no cause to doubt; but Wesley would never have approached her with Whitefield's servile consciousness of inferior
rank.

However earnestly the two strove to persuade themselves of
their mutual love, each found plentiful source of irritation in the
other, and their respective supporters found even harder the
ways of toleration. In 1752 Whitefield professed to be sure that
'poor Mr Wesley' was losing the doctrinal battle, 'striving against
the stream'. He wagged a pious dogmatic finger in amplification:
'Strong assertions will not go for proofs with those who are
sealed by the Holy Spirit even unto the day of redemption'[6] –
which, reduced from its canting verbiage, presumably meant
simply, 'It's no good arguing with the elect.' Yet Whitefield was
obliged to concede the superior cohesiveness of the Wesleyan
network. 'My brother Wesley acted wisely', he once remarked:
'the souls that were awakened under his ministry he joined in
class and thus preserved the fruits of his labours. This I neglected
and my people are a rope of sand.'[7]

In December 1752 he told Charles Wesley (who was nearer to
him in many ways, including, alas, prose style) that he thought
brother John was 'still jealous' of him and his activities. Certainly
Wesley took umbrage at what was reported to him of the contemptuous 'scoffing', both at himself and Charles, expressed by
some of Whitefield's preachers at his new Moorfields Tabernacle,
with their retailing of 'an hundred shocking stories . . . as un-
questionable facts, and propagating them with an air of triumph
wherever they came'.[8] In the following spring a meeting in
Leeds of forty-odd Wesleyan preachers requested Wesley to
remonstrate against these slanders. As Whitefield's 'dear brother'
and 'affectionate fellow-labourer' he complied, and added:

> Two or three of our brethren afterwards desired me in private
> to mention farther that when you were in the North your con-
> versation was not so useful as was expected; that it generally
> turned not upon the things of God, but on trifles and things
> indifferent; that your whole carriage was not so serious as they

could have desired, being often mixed with needless laughter;
and that those who . . . endeavoured always to speak and act as
seeing God, you rather weakened than strengthened . . . I am
persuaded you will receive these short lines in the same love
wherein I write them . . .'

There were lulls in the battle, unofficial armistices celebrated
by further gestures of respect and co-operation, but never a
treaty of peace. 'Mr Whitefield called upon me', the *Journal* notes
on 5 November 1755: 'disputings are now no more; we love one
another, and join hand in hand.' But when in 1755 James Hervey,
one of Wesley's old Oxford pupils, sent him for comment the
manuscript of a bulky set of theological dialogues he had composed, Wesley, rather as though Hervey was still *in statu pupillari*,
returned the opening chapters with so many corrections, in
particular relating to election and predestination, that Hervey
took offence and returned no reply – though he did *write* one,
and it was published a few years later, after his death. Long
before that Wesley, unable to let so vital a doctrinal matter rest,
advanced into print himself. To believe that God consigned
'unborn souls to hell, and "damned them from their mother's
womb" ', he wrote, '. . . I would sooner be a Turk, a deist, yea
an atheist, than I could believe this. It is less absurd to deny the
very being of God than to make him an almighty tyrant.'

During the early 1760s, a time of turmoil inside some of
Wesley's own societies (arising from some fanatical interpretations
of his doctrine of Christian perfection) there were those among the
predestinarians who professed to see the imminent demise of his
brand of Methodism. The evangelical preacher William Romaine
wrote:

> I pity Mr John [Wesley] from my heart. His societies are in
> great confusion; and the point which brought them into the
> wilderness of rant and madness is still insisted on as much as
> ever . . . I fear the end of this delusion . . . Perfection is still the
> cry . . . May their eyes be opened before it is too late!

This was in reply to a letter from Lady Huntingdon which
enclosed one *she* had just received, full of aggrieved reproof, from
'poor Mr John':[10]

> My Lady, – For a considerable time I have had it much upon
> my mind to write a few lines to your Ladyship; although I cannot

learn that your Ladyship has ever inquired whether I was living or dead. By the mercy of God I am still alive, and following the work to which he has called me; although without any help, even in the most trying times, from those I might have expected it from. Their voice seemed to be rather, 'Down with him, down with him, even to the ground.' I mean (for I use no ceremony or circumlocution) Mr Madan,* Mr Haweis, Mr Berridge, and (I am sorry to say it) Mr Whitefield. Only Mr Romaine has ... acted the part of a brother ...[11]

When in April 1764 he paid a visit to one of his converts and former supporters, Dr Richard Conyers, he reported unhappily:

By the books lying in the window and on the table, I easily perceived how he came to be so cold now, who was so warm a year ago. Not one of ours, either prose or verse, was to be seen, but several of another kind. O that men were as zealous to make Christians as they are to make Calvinists.[12]

And when, that same year, he sent out to fifty or so clergy of an evangelical persuasion a letter begging for some show of unity on a live-and-let-live, agreeing-to-differ, basis, only three chose to reply. He had asked: could they not at least all consent to stop speaking evil of one another, and so deprive their enemies 'in the poor blind world of their sport, "Oh, they cannot agree among themselves" '? And might they not, leaving aside contentious matter (not something, in fact, Wesley was notably good at), concur in a 'common core' of belief in three essentials, original sin, justification by faith, and 'holiness of heart and life'? 'Who knows', he wrote to Lady Huntingdon, 'but it may please God to make your Ladyship an instrument in this glorious work? in effecting an union ... I own freely I am sick of disputing. My whole soul cries out, "Peace! Peace!" – at least, with the children of God.'[13]

But he cried something rather other than peace when he found that Lady Huntingdon was not proposing to treat him and Charles on terms of equality with her favoured Calvinist preachers. At her new chapel in Brighton, for instance, he could not fail to notice

* Later, to Lady Huntingdon's distress, the author of *A Defence of Polygamy*.

that Mr Whitefield, Madan, Romaine, Berridge, Haweis were sent for over and over, and as much notice taken of my brother and me as a couple of postillions. It only confirmed me in the judgement I had formed for many years, I am too rough a preacher for tender ears. 'No, *that is not it*: *but you preach Perfection.*' What! without why or wherefore? Among the unawaken'd? Among babes in Christ? No. To those I say not a word about it . . . I am grieved for your Ladyship. This is no mark of a catholic spirit, but of great narrowness of spirit.

In January 1766 Whitefield visited Wesley, who found that he 'breached nothing but peace and love'. Again in 1767 there were pipings of peace. Wesley adopted Lady Huntingdon's suggestion that he should accept the honorary chaplaincy offered by her ally in piety the Countess of Buchan. (It was in this kind of polite company that Horace Walpole heard him preach at Bath, 'a clean elderly man, fresh coloured, his hair smoothly combed, but with a little soupçon of curls at the ends . . . He spoke his sermon, but so fast, and with so little accent, that I am sure he has often uttered it, for it was like a lesson.') Wesley reciprocated these signs of goodwill by expressing his readiness to let Lady Huntingdon's preachers make as full and free use of the Methodist Room at Bath as his own followers. But he was never wholly at ease, preaching to those of the upper classes to whom Lady Huntingdon and her preachers gave special attention. 'I find', he wrote to Charles, 'a wonderful difference in myself when I am among those who are athirst for God and when I am among fashionable Methodists. On this account, the North of England suits me best, where so many are groaning after full redemption.'[14]

The Countess was at this time in process of establishing her own theological college at Trevecca in Breconshire, and it certainly might have looked like a conciliatory gesture on her part when she appointed to superintend it the vicar of Madeley in Shropshire, the Swiss-born John Fletcher – an anti-Calvinist to preside over what was to be a seminary for Calvinist preachers. It was opened by Whitefield in the summer of 1768. However, Wesley's devotion to seminaries began and ended with his beloved, if exasperating, Kingswood. Writing to his brother, he does not sound as though he hoped for much from Trevecca, or even wished it particularly well: 'Did you ever see anything more queer than their plan of institution? Pray, who planned it, man or woman? I am afraid the Visitor [Fletcher] too will fail'.[15] But he attended and preached at Trevecca's week-long celebration of its first anniversary in 1769, in apparently fraternal amity with John Fletcher; with Howel Harris, Daniel Rowlands and other leading Welsh Calvinists; with the Countesses of Huntingdon and of Buchan, and other fine ladies of Methodist inclination; and with Lady Huntingdon's cousin, who was also one of her staff of chaplains, the Hon. and Rev. Walter Shirley.

These undisputatious events, however, proved to be only the prelude to doctrinal controversy which was to rage furiously all through the 1770s.

Side by side with this obstinate Calvinist-Arminian argument, there were during the fifties and sixties spasms of internal disorder within the Wesleyan body itself. The volatile zeal of the lay preachers, often accompanied by a certain shallowness of education yet considerable popular appeal, made it highly likely that from time to time one or other of them would take off into his own evangelical empyrean, bearing with him a cloud of local devotees. There were several such fanatics almost from the beginning. In a small way Wesley's brother-in-law Hall affords an example, but the most troublesome of these early Wesleyan schismatics was James Wheatley.

An itinerant since 1742, though one whose preaching Wesley came to think 'an unconnected rhapsody of unmeaning words',[16] he commanded ready admiration among those easily given to exaltation. Like Hall, he seems to have graduated through Moravianism to something near to outright Antinomianism. A dozen women from various parts of Wiltshire eventually volunteered to Charles Wesley charges concerning Wheatley's sexual liberality. He, while admitting 'little imprudences' and promising reformation, conceived attack to be the best defence, and lodged accusations of offences similar to his own against a fair number of his fellow preachers. However, when confronted by these gentlemen in Wesley's presence, he declined to substantiate his allegations. He was accordingly presented with a notice of expulsion signed by both brothers Wesley. He had 'wrought folly in Israel' (i.e. in Wiltshire and the West country), and until visibly sincere repentance and/or the next annual Conference, he was 'to abstain both from preaching and from practising physick'.

A man such as Wheatley, however, was not dealt with quite so easily. Indeed he had barely begun his evangelizing career. Transferring to Israel's more easterly confines, he proceeded to wreak substantial further folly in the neighbourhood of Norwich; preached there before enthusiastic congregations; and so, arousing the same sort of local hostility and derision that Methodist preachers were everywhere liable to, caused repeated outbreaks of rioting. On one occasion a victim of the mob was crowned with thorns and scourged; on another a lamb was paraded through the Norwich streets on a pole, while the crowds yelled 'Behold the Lamb of God!' Among Wheatley's new devotees, one woman suffered multiple rape; another who was pregnant was kicked to death; and many experienced physical assault and serious damage to property. Yet when Wheatley's tabernacle was largely destroyed, money was soon forthcoming to build a new and bigger one. He never lacked for congregations or support. Even after an ecclesiastical court in 1754 had found him to be 'lewd, debauched, incontinent, and adulterous' and he had been obliged to shelter awhile abroad, he was able to continue as pastor to his lambs and enjoy the support of divines and ministers of varying persuasions including Whitefield. And when Wesley – to whom Wheatley's lambs were no lambs, but 'bullocks unaccustomed to the yoke'[17] – protested against Whitefield's giving succour to this 'hypocritical' rebel, Whitefield blandly replied that his time was too precious to be spent in listening to 'the false and invidious insinuations of narrow and low-life informers'. He added, 'Sin, I hope, has been prevented, errors detected, sinners convicted, saints edified, and my own soul sweetly refreshed.' He further hoped Jesus would give everybody – and not least, it was implied, Mr Wesley – 'a right judgement in all things'.[18] Between 1758 and 1763 Wesley struggled to regain spiritual authority over these errant Norwich Methodists, but unsuccessfully. Later, Wheatley's tabernacle and its ministers came under the control of trustees appointed by Lady Huntingdon.

After the Wheatley scandals had first flared up in 1751, Wesley commissioned his brother to organize a cleansing purge among their other preachers. Worst infected of all, John and Charles both thought, were those in Ireland. And what was the prime cause of the hearts of so many of their helpers being 'eaten out'? Why, said John, *idleness*; 'absolutely idleness, their not being

constantly employed'. So they should be given a choice: 'Either
follow your trade, or resolve before God to spend the same hours
in reading, etc., which you used to spend in working.'[19] The
purge was to be achieved in part by means of an *ad hoc* one-day
conference held at Leeds, and additionally by private enquiry.
It would not have been like Charles to preside at an *ad hoc* conference without writing an *ad hoc* hymn, and the Leeds proceedings
began with the singing of a dozen or so verses from this characteristic run-of-the-mill Charles Wesley composition:

> Arise, thou jealous God, arise;
>   Thy sifting power exert.
> Look through us with thy flaming eyes,
>   And search out every heart.
>
> Our inmost soul thy spirit knows.
>   And let him now display
> Whom thou hast for thy glory chose,
>   And purge the rest away . . . etc.

The conference rebuked the Scottish pedlar-shoemaker
William Darney, who had received support from Grimshaw of
Haworth and formed his own societies in Yorkshire and Lancashire, for 'railing, begging, and printing nonsense' (his *Collected
Hymns*); and then various investigations, pursued by both
brothers, found several more preachers, including John Bennet,
doctrinally unsound or suspect. As Wesley wrote, in that biblical
lingo of his which has become now in these secular times so
remotely esoterical: 'I see plainly the spirit of Ham, if not of
Korah, has fully possessed several of our preachers.' They had
been led astray from 'the scriptural way, the Methodist way, the
true way'.[20] Of these sons-of-Ham-if-not-of-Korah, only Wheatley
was formally cast out, but between 1751 and 1755 twenty-four
more preachers 'resigned' – some at least of them from a conviction that they had no business subscribing to a movement
still tied, however fractiously, to the Church of England. These
defections posed for a time a likelihood of preacher shortage,
but both brothers agreed it was preferable to have 'ten, or six . . .
of one heart with us and with one another, than fifty of whom we
have no such assurance'. They then put their joint signatures to
an agreement to decide between them the admissibility of their
preachers, with provision in case of a difference arising, for

arbitration by their friend the vicar of Shoreham in Kent, Vincent Perronet.[21]

Further disciplinary measures became imperative a few years later, after a dangerous enthusiasm had taken hold at the very centre of Wesley's connection in London. To some extent the trouble this time was of his own making, since it arose from a perverted interpretation of his teaching on 'Christian perfection', or as Whitefield called it, 'sinless perfection'. (Wesley never used this latter expression, but disclaimed any objection to it.)

Once a man is justified, he does not sin. No other doctrine Wesley taught came in for more general and often furious denials, or caused more questioning even among his own supporters, not least his brother. A major part of his polemical energies during his middle and later years seems to have been taken up in stating, explaining, defending, qualifying, but certainly never retracting this dogma.[22] Though no one is so perfect in this life as to be free from (for example) ignorance or mistake or other things 'unessential to salvation', yet 'we may safely affirm with St John that, since the Gospel was given, "he that is born of God sinneth not" '.[23] 'Christians are saved in this world from all sin, from all unrighteousness; . . . they are now in such a sense perfect as not to commit sin, and to be freed from evil thoughts and evil tempers.' Over and over again he expounded it, preached it, wrote it, rewrote it. ' "Whosoever is born of God doth not commit sin . . . He cannot sin, because he is born [i.e. newly born, 'justified'] of God" . . . This is the glorious privilege of every Christian'[24] – 'Christian' of course here implying the exclusion of the heathenish majority of *so-called* Christians.

Unfortunately the simple enunciation of this doctrine ran straight into many difficulties and pitfalls. For one thing, there was an uncomfortable number of biblical texts that seemed flatly to contradict it. ('If we say that we have no sin we deceive ourselves', 1 John i. 8; et cetera.) The uncommitted reader may find difficulty in persuading himself that Wesley's ingenious attempts at textual reconciliation carry conviction; he seems often to be fighting hard with his back to the wall. Then, Old Testament figures such as King David, plainly something of a sinner, had to be detached from the operation of the proposition, which Wesley confines to times 'since the Gospel was given' – reasonably enough for *Christian* perfection. Again, the concept of 'sin' itself needed to be defined, and not everyone could easily accept Wesley's simple assertion, 'Nothing is sin, but a voluntary transgression of a known law of God', or as he put it on another occasion, of 'the revealed written law of God'.[25]

And what was to be understood by 'perfection', that blessed condition which the justified – and of course only the justified – might inherit, perhaps on this side of the grave and certainly on the other? In 1762 Wesley explained carefully to his brother: by perfection he meant 'the humble, gentle, patient love of God and man, ruling all the tempers, words, and actions: the whole heart and the whole life'. He believed that, though this perfection was always 'wrought in an instant', a 'gradual work' both preceded and followed it. 'I believe this instant generally is the instant of death, the moment before the soul leaves the body. But I believe it may be ten, twenty, or forty years before death.'[26]

Under attack, he was obliged to admit that during their process of 'sanctification' the 'sinless' justified ones would need constantly to resist backsliding and 'proneness to depart from God'. And when he was pressed – Was this proneness not itself sin? he seems to have fallen back on his theological small print. In a sense *Yes*, he answered in effect, since it manifested man's natural tendency to evil; but basically *No*, for such sins were what Luther called dead sins, bringing neither condemnation nor despair.

Again, under pressure, he explained that perfection must not be taken to mean *absolute* perfection – a qualification which for a semantic purist seems to rob the word of its meaning. (To the enquiry – Would not some term like 'excellence' have done instead? Wesley's reply would have been firm: 'Christian perfection' was not a new doctrine; Wesley did not believe in the possibility of *new* doctrines which were also *true*; and besides, the terms 'perfect', 'perfection', were *scriptural*.) More strangely still, Wesley conceded that perfection was not irreversible. Just as, equally mysteriously, the justified man might become 'de-justified' and have to start all over again, the 'entirely sanctified' man might 'yet fall and perish'.[27]

Was not Christian perfection then explained away to nothing? It was certainly not for Wesley. He adhered doggedly to what he had first enunciated, never conceding any self-contradiction or want of logic. His first detailed defence of his tenet was entitled, with challenging insistence, *A Plain Account of Christian Per-*

*fection as Believed and Taught by the Rev. Mr John Wesley from the
Year 1725 to the Year 1765*; and in the 1777 edition he republished
his words of 1739 and 1741 concerning the man who had attained it: 'Love has purified his heart from envy, malice, wrath,
and every unkind temper'; he had 'put on bowels of mercies,
kindness, humbleness of mind, meekness, long-suffering'. The
most Wesley would concede in 1777 was that on a minor point
(perfection freeing a man from 'wanderings in prayer') his words
had been 'far too strong'.[28]

The value he attached to this doctrine grew as clergy in all
quarters attacked and controverted it. Failure to preach it in
Cornwall, he thought, had caused believers to 'grow dead or
cold'; in Bristol membership had fallen away because perfection
had 'been little insisted on'; at Tiverton it had been preached
'only in general terms'. Wherever it was not *earnestly* taught, the
work of God did not prosper.[29]

But neither unfortunately did he find God's work prospering
when he saw the upheaval threatened by the corrupted version
of this doctrine being spread by some of his more fanatical followers in London and parts of the south-east.

Thomas Maxfield had long been one of Wesley's foremost
disciples. His origins in Bristol had been humble, but once his
conversion had been accomplished (following some sensational
preconversion hysteria) he advanced, not only in piety and study,
but also in reputation as a preacher. He had strongly impressed
Lady Huntingdon, and it was in listening to him that old Mrs
Wesley had been persuaded that lay-preaching was in accord with
God's will. Maxfield in fact had become Wesley's first *regular*
lay preacher. It was Wesley who introduced him to the very
well-to-do woman who became his wife, and again Wesley who
through an intermediary induced the bishop of Derry to ordain
him priest. Many times he expressed something more than mere
esteem for Tommy Maxfield. He loved the man. So by the 1750s
he had become one of Methodism's leading figures. When Wesley
was away on his travels it was Maxfield who was left in charge at
Moorfields.

But between 1760 and 1762 he gradually involved himself in
the activities of a group of 'entirely sanctified' Methodists who
had carried Wesley's teaching on perfection to extremes, and on

the evidence of dreams, visions and other vouchsafings, regarded themselves as in intimate contact with God's especial favours, as having already taken up residence in his bosom.

There began to be complaints from some of the other London preachers, but when there was an accusation made against Maxfield at the 1761 Conference Wesley spoke in his defence, contenting himself with subsequent private, and mild, warnings. Far from holding back, Maxfield continued to recruit his own following. He protested to Wesley that he had no wish to separate, but did wish to see his old master set on the right road to perfection, with his 'heart set at full liberty', adding rather inelegantly: 'I know you will then see things in a wonderful different light from what it is possible to see them before.'[30]

'If Thomas Maxfield continue as he is, it is impossible that he should long continue with us', Wesley had already concluded; 'but I live in hope of better things.' Perhaps if the trouble had centred round anyone but Maxfield, he would have moved with greater decisiveness. But for months he strove to be forbearing, trying to argue Maxfield out of his folly; and meanwhile the London societies degenerated into unruliness and faction.

The situation eventually grew more than a little insane, with the irruption on the scene of one George Bell, an ex-corporal in the Guards recently made 'perfect', a ranter of highly eccentric convictions and fanatical zeal. He and his close associates claimed to be holier than their first parents before the Fall. Being in such potently intimate contact with the Deity, Bell was ready to essay miracle-working: he tried to restore a blind woman's sight. Finally he committed himself to go for the prophetic jackpot, announcing a firm date for the impending end of the world, on 28 February 1763. Maxfield later claimed that he tried to moderate Bell's wildness, but the two men were certainly closely associated in their activities and beliefs. Between them, said Wesley, they 'made the very name of Perfection stink in the nostrils even of those who loved and honoured it before'.[31] Satan, wrote Charles, had made 'mad havoc'; there was acute danger of their whole movement being overwhelmed in 'a flood of enthusiasm'. And when Wesley began to intervene personally in the London society he found the Bell-Maxfield following militantly hostile. 'The mask is thrown off', he wrote to Charles; and to Maxfield:

The breach lies wholly upon you. You have contradicted what I taught you from the beginning . . . O Tommy, seek counsel, not from man but God; not from Brother Bell, but Jesus Christ![32]

The archangel of the Lord, had he appeared in fulfilment of Bell's prophecy, would have had to search him out in the jail to which a Southwark magistrate had taken the precaution of committing him the day before the world was due to end. Wesley had done his best to protect Methodism's reputation by disowning Bell and his follies in a letter to the *London Chronicle*, reckoning that 'not one in fifty, perhaps not one in five hundred of the people called Methodists' believed the nonsense any more than he did himself.[33] But he did improve the occasion on the evening of 28 February by preaching at Spitalfields upon an apposite text: 'Prepare to meet thy God'. If Bell's notions were ridiculous, the idea of a *Dies Irae* was, after all, not something to be written off or trifled with. As for expecting the apocalypse in an hour or two, he reassured his congregation.

But notwithstanding all I could say, many were afraid to go to bed, and some wandered about in the fields, being persuaded that, if the world did not end, at least London would be swallowed up by an earthquake. I went to bed at my usual time, and was fast asleep about ten o'clock.[34]

The number of those who followed Maxfield out of the London society Wesley put at 600. George Bell survived long, if obscurely, deserting the lunatic fringe of Methodism for an atheist radicalism which in Southey's judgement, at least, was no less deplorable; the 'ignorant enthusiast' turned 'ignorant infidel'.[35]

Besides errant Methodists and Calvinists, there was never any shortage of mistaken Christians, ill-informed Christians, corrupted Christians, to be exposed or controverted, and Wesley's pen was never idle. In 1758 he issued his *Preservative against Unsettled Notions in Religion*, partly a compilation but in the main his own work and intended particularly for the guidance of his own young preachers. Among those challenged or condemned therein, he differentiated between true Christianity's most dangerous enemies – Deists, Socinians, Unitarians, Papists – and those 'not so dangerously mistaken' – Quakers, Anabaptists, mystics, Presbyterians, predestinarians and Antinomians. (To

find the last in the less heinous category is surely a surprise.)
When he met James Hutton again after a gap of many years he
was happy to exchange friendly words, but as for the Moravians
in general, they were still 'so infatuated as to believe that theirs
is the only true church on earth', using 'a continued train of
guile, fraud and falsehood of every kind'. In 1757 he published a
tract in condemnation of the Sandemanians, who interpreted
faith *merely* as acceptance of the gospels' truth. He accused them
of 'peculiar pertness, insolence, and self-sufficiency'.

His *Doctrine of Original Sin, according to Scripture, Reason, and
Experience* was an altogether weightier onslaught – 500 pages of
it, though with his customary liberal extracting from other
authors – on the 'deadly poison' of the Socinians, who professed
'nothing but old Deism in a new dress'. There was his hundred-
page *Letter to the Rev. Mr Law*, whose earlier writings he still
admired for their strength and purity of style and for their
'practical divinity' but whose mysticism he thoroughly deplored.
'You would have a philosophical religion,' he told Law, 'but
there can be no such thing . . . So far as you add philosophy to
religion, just so far you spoil it.'* Such an objection, however,
constituted no bar to the issue of his own 'compendium of
natural philosophy' entitled *A Survey of the Wisdom of God in
Creation* (begun 1758, third edition, five volumes, 1777; the most
complete thing of its kind, he told his preachers, in the English
language). Then there was his reply to *The Doctrine of Grace*, a
full-scale attack on him and his 'abuses of fanaticism' by the
bishop of Gloucester, Warburton, who courteously allowed
Wesley to see the manuscript before printing, to correct possible
error. Wesley says: 'After correcting the false readings, improper
glosses, and other errors, I returned it.' 'I was a little surprised
to find Bishop Warburton so entirely unacquainted with the
New Testament; and notwithstanding all his parade of learning, I
believe he is no critic in Greek.'

Warburton 'tore up by the roots all real, internal religion'. So
Wesley declared in a letter to the author of *Paradise Restored*,
Thomas Hartley, who shared his disapproval of Warburton, but

---

* There was nothing mystical about Law's comment on this *Letter* of
Wesley's: 'empty babble, fitter for an old grammarian who has grown blear-
eyed mending dictionaries, than for one who has tasted the powers of the
world to come'.

not of Law and the mystics who, he considered, taught 'the way to Christian perfection on surer principles' than Wesley. Hartley was a millenarian, and here at least Wesley could see eye to eye with him. Jesus would come a second time – though none might predict when – and reign on earth for a thousand years, during which peaceful millennium his saints would be raised and restored to the perfection of the first man, Adam. Wesley wrote praising Hartley's 'seasonable confirmation' of that 'comfortable doctrine, of which I cannot entertain the least doubt, as long as I believe the Bible'.[36]

This formidable outpouring of the printed word never ceased: volumes of theology, anthologized compilations, religious polemics conducted in pamphlets both popular and learned, in the press, or by private correspondence; collections of hymns; ten-or-twelve-page 'Thoughts' on every subject under the sun. Among these last was one of 1765, on which Luke Tyerman, Wesley's Victorian biographer, comments with unusual censoriousness. (Unusual, that is, in respect of Wesley; he is often enough censorious of Wesley's critics.) 'This is a queer tract', he writes, 'and the less said about it the better.'[37] It was *Thoughts on a Single Life* – which, it declared, were 'just the same as they had been for the previous thirty years, and the same they must be, unless I give up my Bible'. 'A man holding such sentiments', pronounced the Rev. Tyerman severely, 'had no right to have a wife.'

CHAPTER 12

Marriage

BY THE TIME HE WAS writing these *Thoughts*, Wesley had been a
married man for fourteen years. Only six months after he finally
lost Grace Murray, he had suddenly, to every appearance im-
pulsively, and more than a little mysteriously, wedded a forty-one-
year-old widow, Mrs Molly Vazeille, of Threadneedle Street in the
city of London and Wandsworth in Surrey. (Only a few days
before the ceremony, he had addressed the single men of the
Moorfields society on the advantages of celibacy.) As to his
motives for taking this as it proved unwise step, among much
that is uncertain one thing at least is not: he did not marry Mrs
Vazeille for her money, which however was quite substantial,
£300 a year from £10,000 in government stock. He was scrupulous
in having this settled on his wife and her four surviving children.

Of itself, his wish to marry seems in no way strange. He had
always demanded feminine companionship, and at the age of
forty-seven wanted something more durably satisfying than the
pious intimacies of confession and counsel which he was for ever
exchanging with the Methodist sisters. He had always been both
attentive and attractive to women. Meeting countless people
year in year out, busy among a thousand friends and fellow-
labourers, he could still at bottom be lonely. Even with Charles
the old close understanding was not what it had been; minor,
and not so minor, suspicions mounted troublesomely between
them. In any case, Charles was now married and building his own
little independent realm of domestic happiness. Wesley longed
for one of his own, while never beginning to contemplate the
smallest deviation from his essentially undomestic, peripatetic
routine.

It seems that he had gone for guidance to his friends Ebenezer Blackwell the London banker and Vincent Perronet the Kent parson, and that they confirmed him in his persuasion that he needed a wife. One of them may even have first suggested who she should be, for the lately deceased Mr Vazeille, like Perronet, had been of Huguenot origins, and his Threadneedle Street merchant's establishment was probably well known to Blackwell.[1] One person whose advice was *not* sought, though he was already well acquainted with Mrs Vazeille, was Charles; and when Wesley informed him that he was resolved to marry, he pointedly did not say whom. It was left to Perronet's son Edward to do that, whereupon Charles was plunged, by his own account, into such a state of groaning consternation that he failed to eat or sleep properly for days.[2] On this occasion, however (one must say unfortunately), he did not rush in to stop the marriage. It seems likely in any case that this time his brother would not have let him.

On 10 February 1751 Wesley preached at the Foundry at five in the morning as usual. He was planning to set off the following day on a northern tour, but damage to an ankle, painfully twisted as he hurried over a frost-covered London Bridge on the way to a preaching engagement in Southwark, enforced a postponement. On 11 February he transferred his quarters from the Foundry to Mrs Vazeille's in Threadneedle Street, where he settled down to nurse his swollen ankle, continued work on his *Short Hebrew Grammar* and *Lessons for Children* – and at the end of a week married his hostess. Nobody is sure where, or even exactly when: *The Gentleman's Magazine* and *The London Magazine* carried differing dates in their announcements of the event; and Wesley's *Journal* does not mention it at all. His brother was not told of it for some days, and it was only by a signal exercise of Christian charity that he brought himself a month or so later to proffer his new sister-in-law a kiss of rather precarious peace.

Molly Vazeille surely could not have properly understood the terms implied in her contract of union with Wesley; or else briefly deceived herself into thinking she could fall in with them. By temperament, conviction, and long habit, he was a nomad. There was small prospect of his settling down at home, as Charles was already beginning to do, in a comfortable *gemütlich* atmosphere. (Charles continued preaching and hymn-writing, but travelled less and less; there were times when his brother felt he was being deserted.) John considered that no Methodist preacher, least of all himself, should 'preach one sermon or travel one day less in a married than in a single state'.[3] His own wife he would expect to act as helpmeet in his great mission, and be ready to submit to its hardships and hazards. Grace Murray had been prepared for this sort of contract. Probably Mrs Vazeille began by honestly thinking she was too. But in marrying her Wesley was committing a sort of bigamy. He had long ago linked his wiry body and ardent soul in indissoluble union with the cause of Methodism.

Molly Wesley was no more than conventionally religious and, though she had once been a domestic servant, had been long accustomed to the amenities of a settled middle-class family life. With Wesley she soon found herself obliged to choose between being left on her own while he evangelized through the length and breadth of the land, and accompanying him on his journeys, which meant many a mile riding over rutted roads, and facing traveller's luck with the weather, the sleeping arrangements, the overnight hosts, the food, even (in 1752 with her husband and her daughter Jenny) the miseries of sea-sickness on the tiresome passage from Whitehaven to Dublin. Just over a year after their wedding, by which time Mrs Wesley had roughed it over two long tours of northern England and another of Cornwall, Wesley was wearing a brave, but obviously false, face in a letter written from Epworth to Ebenezer Blackwell:

> My wife is at least as well as when we left London: the more she travels the better she bears it. It gives us yet another proof that whatever God calls us to he will fit us for ... I was at first afraid she would not so well understand the behaviour of a Yorkshire mob; but there has been no trial: even the Methodists are now at peace throughout the kingdom ...[4]

This last was not quite true either: within a fortnight he had run up against a hostile mob of 'several thousands' at Hull (as usual, the stones they threw 'neither touched nor disturbed' him), and then found 'bitterness' from 'several who met us in the street' at Pocklington.[5]

Blackwell is not likely to have been wholly convinced by Wesley's report of his wife's 'bearing it'. He already, like numerous others, knew how things stood between the two of them, for

Mrs Wesley was not the kind of woman to essay any sort of false façade. Only four months after the wedding she had complained tearfully of her situation to Charles, whom she can hardly have thought of as a friend of first resort. He had given marriage-guidance counsel first to her, then to John, then to both together;[6] but the prayerful peace in which this 'affectionate conference' terminated had proved of short life. Wesley's friends and his enemies soon knew how the wind blew.

Although the reputation Molly Wesley was to earn as a jealous scold was not undeserved, it must be conceded that she had grounds for complaint. For one thing, there was Wesley's authoritarian view of matrimony. Did a wife not take the most solemn of vows to obey her husband? After nine disillusioning years and at least one walk-out by Molly, he spelled out to her what he considered such an undertaking should have meant:

> Alas, that to this hour you should neither know your duty nor be willing to learn it! Indeed, if you was a wise, whether a good woman or not, you would long since have given me a carte blanche: you would have said, 'Tell me what to do, and I will do it; tell me what to avoid, and I will avoid it. I promised to obey you, and I will keep my word. Bid me to do anything, everything. In whatever is not sinful, I obey. You direct, I will follow the direction.'
>
> This it had been your wisdom to have done long ago, instead of squabbling for almost these ten years. This it is both your wisdom and your duty to do now; and certainly better late than never. This must be your indispensable duty, till (1) I am an adulterer; (2) you can prove it. Till then I have the same right to claim obedience from you as you have to claim it from Noah Vazeille [her son]. Consequently every act of disobedience is an act of rebellion against God and the King, as well as against
>
> Your affectionate Husband.[7]

Molly Wesley did initially make an effort to fall in with her husband's mode of life. For four years she did her best, if spasmodically and not without grumbling, to fulfil her required role of evangelist's assistant. Wishing to encourage her and to minimize differences and difficulties, he struggled for some time to persuade himself, and her too if he could, that she *was* being a success. 'Give the glory to God', he wrote to her from Newcastle when she was away in Bristol visiting her son Anthony, who was ill:

Your name is precious among this people. They talk of you much, and know not how to commend you enough, even for those little things, your plainness of dress, your sitting among the poor at the preaching, your using sage-tea [i.e. not the ordinary noxious brew], and not being delicate in your food. Their way of mentioning you often brings tears into my eyes. Bless God for all his benefits.

But then comes strange matter indeed. He blames himself, not because he has failed to give her enough of his company, but because he has not 'conversed' with her as seriously as he ought:

I ought always to speak seriously and weightily with you, as I would with my guardian angel. Undoubtedly it is the will of God that we should be as guardian angels to each other. O what an union is that whereby we are united! The resemblance even of that between Christ and his church. And can I laugh or trifle a moment when with you? O let that moment return no more![8]

It may easily be imagined that this relentlessly earnest line of attack might be hard to endure. He could never for long stop preaching, even when he was writing to give her instructions concerning printing or other business arrangements. When, after six years, he was writing to tell her just how sincerely he was still her 'affectionate husband, lover, and friend', he could not resist using half his letter's space on one more moralizing exhortation:

. . . My dear Molly . . . be . . . as diligent as ever you can. This is one of the talents which God has given you. O use it to the uttermost! Put forth all your strength in things temporal as well as things spiritual. Whatsoever your hand findeth to do, do it with all your might. What a blessed rule is that of Kempis. 'Do what is in thee, and God will supply what is lacking!' Only, my love, watch over your own spirit! Take heed that it be not sharpened. Fret not thyself because of the ungodly, but in quietness and patience possess your own soul.[9]

Quietness and patience were not however among Molly Wesley's foremost virtues – except, Wesley once conceded, in 'assisting the sick', where she showed 'patience, skill, and tenderness'. That she did possess virtues Wesley was eager to admit, even when the marriage had all but disintegrated. 'I still love you', he wrote, painstakingly trying to be fair, 'for your

indefatigable industry, your exact frugality, your uncommon
neatness and cleanliness, both in your person, your clothes, and
all things round you.'[10] But hardly for 'quietness and patience';
not at least in her relations with *him*; instead, wrangling, bitterness, suspicion, jealousy, tantrums;* altogether, as Vincent
Perronet was quick to discover quite soon after the marriage, a
'melancholy situation'. Molly's, he now saw too late, was 'an
angry, bitter spirit', and Wesley's own case 'mournful enough'.
Yet, of the two, it was Molly he was sorrier for.[11]

This was perceptive of him. Wesley's was not the married
misery of the husband returning each evening to find the morning's
resentment still smouldering. He never lacked avenues of escape.
He would be off, to widen or freshen the pastures of his enormous
parish – off to Bristol, to Cornwall, to Newcastle and the north,
to the Midlands, to troublesome Norwich, to overwhelmingly
papist Ireland, to stubbornly Calvinist Scotland, indeed to almost
every sizeable town in the kingdom and a prodigious number of
its townlets and villages. This was his life and his happiness. In
London itself there was a mountain of work to be done from his
headquarters at the Foundry; but when he could leave it – and
his wife – behind him and begin yet another of his innumerable
peregrinations, 'I leap', he wrote to Blackwell, 'as broke from
chains.' This was from Redruth in 1755:

> In my last journey into the north [with his wife] all my patience
> was put to the proof again and again, and all my endeavours to
> please, yet without success . . . I am content with whatever
> entertainment I meet with, and my companions are in good
> humour 'because they are with me'. This must be the spirit of all
> who take journeys with me . . . By the grace of God I never fret,
> I repine at nothing. I am discontented with nothing . . . I see God
> sitting upon his throne and ruling all things well.[12]

He simply did not mind the pouring rain and driving wind, the
occasional spills from his horse, the unpalatable meals and uncomfortable beds. (He drew the line only at being asked, as he
was once, to sleep in the same room as a man and his wife.)
Sometimes a 'flux', or toothache, or hoarseness, or weakness in

---

* Whether these ever involved dragging him round the floor by his hair,
as his follower Hampson vowed to once witnessing, has had some doubt
cast upon it. Nearly all Wesley's early and Victorian biographers retailed the
story without hesitation, in properly shocked tones of anguished outrage.

the limbs he would self-medicate with whatever home-made simple the affliction demanded, or banish by the powerful medicines of willpower and prayer. And though he was always gratified by receptive attention from the large crowds who congregated to hear him, there was that in him which positively relished the challenge of Satan's minions and the drunken sons of Belial, the stones and dirt, the organized drowning of the fervent message. All this was immeasurably preferable to having to endure 'persons at my ear fretting and murmuring at everything', which was 'like tearing the flesh off my bones'.[13]

Charles, writing in April 1755 to tell his own 'dearly loved partner' he would be joining forces that evening with John at Birstall in Yorkshire, added significantly, 'I pity his poor wife, if now upon the road. There she is likely to stick till the warm weather comes. The roads are almost impassable for wheels.' When John set off for Ireland once more in 1756, his wife did not this time go with him. 'Molly, let us make the best of life', he exhorted her from Limerick, where between evangelizing he was working on his *Original Sin*. 'O for zeal! I want to be on the full stretch for God!'[14] How admirable, but how unimaginative of him to have expected a woman of unheroic ambitions, of ordinary capacities and desires, to be able to share such a life harmoniously, and how seriously she too had miscalculated when she abandoned the comforts of respectable widowhood in Threadneedle Street.

Charles, who never managed to like his sister-in-law (even before her later behaviour became so outrageous), made a considerable point nevertheless of trying to love her. He *must*, he resolved, pray to that end, or else he would 'sink into the spirit of revenge'. He meanwhile adjured his wife Sally to pray too: 'What shall you and I do to love her better? . . . I fear you do not *constantly* pray for her.' When it was supposed that Wesley might be dying, in December 1753, he begged his wife and Charles to forget what was past history between them; to which they agreed, in his presence. But, not long after, Charles thought worth recording the fact that he managed two minutes' conversation with her at the Foundry without quarrelling. Loving one's enemies, he regretfully concluded, was beyond human capability. Nevertheless, and oddly, he decided not only that he *must* but that he *could* love his sister-in-law, and even desired 'to love her more' – but only it seems if she kept her distance. On the whole he was obliged to content himself with pitying her, praying for her, and advising his wife 'to be courteous to her without trusting her'.[15]

If Wesley rued his misjudgement in marrying, as he must often have done, he was much too busy to be depressed by it. He was even ready to try persuading himself there was good to be dredged up from his wife's complaints and outbursts. 'Where she is I cannot tell', he writes to Ebenezer Blackwell from Yorkshire,

> for she says not a word whether she intends staying at London or coming forward . . . If anything in the world recovers her, it would be exercise and change of air. But I must not press her to it; for if I did, I should hear of it another day. What a blessing it is to have these little crosses, that we may try what spirit we are of! We could not live in continual sunshine. It would dry up all the grace of God that is in us . . .[16]

Towards the end of 1757 Wesley appointed as housekeeper, or matron, of his Kingswood school Mrs Sarah Ryan, a convert to Methodism three years previously at the age of thirty. She was one of those reclaimed sinners whose spiritual preservation became of much importance to him. One is distantly reminded of Gladstone in his missions of rescue on the West End streets. Not that Mrs Ryan – whatever she meant by her penitent confession of having 'often loved' – had been the prostitute implied in Luke Tyerman's description of her as a 'converted magdalen';[17] but the course of her early life had hardly been such as might conventionally have recommended her for the post Wesley put her into, and certainly might have aroused some apprehension in a wife a good deal less censorious than Molly Wesley.

Sarah Ryan's history before conversion is almost too involved for lucid summary. Reared in poverty, becoming a domestic servant, she married at nineteen a man who deserted her and proved in any case to have been married to another. She then went successively through ceremonies of marriage with two other men, both sailors who in the manner of sailors came and went, one the Irishman whose surname she bore, one an Italian who lived with her before she was claimed as lost property by the returning Irishman, who ill-treated her and eventually left her again, this time to emigrate to America. Rather than risk following him there, she managed to maintain herself and her mother by menial domestic labour. Then she heard Wesley at Spitalfields, 'found peace with God', went to board with Mrs Clarke's 'conclave of Methodist females' close to the Moorfields Foundry, and so impressed Wesley with the seriousness of her reformation and the earnestness of her intentions that in less than three years he had put her in charge at Kingswood, against much criticism.

Wesley then proceeded to discharge at her a volley of passionately phrased letters of exhortation and fortification. Though she was but a novice in the ways of God, without 'knowledge of the people', 'advantages of education', or 'large natural abilities', yet on what a pinnacle (matron of Kingswood!) did she stand! Perhaps 'few persons in England' had ever been 'in so dangerous a situation'!

> You have refreshed my bowels in the Lord . . . I not only excuse but love your simplicity; and whatever freedom you use, it will be welcome . . . Do you continually see God, and that without any cloud or darkness or mist between? Do you pray without ceasing? . . . Are you never hindered by . . . the power or subtlety of Satan, or by the weakness or disorders of the body pressing down the soul? . . . I can hardly avoid trembling for you still . . . What can I do to help you? . . . The conversing with you, either by speaking or writing, is an unspeakable blessing to me. I cannot think of you without thinking of God. Others often lead me to him; but it is, as it were, going round about; you bring me straight into his presence.[18]

The instalment of these letters containing, among other matter at a tenderly exalted level, those last three sentences was written on Friday morning, 20 January 1758. Wesley left it unsealed, ready for the post, in a coat pocket while he went to preach in the evening. He next wrote to Sarah Ryan a week later:

> Last Friday, after many severe words, my wife left me, vowing she would see me no more . . . In the evening, while I was preaching at the chapel, she came into the chamber where I had left my clothes, searched my pockets, and found the letter there . . . While she read it, God broke her heart; and I afterwards found her in such a temper as I have not seen her in for several years . . . So I think God has given a sufficient answer with regard to our writing to each other . . .

Then, unabashed by this contretemps, his epistolatory assault
upon Mrs Ryan continued, in a renewed torrent of questioning,
some of it hardly answerable:

> ... Since we parted ... has nothing damped the vigour of your
> spirit? Is honour a blessing, and dishonour too? The frowns
> and smiles of men? ... What kind of humility do you feel? What
> have you to humble you, if you have no sin? ... What time have
> you for reading? I want you to live like an angel here below ...
> Woman, walk thou as Christ walked; then you cannot but love
> and pray for
> Your affectionate Brother.

This was the atmosphere in which Wesley liked to conduct his
emotional affairs, amid intimacies of the soul where his masculine
authority was not in question, where he had no need to convince
himself – if rather more difficulty in convincing a jealous wife –
that his intentions were wholly pure, arising from a kind of
spiritual philanthropy.

Whatever he may have meant by 'God giving a sufficient
answer', it was hardly reasonable to expect that Mrs Wesley
would view his relationship with Sarah Ryan simply as an
exercise in soul-therapy. There was more to it, she was sure, than
agape. Already, a month or two earlier, she had made clear her
attitude towards this younger rival with the so-chequered past.
At a Bristol conference she had come into the room where Mrs
Ryan was presiding at dinner with Wesley and sixty or seventy
preachers, and had embarrassed the company by shouting, 'The
whore now serving you has three husbands living!' If 'whore'
may be regarded as merely a handy term of abuse, it was indeed
no more than fact. Sarah Ryan, sustained though she now was
(and was to remain) in all manner of godliness, and extenuable
as her previous conduct had doubtless been, had after all been
excessively casual with the criminal, even if not the moral, law.
It was, to say the least, an extraordinarily incautious appointment.

According to Mrs Wesley, her husband's last words to her on
her departure were, 'I hope I shall see your wicked face no more.'
This he denied. In return for 'the kindest words I could devise',
so he told Mrs Ryan, he had been 'continually watched over for
evil' – his letters to sister Crosby had also given offence – and
been worn down by 'a thousand tart, unkind reflections ...

"like drops of eating water on the marble" '. But he was immediately back, relentlessly, searchingly, at his questionnaire:

> . . . How do you look back on your past sins . . .? What tempers or passions do you feel while you are employed in these reflections? Do you feel nothing like pride while you are comparing your present with your past state . . .? How is it that you are so frequently charged with pride? . . . Is your eye altogether single? Is your heart entirely pure? . . . *et cetera.*[19]

Molly, this time, soon came back, and continued to annoy Wesley by opening all his letters before forwarding them, as indeed he had once in the first few trustful days of their marriage actually invited her to do.[20] She also broke open his bureau and showed his 'private letters to more than twenty different persons on purpose to make them have an ill opinion' of him. 'And I have no friend or servant where she is', he complained from Ireland to Ebenezer Blackwell, 'who has honesty or courage to prevent it. I find since I left England all my domestics have changed their sentiments, and are convinced she is a poor, quiet creature that is barbarously used. I should not wonder at all if my brother and you were brought over to the same opinion.' And he was soon, with unusually bitter sarcasm, charging Blackwell with indeed being taken in by Molly: 'you have so eloquent a person at your elbow'. Caught between two fires, Blackwell tried to explain how angry Mrs Wesley was, which made Wesley no less angry: 'What *I* am is not the question . . . but what *she* is; of which I must needs be a better judge than you, for I wear the shoe: as you must needs be a better judge of Mrs Blackwell's temper than I.' Contrition was not in the air: 'I certainly will, as long as I can hold a pen, assert my right of conversing with whom I please. Reconciliation or none, let *her* look to that . . .'[21]

He did, however, at length consent to break off 'conversation' with sisters Ryan and Crosby. Then, for a while, as he told Molly,

> having gained your point, you was in a good humour. Afterwards it was just as I said. You robbed me again; and your sin (as before) carried its own punishment: for the papers you stole harrowed up your soul and tore your poor fretful spirit in pieces . . . You could not refrain from throwing squibs at me even in company, and from speaking with such keenness when we were alone, as I

think no wife ought to speak to a husband ... Perhaps ... having
stripped me of all my papers, you imagine it is absolutely impossible for me to justify myself. But you are under a mistake.
To all that know me my word is a sufficient justification ... [22]

For many more years yet, until Wesley was in his early seventies,
his marital history pursued its thorny course: a marriage largely
nominal and often almost irrelevant; separation frequent but
never final until 1776; perennial mutual resentment. John
Berridge, the eccentric evangelical vicar of Everton in Bedfordshire, perceived in this seemingly unhappy situation the mysterious
wisdom of God: 'No trap so mischievous to the field preacher as
wedlock ... Matrimony has quite maimed poor Charles [Wesley],
and might have spoiled John and George [Whitefield], if a wise
Master had not graciously sent them a pair of ferrets.' (Tormented
by housekeepers, Berridge had once almost succumbed to 'a
Jezebel' himself, but on his knees had sought and been rescued
by 'divine intelligence'.) Wesley sometimes pleaded with his
wife, sometimes lectured her, and for long periods was able to
ignore her – though when he heard in 1768 that she was seriously
ill at the Foundry, he posted immediately from Bristol to London,
arrived at 1 a.m., discovered that she was better, and started back
at 2 a.m., arriving at Bristol that same evening as fresh as a
daisy. Mrs Wesley lost no opportunity of justifying herself,
blackened her husband's reputation before all who would listen,
and even took to handing over what she thought damaging
documents to his doctrinal opponents. 'You totally lose my
esteem', he wrote to her in November 1759; 'you violently shock
my love: you quite destroy my confidence. You oblige me to
lock up everything, as from a thief ... You cut yourself off from
joint prayer. For how can I pray with one that is daily watching
to do me hurt ... O Molly, throw the fire out of your bosom!
Shun as you would a serpent those that stir it up.'

The month before this, he had written to her methodically
itemizing ten principal complaints against her: stealing from his
bureau – including possibly money, for 'he that will steal a pin
will steal a pound' – and showing his private papers and letters
without leave (Items 1, 5); not letting him invite such friends as
he wished 'to drink a dish of tea', and 'extreme immeasurable
bitterness' to all who tried to defend his character (Items 2, 10);
being 'a prisoner in his own house, having his chamber door

watched continually', and having to give her an account of
everywhere he had been (Items 3, 4); browbeating, bullying and
using fishwife's language towards his servants (Item 6); habitual
lying, particularly in maliciously slandering him. Notwithstanding
all this, he would do everything she desired, he promised,
provided it did not hurt his own soul, or hers, or the cause of
God – upon examination pretty comprehensive escape clauses;
and nothing, he said, would delight him more than to have her
always with him, 'provided only' – again a considerable proviso –
'that I could keep you in good humour, and that you would not
speak against me behind my back'.

Certainly life was not easy for Molly Wesley. In addition to all
the unhappy marital bickering, she suffered painful illnesses. She
was defrauded of much of her money. Her daughter, though
described as 'dutiful', was sickly. One son had died, another
proved a 'grievous cross', and the third, at least so Wesley
thought, showed signs of being no better. Let her then consider,
Wesley wrote to her from Whitehaven in April 1760 (still 'with
much sincerity, your affectionate husband'), whether such
afflictions were not perhaps sent by God 'to break the impetu-
osity and soften the hardness' of her spirit: a suggestion unlikely
to have been received with much pleasure.[23]

Throughout the years of his so unsatisfactory marriage Wesley
continued to maintain a 'conversation' with the feminine sex –
as always had been his habit since those delightful early contacts
in the Cotswolds – no less charming, and infinitely safer, for
being of a platonic, paternal, or so to speak tutorial nature. Mrs
Ryan had been merely one of a fair number of young women in
whose spiritual wellbeing he became intimately absorbed. Sally
Ryan, in fact, soon ran out of her stock of his special favour.
She became righteous overmuch, even for Wesley. A year or
two before her early death, when she had left Kingswood to live
at Leytonstone with the wealthy Mary Bosanquet and her circle of
godly Methodist ladies, he wrote to her in his usual straight-
from-the-shoulder manner, 'You appear to think . . . that none
understands the doctrine of Sanctification like you, and to
undervalue the experience of almost every one in comparison
with your own . . . I am afraid you are in danger of enthusiasm.'[24]

But there were many others, most young enough to be his

daughter or granddaughter, who leaned earnestly upon his ever-forthcoming guidance, whether upon points of doctrine, matters of daily conduct, or emotional involvement. He would animatedly respond with a steady fire of questions, warnings, adjurations, flatteries. 'I thought it hardly possible for me to love you better than I did before I last came to Newcastle', he wrote to Peggy, one of the three Dale sisters of that city; 'but your artless, simple, undisguised affection exceedingly increased mine.' 'By conversing with you', he told her, 'I should be over-paid for coming two or three hundred miles roundabout.' 'I found a particular love to you', he confided to Hannah Ball, 'from the time that you spoke so freely to me on that nice subject . . . Christ is yours! . . . Draw not back! . . . and love for His sake, my dear sister, your affectionate brother John Wesley.'[25] (Hannah Ball was soon pioneering a Sunday school in High Wycombe.)

Guidance for those contemplating or newly launched in wedlock was something of a speciality. For instance, there would be danger, he warned the newly married Jenny Barton, of whiling away time in the sort of communication with her husband that did not 'quicken souls'. Jenny had been one of his best-loved protégées. 'You can tell *me* all that is in your heart', he assured her. 'I write often because I know you are weak and tender and in need of every help.' Like all the others Jenny received her share of spiritual bombardment. 'Are your thoughts continually fixed on the God of your salvation? Do you pray without ceasing? Does He preserve you even in your dreams?' 'The more free you are with me, the more welcome', he wrote to Philly Briggs, Vincent Perronet's granddaughter, against whom, it appears, 'all the powers of hell' were currently engaged. 'In the *Thoughts upon a Single Life* you have what has been my deliberate judgement for many years . . . I do not know whether your particular case be an exception to the general rule. It is true your temper is both lively and unstable, and your passions are naturally strong. But that is not much: the grace of God can totally subdue the most stubborn nature.'[26]

Perhaps it was Nancy Bolton (living with her brother, the proprietor of Blandford Park, Witney, where Wesley stayed frequently), whose earthly welfare and eternal salvation exercised him most delightfully. Best of all, he told her, would be an undistracted celibate life devoted wholly to God; but if she had not the resolution and steadiness for this, then second best would be to 'marry a man of faith and love'. He was almost as concerned for her physical as her spiritual wellbeing. 'You must take care', he told her,

> to have enough air at night: it would not hurt you to have the window a little open. When you have the tickling cough, chew a small bit of bark (as big as half a peppercorn), swallow your spittle four or five times, and then spit out the wood . . . Try if red currants agree with you; if they do, eat as many as you can.
>
> O Nancy, I want sadly to see you: I am afraid you should steal away to paradise . . .

'I rejoice over others', he wrote to her, 'but over *you* above all. How unspeakably near you are to me.' 'Look up, my sister, my friend! Jesus is there!'[27]

Wesley's relationship with his wife was not altogether without its sunny intervals. In July 1766, for instance, like one basking in a brief heat wave during a stormy season, he confided to his brother: 'My wife continues in a amazing temper. Miracles are not ceased. Not one jarring string. O let us live now!'[28]

Four and a half years later Molly Wesley walked out again. The *Journal* is laconic: 'January 23. For what cause I know not, my wife set out for Newcastle, purposing "never to return". *Non eam reliqui: non dimisi: non revocabo*' ('I have not left *her*. I have not sent her away. I shall not ask her to come back.')[29] Molly had presumably gone to be with her daughter, by then the wife of a prominent Newcastle Methodist. Inevitably to Newcastle Wesley's evangelizing must take him before long; in fact he was there just over a year later, in 1772; and when from Newcastle his non-stop mission brought him south again to Bristol, his wife was once more in his company, and of course the complaints and quarrels were ready to begin all over again. Wesley told her she should count herself fortunate, after all the 'thousand treacherous wounds' she had given him, that she had a husband who knew her temper, who could 'bear with it', and was willing to forgive everything – 'only not while you have a sword in your hand'. He was 'as clear from all other women', he protested, as

the day he was born. 'At length, know me, and know yourself . . .
Leave me to be governed by God and my own conscience. Then
I shall govern you with a gentle sway, and show that I do indeed
love you, even as Christ the church.'[30]

Molly however remained as difficult as ever to govern with
any kind of sway; still as full of grievances as he of reproaches.
For instance, there was the malice shown her, so she alleged,
and the lies told of her, by some of Wesley's preachers and by the
Methodist sisters in Bristol. Certainly almost all the early and
Victorian biographers of Wesley wrote her down simply as a
jealous, hysterical termagant, a millstone round the neck of a
noble, patient, selfless man of God; but we should perhaps not be
surprised to find that she saw herself as 'a poor, weak, woman,
alone against a formidable body'. 'My dear friend', she begged
Wesley in a letter of May 1774, 'for God's sake, for your sake,
put a stop to this torrent of evil that is poured out against me.'

Attempts at mutual accommodation persisted into 1775, but
after 1776 husband and wife appear to have seen no more of one
another. 'The water is spilt, and cannot be gathered up again', he
told her in September 1777:

> All you can do now . . . is to unsay what you have said. For
> instance, you have said over and over that I have lived in adultery
> these twenty years. Do you believe this, or do you not? If you do,
> how can you think of living with such a monster? If you do not,
> give it me under your hand. Is not this the least you can do?[31]

His last letter to her, of 2 October 1778, doubted whether they
would meet again in this world: 'If you were to live a thousand
years, you could not undo the mischief that you have done. And
till you have done all you can towards it, I bid you farewell.'[32]

Three years later, after returning on 12 October 1781 from one
of his west of England tours, he made the following entry in his
Journal: 'I came to London, and was informed that my wife died
on Monday. This evening she was buried, though I was not
informed of it till a day or two after.' She bequeathed none of her
property (reduced to some £5000) to her husband, except for a
ring.

However, it seems that unhappy, no less than happy, marriages
may be made in heaven. The considered judgement of the aged
Wesley on his thirty years' war with Molly – as 'repeatedly' told

to Henry Moore, one of his disciples and an early biographer –
was that 'he believed the Lord overruled this painful business for
good; and that, if Mrs Wesley had been a better wife, he might
have been unfaithful to the great work to which God had called
him, and might have too much sought to please her according to
her own views'.[33]

CHAPTER 13

Brother Charles and Pope John

THERE NEVER HAD BEEN a time when the Wesley brothers did not feel free to criticize one another, often with a pointed directness to be easily accepted only between two so closely bound together. Their marriages, following the painful imbroglio over Grace Murray, weakened the fraternal bond without breaking it. Both sides of this coin are well shown by some lines Charles wrote in February 1759 to his own 'Dearest Creature' Sally, just after John had preached to some elevated company at Lady Huntingdon's (not without reservation concerning the spiritual emptiness of their wealth): 'My brother', wrote Charles '. . . won all hearts. I never liked him better, and was never more united to him, since his unhappy marriage.' During those eight years there had been a good deal of mutual suspicion and expostulation, and even the real possibility of a rift.[1]

Charles, domestically content, gradually withdrawing from itinerant preaching, was immovably High-Anglican, and correspondingly hostile – fiercely hostile – to Dissenting tendencies among Methodist preachers whom he thought his brother tolerated too easily. From their side many of the preachers were no less mistrustful of Charles on account both of his rigid Church of England traditionalism and of his close links with the Countess of Huntingdon, Whitefield, and (it was suspected) the doctrine of predestination. Already in August 1752 John was requesting Charles, with tart politeness, to write 'without delay . . . explicitly and strongly to deny allegations made by some of our preachers' that 'you neither practise, nor enforce, nor approve of the rules of the bands'.[2] The following year John wrote again:

> Take one side or the other. Either act readily in connexion with
> me, or never pretend it . . . By acting in connexion with me, I
> mean, take counsel once or twice a year as to the places where
> you will labour . . . At present I do not even know when and
> where you intend to go . . . You told William Briggs that you
> never declined going to any place because my wife was there. I
> am glad of it. If so, I have hope we may sometimes spend a little
> time together . . .[3]

By the mid-fifties, when some of Wesley's preachers were in
favour of a clean break with the Church of England, and more
were urging that Wesley should allow them the right to administer the sacraments, Charles's strictures upon them were
angry and explosive. Among these preachers were Thomas
Walsh, an eloquent Irishman who evangelized in his native tongue
as well as English – he died young; Joseph Cownley; and the
brothers Perronet, sons of Wesley's old friend the vicar of
Shoreham. Charles ranted against them: 'pride, cursed pride'
had perverted them. 'What a pity that such spirits should have
any influence over my brother! They are continually urging him
to a separation; that is . . . to put a sword in our enemies' hands, to
destroy the work, scatter the flock, disgrace himself and go out –
like the snuff of a candle.'[4]

At the Leeds Conference of 1755 a three-day debate arrived
eventually, in the manner of so many Conferences, at a tempor-
izing formula: that whether or not it was lawful, it was 'no ways
expedient' for Methodism to separate from the established
Church. Not surprisingly this conclusion was susceptible to
contrary inferences. 'Dear Brother', wrote John to Charles,

> Do you not understand that they all promised by Thomas Walsh
> not to administer [the sacraments], even among themselves? I
> think that a huge point given up . . . The practical conclusion was,
> 'Not to separate from the Church.' Did we not all agree in this?
> Surely either you or I must have been asleep, or we could not
> differ so widely in matter of fact! Here is Charles Perronet raving
> 'because his friends have given up *all*'; and Charles Wesley
> 'because they have given up *nothing*'; and I in the midst, staring
> and wondering both at one and the other . . . We have not one
> preacher who either proposed, or desires, or designs (that I
> know) to separate from the Church . . . Their principles (in the

single point of ordination) I do not approve; but I pray for more and more of their spirit . . . Driving me may make me fluctuate; though I do not yet . . .[5]

The dilemma was plain. And there *were* of course preachers who 'desired or designed' to separate; in asserting otherwise to Charles he was being less than frank. In fact in a letter to Samuel Walker, the vicar of Truro, he not only listed the secessionists' arguments – they included the accusation that many of the Church's canons and decretals were 'as grossly wicked as absurd', 'throughout popish and antichristian' – but also freely acknowledged that he could not answer them to his own satisfaction. And if Methodists were 'pushed' into giving up any one of the four essentials – field-preaching, lay-preaching, praying extempore, and forming societies – they would be left with no option but to separate. The first of these four essentials was above everything vital. 'It is field-preaching which does the execution still', Wesley wrote; 'for usefulness there is none comparable to it.' And after addressing an 'immense' and 'deeply serious' congregation in Moorfields he reflected:

> What building, except St Paul's Church, would contain such a congregation? And if it would, what human voice could have reached them there? By repeated observations I find I can command thrice the number in the open air than I can under a roof. And who can say that the time for field-preaching is over, while (1) greater numbers than ever attend; (2) the converting as well as the convincing power of God is eminently present with them?[6]

As for lay-preaching, it was absolutely indispensable: if it ceased, 'thousands of souls would perish everlastingly'.[7]

In short, as he put it to another of his clerical (but critical) sympathizers, Thomas Adam of Wintringham: 'We will not go *out*; if we are *thrust out*, well': an attitude he reckoned was shared by nineteen out of every twenty Methodists.

It was certainly not shared by Charles Wesley, or by Grimshaw of Haworth, who threatened to desert Methodism if Methodism deserted the Church. Charles, fighting hard to secure the movement irremovably to the Church, maintained that he would have 'broken off from the Methodists' four years before, but for a written undertaking signed by himself, by his brother, and by the leading preachers Nelson, Downes, Shent and Jones, 'never to leave the communion of the Church of England without the consent' of *all* these six. He now thought that 'every preacher should sign that agreement, or leave us'; and no new helpers should be enlisted till the existing ones had been 'regulated, disciplined, and secured'. What he feared was that John would continue to 'trim' until swept away 'into the gulf of separation'. 'I stay not so much to do good as to prevent evil. I stand in the way of my brother's violent counsellors, the object of both their fear and hate.'[8]

In the autumn of 1756 Charles Wesley set forth from his comfortable Bristol home on his last considerable preaching tour, into the North country. It was this time a journey with one reiterated passionate message: to beware the 'treacherous sons of the gospel' who would betray Methodism, and cause 'our children, after our departure', to run 'into a thousand sects, a thousand errors'. There was, he literally believed, 'no salvation out of the Church'; a severe doctrine indeed, but one he feverishly propounded.*

Among the torrent of pamphlets issuing unceasingly from John's pen, one was published in 1758 entitled *Reasons against a Separation from the Church of England*. In fact it appeared in pamphlet form only because the rest of what he had written, intending a book, was withheld from the printer after Wesley had been advised by his friend Samuel Walker – himself no mean evangelist, but of Charles's persuasion – that it constituted rather reasons *for* than *against* separation. In it, Wesley had conceded the justice of Dissenters' objections to ecclesiastical courts, to parts of the Anglican liturgy, and above all to the spiritual deadness of many of the clergy.

By 1760 Charles was declaring, 'We are come to the Rubicon' – though he had been acting as though they had been there for at least the previous eight years. John's new young preachers, he now alleged, were 'raw, unprincipled men. Upon the whole, I am fully persuaded, almost all our preachers are corrupted already. More and more will give the sacrament, and set up for themselves even before we die'; and all, except the few that get

---

* Albeit his definition of 'the Church' seemed somewhat blurred at the edges and left plenty of room for argument: 'the mystical body of Christ, or the company of faithful people'.

orders, will 'turn Dissenters before or after our death. You must wink very hard not to see all this.'

Wesley did indeed continue winking hard and often. It was only when his preachers got outrageously out of step, as with Wheatley in Norwich or Maxfield and Bell in London, that he would exert the full discipline of his control. The Thirty-Nine Articles had to come in for some winks too. Wesley was obliged to admit for instance that he and his fellow-Methodist clergy, by allowing men to preach who were not episcopally ordained, were flouting Article 23. But they had subscribed to it, he claimed, only 'in the simplicity of their hearts' when they knew no better, and did there not always remain a Supreme court of appeal? 'In every point of an indifferent nature they obey the bishops for conscience' sake, but think *episcopal* authority cannot reverse what is fixed by *divine* authority. Yet they are determined never to renounce communion with the Church unless they are cast out headlong.'[9]

Then there was the question of allowing women Methodists to preach. Of course it was impermissible. Yet surely he ought not to censure, for instance, that godly sister, Sarah Crosby, one of his class visitors, who had stood before a company of two hundred at a Derby meeting and exhorted them to flee from sin? The advice he sent her displays admirably that talent of his – of which Charles so disapproved – for bending rules. 'I do not see that you have broken any law', he told her. 'Go on, calmly and steadily.' She should next time 'tell them simply, "You lay me under a great difficulty. The Methodists do not allow of women preachers; neither do I take upon me any such character. But I will just nakedly tell you what is in my heart".' That would 'in a great measure obviate the grand objection' and prepare the way for the coming of the man preacher.[10] A few years later, he ruled that if a woman had an 'extraordinary' call, this might legitimately relax ordinary rules of discipline. There was a scriptural precedent: even St Paul, though denying in general the right of women 'to speak in the congregation . . . made a few exceptions; at Corinth in particular'.[11] Both to Elizabeth Hurrell and to Sarah Mallet, Methodist women preachers, he gave cautious private encouragement. 'You must expect to be censured', he told Sarah Mallet; but she should 'go on' nevertheless, and 'fear nothing but sin'.[12] By 1787 he would be ready, through the Conference, openly to authorize John Fletcher's widow (who as the philanthropic and pious Mary Bosanquet had earlier kept an orphanage in her own house and been one of the leading Methodist ladies) to be an itinerant preacher 'so long as she preaches our doctrine and attends to our discipline'.

It was intolerable to Wesley to think that he and Charles might ever break with one another. He laboured to persuade him; he rallied Charles's energies, less untiring than his own; he sought to reconcile him to the difficult middle course he was trying to steer. 'I think you and I have abundantly too little intercourse with each other', he wrote in June 1766. 'Have we not known each other for half a century? and are we not jointly engaged in such a work as probably no two other men upon earth are? Why, then, do we keep at such a distance? It is a mere device of Satan.'[13] After they *had* met, and talked together, 'you *seemed*', John complained, 'at least to be of the same mind with me, and now you are all off the hooks again! – unless you only talk because you are in a humour of contradiction; and if so, I may as well blow against the wind as talk with you'.[14] In May 1768 he admitted:

> I am at my wit's end with regard to two things – the Church and Christian Perfection. Unless both you and I stand in the gap in good earnest, the Methodists will drop them both. Talking will not avail. We must *do*, or be borne away. Will you set shoulder to shoulder? If so, think deeply upon the matter, and tell me what can be done. *Age, vir esto!* . . . [Act, be a man!] Peace be with you and yours . . .

And a few weeks later:

> . . . What shall we do? I think it is high time that you and I at least should come to a point. Shall we go on in asserting Perfection against all the world? Or shall we quietly let it drop? . . . I am weary of intestine war, of preachers quoting one of us against the other. At length let us *fix* something for good and all . . .[15]

This was rather more than was to be expected. Charles would never share his brother's interpretation of the doctrine of Perfection, or his enthusiasm for it. Charles set perfection *too high*, said John, and thus 'effectually renounced it'.[16] To the end of his days he would retain his mistrust of the lay preachers and their hankering to have done with the Church of England; and his

fear would indeed be vindicated that in the end his brother would
be powerless to prevent a separation. By this time (1768) Charles
was sixty, not in the best of health; shortly to move from Bristol
to a fine house in London;* largely absorbed in the affairs of his
family; soon to be proud of the brilliant success, musical and
social, of his sons Charles and Samuel (whose subscription
concerts, given at their father's house, John looked on as errant
trifling); still writing his hymns; still preaching twice every
Sunday, though only from the pulpit and it seems with waning
power; still emphatically a Methodist – was it not he, after all,
who had founded the movement? – but increasingly out of touch
and out of sympathy with the course his brother was permitting
Methodism to pursue. And from his side John continued to
complain of a lack of whole-heartedness in Charles's loyalty to
the movement and to him personally: 'Nay', he protested to him
in May 1773, 'but you have *intended* again and again to stand by
me at this and that Conference, and then left me to stand by
myself.'[17]

If Charles complained that John's exercise of discipline was
too lax, there were many who reckoned it much too autocratic.
The jibe of 'Pope John' was widely enough known and repeated
for Wesley at his 1766 Conference specifically to dismiss it. He
proceeded in detail to defend the necessarily despotic nature of
his authority.

This arose, he explained, simply from the circumstances of
1738. Like others resorting for their justification to 'the facts of
history', he propounded a version of them not easily contro-
vertible, if a shade subjective:

> In November 1738, several persons came to me in London, and
> desired me to advise and pray with them. I said, 'If you will
> meet me on Thursday night, I will help you as well as I can.'
> More and more then desired to meet with them, till they were
> increased to many hundreds . . . It may be observed the desire
> was on *their* part, not mine. My desire was to live and die in
> retirement. [This last, surely, was an improbable story.] But I

---

* In Chesterfield Street, Marylebone. Mrs Gumley, the wealthy Methodist
benefactress, made him a present of the house (with over twenty years'
residue of the lease), complete with its furniture and 'everything a family
could need'.

did not see that I could refuse them my help, and be guiltless before God.

Here commenced my power; namely, a power to appoint when, where, and how they should meet; and to remove those whose life showed they had no desire to flee from the wrath to come. And this power remained the same, whether the people meeting together were twelve, twelve hundred, or twelve thousand . . .

His first preachers, he said, had desired to serve him 'as sons'. Naturally, therefore, he derived authority 'to appoint each of these, when, where, and how to labour; that is, while he chose to continue with me; for each had a power to go away when he pleased . . . They do me no favour in being directed by me'. Those who were asked to attend the first Conference in 1744 had been sent for 'to advise, not govern me. Neither did I . . . divest myself of any part of that power above described, which the providence of God had cast upon me, without any design or choice of mine'. Possibly after his death the annual Conference might determine matters by majority voting, but 'not while I live'. Was such power to be deemed arbitrary, as some complained? It was indeed *single*, he admitted; but '*arbitrary*, in this sense, is a very harmless word. If you meant unjust, unreasonable, or tyrannical, then it is not true . . . All talk of this kind is highly injurious to me, who bear this burden merely for your sakes . . .'[18]

While he continued to insist frequently that he was sick of controversy and dispute, his hunger for doctrinal correctness and his desire to have the Methodist position – *his* Methodist position – properly publicized meant that he was endlessly engaged in writing treatises and tracts, publishing replies to the many attacks that appeared in *Lloyd's Evening Post*, *The Westminster Journal*, *The London Chronicle* and other journals, and generally sustaining before the reading public an authoritative account of Methodism. And of course, there was always the *Journal*, appearing in instalments three or four years in the rear of events. His preachers were not allowed to publish anything which had not first obtained his imprimatur.

He would tolerate within his flock neither serious doctrinal divergence nor significant moral backsliding. The widespun web of his organization was not perfect, but its lines of communication, through class leaders, band leaders, stewards, through the lay preachers, through the annual Conference (admission by invitation) all led ultimately back to John Wesley – one begins to write 'at the centre'; but indeed he was seldom at the centre for long at a time. Instead, he was covering his four or five thousand miles every year and, in the course of all this tireless evangelizing, was busy repairing where he might those places where the web, the 'connexion', had fractured. Personal inspections and, where necessary, drastic expulsions were always part of the Wesley routine. 'A few violent predestinarians' at Alnwick had broken away, so the *Journal* records. 'It was well they saved me the trouble, for I can have no connexion with those who will be contentious.'[19] Or of course with those of whom the class leaders reported 'disorderly walking' – a term which might include many offences, from adultery to Sabbathbreaking, from habitual swearing or persistent drunkenness to absenteeism from meetings and services; or even such reprehensible though in many parts accepted practices as smuggling. (In the early 1780s drilling with the militia on Sundays, or even *watching* the Sunday drilling, was added to the list.) The prevalence of smuggling in Cornwall for example, where there were more Methodists per head of the population than anywhere else (Yorkshire perhaps excepted) shocked Wesley. It was 'an accursed thing'. They would see his face no more, he told them at St Ives, if they did not 'put this abomination away'. Up in Sunderland he expelled from the local society all who would not give an undertaking to refrain from 'robbing the King'. And on this subject too there followed of course, in time, the inevitable tract (*A Word to a Smuggler*, 1767); this one with the accompanying instruction, *Not to be sold, but given away*.

The jibe of 'Pope John' contained an imputation of autocracy merely. It implied no sympathy for Roman Catholicism. Yet surprisingly Wesley was still in some quarters being accused of just that, as he was in the days when he first came to prominence, and again in the days of the Jacobite scare. The Methodists and Papists were 'in constant correspondence with each other', so it was declared in a book by an Anglican archdeacon; 'the Popish party boast much of the increase of the Methodists'. It was of course a ridiculous assertion and showed, as Wesley wrote, 'amazing ignorance, not to say impudence', in view of the abundant contrary evidence of his writings. Just to underline the absurdity he now, in 1768, repeated what his *Journal* had first declared as early as 1739: No Romanist could expect to be saved.[20]

However, the impartiality of such pronouncements by him must be noted, as well as their rigour. If there were to be no Papists in paradise, the eternal prospects of his own backsliders and disorderly walkers were, if possible, more disturbing still: 'the Methodists that do not fulfil all righteousness', he declared, 'will have the hottest place in the lake of fire'.[21]

CHAPTER 14

'The Gospel Trumpet'

METHODIST NUMBERS GREW during the third quarter of the century, but neither very fast nor at all steadily. By 1767 society membership had reached a little under 26,000, and it was not until the years immediately before and just after Wesley's death that any spectacular leap in membership was to be seen. In 1767 London accounted for 2250, a number temporarily much reduced by the defection of Maxfield's following. Yorkshire was strongly represented with over 6000, almost a quarter of the national total; here it was Methodism's rivals, notably Ingham's adherents, who had lost ground. Lancashire had 1875, the Newcastle district 1873, Bristol 1064. Cornwall (2160) had provided much more rewarding territory than Wales (232), where it was the Calvinist variety of Methodism that prospered. The Scots too, though Wesley found them generally civil and quick to appreciate a good sermon – the 'best hearers in Europe' he thought – remained on the whole loyal to their 'dry' Presbyterianism. His five circuits there could number between them only 468 members. He complained, moreover, of the reluctance of these to contribute the wages of their preachers. 'Scotch bigots', he wrote, 'are beyond all others, placing Arminianism (so called) on a level with Deism, and the Church of England with that of Rome.' From the non-Catholic minority of Ireland, on the other hand, Methodism had by 1767 recruited 2801.[1]

The movement showed continuous ebb, as well as flow, over these years. Wesley realistically recognized it: 'Everywhere', he wrote, 'the work of God rises higher and higher till it comes to a point. Here it seems for a short time to be at a stay. And then it gradually sinks again.'[2] 'I wonder we should ever expect half of those who "hear the word with joy", will bring forth fruit unto perfection.' When a profane drunkard at Rye in Sussex, 'wounded' into a realization of his sin, turns up to 5 a.m. service, Wesley's comment is 'Surely, thus far has God helped him; but, a thousand to one, he will "return as a dog to his vomit".' Though such realism never engendered despondency – his temperament was too sanguine and active for that – yet two directly contrary impressions do arise simulataneously from reading Wesley's own account of his mission. One is all optimism and success and glory. He preaches before multitudes which are 'huge', 'immense', outdoor crowds which are 'serious and attentive', 'such a congregation as I never saw before', overflow meetings because of the crush, twenty thousand people perhaps at Gwennap Pit in Cornwall. He recounts story upon story of conversions achieved, deaths 'triumphantly' gone to, Christian perfection gloriously attained. He reports town after town where he had formerly met hostility and violence, now meek and receptive. 'What a change!' he exclaims, at Sheffield, at Warrington, at a score of other such places. He discovers towns like Bedford where, thanks to Methodism (and an enlightened magistrate) 'no open wickedness of any kind' is any more to be seen. There is no difficulty in exhibiting by selective quotation a glowing picture of moral revival, of a new age of faith replacing the bad old days of unbelief, cynicism, and corruption. The hungry sheep look up and, behold, they *are* being fed.

But although the *Journal* is in considerable measure a work of propaganda as well as of autobiography, it presents a picture altogether less simplified and more honest than this. It rides up and down with the author's spirits as he meets discouragement as frequently as success. At Whitehaven many have 'waxed cold'. At Newcastle he does not find things 'in the order I expected'. Birmingham is 'a barren, dry, uncomfortable place', where most of the seed which has been sown for so many years the wild boars (he singles out in particular Antinomians and 'mystics') have rooted up. In one part after another he finds 'dry bones'; 'shattered', 'scattered', 'dejected' societies; 'dead, senseless people' – at Epworth for instance, where earlier he had thought wickedness to be on its way to extinction; places where the work of God was 'exceedingly shallow'.[3] 'Of those who received the blessing here [in London] in 1762 and 1763', he writes in November 1776, 'I fear we have hardly a sixth part that have not been moved from their steadfastness.' The Yarmouth society, no less 'fickle' than that other East Anglian centre of trouble, Norwich, had been 'wellnigh torn to pieces' by the maleficent activities of Calvinists and Antinomians. Several times on the very same page of the *Journal* where he celebrates the decline in anti-Methodist rioting and 'persecution' since the violent days of the 1740s and early '50s, he proceeds to recount a few lines later some unpleasant new hostility. Thus, immediately after finding Walsall 'earnestly attentive' (how the 'wild beasts' had been tamed) he straightway runs at Derby into 'the beasts of the people . . . hallooing and shouting on every side'. Similarly in Ireland: Cork 'serious and deeply attentive. What a change!'; and the Barrack Square congregation in Dublin quiet as mice ('What a change since Mr Whitefield attempted to preach in this place!'); but then, in no time at all, in County Wicklow, 'more noise and stupid, senseless ignorance than I have found since I left England'. The Irish, he decided, were as fickle as the people of Norwich.[4]

While the severer disturbances did gradually abate, he was, during the fifties, sixties and seventies always liable still to be met anywhere, in town or village, in Britain or Ireland, by organized hooliganism and heckling, as at North Tawton in Devon in 1766 where he was confronted by the local clergyman, 'with two or three (by the courtesy of England called) gentlemen', a huntsman with his hounds (which however turned Methodist and refused to bay), and much abusive 'roaring' which prevailed against him; or shortly after this at Faversham in Kent, where he found that 'the mob and the magistrates had agreed together to drive Methodism out of the town'.[5] Yet such enemies of the Lord as these were not only putting their immortal souls at hazard, but also in their blind folly risking peremptory mortal danger:

> How quiet is this country [round Sheffield] now, since the chief persecutors are no more to be seen! How many of them have been snatched away in an hour when they looked not for it! Some time since a woman of Thorpe often swore she would wash her hands in the heart's blood of the next preacher that came; but before the next preacher came she was carried to her long home. A little before John Johnson settled at Wentworth, a stout

healthy man, who [promised to silence the preachers arriving after May Day], before May Day was silent in his grave. A servant of Lord R[ockingham] was as bitter as him, and told many lies purposely to make mischief; but before this was done, his mouth was stopped. He was drowned in one of the fishponds.[6]

And after being received 'very quietly' in Devizes, where Charles had once been besieged by a vicious mob, it was in admiration of God's justice, and not entirely without sober satisfaction, that he was able to write that most of the 'old persecutors' had failed to live out half their days. 'Many were snatched away in an hour when they looked not for it.'

The almighty president over human destiny was never inactive, nor slow to intervene even in the minor difficulties and inconveniences of his faithful servants. Becalmed in 1758 while crossing from Liverpool to Dublin, having first made sure by 'speaking' to his fellow passengers that 'no oath, immodest or passionate word' should pass their lips, and

> having no wind still, I desired our brethren to come upon the quarter-deck; where we no sooner began singing a hymn than both passengers and sailors gladly assembled. The wind sprung up almost as soon as I began, and about nine the next day we entered Dublin Bay, after so smooth and pleasant a passage as the captain declared he had not had at that time of the year for forty years.[7]

And again two years later, on the passage from Dublin to Parkgate (the port for Chester), twice when they were becalmed his sermons succeeded in raising a favourable breeze. In London during October 1770, so rainy a week he had seldom seen, yet his outdoor work had met hardly a shower. 'Poor reasoners', he exclaims, 'who think any instance of providence too *small* to be observed or acknowledged.'[8]

It has commonly been asserted that, while the anti-Methodist violence gradually declined after the first noisy decade of the Methodist mission, the evidences of psychological disturbance, frequent at meetings during the early years, similarly faded into insignificance. There is little in Wesley's own writings to lend this proposition much support. As he told one of his preachers, 'The bulk of our hearers must be purged before they are fed.' Before the unawakened could properly appreciate the love of God they must be *torn in pieces*.[9]

After about 1747, according to Southey's *Life of Wesley*, the convulsions, physical collapses, and other sensational phenomena that accompanied the earlier Methodist conversions were 'rarely met with'. The later Wesley, writes Southey, 'neither expected paroxysms of this kind nor encouraged them'.[10] This view seems to have become widely accepted, yet there is a good deal in Wesley's own account of events to bring it into question.

It is true that he objected to the *screaming* which accompanied some Methodist services, and sometimes reprimanded, sometimes ridiculed, those among his preachers who indulged in it. He also deprecated such religious antics as those of the 'Welsh Jumpers', who in their worship would leap, men and women, repeatedly into the air and violently agitate their bodies while singing the same verse of a hymn thirty or forty times over until they were exhausted. He was distressed to discover some of his own people behaving similarly – first screaming in concert as loud as they could, and then shouting ' "Glory! Glory!" perhaps twenty times together – bringing the real work into contempt'.[11] His explanation of such enthusiastic practices was characteristic: the Welsh Jumpers were good people but simple, and Satan took advantage of their simplicity 'in order to wear them out and bring discredit on the word of God'.[12] Again, it was the Devil who might also implant false visions and prophetic dreams. That was not to say that *all* such dreams of the future were false; there were genuine visions, as there were honest ghosts. But 'how frequently do men mistake herein! How are they misled by pride, and a warm imagination, to ascribe them to God! . . . Now all this is pure enthusiasm.'

And therefore of course to be condemned. By definition everything Wesley *rated* as enthusiasm was to be condemned. But that he grew to show distaste for the psycho-physical disturbances which on the evidence of his own *Journal* were far from being 'rarely met with' after 1747 seems to be quite untrue. As for 'outcries, convulsions, visions, trances', no, he declared, they were not *essential* to the 'inward work', but the danger was 'to regard them too little, to condemn them altogether; to imagine they had nothing of God in them', and were a hindrance to his work. 'Enthusiasm' might be interpreted altogether too sweepingly. Upon reading the *Essay on Fanaticism*, by the Mennonite John Stinstra, he commented that doubtless the author was 'a well-meaning man', but he was deeply ignorant of his subject: his principles would prove the Bible to have been written by fanatics, and the Apostles to have been fanatics to a man. 'The very thing which Mr Stinstra calls fanaticism is no other than heart-religion; in other words righteousness, and peace, and joy in the Holy Ghost.'[13]

'One or two felt the edge of God's sword and sank to the ground, and indeed it seemed as if God would suffer none to escape him.' That was in Cornwall in 1755. At Grimsby, in 1757, several listening to his sermon 'sunk down and cried aloud for mercy'. 'Much pleased' with the congregation at Newry in Ireland in 1758, he records how in mid-service a young man 'dropped down as dead'. At Cork later that year those involved were younger still, children 'so affected that they could not refrain from crying aloud to God. When I began to pray their cries increased, so that my voice was soon lost. I have seen no such work among children', he adds with satisfaction, 'for eighteen or nineteen years.' Back home at Moorfields he notes 'God made bare his arm', and 'there was a great cry among the people'. Then in 'a large and earnest congregation', first there were 'silent tears', then much 'weeping aloud', and finally 'a stout young man dropped down and roared as in the agonies of death'. Wesley's comment here is hardly disapproving: 'What a day of jubilee was this!' At Wrestlingworth in Bedfordshire, women listening to his sermon 'dropped down as dead', and other were 'struck' at neighbouring Everton.

The neighbourhood of these two villages soon gained a special notoriety for the extremity and contagiousness of their 'enthusiasm'; but Wesley, far from expressing disquiet at the sensational occurrences there, felt deeply rewarded by being allowed to assist the local clergy, John Berridge and William Hicks, in furthering them. The accounts he provides of the extraordinary series of trances, convulsions, vision, agonies of body and soul, shriekings, roarings, bursts of unnatural laughter, 'heavings of the breast I suppose equal to those of a woman in travail', congregations 200 strong 'crying aloud for mercy' – these are for the most part not his own, but came from eye-witnesses known to him. However, he prints at length their story of how the work of God prospered under these preachers in Bedfordshire and Cambridgeshire, implicitly approving the narrators' laudatory and often ecstatic tone.[14]

When he returned to Everton in the summer of 1759, by which time it was reckoned that Berridge and Hicks had garnered 2000 souls, he found the incidence of sensational phenomena on the decline, though still there were people liable to fall to the ground 'extremely convulsed' as he preached. Then at Otley in Yorkshire the travail of his hearers' souls 'burst out into loud and ardent cries' for two hours on end; there were 'dismal shrieks, one crying "I am in hell, O save me, save me!" ' At Pocklington 'their tears fell as rain'. At Stroud, two young men were 'convulsed, yet quite sensible', one of them crying 'I am damned!' At Limerick, as 'many more were brought to the birth', they were 'all of them lying on the ground', weeping, praying, 'roaring'. At Warrington on Easter Day 1780 'some fell to the ground; some cried aloud for mercy'. So it continues, well into Wesley's old age, as the power of the Lord was manifested 'to wound and to heal'. (The 'wounding' so constantly referred to came of course from the mental and bodily trauma, often too much for the frame to bear, as God battled to expel the Devil and his cohorts.) Wesley was even prepared publicly to single out for God's notice a potential victim of the wounding blade. In 1772, preaching in Sunderland, when he was nearing seventy, he suddenly felt moved to make a direct thrust *ad hominem*:

> . . . An eminent backslider came strongly into my mind, and I broke out abruptly, 'Lord, is Saul among the prophets? Is James Watson here? If he be, show thy power!' Down dropped James Watson like a stone, and began crying aloud for mercy.[15]

That at least is the *Journal*'s story, though we ought perhaps to remember that Wesley was not above simplifying to his own advantage his account of events. This incident followed hard upon a Methodist campaign among the lead miners of Weardale, conducted not by Wesley himself but by three of his preachers, which produced sensational happenings no less startling than those in Bedfordshire earlier. There is not the slightest hint of disapprobation in Wesley's account of them. Very much the reverse: in fact, the manifestations at Everton inspired by the non-Methodist, Calvinistic Berridge having by then had thirteen years to fall into perspective, Wesley underlines the superiority of the recent work in Weardale – a higher percentage of successful conversions; fewer devil-counterfeited visions; a better 'guiding of souls'; Everton shallow, Weardale deep.[16]

The new Oxford edition of Wesley's *Works* (xi. 24n.) quotes the *Journal* entry of 3 April 1786 to illustrate what it claims to be his 'dislike of the dramatic accompaniments of revivalism' in his latter years. He certainly deprecates there, as he occasionally does elsewhere, the antics of some of his followers (jumping and screaming always offended him); but such condemnation is by no means consistent. He usually reports individual or collective 'drama' or hysteria at services, either without further comment or with apparent approval. Only two months before the 'screaming' incident above, when he was preaching at City Road, at eighty-two no youngster, he notes that 'God spoke aloud . . . so that the stout-hearted trembled', and two voices could be heard even above the 'general cry' of the congregation, one of them 'shrieking as in the agonies of death'. As 'dislike' of this, Wesley's comment reads strangely: 'The power of God', he says, 'came mightily upon us.'

Nor did the religious fear and emotional turmoil whipped up among the boys and maidservants at Kingswood School during another of its short-lived 'revivals' in 1770 receive anything but approval from its founder. He happened to be present there at the time, helping (as he puts it with a just and careful choice of verb) to enforce upon the children 'the first principles of religion'.

Having first been put into a properly sober frame of mind by being taken to see the corpse of 'Francis Evans, one of our neighbours', and having then sung the hymn 'And am I born to die?', the boys, one reads with no great surprise, began to show increased 'concern'. Two of them were soon 'crying aloud for mercy', then 'quickly another and another, till all but two or three were constrained to do the same; and, as long as [the schoolmaster, Hindmarsh] continued to pray, they continued the same loud and bitter cry'. For the next ten days or so this spiritual blitzkrieg continued, under the direction principally of Mr Hindmarsh. The epidemic of tears, 'strong cries', groans, 'piercing of hearts', 'sinking down as dead', praying and 'wrestling', waiting to be 'set at liberty by the Lord', spread from the boys to the three maids, who also developed 'much distress' – one of them being 'like one at the point to die' – until they too were set at liberty, joyfully ready to take their first Communion.[17]

All this the Wesley of now nearly seventy hailed as a 'wonderful work of grace'. His only regret was that it all proved a Penelope's web. Within a year he was at Kingswood again to find the web unpicked. 'It is gone!' he mourned. 'It is lost, it is vanished away!' – so (with a transmigration of metaphors) they must begin again, 'and in due time we shall reap, if we faint not'.[18] They did not faint. Enquiring into 'the present state of the children' in September 1773, and not wishing to disturb the thirty or so boys 'got to prayer by themselves', he watched through a window as 'three or four stood and stared, as if affrighted. The rest were all on their knees, pouring out their souls before God, in a manner not easy to be described. Sometimes a cry went up from them all; till five or six of them, who were in doubts before, saw the clear light of God's countenance.'[19]

Eleven years later, when he was nearly eighty-one, Wesley was still finding 'an uncommon work of God' in similar scenes of juvenile 'enthusiasm' at Stockton-on-Tees.[20]

Ever since leaving his youth behind him he had been referring constantly to his approaching, even imminent, end. He and Charles, both destined for a ripe old age, both saw death always just round the corner. Not of course that they were apprehensive of it. Indeed, other men's fears of it Wesley found deeply shocking, as when in Ireland, in 1762, at a hanging of four members of a 'Whiteboy' gang condemned for housebreaking, he watched them in their final moments of desperate resistance, clinging to the ladder, one of them shrieking in wild terror (despite, he notes sharply, the priest's absolution), all *dying with fear of death*. How 'inexpressibly miserable' was such bondage![21]

If he was still alive and strong in his sixties – and then seventies – and at last eighties – it could only be that God was preserving him for especial service. From the age of twenty-seven, he said, he had for several years spit blood. More than ten times already, he wrote when he was still only fifty-seven, his health had been supernaturally restored.[22] Although he thought he had been 'brought to the brink of death by a fever' in 1742, it seems likely that the illness he suffered at fifty, when he developed a 'settled' chest pain, a violent cough and persistent fever (and Dr Fothergill, assuming a case of incipient consumption, significantly ordered him asses' milk), provided the only instance until that time of his being seriously ill; ill enough for his friends to give

him up for lost – and for Wesley himself calmly and modestly to
prepare a proper inscription for the tombstone that would, he
thought, shortly mark his grave. That was the time when Whitefield, unable to manage a sick-visit before another week, had
written to express the hope of finding him still in the land merely
of the *dying* rather than the dead. 'If not', he had written, 'reverend
and dear sir, F-a-r-e-w-e-l-ll . . . My heart is too big; tears trickle
down too fast!'[23]

For some months in 1754, recuperating at the Hot Wells in
Bristol, Wesley had remained too unwell to travel or preach,
though well enough to work sixteen hours a day on his *Notes
on the New Testament*. Once four years later he found himself
coughing and again spitting blood, with a pain in his side and
some 'decay of strength'; but this time, we are told, a brimstone
plaster and a linctus of roasted lemon and honey combined to
effect a quick cure.[24] For the rest of his days no one could sound
less like a consumptive, which indeed it is unlikely that he ever
was. In his sixtieth year he was able to record: 'The more I
use my strength the more I have. I am often tired the first time
I preach in a day; a little the second time; but after the third or
fourth, I rarely feel either weakness or weariness.' (In fact, *four*
was rare; and he advised his preachers to stop at two.) Three
years later, after taking breakfast with 'poor George Whitefield' –
who was now suffering from angina – and finding him 'an old,
old man . . . fairly worn out in his Master's service, though he has
hardly seen fifty years', he contrasted his own still vigorous
health at sixty-two: 'no disorder, no weakness, no decay, no
difference from what I was at five-and-twenty; only that I have
fewer teeth, and more grey hairs'. On his birthday in 1770 he
was rejoicing and giving thanks that for many years – though this
was not *quite* true – he had 'known neither pain nor sickness',
and was actually healthier at sixty-seven than he had been at
twenty-seven. 'This hath God wrought'. And exactly a year
later: 'This day I entered the sixty-ninth year of my age. I am
still a wonder to myself.'[25]

'He has generally blown the gospel trumpet', wrote John
Fletcher as Wesley was nearing seventy, 'and rode twenty miles
before most of the professors who despise his labours have left
their downy pillows. As he begins the day, the week, the year,
so he concludes them, still intent upon . . . the good of souls.' The

pattern of those labours, kaleidoscopic as it was in respect of the people, places and situations he met, was yet one of an only narrowly varying routine, at least for that three-quarters of the year he spent in travelling. Up by four; private prayer and Bible-reading, from the Greek Testament or the King James version; ready for morning service by five; breakfast with his overnight hosts, or less usually at an inn; away on horseback, or sometimes by post chaise, towards his next pre-arranged place of meeting, where the local faithful would be ready to welcome and house him, and many of the less faithful at least to turn out and listen to him (for he was a famous figure now) – perhaps some of them still prepared to fling a clod or two. On arrival, more prayers, scripture readings, hymn-singing, conversation and discussion with local Methodists over a dish of tea, questioning of officers, examination perhaps of classes, or sometimes of those claiming to be 'wholly sanctified'; a sermon, probably two sermons, possibly three, whether in the local meeting-house, or – only occasionally, where the clergy were in sympathy – in church, or much more likely in field or town square or on village green. ('What marvel that the devil does not love field preaching!' he wrote. 'Neither do I: I love a commodious room, a soft cushion, a handsome pulpit. But where is my zeal, if I do not trample all these underfoot to save one more soul?')[26] A meal with his hosts; an early retirement; more reading, writing and prayer; bed usually by ten – and sleep by two minutes past. Wesley was not a man to lie awake worrying. At the age of seventy he did once lose a night's sleep, though 'at ease in body and mind'. It was the first time, he declared (even though, again, we know this cannot be *quite* true), such a thing had ever happened in his long life.

Though he had habitually done some of his journeying by chaise, until he was nearly seventy he always regarded horseback as preferable. 'I must be on horseback for life if I would be healthy', he told Ebenezer Blackwell in 1764, by way of ex-horting this rich but recently ill banker to follow his example. ('I really am under apprehensions lest that chariot should cost you your life.')[27] He would read as he rode, with the reins thrown forward on to the mare's neck, to allow her to pick her own way along with her own horse sense. 'I aver', he wrote, 'that in riding about a hundred thousand miles in thirty years I scarce ever remember any horse . . . to fall, or make a considerable stumble, while I rode with a slack rein.' How was it, he reflected, that other riders almost universally neglected this simple precaution?[28] (His journal's not infrequent accounts of spills and contretemps do not perhaps altogether support this theory's infallibility.)

When he was about seventy, however, he began to experience a trouble which made riding painful: a hydrocele, or swelling from fluid in the scrotum. In January 1774 he had it drained, and was soon professing to be right as rain; but in the following May he told Charles that the complaint was increasing 'by slow degrees, much the same as before. It seems I am likely to need a surgeon every nine or ten weeks. Mr Hey, of Leeds, vehemently advises me never to attempt what they call a radical cure.'[29] It was this persisting inconvenience which forced him to exchange, as a general rule, his mare for his private chaise.

Already, eight years before, a wealthy sympathizer, Miss Lewen, had presented him with one, together with a pair of horses; and he had other well-to-do friends who were solicitous to promote all possible comfort for him in the ten hours a day that he estimated he averaged in solitary travel. His chaise was fitted, among other amenities, with a bookcase and desk so that *en route* he might do a good deal of his reading, and even his writing when the condition of the road allowed.

His health in general remained obstinately sturdy, and in April 1776, in a letter to his sister Patty (offering to contribute towards the maintenance of her bastard stepdaughter Suky, now herself a mother), he affirmed:

> Since I recovered my strength after my late fever, I have scarcely known what pain or weakness or weariness meant. My health is far better and more uninterrupted than it was when I was five-and-twenty. I was then much troubled with a shaking hand. But all that is over.[30]

Occupied as he was on the road with his work, or with the *relaxation*, as he put it, of history, poetry and philosophy, he seldom finds much to say of the rural or agricultural scene through which he passes. Every now and then some creation of man or nature will elicit some sentences of lively appreciation – William Shenstone's celebrated gardens at The Leasowes near Halesowen, for instance, 'beautiful and elegant all over. There is nothing grand, nothing costly; no temples, so called; no statues (except two or three, which had better have been spared); but such walks, such shades, such hills and dales, such lawns, such artless cascades, such waving woods, with water intermixed, as exceeds all imagination!'[31] Occasionally he briefly praises some stretch of countryside, as at Gawksholme in Yorkshire – 'I believe nothing on the post-diluvian earth can be more pleasant than the road from hence' – or in the Isle of Wight – 'I never saw a more fruitful or a more pleasant country than the inland part of this island'; but there usually it will stop. His mind and his pen dwelt among other landscapes, upon other seed-sowings and harvests. And if it should happen that his horseback verse-reading was of Edward Young's *Night Thoughts on Life, Death, and Immortality*, as during the latter weeks of 1768, his own thoughts would be already jumping to a consideration of how Young might be improved, didacticized, edited, expurgated of 'everything childishly conceited, prosaically flat, falsely sublime, incurably obscure, or turgid'[32] – and then presented by John Wesley (published in fact at Bristol in 1770) for the edification of the public.

All poetry, all art, must be the handmaiden of morality. If it were not, it should be for the dust-heap. The statues of heathen gods at Stourhead were but 'images of devils'. Moreover, their nudity – and it seems all pictorial nudity – offended against both 'common decency' and (less explicably) 'common sense'. After preaching in 1757 at Chester-le-Street, supping in his host's parlour he noticed some 'not very modest' pictures on the wall. They were indeed 'very fine' pictures; but 'I desired my companion when the company was gone, to put them where they could do no hurt. He piled them on a heap in the corner of the room, and they have not appeared since.' Despite 'blemishes', he rated Homer above Virgil because of his 'fine strokes of morality', 'always recommending the fear of God, with justice, mercy, and truth'.[33]

Similarly with buildings. He might admire, in moderation, the neatness and elegance of, say, St Stephen's Walbrook, or find Dr Taylor's new octagonal meeting-house in Norwich 'the most elegant in Europe', with its thirty-two sash windows, eight 'purely ornamental' skylights in the dome, communion table of fine mahogany and 'the very latches of the pew-doors . . . of polished brass' – but what chance had 'the old, coarse gospel' of gaining admittance in such a house as this? And Beverley Minster was all very fine: beautiful, stately, 'nicely clean'; 'but where will it be when the earth is burned up, and the elements melt with fervent heat?'[34]

Or with music. For him music meant, almost exclusively, vocal music, where the sound was primarily a vehicle for the words, and for the thought and devotion behind them. In 1764 he heard in Thomas Arne's oratorio *Judith*, the *same* words being sung ten times over, a gross affront he decided to common sense; and worse, *different* words being sung by different persons at the same time, a malpractice offensive both to reason and religion, since the words thus rendered unintelligible were in fact 'solemn addresses to God'. Of Dr Arne's music – no comment. Busy about God's business, he had 'no time for Handel or Avison now', he told Charles. He deplored hymns being sung by a trained choir before a silent congregation. By way of contrast, the spirit of the hymn-singing by the select hundred little trebles from the Bolton Sunday schools came second only to that of the 'angels in our Father's house'.[35]

Great estates and stately mansions which he saw in his interminable journeyings regularly elicited from him some Puritan moralizing or apocalyptic judgement upon the insignificance of grandeur. Lord Charlemont's country house near Dublin was one of the pleasantest places he had ever seen; but what was all this if God was not present? Only vanity and vexation of spirit. In Edinburgh Holyrood House merely provoked from him reflections on the transience of human greatness. And what did the beauties of Harewood House do for their proprietor Mr Lascelles – 'beyond the beholding with his eyes'? The evidence of Lord Rockingham's palatial stable block at Wentworth Woodhouse might indeed show that he had been worth £60,000 a year, but 'O how much treasure he might have laid up in heaven with all this mammon of unrighteousness!' At Thornhill in Dumfriesshire, 'how little', he reflected, 'did the late Duke [of Queensberry] imagine that his son would plough up his park and let his house run to ruin. But let it go! In a little time the earth itself, and all the works of it, shall be burned up.' The practised reader of Wesley, following him round the varied glories of Lord Shelburne's estate at Wycombe, is already expecting to be introduced to the serpent in this Eden before he reaches the end. And there of course it is: 'But can the owner rejoice in this paradise? No, for his wife is snatched away in the bloom of youth.'[36] Sometimes his desire to relegate to a lowly plane any beauty which was merely sensuous or terrestrial could lead him to sound as if he positively gloated in its destruction. He narrates how one August Sunday in 1755 he 'dined with one who lived for many years with one of the most celebrated beauties in Europe. She was also proud, vain, and nice to a very uncommon degree. But see the end! After a painful and nauseous illness, she rotted away above ground, and was so offensive for many days before she died that scarce any could bear to stay in the room.'[37]

In worship, the danger of sexual distraction might be at least lessened by segregation. Men and women he always required to sit on separate sides of the chapel or meeting-house. It was his practice also to refuse the Methodist ticket to any woman who wore 'either ruffles or a high-crowned cap'. The particularities of the Quakers were not to be emulated, but the neat plainness of their attire was. 'Wear no gold', he told his woman Methodists; no jewellery, no velvets, silks, laces, or fine linens; 'no super-fluities, no *mere ornaments* . . . nothing apt to attract the eyes of the bystanders'. Nor should the men wear 'coloured waistcoats, shining stockings, glittering or costly buckles . . . expensive perukes'.[38]

He disapproved strongly of the theatre, that 'sink of all profaneness and debauchery'.[39] When he learned in Birmingham that a theatre had been made into a chapel he commented, 'How happy would it be if all the playhouses in the kingdom were converted to so good a use.' Popular merrymaking was likewise to be deplored. Arriving at Otley during the summer of 1766, he found the place 'run mad. Such noise, hurry, drunkenness, rioting, confusion . . . It was their feast day! A feast of Bacchus, or Venus, or Belial? O shame to a Christian country!'[40]

In his youth he had enjoyed dancing; but now he saw that it was alive with danger. 'Be careful', he told a Derbyshire con-gregation, 'that you don't dance yourselves to hell.'[41] Card-playing presented a parallel hazard. Pressed on the possible admissibility of such pursuits – card-playing, dancing, theatre-going – he was at pains to make his attitude crystal-clear. No *Methodist* was permitted them; but allowances must be made for the unawakened. One does not take away a rattle from a child, or he will be angry. 'Give him something better first, and he will throw away the rattle of himself.'[42] 'Of playing at cards', he said, 'I say the same as of seeing plays, I could not do it with a clear conscience. But I am not obliged to pass any sentence on those that are otherwise minded. I leave them to their own Master.' Yet he was quick to pass sentence once in Ireland when he discovered that the local priest, forbidding his flock to *work* on Sundays, was happy to allow card-playing. 'Alas', groaned Wesley, 'for the blind leader of the blind!'[43]

When a Methodist lady wrote to him to enquire whether it was sinful to maintain *hothouses* and *flower gardens*, he first reassured her – 'my reason for judging both of these innocent is because neither of them is forbidden in scripture' – but then proceeded to a massive generalization: 'It is sinful to condemn anything which scripture does not condemn.' Taken literally, this is mind-boggling in its implications, but at least it seems to turn the scriptural tables against the Puritan lunatic fringe.

The scriptures offering no precise condemnation of state lotteries, neither would Wesley. 'I never myself bought a lottery ticket', he said, 'but I blame not those who do',[44] though he had no hesitation in fiercely condemning those who made 'drams, or spirituous liquor'. Wine was altogether different, 'one of the noblest cordials in nature', but all who manufactured spirits – 'liquid fire' – except for medicinal use, were 'poisoners and murderers'. 'The curse of God is in their gardens, their walks, their groves. Blood, blood is there; the foundation, the floor, the walls, the roofs of their dwellings, are stained with blood.'[45]

Inexcusable always was the failure to be serious. Any form of play, of mere amusement, was a squandering of God's time, a dissipation of this life's proffered opportunity to prepare for the next. One of his favourite epithets of opprobrium was 'trifling'. 'Gay' was another. The *Journal* is full of disparaging references to gay (usually young and feminine) triflers. Sometimes it was because they had come, perhaps out of curiosity, to hear him preach; and if, as might well be, coming to scoff they had remained to pray, the success would be thankfully chronicled – as at Fordingbridge in 1770, where 'two young gentlewomen' had only *at first* been 'inclined to mirth'. Irritatingly however there were others who 'retained their mirth to the end', like two at Salisbury 'greatly diverted with hearing of the dead . . . standing before God!' For such young triflers – 'these pretty things' – his scorn was boundless.[46]

When he attended in Ireland a military execution of some deserters, what shocked him was neither the killing itself – like nearly all his contemporaries he never questioned the necessity or the morality of capital punishment – nor the 'numberless crowds' that flocked to witness it. Indeed some of these people might well have benefited ('retained serious impressions', if only 'for four and twenty hours'). What was shocking was the behaviour of the rest of the troops, as merry within six hours as if they had only seen a puppet show.

For such levity he was readier to forgive the poor than the genteel. 'Genteel' is another of his favourite epithets, usually used pejoratively. When he comes upon a respectful audience with a fair sprinkling of the well-to-do among them, the *Journal*'s frequent comment is 'genteel but serious' – gentlefolk who were nevertheless serious presenting a phenomenon unusual enough to deserve mention. At Liverpool in 1764, 'the rich behaved as seriously as the poor. Only a young gentlewoman (I heard) laughed much. Poor thing! Doubtless she thought "I laugh prettily".' 'Even the genteel hearers were decent', he noted at Cockermouth. Compare this faintly sarcastic commendation with his fervour at neighbouring Whitehaven, a town of Cumbrian colliers: 'Surely here above any place in England "God hath chosen the poor of the world".'[47]

He constantly points to the spiritual advantages enjoyed by his rough miners – at Kingswood, on Tyneside, in Staffordshire, in Cumbria, in Cornwall – over their social betters, those 'rich and genteel people throughout the nation' in whom he found 'flippancy, infidelity, and gross ignorance'. 'How hard it is for those to enter the kingdom of heaven!' When he was invited to breakfast, in Bury in 1787, by the calico printer, Robert Peel the elder, who was reported to have turned £500 into £50,000 in a few years, his comment was 'O what a miracle if he lose not his soul!' 'How unspeakable is the advantage, in point of common sense', he reflected, 'which middling people have over the rich! There is so much paint and affectation, so many unmeaning words and senseless customs among the people of rank.'[48] (This last observation was prompted by a consideration of one of his street congregations in County Clare, over nine-tenths of them poor

Papists, fewer than one-tenth well-to-do Protestants.)* Almost at the end of his days, at Shrewsbury in 1790, he was still commenting in the same vein: his noisy audience had made him much ashamed of them – but '*no wonder* they had neither sense nor good manners, for they were gentlefolks!'⁴⁹

He preached many sermons on riches, including one among his very last, in 1790: riches as a hindrance to holiness; as a high road to atheism (since the rich man among his comforts and 'dissipation' feels no need of God: 'Thou fool! Dost thou imagine because thou dost not see God, that he doth not see thee?'); riches as a temptation to seek *idols* in 'poetry, history, music, philosophy, or curious arts and sciences'; riches as a stimulus to 'the desire of the flesh, the desire of the eyes, and the pride of life'. Methodism, of course, was not without its own men of substance, and he fulminated against the hypocrisy and self-deception with which they found excuses for themselves, as that *their* money was intended to provide for their children ('how? by making them rich? then you will probably make them heathens, as some of you have done already'), or that it was tied up in investments, or that it was being saved. If a man received £500 a year and spent £200, *he owed God* £300. If he received £200 and spent only £100, did he 'give God the other hundred?' If not, he robbed him 'of just so much'.⁵⁰

He regarded himself, he said, as God's steward for the poor, accepting that although poverty was essentially preferable to wealth, one might in practice have somewhat too much of it. On the whole, he decided that 'it is most desirable to have neither poverty nor riches'.⁵¹ When he made £200 from his 4-volume *Concise History of England* (extracted 'with various corrections and additions' from other writers)† he gave it all away within a week. When the pious and munificent Miss Lewen died and left him personally the then considerable sum of £1000, he straightway set about organizing its distribution among the needy. When it

* His comments on Irish Catholics were not always as charitable as this. 'I am surprised to find,' he wrote in June 1758, 'how little the Irish Papists are changed in a hundred years. Most of them retain the same bitterness, yea, and thirst for blood, as ever, and would as freely cut the throat of all the Protestants as they did in the last century.' (*Journal*, iv. 268).

† 'Goldsmith's *History* and Hooke's are far the best. I think I shall make them better. My view in writing history (as in writing philosophy) is to bring God into it' (John to Charles Wesley, 13 Jan. 1774).

was almost all given away, he was reminded that among these was his own sister Patty Hall, long abandoned by her reprobate husband. Wesley had told her, some years before, how fortunate she was to be poor; how she must remember that God ordered everything for good; that if she had been well off she would have been afflicted by pride, and 'a legion of foolish and hurtful desires'.[52] Now, however, he wrote kindly to her:

> You do not consider, money never stays with *me*; it would burn me if it did. I throw it out of my hands as soon as possible, lest it should find a way into my heart. Therefore you should have spoken to me while I was in London, and before Miss Lewen's money flew away. However, I know not but I may still spare you five pounds, provided that you will not say, 'I will never ask you again', because that is more than you can tell; and you must not promise more than you can perform . . .[53]

After Westley Hall decamped with one of his mistresses to the West Indies, Patty had settled down in London with her eldest sister Emily (Mrs Harper) in accommodation adjoining his West Street chapel provided by their brother John, who further contributed enough to allow the employment of a maidservant. He and Charles between them also made provision for Patty's one surviving child. But Patty was to understand that if they found a suitable school for this son, she must not subsequently 'interfere', but leave him to her brothers' 'disposal'. It was God, not man, however, who finally disposed: the boy was soon to join his nine dead brothers and sisters. Their father Hall, eventually returned to England, was 'given deep repentance' and forgiven by his wife Patty. He died in 1775, Wesley officiating at his funeral. 'It is enough', he wrote, 'if after all his wanderings we meet again in Abraham's bosom.'

These two sisters, Emily and Patty, whom John at least preserved from penury, proved to a degree disappointing to him. Emily had always had a sharp tongue, and was never prepared to accept either her brother John or Methodism at *his* valuation, however genuinely she loved him. In fact, neither sister, so Wesley complained, would 'join heartily' in his work, as he thought he had a right to expect. Why, he demanded, did they 'cavil' and keep their distance? Could it be that they did not *understand* what he and his brother were about? Or simply that they lacked 'resolution, spirit, patience?'[54]

When he came to consider, the only one of his relations, other than Charles, who had been of the slightest use to him in the furthering of God's work was Hetty, 'sister Wright', who in her latter years of illness and sorrow had found religious consolation and died a pious Methodist. Emily at least continued attending the West Street chapel until her death in 1771; but this grievance of Wesley's never quite vanished. Patty was far from being an irreligious woman. Boswell, who met her in Dr Johnson's company, and noted, incidentally, how closely she physically resembled her famous brother, writes of 'lean, lank . . . exquisite' but also *preaching* Mrs Hall; and she died (a very old lady, in the same year as John) in 'the assurance she had long prayed for'. But in her later years she had been closer to Charles and his family than to John. Charles's musician sons, as they grew up, were hardly to see eye to eye with their uncle – one of them for a time actually turned Papist. In the last months of his life we find Wesley writing in a voice more of pathos perhaps than bitterness to the sister of these nephews, Sarah Wesley junior, pleading with her to join a Methodist class he particularly recommended: 'Let me have the comfort of one relation, at least, that will be an assistant to me in the blessed work of God.'[55]

'I have known those', Wesley wrote, 'who could only afford to eat a little coarse food every other day, and known one picking up stinking sprats from a dunghill and carrying them home for herself and children. I have known another gathering the bones that the dogs had left and making broth of them to prolong a wretched life.' His efforts to relieve destitution could never, as he always recognized, do more than nibble here and there at the edges of so vast a problem. But what he might do, that he must; that he would. In the very severe winter of 1763 for instance, when the Thames froze over, he opened a soup kitchen at the Moorfields Foundry and distributed cash relief. Two years later he was organizing collections to relieve the plight of London's unemployed weavers. On a more regular basis his London stewards distributed at this time about £7 or £8 per week among the 'deserving poor'. There was one period when his book sales allowed him to disburse £1400 in a single year, and indeed towards the end of his life he was annually giving away something like £1000.

At the same time one had to remember that although penury

was a great evil, immorality was a greater. The one brought temporary misery indeed, but the other everlasting woe. It was natural therefore that when a revived Society for the Reformation of Manners was formed in 1757, Wesley became its active and vocal supporter. Long before, his father had, by invitation, addressed an earlier society similarly named. Wesley preached on his father's identical text before its successor. In 1763 he was able to congratulate his fellow campaigners on five or six years' extensive achievement in the cause of purer living: 10,588 cases had been brought before the courts on charges of prostitution, brothel-keeping, Sabbath-breaking, profane swearing, obscene publishing, or unlawful gaming. Of the society's leading 160 members, Wesley reckoned that some 70 were Dissenters, 20 Whitefieldites, 50 Wesleyans, 20 'unconnected' Anglicans; that it did 'unspeakable good'; and that its eventual breakdown in 1766 under the strain of its legal expenses represented a deplorable victory for the forces of unrighteousness.

In other areas of philanthropy and social betterment Wesley was no less decidedly on the side of the angels. He declared the press gang an iniquity. Cock-fighting represented the 'foul remains of Gothic barbarity'.[56] British treatment of French prisoners of war he more than once condemned as disgraceful. The game laws were a scandal. The institution of slavery – not merely the trade – was indefensible. This was another matter on which his views departed sharply from those of Whitefield, who as Bible student and American proprietor of some seventy-five slaves, justified his position by reference to the Old Testament patriarchs. What was right for Abraham could hardly be wrong for Whitefield, who moreover like his fellow slave-owners in the southern states would be quite unable to farm without their black labourers. 'I trust', he added, 'many of them will be brought to Jesus.'*

In England, most of the early running in the battle against slavery, and in particular against the Atlantic slave traffic, was made by the Quakers. In the same year, 1772, that Lord Mansfield delivered the historic judgement which denied legal recognition to the status of slave, Wesley, after reading a book by the Ameri-

* In his will Whitefield bequeathed his slaves, together with the rest of his property in America, to 'that elect lady, that mother in Israel', Lady Huntingdon.

can Quaker, Anthony Benezet, himself attacked the wickedness
of the existing slave trade, for which, he wrote, he could find no
parallel in 'the heathen world, whether ancient or modern', and
whose barbarities exceeded those practised on Christian slaves in
Muslim countries. Two years later he published his *Thoughts on
Slavery*, soon to be issued also in Philadelphia. By the closing
years of Wesley's life, the British anti-slave-trade movement
begun by Granville Sharp, Clarkson and their associates had
recruited its most influential advocate in Wilberforce, and it is
fitting that the last letter Wesley was to write, in 1791, should be
addressed to this man who in many fields was to be his natural
successor. 'My dear Sir,' he wrote,

> Unless the Divine power has raised you up to be as Athanasius
> *contra mundum*, I see not how you can go through your glorious
> enterprise, in opposing that execrable villany which is the scandal
> of religion, of England, and of human nature. Unless God has
> raised you up for the very thing, you will be worn out by the
> opposition of men and devils, but, if God be for you, who can be
> against you? . . . Go on, in the name of God, and in the power of
> his might, till even American slavery, the vilest that ever saw the
> sun, shall vanish before it.
>
> Reading this morning a tract by a poor African, I was parti-
> cularly struck by that circumstance, – that a man who has a black
> skin, being wronged or outraged by a white man, can have no
> redress; it being a *law* in our colonies that the oath of a black,
> against a white, goes for nothing. What villany is this! . . .

It would be unlike Wesley not to have strong views on
remedies for economic distress at home, or, having them, to fail
to publish them. Thus during the severe winter of 1772–3 'the
great council of the land' was publicly advised by John Wesley
the political economist and social moralist, in a 2000-word letter
to the press of London and Leeds[57] (promptly as usual produced
as a pamphlet) to take a variety of steps. They should reduce the
price of wheat by putting a ban on distilling; of oats by taxing
and hence reducing the number of horses and gentlemen's
carriages; of beef and mutton by encouraging the breeding of
more sheep and cattle; of pork and poultry by 'repressing luxury'
and preventing farms of above £100 a year from being let; of
land by a combination of all the above methods; and of £2
million of taxation by discharging half the national debt. It is

not probable that he expected much of this to be acted on, or that he had any confidence that the then government of Lord North was likely to concur in his guiding generalization that the luxury of the rich was 'the grand source' of the wretchedness of the poor. When in 1776 the Commissioners of Excise circulated a polite enquiry to all those possibly suspect of keeping undeclared 'any quantity of silver plate, chargeable by the act of Parliament', Wesley's reply was righteously belligerent: 'Sir, – I have *two* silver teaspoons at London, and *two* at Bristol. This is all the plate which I have at present; and I shall not buy any more while so many round me want bread.'[58]

In 1778 Parliament passed a bill to allow military recruits who were Roman Catholics the right on enlistment simply to take an oath of allegiance. It was only a modest move in the direction of emancipating Catholics from their civic disabilities, but it roused once again the fierce old Protestant cry of 'No Popery', and, in an age of rapidly multiplying political 'associations' produced yet one more in Lord George Gordon's Protestant Association. This militantly anti-Romanist organization fetched out a crowd estimated at 60,000 strong on the day when Lord George presented his *protesting* petition to Parliament. There followed the terrible week of the Gordon Riots, in which Catholic chapels and property were the prime, but far from the only, targets of the looting, fire-raising, drunken London mob, quelled bloodily at last by troops.

Of course Wesley deplored these disgraceful excesses. But he did have the greatest sympathy for Gordon's Protestant Association, which had helped to rouse the rabble and provoke the events of that nightmare week. Wesley himself published at about this time an anti-Catholic broadsheet, *The Increase of Popery*. Praising the Protestant Association, he initiated one controversy in the columns of *The Public Advertiser*, and took a spirited part in another in *The Freeman's Journal*, where his adversary was a no less spirited Father O'Leary, a Capuchin friar of Dublin, who had published a capable and polished pamphlet in reply to Wesley. Wesley denied representing any spirit of intolerance, but he unequivocally condemned the government's Catholic Relief Act, particularly on the grounds that it relied on a Romanist's oath of allegiance, which was necessarily worthless since the Council of Constance in 1414 had pronounced that no faith need be kept with heretics. 'With persecution', he wrote in *The Public Advertiser*, 'I have nothing to do. I persecute no man for his religious principles . . . But this does not touch the point.'

> Setting, then, religion aside, it is plain that, upon principles of reason, no government ought to tolerate men who cannot give any security to that government for their allegiance and peaceable behaviour. But this no Romanist can do, not only while he holds that 'no faith is to be kept with heretics', but so long as he acknowledges either priestly absolution or the spiritual power of the Pope.
>
> 'But the late Act,' you say, 'does not either tolerate or encourage Roman Catholics.' I appeal to matter of fact. Do not the Romanists themselves understand it as a toleration? You know they do. And does it not already (let alone what it *may* do by-and-by) encourage them to preach openly, to build chapels (at Bath and elsewhere) to raise seminaries, and to make numerous converts day by day to their intolerant persecuting principles?[59]

Such was the uncompromising hostility of a man frequently charged by his theological opponents with being himself a Romanist sympathizer.

When a grand jury found a true bill against the inflammatory Lord George Gordon, Wesley exploded with indignation. It was a scandal, a 'shocking insult against truth and common sense'. Gordon being confined in the Tower, Wesley visited him there and found him 'much acquainted with both the letter and the sense of the scriptures'.[60]

Characteristically, seven years after their vigorous public hostilities, Wesley sat down to a friendly breakfast with Father O'Leary in Cork, and discovered him 'not to be wanting either in sense or learning'. His own pamphlet against the Papists, he declared, had been written not out of enmity (though he did on another occasion pronounce them, if they died Romanists, to be incapable of salvation), but 'to preserve our happy constitution'.

Throughout his long life his political convictions remained immovably conservative and paternalist. Authority derived from God alone, as within Methodism it derived under God from Wesley alone. The business of politicians was to give *clean* government – he attacked electoral corruption in his *Word to a Freeholder* and elsewhere – but *self*-government, whether for Englishmen or Americans, would be both impractical and improper. Populist radicalism of the Wilkes variety and the

verbal violence of the *Letters* of Junius, anti-governmental or
hostile to the monarch, he found equally distasteful.[61] He had no
sympathy with such democratic ideas as were beginning to stir
during his later years, and declared uncompromisingly, 'The
greater the share people have in government, the less liberty,
civil or religious, does a nation enjoy.'

He had grown up in a domestic and university climate tending
towards Jacobitism, but the mature Wesley became an unquestioning Hanoverian and the staunchest of conventional
patriots. The Jacobites had been tarred with the French as well
as the Romish brush, and he was particular during the '45
rebellion publicly to condemn them. Loyal Protestant subjects
who feared God must not fail to honour the King. During the
Seven Years War he again advertised his patriotism by publicly
offering to raise funds to support a troop of volunteers. During
the American crisis in 1775, because he judged that the public
was 'in a flame of malice and rage against the King and almost all
that are in authority under him', he reckoned it his duty to help
put out that flame. He appears to have convinced himself that
George III was the object of universal hatred and contempt.

> The bulk of the people in every city, town, and village . . . wish
> to imbue their hands in his blood; they are full of the spirit of
> murder and rebellion . . . It is as much as ever I can do, and
> sometimes more than I can do, to keep this plague from infecting
> my own friends.[62]

Thus we find him at this time lecturing political malcontents
among his own people down at Plymouth.[63]

· It was Plymouth too that afforded evidence of a more reassuring
nature. If the English could not exactly call God their fellow
countryman, at least they might reasonably claim him as the
most potent and reliable of allies – for *why* had the combined
fleets of France and Spain in 1779, when they had this vital port
utterly at their mercy, sailed away leaving the place unscathed?
'The plain reason was, the bridle of God was in their teeth, and
he had said, "Hitherto shall ye come, and no farther".'[64]

Throughout his life he maintained the sort of disapproval of
things French which was characteristic of the eighteenth-century
Englishman. With Wesley this extended as far as a comprehensive
dismissal not only of French literature but of the language itself.

We might no doubt expect that he would find Rousseau a 'consummate coxcomb' and 'cynic all over', his 'brother-infidel Voltaire . . . wellnigh as great a coxcomb' and 'the famous Montesquieu . . . no more to be compared to Lord Forbes or Dr Beattie than a mouse to a elephant'.[65] But our estimation of his good judgement is hardly enhanced by his crotchety condemnation of French as 'the poorest, meanest language in Europe, no more comparable to the Spanish or German than a bagpipe is to an organ', or his assertion that it was 'as impossible to write a fine poem in French as to make fine music on a jew's harp'. Such dicta might sound less foolish if like Johnson's they had been sparks thrown off in the friction of conversation. But Wesley was his own Boswell, and what was written daily in his journal was within a few years unfailingly perpetuated in the published version.

So the *Journal*, as well as being a record of half a century of religious activity, became a miscellany of instant judgements on literature, politics, society, science, history, everything.* Dr Price's *Observations upon Liberty*, if put into practice, 'would overturn all government and bring in universal anarchy'. Hume was an 'insolent despiser of truth and virtue', Leibniz a sour, conceited, and generally lamentable writer, one moreover who regrettably maintained 'without reserve that God had absolutely decreed from all eternity whatever is done in time'. Mary Queen of Scots was 'far the greatest woman of her age', but Elizabeth I about 'as just and merciful as Nero, and as good a Christian as Mahomet'. The histories of Livy and Polybius were no more than fiction, the story of St Patrick an improbable romance, Captain Cook's *Voyages* an invention as little credible as *Robinson Crusoe*. Raphael was 'a poor designer . . . O pity that so fine a painter should be utterly without common sense!' Sterne's *Sentimental Journey* was 'queer, odd, uncouth' (and moreover he objected to the neologism: 'Sentimental? What is that? It is not English!') Ossian, however, the faked epic, was 'little inferior to Homer or Virgil, and in some respects superior to both'. There was 'no reasonable doubt' that England's patron saint

---

* 'He leaps to conclusions,' wrote Ronald Knox (*Enthusiasm*, p. 447); 'is easily taken in, or no less easily repelled, by the last author who has been in his hands; altogether he is not a good advertisement for reading on horseback.'

should have been St Gregory, not St George ('Georgius' having been misread somewhere along the line for 'Gregorius'). And what a pity that the sodomite Frederick the Great was not beheaded by his father in youth, and thus saved from later sin and shame!

When he read that in a revolution in Genoa an unarmed rabble had driven out a disciplined army, he took it as 'plain proof that God rules in all the Kingdoms of the earth'. As for the Irish, their land would probably have 'been wholly desolate before now had not the English come, and prevented the implacable wretches from going on till they had swept each other from the earth'. The Irish language, with its 'intolerable number of mute letters', and the native Irish poetry written in it, were alike insufferable. Electricity was a wonder to be welcomed, in view particularly of its therapeutic powers; but the more he thought about 'modern astronomy', the more his scepticism grew. He doubted whether anybody knew 'either the distance or magnitude' of the sun and the moon and the planets. He did know, however, that after a certain Ann Wheeler, being pregnant, was struck in the forehead by a stone, her child was born carrying the mark of the missile, and retained it 'to this day'. And he was passionately convinced on the subject of witches and witchcraft, which the 'infidels' had 'hooted out of the world'. In the past had not everybody, heathen and Christian, believed in witchcraft? And was not the pert, saucy, indecent manner in which so-called modern-minded Christians rejected it 'extremely offensive to every sensible man who cannot give up his Bible'?[66]

CHAPTER 15

Doctrinal War

THE LIVE-AND-LET-LIVE observed, if precariously, during the 1760s between the Calvinist and anti-Calvinist wings of the Methodist movement did not last. New dissension was brewing from 1768, though it began as a quarrel less between Methodist and Methodist than between Lady Huntingdon's following and the more conventional and conservative elements in the Church of England.

The Countess had subsidized the term-time residence of some of her earnest young acolytes at St Edmund Hall, Oxford, while in their vacations they practised round the country as lay preachers, 'ambassadors of King Jesus'. One of them, a barber-wigmaker, had the ill fortune to live, and the temerity to preach, in his native Shropshire parish where an old St Edmund Hall man happened to be the incumbent. The young barber publicly denigrated his vicar. The vicar contacted his old college. The college reported to the university authorities. The university then expelled the students; whereupon Lady Huntingdon's supporters flew vehemently into print, extending their original protest against the injustice of the expulsion into a spirited defence of the young men's theology. Dr Johnson was among those who thought that their removal from Oxford had been 'very just and proper. What have they to do at a university who are not willing to be taught, and will presume to teach? . . . Sir, they were examined, and found to be mighty ignorant fellows.' Wesley, temperamentally on the side of the young preachers, was nevertheless inhibited by his dislike of their predestinarianism from defending them. Their fiercest champions, soon to be also Wesley's noisiest enemies, were the two pamphleteers Richard, later Sir

Richard, Hill, a Shropshire landowner, and the young Rev. Augustus Toplady, who had once (in an Irish barn) been born anew into Wesley's flock, but had since become a bell-wether of Lady Huntingdon's and an uncompromisingly extreme Calvinist. There was a considerable part of Wesley that dreaded this issue and hoped it might go away. The rest of him knew very well it never would, and could not resist publicly controverting a doctrine he so detested. He tried to persuade both himself and others of how he hated and shrank from polemics. 'Lord, if I must dispute', he wrote 'let it be with children of the devil! Let me be at peace with thy children!'[1] Unfortunately it did not always prove possible to distinguish between these two categories. And must not God demand that his offer of redemption for *all* mankind be shouted from the housetops, and that those who denied it must be out-argued by his faithful children? 'How much rather would I write practically than controversially', Wesley reflected on another occasion, 'but even this talent I dare not bury in the earth.'[2]

In 1769 Toplady published *The Doctrine of Absolute Predestination Stated and Asserted*, being a translation 'in great measure' from the Latin of one Jerom Zanchius. At this, Wesley first took the liberty of abridging Toplady's 134-page pamphlet to make a penny tract, and then added insult to injury by appending a belligerent little coda:

> The sum of all is this: One in twenty (suppose) of mankind are elected; nineteen in twenty are reprobated. The elect shall be saved, do what they will; the reprobate will be damned, do what they can. Reader believe this, or be damned. Witness my hand,
> A.......T......

This was undoubtedly neat; but it was asking for a fight, and it certainly got one. Toplady rushed in again with an attack on Wesley in which no venom was spared. He had a legitimate grievance: 'Why did you not abridge me faithfully and fairly?' he demanded. 'Why must you lard your ridiculous compendium with additions and interpolations of your own, especially as you took the liberty of prefixing my name to it?' Other pamphlets aimed against Wesley sprang up like mushrooms, while the *Gospel Magazine*, under the editorship of William Romaine, maintained an excited onslaught against the man who was

alleged to be seducing true Protestants into believing 'the
doctrines of the mother of harlots, the whore of Babylon, the
Church of Rome'.[3]

Sectarian feathers were already flying before August 1770,
when Wesley after that year's Conference, the twenty-seventh,
decided to *publish* its minutes, which included a new statement by
him of his current attitude to the place of 'works' in the scheme of
salvation. In the footnotes to the standard (1909–16) edition of his
Journal, the annotator loyally comments that these Minutes of
1770, 'with great clearness and precision state the Methodist
position in relation to the extreme form of Calvinism which was
playing havoc in all the Methodist borders and also in the most
fruitful pastures of [Anglicans, English Dissenters and Scottish
Presbyterians]'; and adds that he had 'difficulty in understanding
why they should have created so great a sensation, resulting in a
disastrous controversy'.[4] In fact, clarity and precision are hardly
among the virtues of the 1770 Minutes, whose jottings, ob-
scurities, and hair-splitting give rather the impression of a man
thinking aloud, and still only inching towards conclusions which
– at least on the value of 'works' – were radically at variance with
those he had enunciated in earlier days. One of his pronouncements of 1770 which *was* as clear as it was clearly important was
that Methodists had 'leaned too much towards Calvinism'. It
was further declared that a righteous man who feared God might
be 'accepted of God' even if he had 'never heard of Christ';
and also, more bafflingly, that 'we are rewarded according to our
works, yea, because of our works', yet not by the *merit* of our
works* – so that (mysteriously enough) 'salvation by works' was
to be accepted only in the sense of works 'as a condition'.

If this last is too difficult for non-theologians to puzzle sense
from, there was in it more than enough for the Calvinists of 1770
to sniff heinous heterodoxy. Where now was Justification by
Faith Alone, accepted hitherto as the ark of the covenant for all
Methodists, whether Wesleyan, Whitefieldite, Welsh Calvinist,
or whatever? The Minutes, Lady Huntingdon rather absurdly

---

* That Wesley appreciated he was, in this, treading over bubbles is
indicated by a letter he wrote to his brother a year later. After (wrongly)
claiming that he had not used the word 'merit', he says: 'I ask you . . . a plain
question, and do not cry Murder, but give me an answer. What is the
difference between . . . "deserving" and "meritum"? I say still, I cannot tell.
Can you? Can Mr Shirley, or any man living?'

declared, were 'popery unmasked'; and 'all ought to be deemed papists' who did not disown them.[5]

The Countess and her cousin and chaplain Walter Shirley were in process of organizing the forces of 'real Protestantism' when the news arrived of Whitefield's death in America. In accordance with prior agreement, Wesley was invited to give the commemorative sermon, which he preached before capacity congregations three times, once in Whitefield's Tottenham Court Road chapel, once in his Moorfields Tabernacle, and once at the Greenwich Tabernacle. His address offered a mourning tribute both eloquent and sincere.[6] It also, before the mainly Calvinist audience, pleaded for an end to 'strife, envy, contention'. Let them all stop 'biting and devouring one another'. Let them remember the two fundamental doctrines that summed up the dead preacher's credo: the New Birth and Justification by Faith. But a third doctrine, no less basic, Wesley studiously omitted to mention: predetermined election and reprobation, or in a word, predestination. And when he was attacked on this point in *The Gospel Magazine* by Romaine, who asserted that 'the grand fundamental doctrines' which Whitefield everywhere preached were not as Wesley had said, but 'the Everlasting Covenant between the Father and the Son and Absolute Predestination flowing therefrom', Wesley unconvincingly replied that since Whitefield had never asserted these beliefs when preaching by invitation in his, Wesley's, chapel, therefore he could not have held them to be fundamental.[7]

To Lady Huntingdon Wesley complained that not only she but 'wellnigh all the religious world' had arrayed themselves against him. He was ready to admit the possibility that some lines in the Minutes might have been ill expressed. But the gospel he preached, he still insisted, was the same that he had preached for more than thirty years – and moreover it was 'glaring, undeniable fact' he was arguing from! Despite this, however:

> There may be opinions maintained at the same time which are not exactly true: and who can be secure from these? Perhaps I thought myself so once: when I was much younger than I am now, I thought myself almost infallible: but I bless God I know myself better now.
>
> To be short: such as I am, I love you well. You have one of the first places in my esteem and affection. And you once had

some regard for me. But it cannot continue if it depends upon my seeing with your eyes or on my being in no mistake . . .

He remained her Ladyship's 'truly affectionate but much injured servant'.[8]

By the time the 1771 Conference met in Bristol, some softening of attitudes on both sides looked possible. Wesley and fifty-three of his preachers agreed there to sign a declaration that the previous year's Minutes did *not* indicate approval of Justification by Works; that such a 'perilous and abominable' doctrine was to be abhorred; and that, although 'no one is a real Christian believer (and consequently cannot be saved) who doth not good works where there is time and opportunity, yet our works have no part in meriting or purchasing our salvation'.[9] On his side Shirley, representing his cousin and her party, consented to acknowledge that they had interpreted the Minutes mistakenly. But these mutually presented olive branches failed to usher in any era of peace and goodwill – not altogether surprisingly in view of the fact that Wesley refused Shirley's request that he should cancel the imminent publication of a pamphlet vindicating the Minutes, written by his supporter the vicar of Madeley, John Fletcher.

Wesley made only occasional further sorties into these long-continuing hostilities, leaving the brunt to the Rev. Walter Sellon, to the Welsh shoemaker-preacher-printer Thomas Olivers, and most of all to Fletcher, who had of course by this time severed his connection with Lady Huntingdon's Trevecca seminary. Fletcher was at one time intended by Wesley to be his successor, but he predeceased him. Until 1776, when his health began to fail, his defence of Wesley's theological standpoint ran to many hundreds of for the most part restrained and scholarly pages, notably in *Checks to Antinomianism*. Olivers, sneered at as Tom the Cobbler by his gentlemanly Calvinist opponents, was rather more inclined to trade blow for blow – and the Calvinist blows (above all from Toplady and the two brothers Hill, Richard and Rowland) were sustained and punishing. Wesley was a 'universal meddler and universal miscarrier', 'the most rancorous hater of the gospel system that ever appeared in England', 'a proverb for his contradictions', a 'wicked slanderer', 'an enemy of all righteousness', 'unprincipled as a rook and silly as a jackdaw', an 'apostate miscreant', etc., etc. In 1772 and again in 1773 Wesley let go a few punches in return, though he had earlier professed unwillingness to bandy argument with a 'chimney sweeper' like Toplady. As for Richard Hill: 'his name as a writer is Wormwood'. And the *Journal* in 1772 twice makes exasperated mention of the products of Trevecca College, 'raw, pert, young men (vulgarly, though very improperly, called students)', who were trying to foul the Methodist nest. (There is another reference to these 'striplings' at Grimsby in 1779.) Passing through the village of Trevecca itself he quotes with approval the complaint of Howel Harris the Welsh evangelist (who happened also to be the local squire* and was reckoned a 'moderate' Calvinist himself): 'They preach bare-faced Reprobation [predestined damnation] and so broad Antinomianism that I have been constrained to oppose them to the face, even in the public congregation.'[10]

From their side of the fence, were Wesleyans to believe that all who died firm in their Calvinist beliefs were necessarily damned? It seems that some had misinterpreted Wesley on this important question. In 1776 he briefly set one of his correspondents right on it: 'You misunderstand me. I never said or thought that everyone who lives and dies a Calvinist is damned. I believe thousands [of them] are now in Abraham's bosom. And yet I am persuaded that opinion has led many thousands to hell.'[11]

On a serious theological level, and name-calling apart, the teachings of Wesley and his preachers which gave most offence to Toplady and his fellow-Calvinist extremists were three: *free will*, which they denied; *merit* – that is 'deserving' salvation by good deeds; and *sanctification*, or 'Christian perfection'. His unsoundness on these issues gave them occasion for boundless indignation. This reached a pitch of fury in 1777, after Wesley had preached a sermon at the laying of the foundation stone of his new City Road chapel; 'a wretched harangue', declared Rowland Hill in his *Imposture Detected*, 'from which the blessed name of Jesus is almost totally excluded'. Remove, he said, half a dozen lines from Wesley's sermon, and the shrewdest of readers would be unable to detect 'whether the lying apostle of the Foundry be a Jew, a papist, a pagan, or a Turk'. 'Popery', he asserted rather ridiculously, 'is about midway between Protestantism and Mr J.

---

* In his establishment at Trevecca Harris housed a sort of Protestant monastery, with a 'family' of a hundred or so.

Wesley.' 'When you take Old Nick by the nose', observed *The Gospel Magazine*, 'it must be with a pair of red-hot tongs.' Set beside Hill, even Toplady seemed 'a very civil fair-spoken gentleman', Wesley remarked; but when he replied to Hill's latest attack with another of his penny tracts he was careful to avoid answering abuse with abuse.

Toplady, the ablest of these extreme Calvinists, died in 1778, aged only thirty-seven and protesting to the last his detestation of Wesley and all his works. But the chorus of calumny and vituperation continued unabated – against Wesley, the man whose 'grand design . . . is that of trumpeting forth his own praise', 'a man of cunning, and artifices, and foul aspersions, and quibbles and evasions'; Wesley portrayed as an aspirant to a mitre, as a serpent, as a fox in canonicals, as an ass on its hind legs preaching; as a nostrum-monger, as a quack. His odious name would

. . . stink beyond the grave
And truth proclaim him a recorded knave.

Among these Calvinist contributions to the defence of Christian truth we find *Perfection, A Poetical Epistle . . . to the Greatest Hypocrite in England; The Gospel Shop, A Comedy in Five Acts* by R. Hill, Esq., of Cambridge (featuring Dr Scapegoat, Parson Prolix, Mr Rackett, and Simon Sycophant); and *The Saints, a Satire,* where Wesley

Makes Piety a bawd to aid his work
Outlies Sam Johnson, and outwhores a Turk.[12]

A few months before Toplady died, Wesley decided to launch a periodical of his own, primarily to counter *The Gospel Magazine* and sound the trumpet for 'the universal love of God, and His willingness to save all men from all sin'; '80 pages, in octavo, printed on fine paper . . . will be delivered monthly to each subscriber, at the price of one shilling'. He called his new venture *The Arminian Magazine,* the first number appearing in January 1778. (For its early editing and printing Olivers was responsible, until Wesley dismissed him for permitting 'intolerable and innumerable errata'.) In time the name would be changed to *The Methodist Magazine,* then to the *Wesleyan Methodist Magazine,* and it was destined for a long life indeed.

The shrill acrimony towards Wesley shown by the men of *The Gospel Magazine,* often degenerating into the ludicrous, only

weakened what was then theologically a respectable case. Indeed
in strictly polemical terms it may be doubted whether Wesley
had the better of the argument on predestination. The whole
notion was one which his conviction of God's love and justice
caused him instinctively to reject. Predestination destroyed the
joy of Christianity. It made God worse than the Devil. Yet,
hundred-per-cent scripturalist that he was, he could not ignore
the texts upon which Calvinists founded their determinism, and
he was too honest merely to take refuge in the many available
counter-texts, though he and his aides in the controversy did
make great play with them.[13]

In his sermon *On Predestination* he plunged his head boldly into
the lion's mouth, preaching from the most explicit of all the
Pauline texts of the subject, Romans viii. 29, 30:

> Whom he did foreknow, he also did predestinate to be con-
> formed to the image of his Son. Whom he did predestinate, them
> he also called. And whom he called, them he also justified. And
> whom he justified, them he also glorified.

God, so the plain sense of Paul's words (which Wesley always
absolutely equates with God's words) obliged him to accept, does
foreknow which men will and which will not have faith, and thus
acquire grace and be saved. Yet, he argued, what God knows is
not *made to happen* by his knowledge. (This is precisely the point
made in a letter written him by his mother many years before.)
'Men are as free in believing or not believing' as if God did not
already know the outcome. What Wesley does not attempt to
explain is this: If as he agrees God 'foreknows', even if he does
not 'cause', a man's faith or infidelity, how can that faith or
infidelity, and hence his salvation or damnation, be anything but
predestined?

He seeks a way out of this intellectual difficulty in a line of
explanation which does not readily persuade. To speak properly,
he says, there is no such thing as foreknowledge or afterknowledge
with God, since

> the almighty, all-wise God sees and knows, from everlasting to
> everlasting, all that is, that was, and that is to come, through
> one eternal *now* . . . Yet when he speaks to us ['he', be it noted,
> not St Paul], knowing the scantiness of our understanding, he
> lets himself down to our capacity . . . It is merely in compassion
> to us that he speaks thus of himself, as foreknowing the things

in heaven or earth, and as predestinating or fore-ordaining them. But can we possibly imagine that these expressions are to be taken literally?

If this was not rejecting the reliability of the text it was surely going very near it. Certainly it was a remarkable argument to be employed by so literal a Bible Christian. It might well be thought, if it was not quite severed, his head was not extracted unscathed from the lion's mouth.

On his tour of the Midlands and Cheshire in 1782 Wesley was still finding occasion to complain of the tactics of his doctrinal enemies. 'Coming to Congleton', he records with sarcastic bitterness, 'I found the Calvinists were just breaking in and striving to make havoc of the flock. Is this brotherly love? . . . No more than robbing on the highway. But if it is *decreed*, they cannot help it; so we cannot blame them.'

As the years went by, however, it was his teaching on Christian perfection, challenging as it did the ineradicability of sin, rather than his assertion of free will and 'free grace', which seems to have given most offence to Calvinists. This was partly because the earlier uncompromising interpretation of the Pauline texts propounded by Toplady and his friends of *The Gospel Magazine* gave way with most Calvinist evangelicals to a modification of the doctrine of predestination which, while holding on to predestined election, quietly discarded the fearsome decree of predetermined damnation. (In much the same manner subsequently, many Christians – or as Wesley would have it 'almost Christians' – while retaining some sort of belief in heaven, would come to jettison, or at least de-literalize, the complementary concept of hell.) Despite this controversy surrounding Perfection, relations between Methodism and Calvinistic Anglicanism continued to improve during Wesley's last years and just after. Most of the Calvinistic evangelicals of the 1790s were of a very different kidney from Toplady and the Hills, anxious to stand less on Calvin's *Institutes* than on the Thirty-Nine Articles, and professing a readiness to avoid 'acrimonious reflection on any sect of professing Christians' – as in 1793 the successor to *The Gospel Magazine* proclaimed in its first number. Five years later, and only seven after Wesley's death, the author of *Union and Friendly Intercourse Recommended* was even prepared to claim that Calvinists and Wesleyans had 'ceased to irritate each other'.[14]

CHAPTER 16

The Gordian Knot

THE 1770S, THE PERIOD OF the angriest Calvinist-Arminian contention, were also the decade in which Wesley reached, and sailed serenely past, threescore years and ten. At seventy-five he thought nothing of getting out of the stage-coach London-bound from Chatham as it dawdled up the hill past Strood, and walking five miles before being overtaken and getting in again. ('I cared not if it had been ten. The more I walk the sounder I sleep.') 'He thought nothing' is not strictly right. He thought a great deal, repeatedly making reference to his continuing strength, with reminders to himself, to his correspondents, and to his public in general of the wise regimen which enabled him so wonderfully to keep going: the frugal diet, the constant exercise, the ability to command instant sleep, the early rising. The getting up early became a particular hobby-horse with him.

'Shall I tell you', he wrote at seventy-eight to his niece Sally, (Charles's daughter Sarah), then about twenty, 'what I judge to be the grand hindrance to your [attaining God's favour]? Yea, to your attaining more health of body and mind? . . . I believe it is what very few people are aware of, intemperance in sleep.' There follows, for Sally's benefit, an admonitory little essay on the consequences of exceeding the correct number of hours, namely six or seven for men, seven or eight for women. There would ensue numerous disorders – faintness, nervous headaches, eye trouble, a weakened understanding, a damaged memory, a blunted imagination. All this from the indulgence of one hour's extra sleep; the cocksureness of his punditry is breathtaking. All this, and worse: for that one hour too many 'takes the edge off the soul . . . and infuses a wrong softness, quite inconsistent with the character of a good soldier of Jesus Christ'.[1]

As he grew old and still rose daily at four to prepare for the five o'clock service, it saddened him to see so many Methodists unwilling to follow his example, failing too to observe the weekly fast on Friday, thinking they had done enough if they attended the week-night class meeting, refrained from 'open sin', and went to Sunday chapel. Methodism should mean much more. It should be a school of holiness, a progress from justification and new birth towards sanctification and perfection, to which end the week-long observance of the Methodist way of life was essential. Going to Sunday chapel merely to enjoy a good rousing sermon and give voice to hearty 'luscious' hymns (the expression is Wesley's)* was as little likely to make one a good soldier of Jesus Christ as lying nine hours in bed.

Perhaps we may best be reminded that the ageing Wesley was predominantly engaged, not so much in the *furor theologicus* of anti-Calvinist controversy as in the same old evangelistic activity that had governed his life for the past forty years or so, by opening at random a page of his *Journal* and following him over a run-of-the-mill two or three weeks of his 76th year. There are no sensations; a straight account, relating the good and the bad; a 'mother in Israel', a faith-healing, a 'triumphant' death; the never-ending routine of preaching; the usual thing. Practically any other pages might have done as well, at least until we come to the important milestone of the opening of his City Road chapel, the new and roomier headquarters replacing the Moorfields Foundry.

Fri. 9. I returned to London; and Sunday, 11th, buried the remains of Eleanor Lee. I believe she received the great promise of God, entire sanctification, fifteen or sixteen years ago, and that she never lost it for an hour. I conversed intimately with her ever since, and never saw her do any action, little or great, nor heard her speak any word which I could reprove. Thou wast indeed 'a mother in Israel!'

Tues. 13. I took a little tour into Oxfordshire, and preached in the evening at Wallingford.

Wed. 14. I went on to Oxford, and having an hour to spare,

---

* The singing ought to be 'thoughtful' and 'theological'. A common Wesleyan practice was 'lining out' the hymns – reading each line aloud to point its meaning before singing it.

walked to Christ-Church, for which I cannot but still retain a peculiar affection. What lovely mansions are these! What is wanting to make the inhabitants of them happy? That without which no rational creature can be happy, the experimental knowledge of God. In the evening, I preached at Finstock, to a congregation gathered from many miles round. How gladly could I spend a few weeks in this delightful solitude! But I must not rest yet. As long as God gives me the strength to labour, I am to use it.

Thur. 15. I preached at Witney. Since Nancy B[olton] has been detained here, the work of God has greatly revived. Mysterious Providence! That one capable of being so extremely useful, should be thus shut up in a corner!

Fri. 16. I was desired to preach at Thame, on my return to London. I came thither a little after ten. The mob had been so troublesome there, that it was a doubt with the Preachers, whether the place should not be given up. However, I thought it might not be amiss, before this was done, to make one trial myself. But I found it impracticable to preach abroad, the wind being so exceeding sharp. I went therefore into a large building, formerly used by the Presbyterians. It was quickly filled, and more than filled, many being obliged to stand without. Yet there was no breath of noise; the whole congregation seemed to be 'all but their attention dead'. We had prayed before, that God would give us a quiet time, and he granted our request.

Immediately after a strange scene occurred. I was desired to visit one who had been eminently pious, but had now been confined to her bed for several months, and was utterly unable to raise herself up. She desired us to pray that the chain might be broken: a few of us prayed in faith: presently she rose up, dressed herself, came down stairs, and I believe had not any farther complaint. In the evening I preached at High Wycombe, and on Saturday returned to London . . .

Mon. 26. I set out in the diligence to Godmanchester, hoping to be there by six in the evening; but we did not come till past eight; so, most of the people being gone, I only gave a short exhortation. At five in the morning we had a large congregation, but much larger in the evening.

Wed. 28. About noon, I preached at St Neots, and afterwards visited a lovely young woman, who appeared to be in the last stage of a consumption, and was feebly gasping after God. She seemed to be just ripe for the Gospel, which she drank in with all her soul. God speedily brought her to the blood of sprinkling, and a few days after she died in peace.

I preached in the evening at Bedford, and the next day, *Thursday*, 29th, at Luton. We had a miserable preaching-house here; but Mr Cole has now fitted up a very neat and commodious room, which was thoroughly filled with well-behaved and deeply-attentive hearers. How long did we seem to be ploughing upon the sand here? But it seems there will be some fruit at last. *Fri.* 30. I preached at noon to fifty or sixty dull creatures, at poor, desolate Hertford; and they heard with something like seriousness. In the afternoon I went on to London.

Sunday, November 1, was the day appointed for the opening the New Chapel, in the City-Road. It is perfectly neat, but not fine; and contains far more people than the Foundery: I believe, together with the Morning Chapel, as many as the Tabernacle. Many were afraid that the multitudes crowding from all parts, would have occasioned much disturbance; but they were happily disappointed; there was none at all; all was quietness, decency and order. I preached on part of Solomon's Prayer at the Dedication of the Temple . . .

The following Christmas Day Wesley preached four sermons. 'I felt no weariness or weakness', he once more testifies, 'but was stronger after I had preached my fourth sermon than I was after the first.' His day must have begun at about 3 a.m. At four he held his first service, at City Road, and he was there again in the afternoon before a congregation 'packed in every corner'. In between, he administered the sacraments to several hundred people at his West Street chapel in Seven Dials. Then in the evening he preached at St Sepulchre's, one of London's parish churches. Anglican pulpits had been closed to him for many years, but much more frequently now he was being invited to preach from them – an indication of how in his old age opposition to him was softening, and he was gradually coming to be regarded as a venerable national institution. 'The tide is now turned', he was able to say in 1783; 'so that I have more invitations to preach in churches than I can accept of.'

There were of course Methodists, from both England and Ireland, who had emigrated to the American colonies. Their number was reported to the Conference of 1771 as 316. Two years previously Wesley had responded to a call for preachers from the New York brethren by asking for volunteers, and then dispatching Richard Boardman and Joseph Pilmoor to New York and Philadelphia respectively. By 1774 there were seven itinerant preachers under the general supervision of Wesley's delegate Thomas Rankin, and the membership had grown to over two thousand; American Methodism already held its own annual Conference, the first meeting in Philadelphia in 1773.

As colonial resentments grew and disorders multiplied, Wesley at first contented himself with hoping that God would 'hear prayer and turn the counsels of Achitophel into foolishness'. Until that happier day, his preachers, so he instructed them, were to stick together, to ferret out trouble-makers, yet at the same time (a difficult combination surely) to preserve a judicious neutrality. By June 1775 he recognized in a letter to Rankin that 'ruin and desolation must soon over-spread the land'. There was little *he* could do; ought not Rankin, however, to appoint 'one or more general days of fasting and prayer?'[2]

That same month he sent to the evangelical Lord Dartmouth, Secretary for the Colonies in Lord North's government, a long and pessimistic letter on the American situation. It was far from rich in practical suggestions. The minister was asked, if there was anything to be done, to 'let it not be wanting' – and meanwhile to 'remember Rehoboam! Remember Philip the Second! Remember King Charles the First!' The parallels Wesley thought he saw between America in 1775 and England in 1640 were alarming – though when he considered 'the astonishing luxury of the rich, and the shocking impiety of rich and poor', he doubted whether the nation did not 'demand a general visitation'. Perhaps, indeed, the decree was already 'gone forth from the Governor of the world'. He wished to warn the government that the Americans, according to his information, were 'terribly united' and by no means lacking in an understanding of war. They would not be frightened into obedience; and though as a churchman bred in notions of non-resistance and passive obedience he bore prejudices hostile to the American rebels, nevertheless it was his opinion that an oppressed people had 'asked for nothing more than their legal rights'.[3]*

---

* Most biographers, and also the standard edition of Wesley's *Letters*, represent him as sending an almost identical message to the prime minister, Lord North. But Wesley later specifically denied ever having written to North. (See *Letters*, vi. 330)

That was written in June. Before the autumn he had written
and published a pamphlet, whose sales within three weeks
mounted to the then very high figure of 40,000, taking up a
remarkably changed attitude. In fact it was hardly his pamphlet
at all. In the interim he had read Samuel Johnson's *Taxation No
Tyranny*, swallowed it hook, line and sinker, and then regurgitated
it. Wesley's *Calm Address to the American Colonies* was not merely
in its drift but in much of its very language unacknowledged
Johnson, somewhat abridged. By this time Wesley had become
so habitual a retailer and 'improver' of other men's writings that
he probably saw nothing improper in what was essentially
plagiarism. He sold Johnson as his own wares much as he sold
Smollett, Goldsmith, Rapin, and the rest in his *Concise History*, or
his own father on *Baptism*, or numerous earlier authors in his
Concise Ecclesiastical History. He had come to regard all suitable
writing as grist to his own – which was to say God's – mill; and
he was always quick to point out (as he did now with his *Calm
Address*) that he published nothing for personal profit. It is of
course possible, but unlikely, that he had obtained Johnson's
prior consent – a suggestion some have thought gains support
from a graciously worded letter Johnson sent Wesley later,
thanking him for his 'important suffrage' to the arguments of
Taxation No Tyranny: 'to have gained such a mind as yours may
justly confirm me in my own opinion'.[4] Yet surely, if Johnson
had given permission, some acknowledgement from Wesley
would have been the minimum to be expected.

Naturally the *Calm Address* had a far from calm reception; but
Wesley was not the man to withdraw from battle, once engaged.
The sole concession he made to his opponents whose counter-
tracts were soon in spate, was to preface a reprint with a tardy
admission of his debt to Johnson. When the controversy overflowed into the newspapers he underlined his new-found conviction of where blame lay. The Americans were 'poor deluded
rebels'; they could not be fighting for liberty, for they had it
fully already, both civil and religious. What they contended for –
encouraged and incited by Englishmen at home – was 'the illegal
privilege of being exempt from parliamentary taxation'. In his
Seasonable Address to the Inhabitants of Great Britain (1776), *Some
Observations on Liberty* (1776), and *Calm Address to the Inhabitants*

of England (1777) he continued hammering away at the same nail. George III and his government had no more devoted champion – not that George III would have seen much wisdom in the policy advocated by Wesley in a letter to one of his preachers:

> I see no possibility of accommodation . . . I say, as Dean Tucker, 'Let them drop . . . Four and thirty millions they have cost us to support them since Queen Anne died. Let them cost us no more. Let them have their desire and support themselves.'[5]

The war for independence drove all but one of Wesley's preachers back to England, but also coincided with a rapid spread of American Methodism. The sole surviving preacher was Francis Asbury, a self-taught evangelist of outstanding piety and fortitude and tenacity, whom Wesley had sent out in 1771 and whose preaching record in America was to rival Wesley's own in Britain. Asbury, travelling his five or six thousand horseback miles a year, amid the hardships and hazards of an only half-tamed countryside, would preach in the course of the next forty-five years some twenty thousand sermons.

By the time the American states were at peace again in 1783, they numbered among them nearly 15,000 Methodists, all of them, it could be argued, still nominally members of the Church of England, but of a Church of England battered and weakened by the war. In Virginia, for instance, only 28 clergy remained out of 98, and very few of those were likely to have much sympathy with Methodism. Conversely, American Methodists, citizens now of an independent country, were psychologically readier to sever ecclesiastical relations with a recently hostile one. But they still felt a need for ordained clergy to administer the cardinally important church sacraments, and already by 1780 Asbury was begging Wesley to allow American preachers to celebrate them. Alternatively Wesley might himself assume episcopal powers and ordain an adequate number of preachers for America.

This was the Gordian knot he was as yet unready to cut, though it is clear from what he wrote to his brother in June 1780 that he had convinced himself he had a right to:

> Read Bishop Stillingsleet's *Irenicon*, or any impartial history of the ancient church, and you will think as I do, I verily believe, I

have as good a right to ordain as to administer the Lord's supper.
But I see abundance of reasons why I should not use that right,
unless I was turned out of the Church.[6]

This last was what deeply alarmed Charles: that his brother, by
using this 'right' which he claimed, might excommunicate
himself from the Church – or, as he once put it the other way
round, might excommunicate the Church from Methodism. But
for the time being Wesley would go no further than to appeal to
the bishop of London for a preacher – one preacher – to be
ordained, so that he might fulfil peripatetically the sacramental
needs of America's Methodists. On receiving a refusal, he
chastised the bishop in an indignantly reproachful letter, full of
contempt for the American clergy, most of whom 'knew no more
of saving souls than of catching whales'. He wrote:

> Give me leave, my lord, to speak more freely still: perhaps it is
> the last time I shall trouble your lordship. I know your lordship's
> abilities and extensive learning: I believe, what is far more, that
> your lordship fears God. I have heard that your lordship is
> unfashionably diligent in examining the candidates for holy
> orders; yea, that your lordship is generally at the pains of examin-
> ing them yourself. Examining them! in what respects? Why,
> whether they understand a little Latin and Greek; and can answer
> a few trite questions in the science of divinity! Alas, how little
> does this avail! Does your lordship examine whether they serve
> Christ or Belial? Whether they love God or the world? Whether
> they ever had any serious thoughts about heaven or hell? Whether
> they have any real desire to save their own souls, or the souls of
> others? If not, what have they to do with holy orders? and what
> will become of the souls committed to their care?
>
> My lord, I do by no means despise learning: I know the value
> of it too well. But what is this, particularly in a Christian minister,
> compared to piety? What is it in a man that has no religion?
> 'As a jewel in a swine's snout.'[7]

Before the spiritually deprived condition of his people in
America finally persuaded Wesley to ordain his own clergy,
Lady Huntingdon's Methodists provided him with some kind of
precedent. In 1783 the ecclesiastical courts pronounced against
two of the Countess's preachers who had been prosecuted by the
vicar of Clerkenwell for conducting services, against his wishes,

in a building in his parish not espiscopally consecrated. Lady
Huntingdon and her advisers had then decided that two of their
number who were ordained priests, the Rev. Taylor and the
Rev. Wills (the latter married to Lady Huntingdon's niece),
should formally secede from the Anglican Church, seeking the
protection of the Toleration Act, and then take upon themselves
the responsibility of ordaining further clergy. They were exercising exactly the same 'right' which Wesley had several times in
the past thirty or forty years claimed in theory but had not yet
dared to use. Bishops and presbyters being 'of the same order', he,
like Taylor and Wills, might ordain ministers as freely as any
lord bishop.

By the summer of 1784, the Church of England being no longer
recognized in America and the plight of conscientious Methodists
there being critical, Wesley at last decided on radical measures.
'Being now clear in my own mind, he wrote, 'I took a step which
I had long weighed in my mind', and appointed Mr Whatcoat
and Mr Vasey to go and serve the desolate sheep of America. I
added to them three more; which, I verily believe, will be much
to the glory of God.'[8] That was the *Journal*'s account; but it was a
seriously truncated version of what actually happened. The
vice-gerent he was sending to America was neither Mr Whatcoat
nor Mr Vasey, but the Rev. Dr Coke, one of the few 'presbyters' –
ordained ministers – left among Methodist preachers. (There had
never been *very* many, and then a number of them had parted
company with Wesley over the Calvinist controversies.) Coke,
who eight years previously had been dismissed from his curacy
in a Somerset parish for trying to 'methodize' it, had put himself
forward, at first only for a proposed reconnoitring mission in
America, but later as a suitable candidate to be at the head of the
American branch of Wesley's connection. Wesley agreed; but
then Coke, expecting opposition from Wesley's lieutenant
already in America, Asbury, asked to be ceremonially designated
as American 'superintendent'. If any subsequent odium should
arise, he pointed out, 'you will be obliged to acknowledge that I
acted under your direction, or suffer me to sink under the weight
of my enemies, with perhaps your brother at the head of them'.[9]

So John Wesley not only ordained the named preachers
Whatcoat and Vasey but also as it were re-ordained Dr Coke in
Bristol and delivered over to him the formidably legal-sounding

'letters testimonial' Coke had asked for: 'To all to whom these
presents shall come, John Wesley, late Fellow of Lincoln College
in Oxford, Presbyter of the Church of England, sendeth
greeting . . .' et cetera. 'I have this day set apart as superintendent,
by the imposition of my hands . . . Thomas Coke, doctor of civil
law, a presbyter of the Church of England . . .' et cetera.[10]

It is not surprising that Wesley jibbed at recording all the
details of this transaction in his *Journal*, or that he failed to invite
to the ceremony his brother, who was as it happened also in
Bristol at the time. As a Christian presbyter Wesley might,
arguably at least, claim the right to ordain a layman, but how
might he justify laying hands on Dr Coke and investing him
with greater authority than, as equally a Christian presbyter, he
already had? Only, it seems, if Wesley were indeed to be regarded
as a sort of Methodist pope, as his enemies and the grumblers
among his own preachers had long been saying in fact he was.
'I, John Wesley', his letters testimonial had declared, 'think
myself to be providentially called, at this time, to set apart some
persons for the work of the ministry in America.' His justification
would be the claim of overriding necessity – the same justification
he had given, years before, for lay and field preaching. If souls
called out to be saved, nothing, nothing whatever, must stand in
the way of his striving to save them. If this meant *varying* from
the rule of the Church, vary he must; but he would never admit
that he had *broken* with it or *separated* from it. Many more times
over the remaining seven years of his life he would repeat the
same message: 'When the Methodists leave the Church, God
will leave *them*! I shall not separate from the Church of England
till my soul separates from my body.' Was this wanting to have
his cake and eat it? Most people thought so, whether like Charles
they were bitterly and reproachfully opposed to what he had
done, or, like a numerous company of the movement's rank and
file, they would have welcomed complete separation.

The act of ordination once done, nothing was likely to prevent
it being many times repeated. Nor was the eager Dr Coke, once
arrived in America, inclined to let the grass grow under his feet.
He began, as Wesley had instructed, by ordaining Asbury and
appointing him associate superintendent. Very soon from the
pulpit he was violently attacking the ministers of the lately
deceased Church of England in America, as 'parasites and bottle

companions of the rich and great'. He and Asbury naturally
proceeded to ordain more ministers for the quickly expanding
church, but they also, to Wesley's anger, began to call themselves
bishops and their church the Methodist Episcopal Church of
America. 'How can you, how dare you, suffer yourself to be
called a Bishop?' Wesley demanded of Asbury in 1789. 'For my
sake, for God's sake, for Christ's sake put a full end to this!'[11]
His attitude perhaps showed rather more indignation than logic
– for the Church of England to which he still clung knew nothing
of the office of 'superintendent'. Moreover Coke and Asbury
were his chosen leaders in America; and had he not after all based
his whole course of action on the thesis that 'bishops and presbyters are the same order'? There seems no valid reason why a
presbyter given authority over other presbyters should not
describe himself as a bishop. It was not as if Wesley was an
opponent of authority from above, or would have any truck with
Dissenter ideas of congregational democracy. But that he had
brought into being an American hierarchy wholly separated from
and hostile to the Church of England undoubtedly caused him
unease, of which the omissions in the *Journal* surely provide
evidence. The subsequent unauthorized use of the delicate name
'bishop' made his discomfort that fraction worse.

Some of his actions in the following year, after he had gone on
to ordain three preachers for Scotland, show the same awareness
of the awkward contradictions of the position he now found
himself in. He allowed these men to be fully accredited clerics
only north of the Border. When they were in England they were
instructed to discard their clerical attire and their title of 'reverend';
and when one of them ventured upon a baptism in the Midlands,
Wesley was severely displeased. Some presbyters were apparently
more equal than others. It was proper, he explained, for clergy
of his creation to officiate in Scotland because the established
church there knew no bishops. In England, he found it necessary
to remind his more impetuous, and on the whole unimpressed,
followers, there were 'bishops who have a legal jurisdiction'.[12]
The truth seems to be that his own assumption of an episcopal
jurisdiction, necessary as he emphatically held it to be, had
offended against powerful elements in his own intellectual
constitution, which was essentially conservative. For Wesley, an
innovator perforce, there was never such a thing as a desirable

innovation. Throughout his lifetime every change he initiated he would seek to justify as a return to ancient practice. The law, and the *theory* of the establishment, were always to be respected, even when the establishment's leading practitioners caused him such righteous pain, even when his pen could so run away with him that he could describe the English bishops of his day as 'mitred infidels'.

The most difficult of rebel sons, he would never be able to tear himself from the offended bosom of his mother church. Lady Huntingdon's Methodists, accepting the logic of their rejection by the Anglican establishment, were soon reconciled to becoming legally tolerated Dissenters; not so Wesley. Though he was surrounded by preachers and society members who would have preferred clean secession, and though he almost certainly recognized, realist that he was, that after his death this would come, such a disaster should never occur while he retained control over the Methodist polity.

Eventually Wesley ordained nine more ministers for Scotland, making twelve altogether; ten for the West Indies, Newfoundland and Nova Scotia; and three (Thomas Rankin, Henry Moore and Alexander Mather) for England.

There were now over three hundred Wesleyan chapels, constituting a considerable church within a church, but still not numerous enough to satisfy the spiritual demands of every professing Methodist. Where no chapel existed – or even where one did – Wesley continued advising his followers regularly to attend Anglican services, though he also suggested that they should quietly walk out if the sermon attacked Christian perfection or preached predestination. That he was happiest with the result of his ministry in England's scattered mining and industrial villages is true; but it is not in general true that *in his day* Methodism supplied places of worship where none previously existed. Later, as the industrial revolution ran into top gear after his death, the fast-growing new towns were often to find themselves with Methodist chapels where there were no Anglican churches, but that was not yet. For that overwhelming majority of the Anglican clergy who were *not* Methodist the new chapel put up in the near neighbourhood of the parish church could hardly represent anything but rivalry and intrusion. Venerable patriarch as he was now widely regarded, an honourable, good and even saintly man, Wesley could nevertheless hardly expect to be looked on as the Church of England's favourite son. Even the Church's own evangelical revival, now gathering strength, though it may have owed something to the Methodist challenge, was to be doctrinally closer to the Calvinism of his opponents than to the Arminianism of Wesley.

CHAPTER 17

The Final Years

SOON AFTER HIS EIGHTIETH birthday, while attending his annual Conference, this time at Bristol, Wesley was again put temporarily out of action by a 'continual fever'. As usual on the infrequent occasions when he was ill, he reports his case as having been 'extreme'; but, also as usual, within two or three weeks he was able again to be in full itinerant flow. He had always seemed anxious to speak of his approaching, even imminent, death; but now that he was eighty it could hardly lie many years away. Concerning his own eternal destiny he had no anxiety, but of Methodism's future he was less certain. It had to be faced that among his preachers there were many whose respect for his word was far from total. Some dared an occasional, though usually abortive, rebellion, like Alexander McNab at Bath, who in 1779 'made utmost confusion' by leading a preachers' revolt against Wesley's invitation to a Rev. Edward Smyth (a nephew of the Archbishop of Dublin ejected from his curacy for embracing Methodism), to preach 'every Sunday evening in our chapel while he remained there'. Clearly the local objection was that good lay preachers were being treated by Wesley as second-class citizens, made to stand aside for an ordained cleric. Wesley had to go specially to the West Country and read to his societies both at Bath and Bristol, to which latter city the insurrectionary temper had spread, a paper he had written

> twenty years ago on a like occasion. Herein I observed that the rules of our preachers were fixed by me before any Conference existed, particularly the twelfth; 'Above all, you are to preach when and where I appoint . . . .' In the morning, at a meeting of our preachers, I informed Mr McNab that, as he did not agree to

our fundamental rule, I could not receive him as one of our preachers till he was of another mind.[1]

There was similar trouble at the new City Road chapel in London, where the preachers objected to having to make way for Charles Wesley (no friend of theirs) to preach *twice* every Sunday. They inevitably disagreed among themselves. 'The body of preachers', wrote Wesley, 'are not united; nor will any part of them submit to the rest; so that', and here was the cardinal point, 'either there must be *one* to preside over *all*, or the work will come to an end.' But the three men who in his mind had stood as potential heirs to the succession were for differing reasons all disqualified: John Fletcher because of infirmity (he died in 1785), Thomas Coke because he was in America, Charles Wesley because he was wholly out of sympathy with the preachers and they with him, and in any case he was already in his seventies and ailing.

Wesley therefore decided to make his Methodist Conference itself the trustee for the movement's future after his death; and to this end had a deed of declaration drawn up in 1784 and enrolled in the Court of Chancery. This secured the ownership and administration of all Methodist property (which might on his death have run the risk of being appropriated by the owners of the land on which it stood) and vested responsibility for future discipline and appointments, including the appointment of a president, in the Conference. Further, the Conference, which currently numbered 192 preachers, was to be restricted to 100, to be nominated by Wesley. This made of course a wonderful prescription for disgruntlement among the 92 rejected, especially as among them were men long established in the movement, and among the 'Legal Hundred' there were some relative beginners. Wesley defended the numerical limitation by explaining that during the Conference-time circuits must not be denuded of preachers. For the rest, he rode serenely over the rebellion of a group of the excluded: 'In naming these preachers, as I had no adviser, so I had no respect of persons, but I simply set down those that, according to the best of my judgement, were most proper.'

The well-being and best deployment of his preachers (there were some two hundred itinerants by 1789) occupied his endless close attention and dominated much of his correspondence. They were his children, and were treated as children must expect to be treated by a firm, if generally considerate, father. Many of them had been skilled craftsmen, and Wesley always tried to insist that as far as it was practicable they should continue in their previous work. If they did not, then they ought to spend an equivalent number of hours in study: first and foremost of the Old and New Testaments in Wesley's own editions with his verse-by-verse annotations; then of his other works and abridgements and compilations, voluminous enough to occupy a busy preacher many years of study; then additionally of other carefully selected religious writers. They would not be expected to read much, if anything, in the way of secular literature. Indeed, as Wesley told one of his preachers (a lawyer, looking for subscriptions towards publishing a book of poetry) Methodists as a whole did not care 'to buy or even to read . . . any but religious books', and in particular had 'very little taste for any poems but those of a religious or a moral kind, and my brother has amply provided them with these'. [2]

Preachers would hardly aspire to live in affluence. They were allowed their food where they worked, plus a grant of £12 a year for necessary expenses, with another £10 if they were married; and before Wesley's death a fund had been established to keep, where necesssary, old or infirm ex-preachers and preachers' widows from the workhouse. *Where* they were to work, and in what capacity (assistant, travelling preacher, local preacher), remained entirely in Wesley's hands, though he shuffled them round the various circuits with solicitous concern for individual inclinations, where he thought these practical and not in conflict with local societies' preferences.

His advice to those wishing to marry (whether preachers or Methodist brethren or sisters) seems usually to have been, *Don't*. But he would not go so far as Lady Huntingdon, who forbade any preacher in her connection to marry; and he was obliged to concede, with seeming reluctance, that '*some* single women have fewer advantages for eternity than they might have in a married state'. [3] From time to time he would address meetings of the single members of his bigger societies, men and women separately, to advise them of the advantages of their condition. More than once he tells cautionary tales of preachers who failed to take his advice, married, and were either 'dead within the twelvemonth', or suffered some hardly less signal token of divine disapproval. 'Some years since', he wrote in 1780, 'one of our preachers said, "Mr W. has hindered me from marrying *once*, but I am resolved he shall not hinder me again." Without asking my advice he married a woman of a thousand, who exercised him well while he lived and sent him to paradise before his time.'[4]

In particular for those thought to be consumptive, marriage was 'a sentence of death'. The preacher John Valton, in poor health but still contemplating wedlock, Wesley discouraged as follows:

> Finding Sam. Levick in Dublin of a consumptive habit, having been married some months, I advised him to leave his wife and ride with me round the kingdom. But she persuaded him to remain with her; in consequence of which in a few months she buried him . . . This would be the case with *you* if you married during your present state of health. I think you ought at all events to take a journey of a thousand miles first.[5]

When twenty-one-year-old Thomas Roberts, of Cork, asked Wesley's permission to marry, the reply from his 'affectionate brother' (aged eighty-four) came that 'provided Miss Christian Davenport answers the description of her which you give, and suppose both hers and your parents are now willing', there was no reasonable objection. But when the lady's parents did object, Wesley congratulated young Mr Roberts on his 'deliverance', which afforded yet another instance of the hand of providence, and advised him to resolve upon a permanently single life, not omitting to consult Wesley's *Notes on the New Testament* relating to 1 Corinthians 7, and to remember the wise direction of Kempis: 'Avoid all *good women* and commend them to God'.[6]

With those preachers who were already married, it would be well for their wives to be acceptable both to Wesley and the local Methodist society. Otherwise, like Thomas Wride, long established as an itinerant, they might find themselves in trouble. In 1780 Wride was demoted, thus:

> My dear brother, – When a preacher travels without his wife, he is exposed to innumerable temptations. And you cannot travel with your wife till she is so changed as to adorn the gospel.

It seems, therefore, all you can do at present is to act as a local preacher.[7]

Thomas Wride was later readmitted to his former itinerant status, though he seems always to have carried round with him the handicap of his wife's temperament, and perhaps too of his own unconventionality and contentiousness. Other Methodists accused him of being 'droll, light, trifling and slothful', but Wesley continued to steer him along with fatherly encouragement: 'Dear Tommy', he wrote, 'Be mild, be serious, and you will conquer all things.'[8]

When asked why he himself had married, his answer, given when he was eighty-seven, convinces only in part: 'Because', he said, 'I needed a home' (which sounds true) 'and to recover my health (which sounds improbable, since when he married Molly Vazeille his severest physical symptom seems to have been a swollen ankle – but perhaps by the time he said this he was confusing the year of his marriage with the time of his 'consumption' nearly three years later). The 'knowledge and enjoyment and service of God' might indeed, he said, be found in either a married or a single state, but – and here was the vital point – 'whenever we deny ourselves and take up the cross for His sake, the happier we shall be both here and in eternity'.[9]

This was equally the burden of the advice which he never ceased giving liberally, sought and unsought, to that company of evangelically devout 'sisters' with whom he constantly strove to keep in loving touch. Here too it might naturally concern matrimony, its suitability, advantages, drawbacks. His immense spiritual prestige as father figure to these earnestly religious ladies gave them a towering respect for his word, and if it came down against some prospective suitor on the grounds of his shortcomings, it might well carry the day. In the case, for instance, of his ever-beloved Nancy Bolton, there is no evidence that he on any occasion met the men in question – three of them at different times – or that it was *merely* his disapproval that caused the end of the attachments; but end they did, and he obviously considered that Nancy should praise God for preserving her from 'almost certain destruction', and for allowing her to devote the rest of her days to serving the spiritual condition of the people of

Witney, and of course her own. How put out he became when he thought he perceived some coldness in Miss Bolton's behaviour towards him! It was when she had become engaged to suitor number three (whom Wesley called an 'unbeliever'). Was she perhaps avoiding him? 'My dear Nancy, share all your griefs with your real friend, John Wesley'; 'I cannot tell how unspeakably near you are to me, my dear Nancy'; 'I have read you over with a lover's eye'. She was not well. She must strive towards Christian resignation, and above all realize that there was no such thing as chance; *everything* was providence.[10]

When she proposed to visit Methodist friends in Gloucestershire, or in Bristol, no, he had no objection at all. No objection! He continued to watch from a distance over all her spiritual and bodily travail. ('Drink the bran water, and follow the other advices I have given you.') Since now it sadly seemed a case of 'time was' when 'you took me to be your friend', he gave his thoughtful consent to her new ties with a godly woman Methodist living not too far from her home, 'ready to be consulted on all occasions'. He still protested: 'To speak freely, I have loved you with no common affection. I "have loved you" – nay, I do still; my heart warms to you while I am writing.' It always had, 'since I saw you a slender girl just beginning to seek salvation'. How did she come to be so weighted down with care, *since she had no husband, no children to perplex her?*

A question such as that tells a good deal about the questioner. Here is the same man speaking who once told his sister Patty what a blessing it was that providence had killed all her many children, so that she might the better devote her life to God; who rebuked the young preacher Adam Clarke for 'inordinate affection' because he grieved over the death of his infant daughter; who told John Ogilvie that it 'should be a matter of great thankfulness' to him and his wife that they had 'been enabled to give to God' that 'lovely child' of theirs; who in the name of love and friendship harshly castigated poor Richard Morgan – once, long before, his pupil at Oxford – for the alleged moral failings of Morgan's young daughter Sophia when she lay dying; the same Wesley who once decided that if he married Grace Murray and she had children by him, they should be sent away at the earliest possible moment to be brought up at Kingswood.

Apparently Nancy Bolton must eventually have given up

being a Methodist class and band leader, for in 1790, when Wesley was eighty-seven, she received from him one of those plain-speaking reproofs which were always liable to come the way of his friends. She, once a mother in Israel, had offended the Holy Spirit. Hence God had 'given a commission to Satan' to buffet her, and buffeted she would go on being till she went again to meet her class. 'Woman, remember the faith! . . . Sick or well, go! Go, whether you can or not! Break through! Take up your cross! . . . God will restore your first love! and you will be a comfort, not a grief, to . . . yours most affectionately, John Wesley.' Despite life's whips and scorpions (which he can see no reason for her to complain of), Nancy must persevere, persevere to the end. But *what* an end it might be! 'The joy is to come! Look up, my dear friend, look up, and see the crown before you! A little longer, and you shall drink of the rivers of pleasure that flow at God's right hand for evermore.'

Thus *to* the end – his end as it proved, not hers – he maintained such alternately hortatory and tender conversation with this troubled acolyte. It was not until 1792, the year after his death, when she was well past middle age, that Nancy Bolton was married, to a Mr Conibeer.

Young Jenny Hilton had been more fortunate. She too wrote to Wesley for advice on her proposed marriage. 'You should have spoken to me when I saw you', he replied:

> Is the person a believer? Is he a Methodist? Is he a member of our society? Is he clear with regard to the doctrine of Perfection? Is he athirst for it? If he fails in any of these particulars, I fear he would be an hindrance to you rather than an help. Was not inordinate affection to him one cause of your losing the pure love of God before?

Satisfying her spiritual mentor apparently on these points, she obtained his qualified sanction for a go-ahead, but there were 'two particulars remaining':

> First, have you both the consent of your parents? Without this there is seldom a blessing. Secondly, is he able to keep you? I mean in such a manner as you haved lived hitherto. Otherwise, remember! When poverty comes in at the door, love flies out at the window.[11]

These provisions having been met, Miss Hilton was soon to

become, and long to remain, Mrs Barton, though not before
further formidable catechizing from Wesley.

To the end of his days Wesley retained this deep mistrust of
matrimony. Nothing seemed to him more likely to weaken the
religious resolution of his young disciples, especially of those
earnest young women in whose spiritual interests his emotions
became so strongly engaged. One of the last of them was nineteen-
year-old Jane Bisson, of St Helier, Jersey, with whom he professed great 'union of spirit' and communicated in his accustomed
vein of solicitous, demonstrative affection. 'Precious as my time
is', he said, 'it would have been worth my while to come to
Jersey had it been only to see this prodigy of grace.' Then
suddenly she was Jenny Bisson no longer, but Mrs Cock. He
had to admit, 'When I heard of your marriage it gave me pain.'
'I hoped if you married at all, it would have been one of our
preachers.' He was glad to have it reported to him that she was
still 'alive to God', but he would be 'surprised if she was as much
alive as ever'. 'I cannot deny that you are now acting in a lower
sphere than was originally designed you . . . shut up in a little
cottage and fully taken up with domestic cares!'[12]

Chief among the darlings of Wesley's later years were Elizabeth
Ritchie, born in 1753, a naval surgeon's daughter of Otley in
Yorkshire, and Hester Roe, a clergyman's daughter of Maccles-
field in Cheshire, who was just twenty when Wesley first met her
in 1776.[13] For the rest of his days he always treated Hester with
what she described as 'parental tenderness'. 'He thinks me
consumptive', she said, 'but welcome life or welcome death, for
Christ is mine.' He thought actually that she was dying, and
tactful evasions in such a situation were not Wesley's way at all.
(In fact Hetty Roe later married and lived to be present at Wesley's
own deathbed, surviving to the age of thirty-eight.) 'I am afraid',
he wrote,

I shall hardly see *you* again till we meet in the Garden of God.
But if you should gradually decay, if you be sensible of the hour
approaching when your spirit is to return to God, I should be
glad to have notice of it, wherever I am, that if possible I might see
you once more . . .

In the meantime, see that you neglect no probable means of
restoring your health, and send me from time to time a particular
account of the state wherein you are. Do you find your own will

quite given up to God . . . ? Do you find no stirrings of pride?
no remains of vanity? . . . Does He bid you even in sleep go on?
What do you usually dream of? . . . [*et cetera*]. You see how
inquisitive I am, because everything relating to *you* nearly concerns
me . . . 'I shall not have you long.' Let our Lord see to that . . . Let
us enjoy *to-day*. You are *now* my comfort and joy!'[14]

He wrote no less characteristically to her, six years later: 'I am
not assured that there is not something preternatural in those
pains which you frequently experience. Not improbably they are
caused by a messenger of Satan, who is permitted to buffet you.'[15]
(As he pointed out to his sister Patty, 'It is not wisdom to impute
either our health or any other blessing we enjoy merely to natural
causes.') The letters persist with fears expressed lest Hetty should
be snatched away, 'as those I tenderly love generally have been'.
But when she heard from him in March 1783 how the wheels of
his own life seemed to be running to a stop, and how he had
(following a helpful suggestion emanating from a friend's
dream) been ordering the details of his funeral cortège – 'all our
preachers walking two by two' – it was now her turn to mourn
prematurely, her 'soul overwhelmed in tenderest grief'. In fact it
had been another of those feverish attacks which now came
rather more frequently, frightening his friends and persuading
him every time that he was on the point of death – but from which
his robust frame emerged each time only a little weaker than
before. He was, after all, a mere eighty, with years of busy
activity and decision, thousands more sermons, tens of thousands
more miles of travelling, still ahead of him. On the very day, in
fact, on which he wrote his alarmist letter he was up preaching
'to a crowded audience'.

Equally precious to the ageing Wesley was the intimate
friendship of Elizabeth Ritchie, 'one of our Lord's jewels'; a
class leader at Otley from her early twenties; thought to be
consumptive, like Hester Roe; earnestly evangelical; the very
pattern of what a Methodist should be. Indeed the highest
compliment he could pay Miss Roe or Mrs Bradburn (a preacher's
wife) was to tell them that they were 'kindred souls' with this
passionately esteemed Betsy Ritchie. Of course he was always
assuming that she too was at death's door – as indeed she may
well have been more than once; yet she too survived to become
one of his closest helps and attendants in his last days; married

in middle age; and long outlived him. Just after Wesley's wife died in 1781, there were those who prophesied that Miss Ritchie, fragile though her health then was, would soon be the new Mrs Wesley. It did not happen so. She was more than rewarded by having him as a 'father'; used thus in fact to refer to him; saw in him the personification of all wisdom and authority and goodness. And in return he was continually probing and catechizing and exhorting and counselling her, in those many sternly demanding yet intimately tender letters of his.

'Send me', he commanded her, 'as particular an account as you can of the state of your body and mind.' 'You said Satan had laid a snare for you. What snare was that? I am concerned in whatever concerns you.' She must read the *Life of the Marquis de Renty.** She must be wary of Mme Guyon, who might entice her into mysticism. A serious perusal of Baron Swedenborg was permissible, but there too caution was necessary, for undoubtedly in his later years his faculties were impaired. Did she need helping to understand the meaning of the *plerophory* (full assurance) of faith and of hope? and of the vital significance of the doctrine of Christian perfection?

Though he warned her off the mystics (except for de Renty), he was nevertheless curiously impressed by an experience he believed she had been vouchsafed, in common with only two others, Hetty Roe and Charles, the son of his old friend Vincent Perronet. Of the three, it was Charles Perronet who had first 'beheld the distinct person of the Godhead'; *seen* 'the light of God'; had communion 'sometimes with Christ alone', sometimes with the Father, sometimes with 'the Triune God'; taken leave of earth and hastened to 'another place'. Wesley, being told of these mysteries, proceeded to wonder (by letter) whether Hetty Roe might have experienced any similar phenomena: 'Tell me, my dear maid . . . but do not puzzle yourself about them, only speak in simplicity.' Yes, it seems she had, or said she had; and so also, it eventually transpired, had Miss Ritchie! Nothing might better confirm his conviction of the saintliness of both these ladies; but his eager readiness to accept accounts of such awesome

* *The Holy Life of Monr de Renty . . . sometime Councellor to King Lewis XIII* (English translation 1658). This was a book which had always impressed Wesley; of which he published an abridgement that went into six editions during his lifetime and gave a handle to those critics like Bishop Lavington who accused him of 'recommending popish books'.

visioning from people close to him, though it fits well with his general credulity over heavenly signs and wonders, goes oddly against the grain of his many-times-repeated detestation of mysticism.[16]

He knew only three people, he said, who claimed to have had such direct intercourse with the Godhead; but supernatural visions, communion with spirits, sensing angelic presence, suspension of the terrestrial laws of nature – such things he was never loath to credit, though he would always wish first to conduct his own examination of the evidence. The validity of like phenomena being scripturally attested and therefore undeniable, his predilection was rather to believe than to dismiss.

Margaret Barlow, a servant-girl from Durham County, provides a case in point. She had, she said, seen a most beautiful angel, clothed in white, 'glistening like silver', with utterance 'unspeakably musical', who foretold certain events which did subsequently occur, as well as certain others which had not yet, such as God being 'avenged of obstinate sinners' by destroying them with fire from heaven. Were these the enthusiastic imaginings of an ignorant young girl? Not at all: 'I asked her abundance of questions. I was soon convinced that she was not only sincere, but deep in grace; and therefore incapable of deceit.' The only slight difficulty in her account was that she always referred to her angel as female, whereas scripture unquestionably made angels male. 'Yet', explains Wesley, 'from the face, the voice, and the apparel, she might easily mistake him for a female; and this mistake is of little consequence.'[17]

To the admirable, earnest, knowledge-questing Miss Bishop, who ran a Methodist school at Keynsham near Bristol, he once expounded, as fully as might be, his precise understanding of the communion of earthly saints and angels in paradise. These two classes of being, he told her, constituted 'all one body united under one Head':

> But it is difficult to say either what kind or what degree of union may be between them. It is not improbable their fellowship with us is far more sensible than ours with them. Suppose any of them are present, they are hid from our eyes, but we are not hid from *their* sight. They no doubt clearly discern all our words and actions, if not all our thoughts too; for it is hard to think these walls of flesh and blood can intercept the view of an angelic

being. But we have in general only a faint and indistinct perception of their presence, unless in some peculiar instances, where it may answer some gracious ends of Divine Providence. Then it may please God to permit that they should be perceptible, either by some of our outward senses or by an internal sense for which human language has not any name. But I suppose this is not a common blessing. I have known but few instances of it.[18]

Happily, however, angels might well be on hand as God's agents to protect mortals even from quite minor misfortunes. Twice, when he slipped down a few stairs and picked himself up more or less unhurt, he attributes his preservation to angels.[19] And there was the rather less trivial occasion when near Newcastle his coachman fell off the coach-box and the carriage horses bolted, with Wesley and his step-daughter's two little girls carried helpless over fields and through gates – one of them a *closed* gate – to the edge of a 'steep precipice' (Wesley never underplayed a hand like this), where the girls' father galloped in to stop and save them. Blessed be God, wrote Wesley, he felt no more fear or care than if he had been sitting at home in his study! – adding rather more than half a page of 'circumstances' to support his persuasion that 'both evil and good angels had a large share in this transaction; how large we do not know, but we shall know hereafter'.[20]

It was for Mary Bishop's enlightenment, again, that he pictured the eternal dwelling place of the good angels. Heaven, he explained, was both a *state* and a *place*; 'there is no opposition between these two':

It is the *place* wherein God more immediately dwells with those saints who are in a glorified *state*. Homer could only conceive of the place that it was paved with brass. Milton in one place makes heaven's pavement beaten gold; in another he defines it more sublimely 'the house of God, star-paved'. As full an account of this house of God as it can yet enter into our hearts to conceive is given us in various parts of the Revelation. There we have a fair prospect into the holiest, where are, first, he that sitteth upon the throne; then the four living creatures; next, the twenty-four elders; afterwards the great multitude which no man can number; and, surrounding them all, the various myriads of angels, whom God hath constituted in a wonderful order.

But what is the essential part of heaven? Undoubtedly it is to

see God, to know God, to love God. We shall then know both
His nature, and His works of creation, of providence, and of
redemption. Even in paradise, in the intermediate state between
death and resurrection, we shall learn more concerning these in an
hour than we could in an age during the stay in the body. We
cannot tell, indeed, how we shall then exist or what kind of organs
we shall have; the soul will not be encumbered with flesh and
blood; but probably it will have some sort of ethereal vehicle,
even before God clothes us 'with our nobler house of empyrean
light'.[21]

This Mary Bishop was yet another of the 'jewels' bringing
reward and comfort to Wesley's latter years; but it was Betsy
Ritchie and Hetty Roe (now Hetty Rogers, having married one
of the City Road preachers) who were the women closest to him
in this final chapter of his life. Together with his niece Sally,
they became accepted members of what he sometimes now
referred to simply as his family.

A woman of Miss Ritchie's correct discernment and educated
judgement might serve her revered and at long last somewhat
failing teacher in a multitude of ways. As his sight deteriorated,
she could read to him. Then again, she was one of a very few
select friends who breakfasted with him during his last Conferences, when improprieties in preachers' dress were among the
subjects discussed. Over breakfast Wesley complained of the
Rev. Peard Dickinson, one of his London helpers, who had worn
ruffles on his shirts. Endeavouring, said Miss Ritchie, to soften
matters, she was commissioned to deal with Mr Dickinson via
his wife. This she proceeded to do, in a letter nicely calculated to
obliterate the offence without too much offending the offender.
No doubt, she suggested, Mrs Dickinson had already proposed to
remove these extravagances, but had been prevented. 'My dear
sister, let me beg of you then, never to let Mr Dickinson wear a
ruffled shirt again. You both love our dear father too well to
grieve him. Yours in Jesus, Elizabeth Ritchie.'[22]

In October 1779 Wesley had slept for the first time in the new
building adjoining his City Road chapel. He had four rooms in
this house, which also accommodated four of his London
preachers. But of course it was always more a base and headquarters than what most people would think of as a home. Here
certainly, on the first floor, were his parlour, his bedroom, his

study, his books and files, his closet reserved for prayer; here he
would spend perhaps three months, in sum, of each year; but
still, to the end of his days, he was nearly always on the move,
adding week by week to that tally of miles which loving and
meticulous mensuration has computed to amount, over all his
half-century of mission, to something like a quarter of a million,
approximately the distance from earth to moon.

His itinerant energy showed hardly any decline. The rounds of
preaching and of examining and rallying the local societies
continued as ever, in all parts of England and Wales, in Scotland,
in Ireland (which he toured four more times in his last eight
years), in the Channel Islands, even in Holland, where he spent
three weeks when he was eighty. At eighty-two he applied himself to writing the life of the saintly Fletcher, for which task he
gave himself just two months. 'To this', he says, 'I dedicated all
the time I could spare . . . from five in the morning till eight at
night. These are my studying hours; I cannot write longer in a
day without hurting my eyes'! Sometimes his voice would give
out after he had been over-exerting it, and sometimes we read
of a feverish infection or an 'impetuous flux': but on his eighty-
second birthday he was claiming that it was eleven years since he
had 'felt any such thing as weariness'.[23] And still in his eighty-
fifth year he could report extraordinary vigour:

> I considered, What difference do I find by an increase of years?
> I find (1) less activity; I walk slower, particularly uphill: (2) My
> memory is not so quick: (3) I cannot read so well by candle-light.
> But I bless God that all my other powers of body and mind
> remain just as they were.[24]

If the roads should prove impossible for his chaise, still the
sermon must be preached, and some means found therefore of
delivering him in time at his scheduled destination. At least once
this involved jolting his venerable bones the last miles in an old
farm cart.

At the end of February 1786, taking he says 'solemn leave' of
his City Road and West Street congregations (he never failed to
remind both himself and his friends that each new setting forth
might be his last), he proceeded, he relates, through Brentford,
and

> went on to Newbury, with little interruption from the snow, and

I had a . . . large and serious congregation. But I have not passed such a night these forty years, my lodging-room being just as cold as the outward air. I could not sleep at all until three in the morning. I rose at four, and set out at five. But the snow which fell in the night lay so deep, it was with much difficulty that we reached Chippenham. Taking fresh horses there, we pushed on to Bath, and found a larger congregation than could well be expected.

March 1, Wed. I had appointed to preach in Trowbridge at noon; but we could not get thither till half an hour after. I then preached without delay, and in the evening in Bristol on 'O Death, where is thy sting? O grave, where is thy victory? . . . In the afternoon I went over to Kingswood, and found the school in excellent order [a welcome contrast with five years before, when Satan seemed to be poised for victory].

Sun. 5 – I read prayers and preached and administered the sacrament to about five hundred communicants. At three I preached in Temple Church; at five in the New Room.

Mon. 13 – I left Bristol . . . In the evening I preached at Stroud; Tuesday the fourteenth at noon in Painswick, with uncommon liberty; and in the evening at Gloucester . . .

Wed. 15 – Much snow fell in the night, and quite blocked up the road. Yet, with some difficulty, we got through to Tewkesbury, where I preached at noon. Abundance of snow likewise fell in the afternoon; but we pushed through it to Worcester.[25]

A routine winter fortnight's work, of the kind he was to be doing for nearly another five years yet.

In 1787 Charles Wesley completed his eightieth year. He had long been unwell, but continued preaching his two Sunday sermons and writing, every day or two, yet another hymn to swell his already vast output.

As the Victorian author of *The Methodist Hymnbook and its Associations* (1872) very fairly observed, 'Charles Wesley's hymns were not the product of a lively imagination . . . nor were they the fruit of hard mental toil. They were the spontaneous effusions of his heart.' His brother's introduction to the 1780 collection, that 'little body of experimental divinity', firmly claimed 'Here is no doggerel'. Perhaps today only the most dedicated of Methodists will be consistently transported by these hymns to 'the courts of heaven' or find in them 'the music of the archangels'.[26] Others may sometimes feel themselves uncomfortable intruders in a spiritual hothouse. Fervent sincerity these hymns undoubtedly do have. Sometimes too they illuminate, however embarrassingly to a corrupt modern ear, the writer's own stumblings and depressions:

> This is my shame, my curse, my hell;
> I do not love the bleeding lamb.

Sometimes he puts altogether too heavy a strain upon the readiness of today's reader to make allowances, as when he writes:

> Let the bowels of Thy love
> Echo to a sinner's groan

or a line as disastrous as

> And worms attempt to chant Thy praise.

But Charles Wesley wrote in all between six and seven thousand hymns, as well as hundreds of occasional poems (a large proportion of them funerary tributes); no one ought to expect uniform excellence. During his lifetime, and for the best part of a century after his death, the overwhelming majority of hymns sung at Methodist services were his. (In John Wesley's 1780 collection there were about 500 of Charles's in a total of 525.) John's contribution was trifling by comparison, consisting mainly of translations from the German. And although most of Charles's hymns have faded quietly away, there are enough admired favourites in the still substantial residue to attest his quality: among these, *Jesu, Lover of my Soul, Hark the Herald Angels Sing* (originally *Hark how all the Welkin Rings*), *Soldiers of Christ Arise, O for a Thousand Tongues to Sing, Love Divine All Loves Excelling,* and *Lo, He comes with Clouds Descending.* Perhaps *Gentle Jesus Meek and Mild* must now be accounted an *ex*-favourite.

Charles Wesley had by now been married thirty-eight years, enjoying one great blessing denied to John, the companionship of a loving and compatibly-minded wife. (She was to survive to the age of ninety-six, outliving her much older husband by thirty-four years.) Of their eight children, five had died in infancy. The surviving daughter Sarah (Sally), unmarried, was living at home. The two sons were both launched upon notable musical careers, both as executants and composers. At twenty-two the elder, another Charles, was seen by his uncle John as

'just launching into life' and in pressing danger of looking to the
'shining baubles' of the elegant world for his happiness rather than
to God. 'Unless you are born again', he warned, 'you cannot
see the kingdom of God! . . . But as your *business*, rather than
your *choice*, calls you into the fire, I trust that you will not be
burnt.'[27] Charles was in time to become organist to the undoubtedly
fire-charred Prince of Wales, and musical preceptor to his daughter
Princess Charlotte. The younger brother Samuel, another outstanding organist – who (laments Tyerman) was 'seduced into
the popish church before he was twenty and thereby brought the
grey hairs of his father with sorrow to the grave'[28] – has the
distinction of being co-editor of the first copy ever to be printed
in England of the at that time almost forgotten J. S. Bach's
Well-tempered Clavier. It was this Samuel who, in his mid-forties,
was to father, out of wedlock, Samuel Sebastian Wesley, the
most eminent of all mid-Victorian composers of sacred music.*

In his old age Charles Wesley, not so fortunate as his brother,
became seriously enfeebled. John thought he was too little
inclined to be out of doors, partly perhaps because of the expense
of carriage travel, which he therefore volunteered to defray
himself. 'Do not die to save charges', he wrote; and then a few
weeks later:

> I hope you keep to your rule, of going out every day, although
> it may sometimes be a cross. Keep to this but one month, and I
> am persuaded you will be as well as you was at this time twelve-
> month.[29]

But Charles was by then too ill to put pen to paper, and his
daughter Sally became his scribe. It was to her that John Wesley,
that never-failing cornucopia of medical wisdom, continued his
counsel:

> When my appetite was entirely gone, so that all I could take at
> dinner was a roasted turnip, it was restored in a few days by
> riding out daily, after taking ten drops of elixir of vitriol in a
> glass of water. It is highly probable, that would have the same
> effect in my brother's case . . .

* Thus the four Samuel Wesleys in consecutive generations are the Rev.
Samuel Wesley (1666–1735), poet and rector of Epworth; the Rev. Samuel
Wesley (1690–1739), poet and schoolmaster; Samuel Wesley (1766–1837),
organist and composer; and Samuel Sebastian Wesley (1810–76), also
organist and composer.

Mr Whitefield had, for a considerable time, thrown up all the food he took. I advised him to slit a large onion across the grain, and bind it warm to the pit of his stomach. He vomited no more. Pray apply this to my brother's stomach the next time he eats.

One in Yorkshire, who was dying for want of food . . . was saved by the following means: Boil crusts of white bread to the consistency of a jelly; add a few drops of lemon juice, and a little loaf sugar; take a spoonful once or twice an hour. By all means let him try this.

If neither of these avail (which I think will not be the case) remember the lady at Paris, who lived several weeks without swallowing a grain by applying thin slices of beef to the stomach.[30]

He wished, he said, that his brother might try being 'electrified; not shocked', that is, 'but only filled with electric fire'. However, neither electric fire nor sliced beef not vitriol elixir nor bisected onion nor jellied bread nor the more conventional medicaments of Dr Whitehead availed. 'I am persuaded', Wesley wrote, 'there is not such another physician in England as Dr Whitehead; although, to confound human wisdom, he does not know how to cure his own wife.' Charles Wesley's case too was beyond his powers to arrest. He died on 29 March 1788, and John published the following obituary notice:

Mr Charles Wesley, who, after spending fourscore years with much sorrow and pain, quietly retired into Abraham's bosom. He had no disease; but after a gradual decay of some months
The weary wheels of life stood still at last.[31]

By the end of the year he had assembled and where necessary *corrected* Charles's last hymns and poems, to complete a five-volume quarto edition of over eighteen hundred pages; and praised Charles's 'justness and strength of thought . . . beauty of expression . . . keenness of wit on proper occasions, bright and piercing'. He also quickly set about the practical business of providing much-needed financial help for Charles's widow. His private diary, with its terse unfailing daily entries in Byrom's shorthand, shows that in 1788 he gave £210 to his brother's family and £81. 10s between his sister Patty and his nieces.

He could hardly fail to be affected by the death of the companion who, whatever the sharp differences which had come between them over the past nearly forty years, had nevertheless, over all that time and more, been his loyal collaborator; who had been, strictly speaking, the founder of the Methodist movement; who, however distressed and exasperated he had become at its development, had always felt himself to be incapable of breaking with his brother. At Bolton a fortnight after Charles's death, John was in the pulpit announcing a hymn, when he found himself reading the lines

My company before is gone
And I am left alone with Thee.

Overcome by their relevance, he broke down, wept, sat down, and for a time buried his face in his hands before recovering to continue the service.

He had been in Cheshire when the news of his brother's death arrived, and was unable to get to London in time for the interment, which on Charles's instructions was in the episcopally consecrated churchyard of his parish church of St Marylebone, and not, as John had wished, at his own chapel in City Road – which, he protested, had a burial ground as 'holy as any in England'. He would of course be buried there himself – how soon! he kept repeating – and had hoped to lie next to his brother. He felt the disappointment and implied slight strongly enough to write for his *Arminian Magazine* an article which asserted that, following the precedent of the purest ages of the Church, a clerk or sexton had as much right as a bishop to consecrate a churchyard. Wesley was never quite capable of humour,* but this article has a characteristic example of his dry, colloquial, sarcastic style of polemic, which is at least allied to wit:

You say, This is consecrated ground, so many feet broad, and so many feet long; but pray how deep is it? 'Deep! what does that signify?' O, a great deal! for if my grave be dug too deep, I may happen to get out of consecrated ground! And who can tell what unhappy consequences may follow from this!

The scouting of Wesley's authority by rebel preachers and independently inclined local societies became a growing problem

* Except of the unintentional variety, of which he was something of a master. He writes in the *Journal* on 23 January 1781: 'I went to Dorking, and buried the remains of Mrs Attersal, a lovely woman, snatched away in the bloom of youth. I trust it will be a blessing to many, and to her husband in particular.' And on 3 August 1784: 'Our Conference concluded in much love, to the great disappointment of all.'

as during the 1780s Methodist numbers themselves increased steeply. In many places he strove, with only partial success, to stop chapel services being held during the same hours as Anglican church services. This practice, in which the Dublin society was one of the most troublesome offenders, signified all too obviously *de facto* separation; and separation he would, literally to the death, refuse to admit. Then parts of Scotland, at the instigation apparently of his Edinburgh assistant, John Pawson, seemed to be adopting native colours. 'Sessions! Elders!' Wesley exploded to his man in Dalkeith:

> We Methodists have no such customs ... I require you, Jonathan Crowther, immediately to disband that session (so called) at Glasgow ... And if they will leave the society, let them leave it. We acknowledge only preachers, stewards, and leaders among us, over whom the assistant [i.e. superintendent] in each circuit presides. You ought to have kept the Methodist plan from the first. Who had any authority to vary from it?[32]

And, of course, as to another he once more insisted:

> As long as I live, the people shall have no share in choosing either stewards or leaders ... We are no republicans, and never intended to be. It would be better for those that are so minded to go quietly away.[33]

There was trouble too in Nottingham, in North and South Shields, and most gallingly of all in Dewsbury where, in Wesley's indignant words, self-appointed trustees *robbed* him of his chapel and of its flock, and appointed that scheming 'traitor', his London book-steward John Atlay, to be their preacher.

Yet such difficulties provided only one face of what was for the most part a decade of heart-warming success. Statistically, including America in the count, progress made during the 1780s was greater than that of the previous four decades together. In 1780 Wesley's connection in the British Isles and America numbered some 52,000 members; by 1790, nearly 130,000. In the British Isles alone, enrolled membership rose from 43,380 in 1780 to 71,568 in 1790. As with that parallel phenomenon the new industrial revolution, the 1780s were the decade of 'take-off'; and no doubt the synchronization was not merely coincidental. The appeal of Methodism had always been strongest in the semi-urbanized industrial and mining districts. Wesley's last

years and the decades to follow were just the time when iron and
coal and steam, the factory and the mine, were most rapidly
transforming the old Britain of parson and squire; when the
mushroom growths of Dickens's Coketown, murky as they were,
were to give the Methodists, schisms or no schisms, fields
'white unto harvest'. But, of course, both Coketown and the
Methodist heyday were still some distance away from the octo-
genarian Wesley.

His was an ingrained pessimism concerning the merely terrestrial prospects of humanity. 'Wherever I have been', he wrote
in 1773, 'I have found the bulk of mankind, Christian as well as
heathen, deplorably ignorant, vicious, and miserable . . . Sin and
pain are on every side.'[34] To believe as he passionately did in
'Christian perfection' for a necessarily small number of the 'wholly
sanctified' was a very different thing from believing in human
perfectibility, or even in 'progress'. Earthly existence would
always, for the mass of mankind, be pursued through a vale of
tears. Yet the great message remained: everyone, *everyone*, might
hope for salvation. *None need* perish (the emphasis was equally on
both those words), 'for we have an almighty Saviour'.

In his last years he even saw some grounds for a more immediate optimism, not least in the encouraging growth in his
followers' numbers. 'Never was there, throughout England,
Scotland and Ireland, so great a thirst for the pure word of God
as there is at this day', so he said in 1790.[35] Even the recent
revolution in France, which had not yet acquired its later in-
gredients of tyranny, paganism and terror, seemed to promise
well for the future. He might even briefly persuade himself to
hope that a time might be coming when the earth should be
filled with the knowledge of the glory of the Lord. As for England,
under the benign rule of George III and Mr Pitt ('I suppose
everyone that loves King George loves Mr Pitt')* – 'I do not
know that England was ever before in so quiet a state as it is
now.'[36]

He continued to offer, for his friends, for the public, for all
who cared to listen, his opinions on any and every aspect of the

---

* Because some Methodists were still being 'persecuted' under the
Conventicle Act by being fined for preaching without registering as
Dissenters, Wesley wrote to his esteemed young friend William Wilberforce,
'If you will speak a word to Mr Pitt on that head, you will oblige.'

age into which he had survived. The villainy of the slave trade; the corrupting influence of increasing wealth, not least among Methodists; the ubiquity of Satan, and his part in promoting human disease, for instance in Wesley's friend Alexander Knox (the same enemy was clearly involved in the newly fashionable practice of 'animal magnetism', or mesmerism, which was 'diabolical from beginning to end'); the absurdity of publishing books in the Manx language ('we should do everything in our power to abolish it from the earth – all Methodists should speak English'); the misguided attempts to modernize the language of the Lord's Prayer (in altering for instance its third word from *which* to *who* – 'I love the old wine best'); the infamous, and indeed poisonous, habit of spoiling ale by adding hops (protracted correspondence in the *Bristol Gazette*); the growing fashion for self-destruction, to discourage which the bodies of suicides should be hanged in chains on public display. And all Bristol Methodists who had a vote would, he trusted, give it to the *government* candidate in 1789.[37]

The preacher John Hampson, junior, one of his earliest biographers, wrote of the aged Wesley:

> A clear, smooth forehead, an aquiline nose, an eye the brightest and most piercing that can be conceived; and a freshness of complexion scarcely ever to be found at his years . . . In dress, he was a pattern of neatness and simplicity. A narrow, plaited stock; a coat with a small upright collar; no buckles at his knees; no silk or velvet in any part of his apparel, and a head as white as snow, gave an idea of something primitive and apostolic . . .[38]

Another who heard him in these last years, preaching in York, conveys something of the intimate didactic informality liable to invade any chapel service he was conducting:

> During the singing some discordant notes grated harshly on Wesley's ear . . . At the end of the verse, he said, 'Now listen to brother Masterman,' who was the leading singer. As this did not produce the desired effect, he stopped again and said, 'Listen to me.' But the cracked voice of the old man of nearly ninety [nearly eighty-seven] failed to do its office . . .[39]

Mortality was at last in close pursuit of him. His left eye had a 'pearl' on it. From 1789 he began to suffer from diabetes; still, he 'crept round a little', he said, 'and made shift to preach once a day'. 'I am now an old man', he wrote on 1 January 1790, 'and decayed from head to foot; my eyes are dim, my right hand shakes much; my mouth is hot and dry every morning; I have a lingering fever almost every day; my motion is weak and slow. However, blessed be God, I do not slack my labour; I can preach and write still.' He might have added, 'and travel' – for he was soon off once more to the West Country, the Midlands, Lancashire, Yorkshire, the North-East, Scotland; then back to Hull, Lincoln, Epworth, Bristol (for the Conference), South Wales, Bristol again, the Isle of Wight, Sussex, Kent, Essex, Suffolk, Norfolk. Even rebellious Norwich, which had long given him so much trouble, seemed to welcome him. 'The house would in nowise contain the congregation', he recorded. 'How wonderfully is the tide turned! I am become an honourable man at Norwich. Scarce any but Antinomians open their mouths against us.'

Two days later he was at Lowestoft, where the poet Crabbe was among those who heard him preach in a hot, overcrowded chapel, and noted his 'reverend appearance, his cheerful air, and the beautiful cadence he gave' to some lines he quoted from a translation of Anacreon ('Poor Anacreon, thou growest old . . . 'Tis time to live, if I grow old'). Not many days before, the young Henry Crabb Robinson had listened to him preaching at Colchester, standing

> in a wide pulpit, and on each side of him stood a minister, and the two held him up, having their hands under his armpits. His feeble voice was barely audible; but his reverend countenance, especially his long white locks, formed a picture never to be forgotten. There was a vast crowd of lovers and admirers. It was for the most part pantomime, but the pantomime went to the heart.[40]

By 22 October 1790 he was back in London, and two days later, a Sunday, preached sermons at Spitalfields and Shadwell. It proved the last day's activity to be recorded by that great long-distance runner the *Journal* (fifty-five years, a million words); but it was not yet the end of his journeyings or labours. The shorthand diary gives an account of four more busy months of work in London and through several of the home counties – to within a week of his death.

He made his will in February 1789. He was leaving no money,

he first said, because he had none. 'But now, considering that whenever I am removed, money will soon arise by sale of books, I added a few legacies.' One of these was of £40 to Patty, who survived him by only a few months. He left the bulk of his book revenues in trust for the Methodist Conference, subject to an annual deduction of £85 to help support Charles's widow and her sons. The contents of his bureau, including any coins there, were to go to his step-daughter's two daughters; his watch to the preacher Joseph Bradford, his gold seal to Elizabeth Ritchie. Six pounds was to be divided among 'six poor men . . . who shall carry my body to the grave'. Three 'faithful friends' (two merchants and a stockbroker) were to be his executors, 'for which trouble they will receive no recompense till the resurrection of the just'. 'Lastly, I give to each of those travelling preachers who shall remain in the connexion six months after my decease, as a little token of my love, the eight volumes of sermons.'

The Conference of 1790 appointed James Rogers to London, intending that he should accompany the infirm Wesley on his daily journeys and that his wife Hester (*née* Roe) should supervise the domestic economy of the City Road chapel-house. However, Mrs Rogers's health being again poor, Elizabeth Ritchie (visiting London in time for 'dear Mr Wesley's meeting the classes') was prevailed upon to lodge at City Road and undertake the housekeeping duties. 'How good is the Lord', Wesley said to her, 'to bring you to me when I want you most. I should wish you to be with me in my dying moments: I would have you to close my eyes.' 'Betsy', he told her, 'you must be eyes to the blind'; 'I therefore rose with pleasure', she wrote, 'about half-past five o'clock, and generally read to him from six to breakfast time.' She considered herself forever rewarded by sharing his conversation during these final two months.

From about 17 February 1791 his weakness and feverishness grew worse. On the 22nd, he was driven to Leatherhead and preached what proved to be his final sermon, in the house of a family who had 'lately begun to receive the truth'.

Back in City Road, he managed one or two little rallies, but was clearly near death, and both knew it and spoke freely of it. On 1 March, after a very restless night, he said to Miss Ritchie that he wished to write. In her words,

I brought him pen and ink, and on putting the pen into his hand, and holding the paper before him, he said, 'I cannot.' I replied, 'Let me write for you, sir; tell me what you would say.' 'Nothing,' returned he, 'but that God is with us.'

He then astonished those present by breaking into song, to the words of Isaac Watts,

I'll praise my Maker while I've breath . . .

He lived into the following day, part of the time delirious, more than once summoning his little remaining strength to declare loudly, 'The best of all is, God is with us.' James Rogers and two others sat with him through the last night, hearing Wesley repeat, 'at least some scores of times', 'I'll praise – I'll praise – ', the first words of the verse he was too weak to get any further with. When he died, quietly, the following morning, there were present 'kneeling around his bed, according to his often expressed desire', Rogers and three others of the London preachers, Dr Whitehead and two more friends of Wesley, his niece Sally, Hester Rogers and her little boy, and Elizabeth Ritchie. 'This awful event', Rogers wrote, 'had a good effect on our society in London. Our chapels were much crowded, the classes and bands were exceeding lively, and the Lord added daily to his church; so that when I came to visit the classes in May, I found upwards of an hundred new members.'[41]

'. . . to the Latest Posterity'

WIDE-RANGING CLAIMS have been made for Wesley's influence and importance; some of them, it must be said, of considerable extravagance. The standard eight-volume edition of his *Journal*, having first declared comprehensively that he 'saved the nation from popery, atheism and revolution',[1] proceeds later to embellish this claim: the work of Wesley 'saved England, helped to save Scotland, to some extent saved Ireland, also Wales, Holland, even France* herself, and certainly America – saved them from Voltaire and Frederick the Great'.[2] And if we turn from this devotedly partisan view to a leading Oxford historian writing at the same time (1911, in a book popular enough to be reprinted seventeen times by 1949), we still read, 'Methodism and the French Revolution are the two most tremendous phenomena of the eighteenth century.'[3]

This was a century, we may recall, which saw new peaks scaled in almost every department of the arts and many of the sciences; the European 'enlightenment', the British beginnings of modern industrialization; the rise of Prussia and Russia; the independence of the United States of America; a world-wide acceleration in British commercial, naval and imperial power; and other developments of hardly less profound importance. Amid such competition, can there really be room at the top for Methodism? Is it even tenable, as the last-quoted passage proceeds to assert and many more have claimed, that Wesley 'kept the English people Christian'?

Wesley of course would have maintained that they had not

---

* There were, when this was written, about a thousand Methodists in France.

previously *been* Christian; but, that apart, it is undeniable that
Methodism did have a considerable share in preserving the forms
of religion among the rapidly multiplying urban working class.
That is not quite the same thing as saying that 'Wesley's Methodism became the religion of the neglected poor'.[4] A *majority* of the
neglected poor in fact continued themselves to neglect all forms of
church- or chapel-going, and remained hardly more affected by
Christian teaching than Wesley had earlier found them. This
stayed true through the Victorian era, that heyday of middle-
class religious observance, and of course is still true today, even
if the neglected poor are not quite as neglected as they once were.

As the Methodist chapels tended to outnumber the Anglican
churches in the new industrial towns, they did much to rob the
Church of England of its earlier unquestioned primacy in the
nation's ecclesiastical affairs. And as the nineteenth century
progressed there were not many sizeable country villages either,
at least in England, without their Methodist chapel, or very
likely two Methodist chapels of rival connections. Whereas before
Wesley nineteen out of every twenty English worshippers had
attended Anglican services, eventually, after Methodism had
grown to full stature, the proportion fell to only a little over half,
since Methodists of whatever sub-denomination had all now to be
numbered among Nonconformists. That in this simple numerical
sense Wesley weakened the Church of England is obvious. To
what extent his influence operated also in an opposite direction
by helping to stimulate the evangelical revival within the Church
is more arguable. In terms of challenge-and-response probably a
good deal. But although most of the leading Evangelicals shared
Wesley's puritanism, his moral earnestness, his emphatic insistence on the value of prayer and of works, they rejected his
chosen methods, in particular lay and open-air preaching, and
much that was crucial to his theology, notably free grace and
Christian perfection. Pre-Victorian and Victorian evangelicalism
probably owed rather more to Wesley's Calvinist opponents
than to Wesley.

But whether his influence on the Church of England is regarded as on balance harmful or beneficial, he had undoubtedly,
in spite of his own so often professed intention, in effect founded
an important new church. True, it was composed of very dis-

parate elements and ripe for the schisms which soon afflicted it.*
It was nevertheless young, vigorous, well-organized, and 'matched
with its hour'. It and the new industrial revolution were made for
one another.

A hundred years after Wesley's death, at about the time when
the ratio of Methodist membership to total population had
reached a peak, there were altogether in the English-speaking
world a little short of six million Methodists of one connection
or another, about half a million of them British Wesleyans. By
the 1970s the world-wide total, drawn from more than seventy
nations, was estimated at eighteen million, about two-thirds of
them in the United States, where the United Methodist Church
formed the second largest branch of Protestant Christianity. Of
course during the present century Methodism's influence, and
its numbers proportionate to population, have shrunk, along
with most other Christian denominations; and no doubt, too,
most living Methodists would in honesty find a great many of
Wesley's beliefs and attitudes now quite untenable. Yet are not
the simple figures just cited alone sufficient to establish Wesley
as the single most influential Protestant leader of the English-
speaking world since the Reformation?

If that is so, it is not necessary to load him with more doubtful
honours. He could do a little, but only a little, to retard the
progressive laicization of society and secularization of thought
that have marked the past three centuries. He could not 'save the
nation from popery', since there was not the slightest risk of the
nation's embracing it; nor 'from atheism', which was far too
positive an 'ism' for the English to be in any danger of adopting
it.

As for saving the nation from revolution, this follows a theory
once popular but now, if not totally rejected, at least needing the
severest qualification. It is true that the Methodists of the last
thirty years of George III's reign, the generation immediately

* The first came in 1797, when the rather democratically inclined New
Connexion, sometimes called Tom Paine Methodists, seceded. By 1810 two
more groups had broken away, the Primitive Methodists and the Independent Methodists. There followed the Bible Christians, or Bryanites, in
1815; then the Wesleyan Association in 1836 and Wesleyan Reform Association in 1849, subsequently amalgamated into United Free Church Methodists.
Further amalgamation in 1907 reduced the number of groups to three, and
since 1932 there has again been one united Methodist Church. Similar pro-
cesses of secession and re-unification have occurred in the United States.

following Wesley's death, were on the whole politically conservative. 'Tom Paine Methodists' formed only a small minority.
But however loyal and law-abiding Wesley's followers were
taught to be, they can hardly, at one or two per cent of the total
population (and less than that in the southern counties) have
provided more than a minor influencing factor. Moreover, the
subsequent history of British radicalism, of Chartism and trade
unionism, showed that a Methodist upbringing was far from
necessarily implying political passivity, even during years when
the Methodist Conference continually pontificated against
radicalism and urged its rank and file to resist democracy as
they would Satan himself. The most in this respect that can be
said of the post-French Revolutionary period is that Wesley had
hated democracy and feared the foolishness of popular power;
that his followers, like most of their countrymen, and as Wesley
surely would have approved, rallied to the flag and patriotically
hated the French; that there were plenty of other reasons unconnected with Methodism why there was no British Revolution;
and that the breakaway Methodist churches proved more democratically inclined than the Wesleyans.[5]

Another well-aired proposition is that the Labour movement in
Britain owes less to Karl Marx than to John Wesley – a thesis
which appears at first to be in clear conflict with the theory of
Methodism as preventive of revolution but perhaps on examination is not, British socialists having in general been markedly
*un*revolutionary. A number of working-class leaders during the
nineteenth century and after did indeed come from Methodist
backgrounds. Wesley himself certainly despised the values of an
'acquisitive society', even if he had never heard it so described.
He did stand, too, for a spiritual, if never a political or social,
egalitarianism. The Cornish tinner or Northumbrian coal-miner
weighed equally in God's scales with Wesley's merchant or
banker Methodist friends whose very wealth he saw indeed as
placing them in the severer danger. It is not difficult to imagine a
time-transposed Wesley approving of the basic ideology of the
welfare state. However, this hardly makes him any kind of
socialist forerunner. He deemed it the duty of the rich to relieve
poverty by generous charity; but it was the state not of men's
bodies but their souls that was his overwhelmingly chief concern.

In his early years, a preoccupation with the health of his *own* soul, a constant fussing over his spiritual temperature, had produced in him a degree of religious hypochondria. Until he was thirty-five he had been obsessively concerned with his own salvation. Released from fretting over this by the 'joyous assurance' that came upon him during his thirty-sixth year, when at last (as he said) Heaven sprang up in his heart, his powerful ego and outward sympathies were set free. From that time it is only on the rarest occasions that his confidence seems in the slightest danger of stumbling. True, he could once, in his sixties, write to his brother, 'I do not love God. I never did. Therefore, I never believed in the Christian sense of the word. Therefore I am only an honest heathen, a proselyte of the Temple'. But such onsets of apparent or professed spiritual malaise were of the rarest occurrence. Once he was finally convinced that he had received and accepted that sublimely heart-warming message, 'Thy sins are forgiven, accepted thou art', he was able to discard the enfeebling remnants of self-doubt and introversion, and become for the ensuing half-century the never-failing dispenser of doctrinal truth and retailer of practical wisdom, the tireless chapman not only of God's wares but also of Mr Wesley's own personally recommended specialities and nostrums.

It is easy – perhaps too easy – to load the debit account against Wesley. He was credulous and in some respects superstitious, always loath to accept a natural explanation of events if a supernatural one seemed appropriate. His thought never escaped from its scriptural straitjacket. He was habitually self-justifying and self-laudatory. He was dictatorial. Though certainly he did not lack sympathy for the poor and oppressed, a want of empathy and narrowness of imagination could lead him on occasions to behave with blundering insensitivity. If in his love of plain speaking he spoke plain words which sometimes fetched blood, the sufferers must learn to lick their wounds. Perhaps, for all his protestations to the contrary, he *was* sometimes guilty of encouraging 'enthusiasm'. Not only was he devoid of humour, but he made a virtue of that deficiency, considering humour a form of 'trifling'. His views on children's education were narrowly illiberal, his moral attitudes restrictive and puritanical, his philosophy of literature and the arts utilitarian and philistine. He was unrelentingly didactic. Confident, despite a succession of failures in his personal and domestic relationships, that he had discovered the paths of truth and habits of wisdom in his own affairs, he never ceased trying to manage other people's. And the more closely he was attached to them, the more imperative and detailed such direction had to become. Hence those innumerable entreaties and questionings and soul-searchings, benevolently paternal, solicitously pastoral, sharply reproving, but always *de haut en bas*, in his letters to preachers and society members.

Yet, two hundred years on, he still commands a wondering, indeed sometimes an astonished, respect. His faith was matched by his courage, his single-mindedness by his tireless energy. His sense of mission, his hunger to save souls, defied alike the rebuffs of detractors and the passage of years. He combined to an unusual degree strength of mind, force of character and power of will. Together with his uncompromising and sometimes unsparing directness went an essential honesty and goodness. Not less essential was his unshakable conviction of the goodness and justice of God, the foundation of that 'religion of the heart' which he proclaimed, and which denied – *must* deny, all counter-argument notwithstanding – the hideous doctrine of predestinate damnation.

The power of his personality and might of his eloquence could command passionate and often awestruck devotion. One has only to read the testimony of John Nelson or Adam Clarke or Elizabeth Ritchie, or indeed of any number of others among his followers, to be in no doubt of the capacity of their great man to inspire the intensest veneration. And at least by the last decade or two of his life he had reaped a broader, nationwide recognition and esteem.

There was nothing very unusual about his original Methodist-Moravian society when it was set up at Fetter Lane in 1738. At that time there were in London alone some thirty broadly similar religious societies – a fact which incidentally in itself tends to argue against the prevalence of quite the total godlessness from which he is commonly alleged to have rescued Georgian England in its 'age of reason'. But why were these other societies lost in oblivion when Wesley's was able to survive and multiply throughout the British Isles and eventually far beyond? The answer must surely lie nowhere but in Wesley's own formidable combination of ability, personality and zeal, married to a fortunate longevity; in his success in stimulating and capturing, yet at the same time holding within tolerable bounds, those potent forces of religious ardour always latent in every age; in the unexclusiveness of his societies; in his adventurous readiness to adopt evangelistic methods not new or original but taboo within the Church of England; in the practicality and pragmatism of his generalship, and his tactical acumen in developing an easily extendable system of organization which allowed some of the advantages of local democratic initiative without sacrificing any of his own benevolent autocracy.

The extent of his achievement was already being recognized in the obituary notices of 1791. 'His eminent abilities in every branch of politics and sacred literature', wrote the *Public Advertiser*, 'being directed by the grace of God to the most important and valuable ends, not only rendered him the ornament of his own age and country, but will also endear his name to the latest posterity.' And as the *Gentleman's Magazine* declared:

> Whatever may be the opinions held of his inspiration it is impossible to deny him the merits of having done infinite good to the lower classes of the people . . . He was one of the few characters who outlived enmity and prejudice, and received in his later years every mark of esteem from every denomination . . . His personal influence was greater perhaps than any private gentleman in the country.

References

The following abbreviations have been used:

JJW: The Journal of John Wesley, ed. Nehemiah Curnock.
LJW: The Letters of John Wesley, ed. J. Telford.
JCW: The Journal of Charles Wesley, ed. T. Jackson.
Tyerman JW: The Life and Times of the Rev. John Wesley, by Luke Tyerman.
Tyerman SW: The Life and Times of the Rev. Samuel Wesley, by Luke Tyerman.
YMW: The Young Mr Wesley, by V. H. H. Green.

CHAPTER 1: EPWORTH RECTORY

1   Tyerman SW, 388.
2   Clarke, Memoirs, 106.
3   Tyerman SW, 304.
4   ibid., 329.
5   Susanna to S. Wesley, jun. 11 October 1709.
6   Clarke, Memoirs, 283–327.
7   J. to Susanna Wesley, 28 February 1732.

CHAPTER 2: OXFORD

1   J. to Susanna Wesley, 18 June 1725.
2   Same to same, 29 July 1725.
3   Tyerman SW, 83.
4   Green YMW, 62.
5   Tyerman SW, 395.
6   Stevenson, Memorials, 263.
7   ibid., 271–2.
8   Whitehead, Wesley, i. 399.
9   JJW, i. 466–7.
10 S. to J. Wesley, 21 March and 1 April 1726.
11 Green YMW, 106.
12 LJW, i. 34–9.

13   e.g. Diary, 6 September 1729.
14   LJW, i. 42–3.
15   Green YMW, 215.
16   ibid.

CHAPTER 3: THE HOLY CLUB

 1   Green YMW, 155–6.
 2   LJW, i. 33, 113.
 3   ibid., 102.
 4   ibid., 84.
 5   ibid., 109.
 6   Mrs Pendarves to Ann Granville, 11 March 1732.
 7   LJW, i. 165.
 8   ibid., 120.
 9   ibid., 133.
10   ibid., 183–4.
11   JJW, viii. 147–9.
12   Southey, *Wesley*, ii. 6–8.
13   Whitefield, *Journals*, 45–56.
14   LJW, i. 166–78.

CHAPTER 4: GEORGIA

 1   LJW, i. 188–94.
 2   Charter of 1732.
 3   JJW, i. 121.
 4   ibid., 152, 166–7.
 5   LJW, i. 199.
 6   JJW, i. 138.
 7   ibid., 151.
 8   ibid., 407.
 9   Moore, *Wesley*, i. 311; Church, *Oglethorpe*, 201.
10   JJW, i. 213n.
11   ibid., 379.
12   ibid., 386.
13   ibid., 271.
14   ibid., 234–5.
15   Egmont, *Diary*, ii. 370.
16   LJW, i. 197.
17   JJW, i. 191–2, 258.
18   JCW, i. 1–18.
19   ibid., 6.
20   JJW, i. 192–3.

21 JCW, 17/4/36.
22 Wesley to Oglethorpe, 20 April 1736.
23 JCW, 25/7/36.
24 JJW, i. 291–4, 317.
25 ibid., 325.
26 ibid., 260–4.
27 ibid., 266, 312–13.
28 JCW, i. 57.
29 JJW, i. 280–1.
30 ibid., 286–91.
31 ibid., 323.
32 ibid., 325.
33 ibid., 300.
34 Diary, 9 March 1737.
35 JJW, 3/7/37.
36 ibid., 7/8/37.
37 ibid., 19/3/37.
38 ibid., 12/8/37.
39 ibid., 385–91.
40 ibid., 394.
41 W. Stephens, *Journal*, quoted Tyerman JW, i. 163.
42 JJW, 2/12/37.
43 ibid., 13/12/37.

CHAPTER 5: BY FAITH ALONE

 1 JJW, 24/1/38, i. 418.
 2 ibid., 24/1/38, i. 420.
 3 ibid., 25/5/37.
 4 Böhler to Zinzendorf, February 1738.
 5 JCW, 10/2/38.
 6 JJW, 26/2/38.
 7 ibid., 27/2/38.
 8 ibid., 23/4/38.
 9 J. to C. Wesley 28/6/38.
10 LJW, i. 241–4.
11 Sermon 5, *Justification by Faith*.
12 JCW, 11/5/38.
13 ibid., 17/5/38.
14 ibid., i. 94–5.
15 M. Piette, *John Wesley in the Evolution of Protestantism*, 308.
16 J. to S. Wesley, 30/10/38.
17 LJW, i. 298–307.

18 Sermon 13, *On Sin in Believers*.
19 Clarke, *Memoirs*, 398.
20 JJW, i. 480n.
21 Southey, *Wesley*, i. 173.
22 LJW, i. 251–2, 262–5.
23 JJW, 1/5/38.
24 LJW, i. 251, 257–8.
25 JJW, 10/8/38.
26 LJW, i. 260.
27 Simon, *John Wesley and the Religious Societies*, 237, 257.
28 LJW, iii. 129.
29 JJW, 24/8/76.
30 ibid., 15/6/41.
31 LJW, i. 261.
32 JJW, 11/11/38.
33 Wesley, *Works*, iv. 493.

CHAPTER 6: THE CAMPAIGN BEGINS

 1 JJW, 17/1/39.
 2 ibid., 28/1/39.
 3 Clarke, *Memoirs* 425; Southey, *Wesley*, i. 282–3.
 4 LJW, i. 299.
 5 ibid., 303.
 6 JJW, ii. 203, 386.
 7 ibid., 6/4/48.
 8 Wesley, *Works* (OUP), xi. 392.
 9 LJW, iii. 111, 113.
10 JCW, 9/6/38.
11 Wesley, *Works* (OUP), xi. 390–1.
12 Whitefield, *Journals*, 238, 241.
13 Wesley, *Works* viii. 127; JJW, 12/3/43.
14 Conference Minutes, 1745.
15 JJW, 11/4/48.
16 *Earnest Appeal* . . ., *Works* (OUP) xi. 58–64; JJW, 21/5/41.
17 JJW, 23/4/72, 23/3/77, 19/7/77, 22/4/79.
18 LJW, i. 284–7.
19 ibid., 319–20, JJW, ii. 211–13.
20 JJW, 5/6/39.
21 Green YMW, Appendix 2.
22 JJW, ii. 295–6, 304, 321, 340, 346; JCW, 29/3/40.
23 JCW, 25/8/39.
24 JJW, ii. 298, 324, 327.
25 JCW, 5/8/40.

26 ibid., 4/6/43, 15/6/43.
27 ibid., 5/4/40.
28 J. Hutton to Zinzendorf, 14 March 1740.
29 Clarke, *Memoirs*, 408.
30 Stevenson, *Memorials*, 273–4.
31 LJW, iii. 87.
32 JCW, 14/5/40.
33 JJW, 1/11/39.
34 JCW, 14/5/40, Hutton to Zinzendorf, 14 March 1740.
35 JJW, ii. 369–70, 467; LJW, i. 345–51, 353.
36 JJW, ii. 369–71.
37 Towlson, *Moravian and Methodist*, 111; LJW, i. 352–3.
38 Howel Harris to Wesley, 16 July 1740.
39 Sermon 128, *Free Grace*.
40 Tyerman JW, i. 312–25; Whitefield, *Letter to John Wesley, Journals*, 569–88.
41 JJW, 1/8/41.
42 ibid., 5/11/55.

CHAPTER 7: 'SURELY GOD IS OVER ALL'

1 JJW, 1/2/41.
2 Tyerman JW, i. 333.
3 JCW, 27/8/41, 15/9/41.
4 JJW, 8/3/41, JCW, 30/11/40.
5 JCW, 28/6/41.
6 Whitehead, *Wesley*, ii. 148–9.
7 Wesley, *Works*, viii. 247.
8 JJW, ii. 403–4, 454.
9 ibid., 2/11/50.
10 Tyerman JW, i. 370.
11 J. to C. Wesley, 21/1/41.
12 LJW, ii. 5.
13 JCW, 16/6/38, 27/7/38, 24/9/43.
14 JJW, ii. 10.
15 ibid., 27/5/42.
16 ibid., 30/5/42.
17 ibid., 1/3/43.
18 ibid., ii. 73.
19 LJW, ii. 12.
20 ibid., 13–14.
21 JJW, 13/4/43.
22 LJW, v. 151.
23 JJW, 20/10/43.

24 JCW, 25/10/43.
25 JJW, 20/10/43.
26 ibid., ii. 437, 505, 511; iii. 56, 189–90, 236; iv. 112, 133, 152, 153, 187–8.
27 ibid., 25/12/42.
28 JCW, 18/6/40, 22/6/43, 25/12/43, 24/2/47.

CHAPTER 8: POLEMICS AND ALARUMS

1   *Earnest Appeal, Works* (OUP), xi. 86–8.
2   JJW, 4/3/47.
3   *A Plain Account of Kingswood School* (1781).
4   Tyerman JW, i. 450–2; JJW, 24/8/44.
5   Sermon 129.
6   Tyerman JW, ii. 72.
7   JJW, iv. 117–20.
8   Simon, *John Wesley and the Methodist Societies*, 182.
9   ibid., 212–13; Minutes of Conference, 1744.
10 LJW, ii. 40–1, 52–3.
11 JJW, 31/10/45.
12 *Farther Appeal II, Works* (OUP), xi. 242.
13 ibid., *passim*.
14 ibid., III, Sections 4–10.
15 Wesley, *Works* (OUP), 350.
16 *Letter to . . . Bishop of London, Works* (OUP), xi. 338.
17 Wesley, *Works* (OUP), xi. 359–436.
18 JJW, 29/8/62.
19 ibid., 21/12/51.
20 Knox, *Enthusiasm*, 414.
21 ibid., 415.
22 LJW, ii. 324.
23 ibid., 314–15.
24 P. Johnson, *History of Christianity*, 365.

CHAPTER 9: BODIES AND SOULS

1   Wesley, *Works*, vii. 9.
2   JJW, 12/11/46.
3   LJW, ii. 307.
4   ibid., iii. 78.
5   ibid., v. 132–4.
6   ibid., iii. 102.
7   JJW, 8/2/53.
8   ibid., 3/2/53.

9 ibid., 24/5/49, 26–28/11/53, 7/4/55, 16/2/57, 30/9/57, 10/10/57;
   JCW, 2/12/53; LJW, iv. 108, v. 61, vi. 59, vii. 87.
10 LJW, ii. 308.
11 JJW, 20/1/53, 9/11/56, 19/4/74.
12 Wesley, *Works*, vii. 80.
13 Southey, *Wesley*, ii. 160–1.
14 JJW, 12/8/48.
15 LJW, v. 53.
16 J. Hindmarsh to J. Wesley, quoted JJW, v. 259.
17 LJW, v. 123.
18 H. Walpole to H. Mann, 3/5/49.
19 Same to same, 10/10/66.
20 *Lives of Early Methodist Preachers*, i. 14–19.
21 Telford, *Wesley*, 229.
22 J. Bunyan, *Grace Abounding . . .*, 22.
23 Southey, *Wesley*, ii. 141.
24 LJW, iii. 99–100, 102–4.
25 ibid., 119.
26 ibid., 103.
27 ibid., 120–2; JJW, 28/10/54.
28 LJW, iii. *passim*.

CHAPTER 10: GRACE MURRAY

1 JCW, i. 224–5.
2 LJW, iii. 16.
3 JJW, 25–26/8/48.
4 JCW, 1–7/4/49.
5 The ensuing account follows broadly A. Léger, *John Wesley's
   Last Love* (1910). See also G. E. Harrison, *Son to Susanna* (1937),
   chapters 22–31.
6 LJW, iii. 17–18.
7 JJW, 29–30/9/49.
8 ibid., iii. 435–6n.
9 ibid., 439n.

CHAPTER 11: BREACHES AND PURGES

1 *Life and Times of Selina Countess of Huntingdon*, i. 118.
2 Tyerman, *Whitefield*, ii. 318.
3 *Life and Times of Selina Countess of Huntingdon*, ii. 380.
4 Wesley to Mrs Hutton, LJW, ii. 24.
5 JJW, 25/1/81.

6 Whitefield, *Works*, ii. 428.
7 G. Whitefield to C. Wesley, Tyerman JW, ii. 147.
8 LJW, iii. 101.
9 ibid.
10 W. Romaine to Lady Huntingdon, 21 March 1763.
11 LJW, iv. 206.
12 JJW, 17/4/64.
13 ibid., 19/4/64; LJW, iv. 235–9.
14 LJW, v. 93.
15 Wesley, *Works*, xii. 126.
16 LJW, iii. 83.
17 JJW, 20/1/61, 12/10/64.
18 Tyerman, *Whitefield*, ii. 347.
19 LJW, iii. 71.
20 ibid., 74, 85.
21 Tyerman JW, ii. 126–31.
22 *A Plain Account of Christian Perfection*, various editions 1767–77; *Works*, xi. 351–427; Sermon 40, *Christian Perfection*.
23 1 John v. 18.
24 Sermon 40, *Christian Perfection*.
25 LJW, v. 322.
26 Jackson, *Charles Wesley*, ii. 209–10.
27 Wesley, *Works*, xi. 405; LJW, v. 41.
28 R. Davies, in *History of the Methodist Church in Great Britain*, i. 171.
29 JJW, 15/9/62, 30/9/65, 14/8/76.
30 T. Maxfield to J. Wesley, 16/10/62; JJW, 4/2/63.
31 LJW, v. 38.
32 ibid., iv. 201–2.
33 ibid., 202–3.
34 JJW, 28/2/63.
35 Southey, *Wesley*, ii. 344–5.
36 *Arminian Magazine* 1783, Tyerman JW, ii. 521–5.
37 Tyerman JW, ii. 551.

CHAPTER 12: MARRIAGE

1 Simon, *John Wesley and the Advance of Methodism*, 192.
2 JCW, 2/2/51.
3 JJW, 27/3/51.
4 LJW, iii. 87.
5 JJW, 24–25/4/52.
6 JCW, 21–22/6/51.
7 LJW, iv. 89.
8 ibid., iii. 91–2.

9 ibid., 213.
10 ibid., iv. 101.
11 Tyerman JW, ii. 108.
12 LJW, iii. 138–9.
13 ibid.
14 ibid., iii. 179–80.
15 JCW, ii. 201, 213, 217, 247.
16 LJW, iii. 127.
17 Tyerman JW, ii. 287.
18 LJW, iii. 239–42, 243–4; iv. 3–4.
19 ibid., iv. 6–7.
20 ibid., iii. 61, 65.
21 ibid., iv. 21–3.
22 ibid., 62.
23 ibid., 79–80, 153.
24 ibid., v. 17–18.
25 ibid., 50, 78.
26 ibid., 53, 63, 127, 142, 240, 253–4, 283; vi. 153.
27 ibid., v. 86, 92–3, 309.
28 ibid., 21.
29 JJW, v. 400.
30 LJW, vi. 98–102.
31 ibid., 273–4.
32 ibid., 321–2.
33 Moore, *Wesley*, ii. 175.

CHAPTER 13: BROTHER CHARLES AND POPE JOHN

1 JCW, ii. 219; JJW, iv. 300.
2 LJW, iii. 95–6.
3 ibid., 112.
4 C. Wesley to W. Sellon, 1755.
5 LJW, iii. 132–3, 135–6.
6 JJW, 10/10/56, 23/10/59.
7 LJW, iii. 186.
8 C. Wesley to S. Walker, 21 August 1756.
9 J. Wesley to (?) Lord Dartmouth, LJW, iv. 150.
10 LJW, iv. 133.
11 ibid., v. 257.
12 ibid., viii. 78.
13 ibid., v. 15.
14 ibid., 19.
15 ibid., 88, 93.
16 ibid., 20

17 ibid., vi. 29.
18 Conference Minutes, 1766.
19 JJW, 26/4/53.
20 LJW, i. 278; JJW, 20/12/68.
21 JJW, v. 240.

CHAPTER 14: 'THE GOSPEL TRUMPET'

1 Tyerman JW, iii. 608; JJW, 23/7/55; LJW, vii. 54.
2 JJW, 13/7/56, 15/10/58.
3 ibid., 3/7/48.
4 ibid., 13/12/79, 14/2/81.
5 ibid., 4/9/65, 5/12/65.
6 ibid., 28/7/57.
7 ibid., 18/10/72.
8 ibid., 30/3/58, 24/8/60, 20/10/70.
9 e.g. ibid., 28/8/55, 19/7/57, 29/1/58, 21/5/58, 1/9/58, 25/12/58, 15/7/59, 1/1/60, 16/2/60, 7/1/62, 28/7/62, 4/4/64, 18/3/65, 28/6/69, 5/6/72, 8/9/84, 5/2/86.
10 See also JJW, iv. 347.
11 ibid., 27/8/63, 3/4/86.
12 ibid., 27/8/63.
13 ibid., 8/6/53, 12/8/71.
14 ibid., iv. 317–22, 334–43.
15 ibid., 5/6/72.
16 ibid., v. 465–72.
17 ibid., 15–25/9/70.
18 ibid., 6/9/71.
19 ibid., 10/9/73.
20 ibid., 8/6/84.
21 ibid., 7/7/62.
22 LJW, iv. 108.
23 G. Whitefield to J. Wesley, 3 December 1753.
24 JJW, 4/7/58.
25 ibid., 28/10/65, 28/6/70, 28/10/71.
26 ibid., 24/5/59.
27 LJW, iv. 255.
28 JJW, vi. 260–1.
29 LJW, vi. 81.
30 ibid., vi. 214.
31 JJW, 13/7/82.
32 LJW, v. 117.
33 JJW, 22/6/57, 5/9/69, 12/9/76.
34 ibid., 23/11/57, 19/7/66.

35 LJW, v. 118; JJW, 29/3/64, 19/4/88.
36 JJW, 25/5/59, 11/10/75, 16/7/78, 28/4/79, 20/5/80, 14/7/86.
37 ibid., 3/8/55.
38 *Advice to Methodists with regard to Dress* (1760).
39 Sermon 89, *On the More Excellent Way.*
40 JJW, 8/4/66.
41 Tyerman JW, ii. 195.
42 LJW, viii. 12.
43 JJW, 13/5/62.
44 LJW, viii. 80.
45 Sermon 50, *On the Use of Money.*
46 JJW, 10/10/70.
47 ibid., 11/4/53.
48 ibid., 18/7/56, 29/6/58, 27/7/87.
49 ibid., 26/3/90.
50 Sermons 87, 108, *On Riches, On the Danger of Riches.*
51 LJW, vi. 56.
52 ibid., iii. 199.
53 ibid., v. 108–9.
54 ibid., iv. 156.
55 J. Wesley to Sarah Wesley, 5 October 1790.
56 Sermon 89, *On the More Excellent Way.*
57 LJW, v. 349–54.
58 ibid., vi. 230.
59 ibid., 372.
60 ibid., vii. 46–7; JJW, vi. 299n., 301–2.
61 See *Thoughts upon Liberty; Thoughts concerning the Origin of Power* (both 1772).
62 LJW, vi. 176.
63 JJW, 11/10/75, 11/11/75.
64 LJW, vi. 358; JJW, 31/8/79.
65 JJW, 3/2/70, 21/3/79.
66 ibid., 25/4/48, 4/1/60, 1/1/65, 13/7/65, 29/4/68, 10/11/69, 15/2/73, 12/7/73, 17/12/73, 4/4/76, 24/7/80, 29/1/81, 15/5/84, 18/5/85; LJW, vii. 46–7.

CHAPTER 15: DOCTRINAL WAR

1 JJW, 20/7/61.
2 ibid., 13/1/58.
3 *Gospel Magazine*, May 1771.
4 JJW, v. 380n.
5 *Life and Times of Selina Countess of Huntingdon*, ii. 240.
6 Sermon 53, *On the Death of Mr Whitefield.*

7   *Lloyd's Evening Post*, 26/2/71; LJW, v. 223-6.
8   LJW, v. 258-60, 274-5.
9   Illustration facing JJW, v. 426.
10 JJW, 14/8/72, 7/12/72.
11 LJW, vi. 224.
12 Tyerman JW, iii. 262-6.
13 Sermon 58.
14 *History of the Methodist Church in Great Britain*, i. 298.

CHAPTER 16: THE GORDIAN KNOT

1   LJW, vii. 75.
2   ibid., vi. 142-3, 154-5.
3   ibid., 155-64.
4   S. Johnson to J. Wesley, 6 February 1776.
5   LJW, vi. 199.
6   ibid., vii. 21.
7   ibid., 29-31.
8   JJW, 1/9/84.
9   T. Coke to J. Wesley, 9 August 1784.
10 Quoted fully in Tyerman JW, iii. 434-5.
11 LJW, viii. 91.
12 Quoted fully in Simon, *John Wesley, the Last Phase*, 233.

CHAPTER 17: THE FINAL YEARS

1   JJW, 23/11/79.
2   LJW, viii. 82, 107.
3   ibid., v. 136, viii. 223.
4   ibid., vii. 18.
5   ibid., vi. 43.
6   ibid., viii. 29, 35, 116.
7   ibid., vii. 32.
8   ibid., 301.
9   ibid., viii. 223.
10 For correspondence with Ann Bolton, see LJW vols 5-8, *passim*.
11 LJW, v. 108-9.
12 ibid., viii. 4, 26, 55, 109, 128, 248.
13 For correspondence with Hester Roe (Rogers) and Elizabeth Ritchie, see LJW, vols 6-8, *passim*.
14 LJW, vi. 216-17, 222-3, 231-2.
15 ibid., vi. 223, vii. 100.
16 ibid., vi. 253, viii. 83.
17 JJW, vii. 398-9.
18 LJW, vi. 26.

19 JJW, 13/8/79, 15/6/82.
20 ibid., 20/6/74.
21 LJW, vi. 213–14.
22 Tyerman JW, iii. 621.
23 JJW, 28/6/85.
24 ibid., 1/3/88.
25 ibid., vii. 142–6.
26 W. F. Lofthouse, in *History of the Methodist Church in Great Britain*, i. 134.
27 LJW, vii. 77–8, 81.
28 Tyerman JW, iii. 361.
29 LJW, viii. 36, 41, 43.
30 ibid., 43, 49.
31 Conference Minutes, 1788.
32 LJW, viii. 136.
33 ibid., 196.
34 ibid., vi. 61–2.
35 ibid., vii. 222.
36 ibid., 113, 199, 204.
37 ibid., vi. 364, viii. 45, 164, 172–3, 189, 208, 212.
38 Hampson, *Memoirs . . .*, iii. 167–8.
39 *Methodism in York*, JJW, viii. 63n.
40 H. Crabb Robinson, *Diary*, i. 120.
41 Elizabeth Ritchie's *Account . . .* in JJW, viii. 131–44.

CHAPTER 18: '. . . TO THE LATEST POSTERITY'

1 JJW, iii. 108.
2 ibid., vi. 370.
3 C. Grant Robertson, *England under the Hanoverians*, 210.
4 G. M. Trevelyan, *British History in the Nineteenth Century*, 25.
5 See, in particular, E. J. Hobsbawm, *Methodism and the Threat of Revolution in Britain*, in *Labouring Men* (1964).

Bibliography

WESLEY J.:
> The Journal of John Wesley, ed. N. Curnock (8 vols 1909–16).
> The Letters of John Wesley, ed. J. Telford (8 vols 1931).
> Works, ed. T. Jackson (14 vols 1831).
> The Works of John Wesley (editor-in-chief F. Baker, 34 vols projected: vol. 11, ed. G. R. Cragg, Appeals to Men of Reason and Religion, 1975).
> Sermons on Several Occasions (ed. J. Beecham, 2 vols n.d.).
> The Standard Sermons of John Wesley (ed. E. H. Sugden, 2 vols 1931).
> Explanatory Notes upon the New Testament (1755).
> Primitive Physick (1747).

WESLEY, J. AND WESLEY, C.: The Poetical Works (ed. G. Osborn, 13 vols 1868–72).

THE ARMINIAN MAGAZINE (1778–91), various articles.

Much of what Wesley published was abridged or adapted from other authors. Above are some of the more important of his own writings. For a complete list, see A Union Catalogue of the Publications of John and Charles Wesley, by Frank Baker (1966).

BAKER, F.: John Wesley and the Church of England (1970).
BOWEN, M.: Wrestling Jacob (1938).
BUNYAN, J.: Grace Abounding to the Chief of Sinners (ed. R. Sharrock, 1966).
CANNON, W. R.: The Theology of John Wesley (1946).
CHURCH, L. F.: Oglethorpe (1932).
CLARKE, A.: Memoirs of the Wesley Family (1823).
CLARKE, E.: Susanna Wesley (1886).
COX, L. G.: John Wesley's Concept of Perfection (1968).
CRAGG, G. R.: The Church and the Age of Reason (1960).
> Reason and Authority in the Eighteenth Century (1964).
DAVIES, R. E.: Methodism (2nd edn 1976).
DAVIES, R. E. AND RUPP, E. G. (eds.) History of the Methodist Church in Great Britain, vol. 1 (1966).

DELANY, MARY GRANVILLE, MRS: Autobiography and Correspondence (ed. Lady Llanover, vol. i. 1862).

Dictionary of National Biography.

DOBRÉE, B.: John Wesley (1933).

EDWARDS, M. L.: John Wesley and the Eighteenth Century (2nd edn 1955). Family Circle (1949).

Gentleman's Magazine (1731–1816).

GREEN, J. B.: John Wesley and William Law (1948).

GREEN, V. H. H.: The Young Mr Wesley (1961).
    John Wesley (1964).

HALÉVY, E.: The Birth of Methodism (transl. B. Semmel 1971).

HAMPSON, J.: Memoirs of the late Rev. John Wesley (3 vols 1791).

HARRISON, G. E.: Son to Susanna, the Private Life of John Wesley (1937).

HAZLITT, W.: On the Causes of Methodism, in The Round Table (1817).

HOBSBAWM, E. J.: Methodism and the Threat of Revolution in Britain, in Labouring Men (1964).

HOLMES, G.: The Trial of Dr Sacheverell (1973).

JACKSON, T.: Life of Charles Wesley (2 vols 1841).
    (ed.) Lives of the Early Methodist Preachers (6 vols, 3rd edn 1865).

JAMES, W.: Varieties of Religious Experience (1914).

KIRK, J.: The Mother of the Wesleys (1866).

KNOX, R.: Enthusiasm (1950).

LAVINGTON, G.: The Enthusiasm of Methodists and Papists Compared (3 vols 1749–51).

LAW, W.: Serious Call to a Devout and Holy Life (1728).

LECKY, W. E. H.: History of Rationalism (1865).
    History of the English People in the Eighteenth Century (1891).

LÉGER, A.: John Wesley's Last Love (1910).

Minutes of the Methodist Conference (vol. i, 1799).

MOORE, H.: The Life of the Rev. J. Wesley (2 vols 1824–5).

MORGAN, J.: The Life and Death of Mr Thomas Walsh (1763).

NELSON, J.: Journal of John Nelson, Written by Himself (1767).

PIETTE, M.: John Wesley and the Evolution of Protestantism (transl. 1937).

Proceedings of the Wesley Historical Society (from 1897).

QUILLER-COUCH, A.: Hetty Wesley, a novel (1903).

RATTENBURY, J. E.: The Conversion of the Wesleys (1938).
    The Eucharistic Hymns of John and Charles Wesley (1948).

SARGANT, W.: The Battle for the Mind, a Physiology of Conversion and Brainwashing (1957).

SCHMIDT, M.: John Wesley, a Theological Biography (English translation, 3 vols 1962–73: this, the most detailed of recent Wesley biographies, carries also an extensive bibliography).

SEMMEL, B.: The Methodist Revolution (1974).

SEYMOUR, A. C. H.: The Life and Times of Selina Countess of Huntingdon (2 vols 1844).

SIMON, J. S.: John Wesley and the Religious Societies (1921).
John Wesley and the Methodist Societies (1923).
John Wesley and the Advance of Methodism (1925).
John Wesley, the Master Builder (1927).
John Wesley, the Last Phase (1934).

SMITH, SYDNEY: Methodism, in The Edinburgh Review (1808).

SOUTHEY, R.: The Life of Wesley and the Rise of Methodism (2 vols 1820).

STEPHEN, L.: History of English Thought in the Eighteenth Century (2 vols 1902).

STEVENSON, G. J.: Memorials of the Wesley Family (1876).

SYKES, N.: Church and State in England in the Eighteenth Century (1934).

TELFORD, J.: The Life of John Wesley (1886).

THOMPSON, E. P.: The Making of the English Working Class (1963).

TOWLSON, C. W.: Moravian and Methodist (1957).

TYERMAN, L.: The Life and Times of Samuel Wesley (1866).
The Life and Times of John Wesley (3 vols 1871).
The Life of George Whitefield (2 vols 1876).
Wesley's Designated Successor (1882).

VULLIAMY, C. E.: John Wesley (3rd edn 1954).

WALSH, J.: Methodism and the Mob in the Eighteenth Century, in Popular Belief and Practice (eds G. J. Cuming and D. Baker, 1972).

WARBURTON, W.: Works, vol. 8 (ed. R. Hurd, 1811).

WEARMOUTH, R. F. W.: Methodism and the Common People of the Eighteenth Century (1945).

WESLEY, CHARLES: Journal (ed. T. Jackson, 2 vols 1849; also ed. Culley 1909).

WESLEY, SAMUEL JUNIOR: Poems on Several Occasions (ed. J. Nichols, 1862).

WHITEFIELD, G.: Journals (ed. I. Murray, 1960).

WHITEHEAD, J.: The Life of John Wesley (2 vols 1793-6).

WILLIAMS, C. W.: Wesley's Theology Today (1962).

Index

Wesley, John [*contd.*]
Fetter Lane 122–4; early differences with Whitefield 124–7; buys 'Foundery' 128; dissension at Bristol 129–30; in South Wales, Cornwall, and Midlands 130–1; purges backsliders 131; Methodist 'classes' 132; relieving poverty and sickness 132–3; employs lay preachers 133–4; takes mission north 135–41; preaches from father's tombstone 140; mission in Cornwall 141–2; riots in Staffordshire 142–4; 'particular providence' again 144–6; toughness and fortitude exemplified 146–8; his *Appeals* 149–50, 156–8; castigates Oxford 150–2; attitude to Jacobitism and the soldiery 153, 155–6; controversies with bishops of London and Exeter, and others 158–63; tracts, dispensaries, views on diet, etc. 164–6; visiting poor, sick, and prisoners 167: *Primitive Physick* 168; electrical machines 169; Kingswood School 169–73; variety and arduousness of his work 173–4; Methodist organization and preachers 174–9; his candour 179–82; and Grace Murray Chapter 10; relations with Whitefield, Lady Huntingdon, etc. 197–205; internal Methodist troubles, and purges 205–8; and Christian Perfection 208–10; breach with Maxfield 210–12; further polemical and theological works 212–14; marries Mrs Vazeille Chapter 12; and Sarah Ryan, etc. 222–9; at odds with Charles 232, 237–8; the question of separation 233–6; and women preachers 236–7; his autocracy 238–41; erratic progress 242–5; later attitude to 'enthusiasm' 245–50; health 250–1, 253; style of life and travel

251–3; miscellaneous judgements 253–9, 267–8, 312; and his sisters 260–1; relieving poverty, attacking slavery 260–3; and Lord George Gordon 264–5; his patriotism and conservatism 265–6; resumed controversy with Calvinists Chapter 15; preaches sermon on Whitefield's death 272; and on predestination 276–7; healthy living 278–9; sample extract from 1778 *Journal* 279–81; and America 281–8; ordains preachers 285–9; treatment of rebellious preachers 291–2, 310; Deed of Declaration (1784) 292; advice to preachers and women Methodists 292–8; Hester Roe and Elizabeth Ritchie 298–301; angels, and heaven 301–3; and City Road Chapel 303–4; a routine fortnight in 1786 304–5; and death of Charles Wesley 307–9; his pessimism and optimism 311; description of the aged Wesley 312–13; his will 313–14; last illness and death 314–15; reputation, influence and importance Chapter 18
Wesley, Kezia (Kezzy) 42, 55, 60, 84, 121, 139n.
Wesley, Maria (Molly) (Mrs Whitelamb) 40, 119
Wesley, Martha (Patty) (Mrs Hall) 25, 38, 41, 55, 56, 60, 62, 89, 119, 121, 134–5, 138–9, 253, 260, 261, 299, 308, 314
Wesley, Matthew 20, 42
Wesley, Mehetabel (Hetty) (Mrs Wright) 17, 25–6, 38, 39, 40, 42, 119, 120, 140, 261
Wesley, Mrs Charles (Sarah Gwynne) 185, 187, 221–2, 232, 308, 314
Wesley, Mrs John (Molly Vazeille) Chapter 12 *passim*, 295
Wesley, Samuel (W's father) Chapters 1 and 2 *passim*, 47,